W9-BJH-597

Hard Disk Management with DOS
2nd Edition

Dan Gookin

Library of Congress Cataloging-in-Publication Data

Gookin, Dan.
    Hard disk management with DOS / by Dan Gookin. – 2nd ed.
       p.   cm.
    Rev. ed. of: Hard disk management with MS-DOS. 1st ed. c1987.
    ISBN 0-8306-8490-5   ISBN 0-8306-3490-8 (pbk.)
    1. File organization (Computer science) 2. MS-DOS (Computer operating system) 3. PC DOS (Computer operating system) 4. Hard disks (Computer science)   I. Gookin, Dan. Hard disk management with MS-DOS. II. Title.
QA76.9.F5G66 1990
005.74—dc20   89-77205
                                        CIP

TAB BOOKS offers software for sale. For information and a catalog, please contact TAB Software Department, Blue Ridge Summit, PA 17294-0850.

Questions regarding the content of this book should be addressed to:

Reader Inquiry Branch
TAB BOOKS
Blue Ridge Summit, PA 17294-0214

Acquisitions Editor: Ron Powers
Book Editor: Mark D. LeSuer
Production: Katherine Brown

Contents

PART TWO

HARD DISK SECURITY

Notices

dBase III	Ashton-Tate
FastBack	Fifth Generation Systems
COREfast	CORE International, Inc.
The Mace Utilities	Paul Mace Software
CUBIT	SoftLogic Solutions, Inc.
ERLL, RLL	Maynard Electronics, Inc.
Ad-PAC 2	Tandon Corporation
IBM, and PC AT	International Business Machines
Lightning	Personal Computer Support Group
POWER TOOLS	MLI Microsystems
SuperKey	Borland International, Inc
VCache	Golden Bow Systems
Lotus 1-2-3/Symphony	Lotus Development Corp.
AutoMenu	Magee Enterprises
Windows	MicroSoft Corp.
GEM	Digital Research
Direct Access	Delta Technology Int.
TM	Norton
Framework	Ashton-Tate
Aboveboard	Intel
Six Pack	AST
DESQview 386	Quarterdeck
WordStar	MicroPro International
MultiMate	Multimate International Corp.
WordPerfect	WordPerfect Corporation
Apple Lisa	Apple Computer, Inc.
The Norton Commander	Peter Norton Computing
The Norton Utilities	Peter Norton Computing
DOSSHELL	Microsoft Corporation
VisiCalc	Visicorp
SideKick Plus	Borland International

*I would like to acknowledge
the contribution of Andy Townsend,
the original coauthor.*

Introduction

A REVOLUTION is taking place in the personal computer industry. While this revolution is driven by technology, it's affecting the type and range of applications for which personal computers are used. At the heart of this revolution is the declining cost of computer power. Dramatic cost reductions have taken place in processing power, random access memory, and data storage. For example, in 1980, the cost of 1 megabyte of storage was over $100. Now, a megabyte costs around $30. At the same time, personal computers have become increasingly powerful and sophisticated. The typical 8-bit, 64K, dual-drive IBM PC that used to be the desktop standard has been replaced by the 32-bit, 640K AT or "'386 machine" with a 40 megabyte hard drive and a 1.44 megabyte floppy drive. Even more powerful machines are just around the corner.

Until recently, personal computers with hard disk drives were too expensive for home and small business use. A 10 megabyte hard drive unit alone used to cost over $1,000. PCs equipped with hard drives were mainly used for applications involving large amounts of data. After all, that's what hard disks are for—storing lots of data, right? But times have changed.

The latest generation of personal computers, with faster microprocessors and increased memory capacities, are changing the applications programs used with microcomputers. Word processing programs, spreadsheets, and database programs are all getting faster, fancier, and bigger. Another trend in software is the move to *integrated programs*, which incorporate the functions of several types of applications into a single package. Such programs tend to be massive.

While many of these programs can still be run on computers having only floppy drives, some recommend the use of a hard disk, and most actually require one. Even if it is possible to run large applications on a floppy-drive-only system, the amount of disk swapping involved makes their use tedious at best. In fact, floppy diskettes have been dubbed "swappy" diskettes by disgruntled users who face the constant task of replacing diskettes every time their software needs to access a different portion of the program. For this reason alone, many personal and small business computer users are switching to hard disk systems.

Paralleling the trend toward larger application programs is the continuing decline in the cost of data storage. The same 10 megabyte hard drive that cost over $1,000 several years ago cannot be purchased today. But it's easy to find a 20 megabyte hard drive for $250. Hard drives that store 40, 60, 80, 100, and 150 megabytes are quite common in business situations. And as technology drives forward, hard drives capable of storing over a gigabyte, or 1 billion characters, of information will soon be commonplace on personal computers.

Finally, small business and departmental computing is on the rise. Where manual systems, time-sharing, and centralized data processing once accounted for much of the data handling of small businesses and individual departments, today most small businesses and departments within large organizations are opting for on-site and distributed data processing.

Clearly, the increasing need for hard disk computer systems to run larger applications and manage more data, coupled with the decreasing cost of hard disk technology, has led to an expanding number of hard disk personal computer systems in operation. Most of these systems are based on the MS-DOS operating system. (PC-DOS is IBM's own version of this widely adopted microcomputer operating system.) In fact, the latest generation of MS-DOS computers, those based on the 80 × 86 microprocessor, are designed to be configured with some form of hard disk. Even their floppy diskette drives store more data.

WHAT THIS BOOK IS ABOUT

This book is about taming your hard disk. The subject of hard disks is a bewildering one. Even experienced computer users can become lost in the maze of megabytes and special commands associated with hard disks. The differences in technology, data storage capacities, and commands separate hard disk computer systems from those employing floppy diskette drives.

On the one hand, hard disks are nothing more than rigid floppy diskettes. There is nothing conceptually different in the way they store data. It's only their rigidity that allows them to store higher quantities, or *densities*, of data. On the other hand, hard disk technology and the increased data handling capacity that goes with it create an entirely new set of problems not encountered with floppy drives.

The special problems associated with hard disks can be broken into three major areas of concern. The first, and most obvious, is the need for some means of organizing the massive storage capacity of a hard disk. Unless the drive is being used to maintain a single, enormous database, it is likely that there will be hundreds, if not thousands, of different program and data files stored on it. Keeping track of programs and data can be a daunting proposition, especially to someone who is unfamiliar with computers.

The first section of this book describes several methods for organizing your hard disk into manageable units. You will learn how to divide your hard disk into partitions and subdirectories. You also will learn how to create professional-looking menus and programs to access your programs and data. These techniques will take the hassle out of your hard disk and leave the power readily available.

A second concern to hard disk owners is the problem of security. The issue of security includes both data and program security. First, of course, you want to make sure your data is secure from accidental loss resulting from a hard disk failure. Hard disks do fail occasionally, and when they do, the data stored on them is usually lost. Also, people sometimes forget and reformat their hard disks by mistake. Again, data might be lost. The second section of this book describes methods for duplicating the data stored on your hard disk to prevent the permanent loss of valuable data.

But hard disk security extends beyond protecting data from accidental loss. If your computer system will be shared by others or if your computer is accessible to unauthorized use, you have a different kind of security problem. On the one hand, you need to ensure that multiple users do not accidentally destroy each others' data. On the other, you need to be sure that confidential data is secure from prying and tampering. Password security and data encryption are two features that can be added to your system to protect confidential data. This book describes a variety of techniques and programs you can employ to protect your data from security violations.

A third concern of hard disk users is performance. When you first use a hard disk, the contrast between a hard disk system and a floppy system is striking. This difference is due to the reduced time required by the disk drive to read in data and programs from the hard disk. Once you get used to this increased performance, you take it for granted. However, for reasons discussed in this book, a hard disk's performance deteriorates as more files are added to it. This deterioration can significantly slow down your computer system. The final section of this book describes a number of techniques and tricks for enhancing the performance of your hard disk.

WHO THIS BOOK IS FOR

Personal computer users are often categorized according to their experience and the amount of time they spend working with computers as novices, advanced users, or power users. Of course, as with any such scheme, there is actually a continuum, and you might fall anywhere between the rankest rookie and the most hardened "tech weenie." I have made every effort to make this book accessible to all readers, including those at both ends of the computer user spectrum.

If you are new to computers or if this is your first hard drive system, you will find a wealth of information describing the technology and terminology involved. You will also find step-by-step instructions for formatting your hard disk and storing programs onto it. You probably will find these instructions easier to follow than those provided with your Disk Operating System manual.

Novice users will also appreciate the information on subdirectories and the various commands associated with multiple directories. The first five chapters of this book are devoted to discussions of hard disk technology, preparation of hard disks for use, and commands associated with subdirectories and paths. As the novice user becomes comfortable working with files and programs stored in different subdirectories, he or she will want to move onto the more advanced subjects covered in later chapters.

Advanced users will find the information on menu systems and batch file programming particularly useful. Using the information and programs provided with this book and the optional supplemental programs diskette, you will be able to design and create professional-looking menu systems for your own use and for use by less experienced users. The topics of data security and improved performance, covered in Parts Two and Three of this book, will also be of interest to advanced users.

Power users will find the utilities provided on the supplemental programs diskette worth the price of the book and diskette. These utilities provide sophisticated file management; a fast, professional menu generator; file encryption and attribute manipulation; and disk storage optimization. Power users will also find some of the tricks for providing file security and logging computer usage of interest. Some of these tricks are not documented in the DOS technical reference manual.

THE SUPPLEMENTAL PROGRAMS DISKETTE

Although you can implement many of the techniques described in this book directly from the text, some of the most powerful and useful applications require special utility programs. A diskette is offered by PC-SIG (see the back of the book) that contains special-purpose programs for creating menus, locating files, hiding and encrypting files, enhancing the performance of your hard disk, and much more. Most of the programs are in the *public domain*; that is, they have been made available to anyone who wishes to use them and can be freely duplicated and passed on to others.

Other programs contained on the diskette are made available to you on a *shareware* basis. These shareware programs are copyrighted and are provided to you for trial use. If you find that you like a particular program and plan to use it on a regular basis, you are asked to send the owner of the copyright a fee. Shareware fees are quite reasonable and are well worth the investment. After you send in your fee, you become a registered user of the shareware program. As improvements are made to the program, you will receive updates automatically. Also, you can call the shareware company directly if you need telephone support.

Remember, shareware programmers are in business just like anyone else. They usually offer excellent products for a fraction of what you would pay for commercial software with similar features. I have tested each of the shareware programs on the diskette and found them to be of high quality. Shareware programs are identified as such either with an initial sign-on message or in a special documentation file. Instructions for registering and the amount of the registration fee are included in the sign-on message or the documentation file.

COMMERCIAL PROGRAMS AND HARDWARE COMPONENTS

In addition to public domain and shareware programs, there is a host of commercial programs available for performing special functions associated with hard disks. Such special-purpose programs are referred to as *utilities*. There are utilities for backing up the data stored on your hard disk, utilities for managing files and data, utilities for creating menus, and still other utilities for improving the performance of your hard disk. Some of these programs are well worth their purchase price in terms of the time and effort they will save you in the long run.

There is also a large market in special-purpose hardware devices for use with hard disk computer systems. Most of these are designed to perform high-speed backup of the data stored on your hard disk. These products include streaming tape units, removable *Bernoulli* drives, and fault-tolerant systems. Other units are designed to improve the hardware performance of your hard disk.

A number of commercially available programs and hardware components are reviewed in this book. I am not making any recommendations regarding any of these products, nor do I receive any financial remuneration from the publishers of these programs. Information has been provided solely for your convenience in determining if you should purchase any of these products for your own use.

WHAT'S NEW IN THE SECOND EDITION

Since this book first appeared in 1987, a lot has changed in the personal computer industry. As far as software applications and DOS goes, it's a similar ball game: the same DOS commands are used, only there are more of them and the old ones have some extra options; hard disks and files are organized the same way (which is nice and consistent, but getting old); and faster and better utility programs exist to help you deal with your files, provide data security, and so on. The programs have gotten smarter and have more capabilities, but new things have been added and old things have changed, which is why a second edition of this book was deemed appropriate and necessary.

Also, since the last version, computers running DOS (which are generally referred to as "PCs" regardless of the machine's model or make) have more or less settled on using DOS version 3.3. Although both MS-DOS and PC-DOS have versions now numbering in the 4's, nearly everyone has agreed that DOS version 3.3 is the way to go. This book now includes DOS 3.3 as the standard version, and all references to DOS are made to that version. Where appropriate, this book also notes commands and comments on the capabilities of DOS version 4—and future releases of DOS—as well.

The big change in recent years has been in computer hardware. Faster computers we could only dream of a few years ago are here now and ready to go. Along with that technological leap comes bigger and faster hard drives. Where a few years ago having a hard drive was a novelty and merely a step up from floppy drives, today it's a technological leap: more storage, faster access to data, and more common than floppy disk systems.

Nearly two out of three computers sold today have hard drives. Half of the 30 million PCs out there have hard drives. It's now the rule and not the exception. Add the technological advances of more storage and suddenly, new and experienced users alike face an interesting situation. This second edition deals with those changes, letting you know how to manage your hard disk in an ever-advancing computer world.

CONVENTIONS USED IN THIS BOOK

Part of the purpose of this book is to educate you about hard disk technology. Although I have done my best to avoid overly technical discussions, it's in your interest to understand the terminology associated with this technology. When a new term is introduced, it will appear in *italics*. The term will be defined in the paragraph in which it is introduced. The primary reference in the index will refer to this initial definition.

Throughout the text of this book, you will be shown new commands. Most of them will be from the PC-DOS or MS-DOS operating system, or from one of the utility programs associated with these operating systems. I have followed the format of the MS-DOS users manual in listing the syntax of commands. Commands are shown in uppercase, with user-supplied information, such as drive designator and file specification, in lowercase. Optional information is displayed in brackets. Optional command parameters are displayed in uppercase within brackets. For example, the syntax of the FORMAT command is shown as:

FORMAT [d:][/S]

I have adopted the convention of displaying commands in uppercase although DOS does not require this practice. When disk drives are referred to in the text, only the letter corresponding to the drive is used. However, in commands, the full drive designator, including the colon, is included. When you are instructed to enter commands, they will appear according to the following format: The computer display will be shown in regular typeface, and the keystrokes you are to enter will be shown in an alternate type. Assume that you are to press the Enter key at the conclusion of each command.

For example, suppose you are to enter the command to format the hard disk, including the option to place the system files on the hard disk. Assume that the A drive is the floppy drive. The command would be displayed as follows:

A>FORMAT C:/S

This book refers to all computers capable of running MS-DOS or PC-DOS as either DOS computers, or just PCs. A PC can be any type of computer running DOS: a PC, PC/ XT, AT, 286, 386, 486, "clone," or compatible. When it comes to the computer's Disk Operating System, it's called "DOS." The differences between MS-DOS and PC-DOS are present but subtle. Therefore, for purposes of reference, let's just call it DOS.

Every attempt has been made to ensure that the information contained within this book is as easy to follow as possible. Although the subject matter is at times difficult and technical, the style of the book is always unintimidating and friendly. I hope that you find this book interesting and useful in helping you tame your own hard disk.

PART ONE
Hard
Disk
Organization

Using a computer with floppy disks only is easy—as far as organization is concerned. You have a pile of program diskettes and a pile of data diskettes. To use a program, you stick its diskette into the disk drive, close the drive's door, type the program's name at the DOS prompt, press ENTER, and—voilá—you're there. For organization, you alphabetized the stack of diskettes. But a hard drive is just one big disk. It holds all your programs and all your data—possibly thousands of files or more. How a hard drive works and keeping it organized is the subject of this part of the book.

1
The Basics of Disk Storage

HARD DISKS, with their massive storage capabilities and "black box" appearance, might seem a bit mysterious to many people—especially novice computer users, who often find the thought of all that storage space intimidating. If you feel this way about your hard disk, don't worry! This book will dispel the mysteries of megabytes, paths, and partitions and put you firmly in command of your hard disk.

This chapter exposes you to some practical theory relating to hard disk technology. Although there is no "how-to" information involved, the concepts and jargon talked about here will serve as the foundation for the remainder of the book. If terms like *sector*, *recording density*, and *access time* are unfamiliar to you, you should read this chapter before proceeding any further. If you already have some understanding of magnetic storage and how hard disks differ from their floppy cousins, feel free to merely skim over this material.

HARD DISK KNOW-HOW

A computer is just a tool, albeit a very powerful one, which you ultimately control. As tools go, your computer is really quite simple to learn and use. However, computers represent a different kind of tool than you might be used to working with. Computers have been referred to as "mind tools," which is an apt description, because they can drive you crazy (but only sometimes!).

Although computers consist of various hardware components, such as keyboards, screens, microprocessors (a computer's brain), and storage devices, what causes them to run the way you want them to is *software*. You can't see software; you can't touch it. Yes, although you can see and hold the floppy diskette that contains the software, the diskette itself isn't the software—just as a compact disc, or CD, isn't the music on the disc. In fact, the musical simile is a good one: your computer is an orchestra and software is the music. Music—the software—is what makes the orchestra—the hardware—productive.

Software is the ultimate "mind tool" because you control it by understanding how it works. As you have probably learned by now, an excellent computer program with poor documentation (a rotten manual) is pretty useless. The software itself is just as good whether it's described well in the manual or not. However, the program's value as a tool is limited by your level of understanding. If you can't read about it in the manual, how can you use the software?

The same concept applies to your hard disk. Whether you've recently upgraded your computer with a hard disk or just purchased a new system equipped with a hard drive, you must gain some basic understanding of how it operates before you can use it successfully. Of course, this is true of any powerful tool. How useful would your car be if you didn't know how to start it, drive it, and maintain it?

Consider the two types of knowledge you need in order to use your car effectively. First, you need "how-to" knowledge—commonly called *know how*. You need to know how to turn it on, operate the various switches and pedals, steer, brake, and so on. But you also need some *know why* knowledge as well. At a minimum, you need to know why the car goes when you press on the accelerator pedal. What would happen if your car ran out of gas on the freeway and you didn't have a clue why it stopped running? (Most people who run out of gas never assume that at first because they think they should know better.)

Your basic understanding of how your automobile works helps you to maintain it in proper working order and diagnose what's wrong when it isn't working. This kind of knowledge is frequently referred to as *practical theory*. Although you don't have to know all the technical details about how your automobile works, a little practical knowledge can go a long way.

BITS AND BYTES

The first step in understanding how computer storage works is to master the concept of *bits* and *bytes*. You've probably heard these two terms used before, and you might know that bytes are made out of bits. Bits are the basic units of data storage. A bit can have one of two values: zero or one. For this reason, computer data is often referred to as *binary,* which is base two. (We count in base 10, decimal.)

The octal and hexadecimal counting bases, shown in *Table 1-1*, are used mostly by programmers. Base 10, decimal, is used by most people for counting, balancing checkbooks, and obeying traffic laws. Binary is base 2, used by computers. Why? Because computers only really have two things to count: an on current (usually 5 or 12 volts) and an off current (no volts). That's the basis of how computers store all information.

Table 1-1. Computer Counting Bases.

Name	Base	Values
Binary	2	0 1
Octal	8	0 1 2 3 4 5 6 7
Decimal	10	0 1 2 3 4 5 6 7 8 9
Hexadecimal	16	0 1 2 3 4 5 6 7 8 9 A B C D E F

However, a zero or a one (an off or on current) does not contain much information. For this reason bits are grouped together in clusters called *bytes* (*Fig. 1-1*).

In the computer world, a byte is composed of eight bits. It takes at least one byte to represent any useful data, such as a character or a number.

Computers generally process whole bytes or groups of bytes when manipulating data. The number of bytes of data a computer can work with at one time is called its *word length* and depends upon the type of microprocessor it contains. Early microcomputers employed 8-bit microprocessors. The IBM AT and other computers using the 80286 microprocessor utilize a 16-bit word length. PCs with an 80386 microprocessor work with 32-bit word lengths. In practical terms, the longer the word length, the more bytes of data a PC can process at a time. (Although, the odd part is, DOS is still written to the lowest common denominator, meaning it still deals in 8-bit word lengths.)

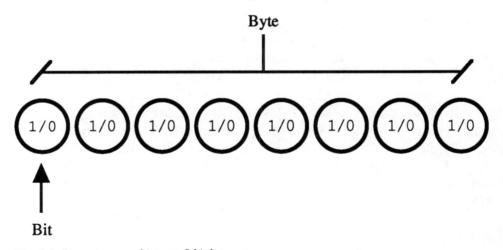

Fig. 1-1. Bits are grouped into an 8-bit byte.

DATA REPRESENTATION

When working with data, your computer is able to distinguish between *alphanumeric* and *numeric* data. Alphanumeric data include text and digits (0 through 9). However, alphanumeric digits have no arithmetic value. A street address, such as "123 Any St." is an example of alphanumeric data. "123" isn't a value. The value 123 also can be stored in a computer, but it is numeric data, not alphanumeric.

To represent alphanumeric data, your computer uses a coding scheme known as *ASCII* (American Standard Code for Information Interchange). It's a system of numbers from 0 to 127, each of which corresponds to a character, that is, a letter, number, or punctuation symbol. There are also codes that represent certain *control characters*, such as the Enter key, the Esc key, Backspace, Tab, and so on.

Every character on the keyboard, including both upper- and lowercase letters, has its own ASCII code value. For example, the capital letter "A" has the ASCII value 65 and the digit "9" has the value 57. Whenever you strike the capital letter "A," the ASCII byte value 65 is transmitted up the keyboard cable to your computer for input. In binary, the 65 looks like this: 01000001. The value for "9," 57, looks like this in binary: 00111001.

Numeric data is coded differently. With numeric data, the bit values represent the arithmetic value of the data—not the corresponding ASCII code. This is accomplished using the binary place values of the individual bits within a byte. *Figure 1-2* shows the binary place values for the first eight bit positions.

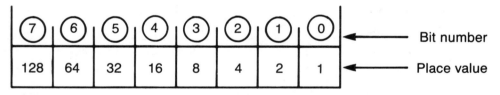

Fig. 1-2. Binary place values for the first eight bit positions of a binary number.

Using this binary arithmetic approach, the number 9 (the value) has the binary code value 00001001. There is a 1 in the eight's place and another 1 in the one's place; all the other bit positions contain 0's. Because 8 and 1 add up to 9, this specific sequence of bits represents the number 9. Notice that the binary coded number 9 differs from the ASCII digit 9. Don't worry if binary arithmetic is not one of your stronger subjects because you won't need to convert decimal numbers to their binary equivalents. The computer converts numbers automatically.

Your computer is able to differentiate between numeric and alphanumeric data according to the instructions of the software you are using. This means that you don't have to worry about data representation. Instead, you just type at the keyboard, or load information from a disk, and leave it to the software and the computer to wrestle with the bits and bytes while you concentrate on the job at hand.

Because the binary number system is the basis for data representation, people who work with computers often compute things in binary. For trivial purposes, *Table 1-2* shows a few common values converted into binary.

Table 1-2. Common Values Converted to Binary.

Common Value	Decimal	Binary
Fingers on one Hand	5	00000101
Planets in the Solar System	9	00001001
Sweet & Sour Pork	16	00010000
Hours in a Day	24	00011000
Baskin-Robins Flavors	31	00011111
States in the U.S.	50	00110010
The National Speed Limit	55	00111011
Squares on a Chess Board	64	01000000
Degrees in a Right Angle	90	01011010
A "C" Note	100	01100100
A Gross	144	10010000
Water Boils	212	11010100

Doesn't binary conversion make the metric system seem easy? But don't let it bother you. Usually it's only the computer types who stick to binary numbers Just consider binary numbers as byte values that can represent characters, letters, and numbers.

Bytes are referenced in groups, just as binary bits are grouped into bytes. These references to bytes are used primarily when dealing with computer storage. The letters used for references are *K, M,* and *G.*

The letter K stands for *kilobyte* and comes from the metric system representing 1,000. A K is not strictly 1,000, it is actually 2 raised to the tenth power, which equals 1,024. Since that's so close to 1,000, most people are willing to neglect the difference and consider 1K to be 1,000. "Close enough for government work" is one way of looking at it.

The letter M, for *megabyte*, means 1,000 K's or 1,048,576. You can compute this by multiplying 1,024 times 1,024. One megabyte is roughly a million bytes of storage. This might seem like a lot of storage until you start thinking in terms of gigabytes.

The letter G is for a *gigabyte*—1,000 M's, which is a whopping 1,073,741,844 bytes. Again, using round numbers, this is roughly equivalent to a billion (who's counting?). These large numbers are used because bytes of data are really quite small compared to the large volumes of data which frequently are processed by computers.

COMPUTER STORAGE

How does your computer keep track of all the bytes of programs and data you use? It must rely on various storage devices to keep track of those bytes. Computers use two different types of storage: electronic and magnetic.

Electronic Storage

Electronic storage, usually in the form of *RAM* (random access memory), is used by the computer while in operation. The computer needs some place to store the program instructions that tell it what to do, and it also must keep track of what has been done. In addition, it might need to remember the results of computations to be used in yet other computations.

Consider a simple example involving a word processing program. Before you can execute the word processing program, it must be loaded into your computer's RAM. The program instructions will be retained in RAM throughout your word processing session. When you begin typing a new document, the processed words are retained in your computer's RAM in a data area designated by the word processing program.

Most forms of electronic storage operate through the use of microscopic gates, or switches, that can be opened or closed according to the instructions of the word processing (or any computer) program. These switch settings remain in effect by electricity. If the power to the computer were interrupted, as in a power outage, the switch settings would return to their original state. This means that the program and the document under construction would be lost. Most kinds of electronic storage, including RAM, are considered to be *volatile* because information is erased everytime the power is disrupted. If you have ever lost important data because you inadvertently turned off your computer before saving (or the power company did it for you), then you know the true definition of volatility.

Another problem with electronic storage is its limited capacity. You are limited in the amount of RAM available to you by two factors: space and DOS. Space is a physical limitation—RAM chips might be small, but they do occupy space in your computer. RAM chips are categorized according to the number of gates they contain. Some common RAM chips contain 64K or 256K bits, or gates. Note that, when referring to RAM chips, the K stands for bits, not bytes. (It's often abbreviated "Kb" for Kilobit.)

Although 256K might seem like a lot of switches to squeeze onto a single chip, it takes nine 256K-bit chips to make up 256K of data or program. Today, many programs require much more memory than what is in RAM in order to run. In addition, you need room to store your data. A single-spaced page of text contains about 4K of data. This converts to roughly 64 pages per 256K of storage. Considering that the Encyclopedia Britannica contains some 20,000 pages (of course, it's not all text, but pictures require even more storage than words), you quickly see that 256K is a rather puny amount of storage. In order to hold a database of any real size, you would need more RAM chips than could fit into the case of your computer. And to think that the first microcomputer had only 4K of RAM!

The second limitation is one imposed by your DOS. Current versions of DOS limit you to 640K of RAM. There are a number of methods for overcoming this limitation, but they require additional hardware, software, or both. Future PC operating systems will expand the limits of RAM into the gigabyte range and even beyond. Even with such advances, unless the bit densities of RAM chips can be significantly increased, the space limitation will continue to restrict the amount of data that can be held in RAM.

Magnetic Storage

Because of volatility and storage limitations, computers usually come equipped with a second type of storage called *magnetic storage*. Magnetic storage usually involves placing a magnetic imprint of the stored data on some medium, such as disk or tape.

Magnetic storage enjoys several advantages over electronic storage. For one thing, magnetic storage media require no power at all because they don't rely on electronic switch settings to represent data. Turn off the power and the data stays on the magnetic media. Also, magnetic media are very space efficient. On a high-capacity disk drive, a single $5^1/_4$-inch diskette can hold 1.2M (megabytes, or a thousand kilobytes) of storage. A high-capacity $3^1/_2$-inch diskette can hold 1.44M of storage. You can store over a gigabyte of data on a single shelf of a bookcase because of the compactness of floppy disks.

The basic principles of magnetic storage are the same for every medium used: tape, floppy diskette, or hard disk. The tape or disk (usually mylar for tape and floppy diskette and aluminum for hard disks) is coated with a thin film containing molecules of ferric oxide (FeO_2) or a similar metallic oxide. The molecules exhibit a property known as *polarity*, which means they have tiny magnetic poles, just like a magnet.

Initially, these polarized molecules are randomly dispersed across the surface of the medium, so that their individual magnetic fields cancel each other. *Figure 1-3* illustrates this random situation. However, by subjecting localized areas of the surface to a strong magnetic force, the poles of clusters of these molecules can be aligned so that they exert a magnetic field of their own. When such a cluster has been created, a bit of data can be represented in that location on the media's surface. The read/write head in the disk drive or tape unit aligns the clusters of ferric oxide molecules on the surface of the medium, as shown in *Fig. 1-4*.

After the data has been stored, it can be read later by passing the surface of the medium under the read/write head. The read/write head detects the magnetic fields of the

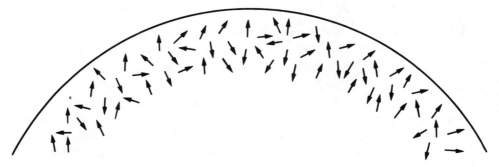

Fig. 1-3. Randomly dispersed molecules of ferric oxide on the surface of a disk.

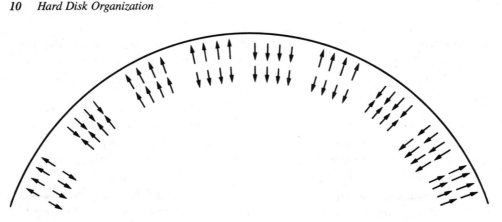

Fig. 1-4. Molecules of ferric oxide that have been aligned by the read/write head.

aligned clusters of molecules. The data will remain on the surface of the storage medium until it is either intentionally changed or the medium becomes damaged.

How can you damage the media or destroy your data? Magnetic storage media can be damaged in a variety of ways, many of which you were warned about when you first learned how to use your computer. Fingerprints, soft drinks, dirt, dust, and exposure to electromagnetic fields can cause data to disappear. The thin film containing the ferric oxide molecules can be scratched or corroded away. In these cases, the oxide molecules are literally lost.

The molecules can become "scrambled" through exposure to errant electromagnetic fields. Even the most innocent-looking appliances, such as telephones and answering machines (which tend to congregate with computers on desktops), can be the source of electromagnetic radiation. (Every phone has a magnet in the mouthpiece.) The mere ringing of a telephone can be enough to scramble data on a nearby floppy disk.

Because data stored on magnetic media can easily be lost, you should create multiple copies, or backups, of your data. You will learn more about creating backups in chapter 12, "Backing Up Data and Programs."

HARD DISKS VERSUS FLOPPY DISKETTES

In the microcomputer world, the two most common magnetic storage media are *floppy diskettes* and *hard disks*.

This wasn't always the case. The earliest microcomputers used cassette tapes to record programs and data. You can still see evidence with the IBM Cassette BASIC stored in the ROM of some early IBM PCs. This version of BASIC appears if you start an IBM PC without putting a DOS disk in the A drive. Although you can successfully enter and run a BASIC program from the keyboard, just try to save the program to disk. You can't. You would need a cassette tape connected to your computer. You might have noticed this connection located next to the keyboard cable input at the back of the IBM PC. (Clone and compatible PCs, as well as IBM's latest models, have dropped the cassette mode.)

Unless you were involved in the pioneering days of the microcomputer revolution, you are probably more familiar with floppy diskettes. Floppy disks are still the most prevalent storage medium for home computers, with business computers nearly always having hard disks. However, as advances in technology and increased production bring prices down, more and more microcomputers are being equipped and sold with hard disks. There are three major advantages of hard disks over floppy disks:

(1) Increased storage capacity
(2) Faster access time
(3) Greater convenience

If you have recently switched from a floppy system to one sporting a hard disk, you're well aware—and possibly quite thankful—of these advantages.

Early Hard Disk History

Interestingly enough, hard disk technology actually preceded floppy diskette technology. Hard disks evolved from magnetic drum storage. In fact, a drum symbol is used to represent auxiliary storage in systems design flow charts, and near the hard drive LED on the face plate of some present-day computers.

Magnetic drums were hard metallic cylinders with an oxide coating. The drum rotated under a read/write head which recorded and read data on its surface. There were many disadvantages to drum storage, not the least of which was the physical size of the drums.

One of the earliest forms of hard disks was developed by IBM in the early 1970's. These disks were capable of storing 30M of data per side. This characteristic quickly gained them the code name "Winchester disks" after the famed 30/30 rifle.

The first Winchester disks were a whopping 14 inches in diameter and today survive only in the form of coffee tables. Contemporary Winchester disks are typically $5^1/_4$ or $3^1/_2$ inches in diameter. However, the basic design concepts of Winchester disks are still employed in most hard disk drive units used with microcomputers.

Fixed Hard Disks

Winchester disks are *fixed disks*. Some computer manuals (notably IBM's) refer to them that way. In fact, FDISK, a hard disk initialization program, stands for Fixed DISK. (You'll read about FDISK in the next chapter.)

Fixed disk means that the disk drive motor, the read/write head, and the disk itself are all enclosed within a sealed unit. For reasons that will become apparent in a moment, hard disk units need to operate in a vacuum. This is one of the reasons that hard disk drives are more expensive than floppy drives. The disk must either be sealed in a vacuum at the time of manufacture, as is the case with Winchester drives, or some method is used to create a vacuum when the drive is in operation.

Rigid Disk Surface. The reason hard disks can store so much more data than floppy diskettes involves the rigidity of the disk. Floppy diskettes are exactly that—floppy. When they revolve in their jacket, they actually wobble. This wobbling effect means that, at any given point in time, the surface of the diskette may be fairly far away from the read/write head. This requires that the magnetic fields recorded on the diskettes be relatively strong in order to be sensed by the read/write head. Due to the strength of the magnetic fields on the diskette's surface, each localized, magnetically recorded bit must be separated from its neighbors. Otherwise, the magnetic fields would interfere with each other, resulting in unreliable data. *Figure 1-5* illustrates this situation.

Hard disks, on the other hand, are rigid. They don't wobble even at high revolutions. For this reason, the read/write head in a hard disk drive can be placed very close to the surface of the disk.

Head clearances in hard disk drives are typically about one-millionth of an inch. As a consequence, the magnetic fields recorded on the disk can be much weaker and can be placed much closer together. Compare *Fig. 1-5* with *Fig. 1-6*, which represents data

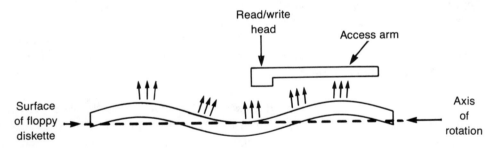

Fig. 1-5. The "floppy" surface of a diskette requires stronger magnetic fields to represent data.

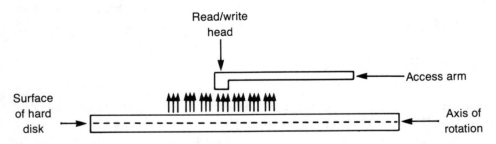

Fig. 1-6. The rigid surface of a hard disk allows the heads to "float" very close to the disk surface, permitting the use of weak magnetic fields to represent data.

stored on a hard disk. The overall result is far greater storage capacity on hard disks than floppy diskettes.

However, there is a price to pay for increased storage capacity. Because the head clearance is so microscopically small, the hard drive must operate in a vacuum (as was mentioned earlier). *Figure 1-7* shows the relative size of some common airborne particles in comparison to the head clearance of a typical hard disk drive. Note that even a fingerprint exceeds this clearance.

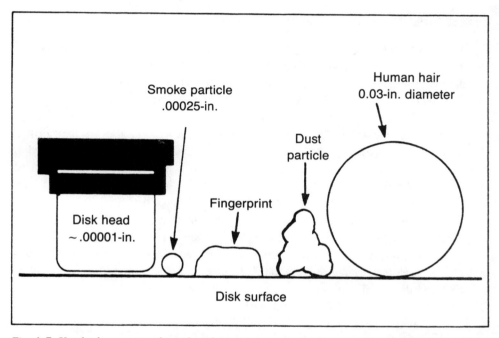

Fig. 1-7. Head tolerances on the order of one micron compared to a variety of airborne particles.

Rapidly Spinning. Due in part to the rigidity, hard disks can revolve very rapidly, often as fast as 3,600 RPM. The read/write heads used in these drives are aerodynamically designed to float, or fly, on the cushion of air created by the rapidly revolving disk.

At such high speeds and with such low tolerances, any particulate matter that gets in the way can cause the head to literally crash into the surface of the disk. The resulting collision will scratch the surface of the disk, rendering it unusable. Because the disk is an integral part of the Winchester drive unit, the entire drive must be replaced. *Head crashes* are by no means unheard of and are one of the primary reasons for making hard disk backups.

Bits Per Inch. One way of comparing the amount of data that can be stored on different media is to measure the number of bits that can be recorded in a given area. This measurement is given in terms of bits per inch, abbreviated bpi. (The inch component actually refers to a one inch segment of the innermost track of the disk; see the following section entitled "Disk Formats.")

Because different manufacturers of Winchester disk drives employ different techniques for writing data to disk, there is a wide variety of bit densities to choose from. Some common recording densities are 6,270 bpi, 7,900 bpi, and 9,300 bpi. Recent advances in recording media have lead to recording densities in excess of 20,000 bpi. Floppy diskette recording densities typically fall in the 5,000 bpi range.

Fixed Disks Versus Removable Disks

The Winchester fixed disk is currently the most commonly used kind of hard disk. As mentioned previously, fixed disk drives include the read/write head, the drive mechanism and the disk itself in a single, integrated, vacuum-sealed unit. Fixed disk technology is well-established, and costs for hard drives have fallen dramatically so hard drives are affordable for even modest computing budgets.

There are limitations to fixed disk technology, however. Because the hard disk is physically "fixed" inside the drive unit, it cannot be removed if it becomes damaged or completely filled with data. A damaged disk means a damaged drive, which must be returned to the factory for repair. And, while you may not believe it right now, someday all those megabytes of storage are going to be used up. Then what?

To overcome these limitations, several different alternative technologies have been developed. All involve some method of separating the hard disk itself from the drive and read/write mechanism. These hard drive units are referred to as removable disks or Bernoulli disks, depending upon the technology employed. Removable disk devices will be reviewed and discussed along with tape backup units in chapter 13, "Tape, Removable Disk, Bernoulli, and Fault Tolerant Systems."

The techniques for hard disk management are the same whether you are working with a fixed disk or a removable disk. For this reason, the term *hard disk* will be used throughout this book to refer to either a fixed or a removable disk.

DISK FORMATS

As was mentioned earlier, the recording surface of the disk consists of a thin layer of randomly dispersed molecules of ferric oxide. Data is magnetically imprinted on the disk by aligning the poles of these molecules. After a byte of data has been stored on the disk, the disk drive must have some method of retrieving that byte. If the surface of the disk was truly uniform, it would be impossible for your computer to locate data after it was recorded. Your computer uses an addressing scheme when storing and retrieving data from disk. This addressing scheme utilizes a series of magnetic markers on the surface of the disk. These markings constitute the disk's *format*.

Tracks and Sectors

Disk formats differ from one brand of computer to another, and even from one version of DOS to another. Despite the seemingly bewildering array of disk formats, certain key elements remain the same in any format. All disk formats employ *tracks* and *sectors* to accomplish addressing schemes.

Tracks consist of concentric rings, which start from the outer edge of the disk and continue inward. Each track is assigned a number, or address, starting with zero for the outermost track. The tracks are further divided into segments called sectors. The sectors within each track are also assigned a number. *Figure 1-8* shows a simplified representation

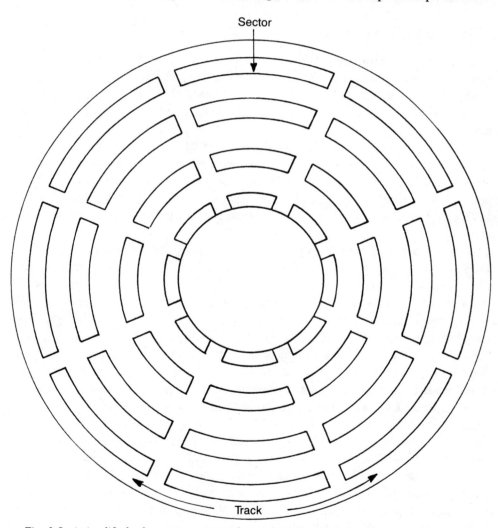

Fig. 1-8. A simplified scheme representing the tracks and sectors of a disk.

of a formatted disk. The number of actual tracks and sectors varies depending upon the disk format.

Disks don't normally come with the tracks and sectors imprinted on their surface. Instead, they are sold blank, or unformatted, so you can use them in any computer you have. You must format blank disks using a special formatting program. (Note: many hard disks are preformatted; more on this in chapter 2, "Preparing Hard Disks.")

IBM PC and XT floppy diskettes are formatted 40 tracks to a side, while both the $5^1/4$-inch high-capacity diskettes and the $3^1/2$-inch microfloppies used with AT-type computers utilize a more sophisticated format with 80 tracks per side. Hard disks usually have hundreds of tracks. For example, most 20M hard drives contain over 600 tracks.

TPI and Disk Density

Surprisingly, the tracks do not cover the entire surface of the disk. In fact, the distance between the outermost and innermost tracks is about 2 centimeters (roughly three-quarters of an inch). The number of tracks per inch, tpi, depends on the disk density. (Note: disk density is related to recording density, or bpi, but is used in reference to tracks rather than bits.)

The standard 360K, $5^1/4$-inch diskettes are referred to as double-density diskettes; 1.2M diskettes are quad-density diskettes. Double-density diskettes, which record 48 tpi, are physically different from quad-density diskettes, which record 96 tpi. Although 360K double-density diskettes may be used in 1.2M drives, they can only be formatted at 48 tpi. In order to format at the higher 96 TPI, you must purchase the special quad-density diskettes.

The number of sectors per track also differs depending upon the format. The original DOS version 1.1 used a format with eight sectors per track. Subsequent versions of DOS (2.0 and above) have a nine sector format. There are 15 sectors per track on quad-density, 1.2M diskettes. Hard disk drives are normally formatted with 17 sectors per track. Each sector contains the same number of bytes, regardless of its location on the disk. The most common sector size is 512 bytes, although some hard disks have 1,024-byte sectors.

Because the width of the sectors remains constant across all tracks, you might think that there should be more sectors in the outer tracks than in the inner ones. However, this would interfere with the addressing scheme, which depends upon a constant number of sectors from track to track. Instead, there are unused gaps between the sectors in the outer tracks. In fact, much of the surface of a disk is unused.

The problem of unused space is exemplified in DOS 1.1, which can only format one side of a floppy diskette. Why? When DOS 1.1 was introduced, most floppy drives contained only one read/write head and could only record data on one side of the diskette. Following the old adage that two heads are better than one, later drives contained read/write heads for both sides of the diskette. Thus, DOS versions 2.0 and higher are capable of formatting both sides of the diskette.

Unfortunately, this situation has given rise to some misleading terminology. Diskettes manufactured for use in drives with only one head are called "single-sided," while diskettes intended for use in dual-headed drives are referred to as "double-sided" or "dual-sided," and are marked as such.

Actually, there's no such thing as a single-sided diskette. Every disk has two sides just as every coin has two sides. During manufacturing, each disk is coated on both sides with an oxide emulsion. However, during quality control inspection, single sided-diskettes are tested on only one side. Double-sided diskettes, on the other hand, get the deluxe treatment and are tested on both sides. Because double-sided diskettes usually cost more than single-sided diskettes, knowledgeable computer users frequently buy single-sided diskettes for use in their double-sided drives. When many people started doing this, and when single-sided disk drives were in a rapid decline, diskette manufacturers dropped their single-sided line of products.

Platters, Surfaces and Cylinders

Hard drive units usually contain a number of disks, or *platters*. The sides of these platters are referred to as *surfaces*. Most hard drives contain two platters. It's possible, though, to purchase disk drives containing many platters. The number of platters contained in a drive unit in part determines the amount of storage it provides. Although a hard disk drive might contain several platters, it's common to refer to these enclosed platters as a single hard disk. Thus, individuals often say, "My hard disk holds 30M of data," when, in fact, the drive they are referring to contains two physical disks.

Track locations on hard disks are described in terms of *cylinders* because the same-numbered track on multiple surfaces essentially constitutes a cylinder in space. Instead of describing the location of data by surface, track, and sector, the surface, cylinder, and sector is used. By using the information provided for a given disk drive, you can determine the amount of formatted storage it can hold.

Consider a disk drive containing two platters with a recording density of 690 tpi (resulting in 612 usable tracks per surface). If the disk is formatted with 17 sectors per track, 512 bytes per sector, that creates 5,326,848 bytes of storage per surface, or 21,307,392 bytes in all. (Remember, the drive contains four recording surfaces.)

DISK ACCESS

In addition to increased storage capacity, hard disk drives have the advantage of providing much faster access to data on the disk. *Access time* is a measure of the time required to locate and retrieve a sector of data. Although data might not come in nice, neat 512 byte blocks, the disk drive always reads and writes a sector at a time. (Technically, this is incorrect. See the section entitled "Directories and File Access Tables" in chapter 3 for a more accurate description.)

Access times for hard disks are typically about 40 milliseconds (one millisecond is ¹/₁₀₀₀ of a second). The original PC/XT hard drive had an access time of 85 to 100 ms. That might seem slow by today's standards, but consider that floppy disk drive access times fall in the range of 175 to 300 milliseconds. Presently, some of the high speed 386 computer's hard drives have access times under 18 milliseconds. Access times keep getting faster and faster. (Non-hard disk technology RAM drives have access times of under one millisecond!)

The reason for the striking differences in access times between hard and floppy drives is due to the mechanical differences between the two kinds of drives. In order to appreciate these differences, you need to have a basic understanding of how disk drives operate. Certain components are common to any kind of drive.

Disks, floppy or hard, are held by a spindle much like a phonograph record. This spindle is rotated by the drive motor. There is a separate read/write head for each recording surface of the disk. Because the read/write head must be able to access data on any of the tracks, it is movable. The read/write head is placed on an *access arm* similar to the arm of a phonograph turntable. The access arm can be directed to move in or out according to the location of the track containing the sector to be accessed. *Figure 1-9* shows how an access arm works on a disk.

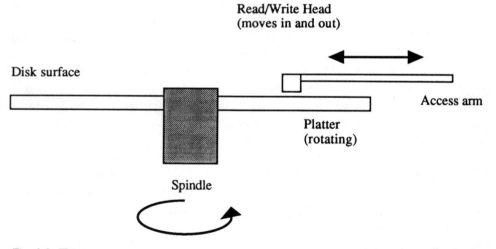

Fig. 1-9. The access arm moves the read/write head across the rotating disk surface, allowing it to access any area of the disk.

The difference in rotation speed between hard and floppy drives is one reason hard drives have faster access times. Hard drives revolve at 3,600 RPM as opposed to 360 RPM for floppy drives. Even though hard drives have twice the number of sectors per track, it takes only one tenth as long to position the read/write head over a given sector on a hard drive. This time lag is known as *latency*.

Another element of access time is the amount of time it takes the access arm to move over the appropriate track. This is referred to as *seek time*. In floppy drives, the read/write head is usually mounted on a pair of rails, and track seeking is accomplished by moving the head in and out through the action of a stepper motor. With most hard disk drives, each read/write head is mounted on its own access arm, and the access arms swing in or out as a single unit. Because of the mechanics involved, seek times tend to be faster for hard drives than for floppy drives.

RANDOM VERSUS SEQUENTIAL FILE STORAGE

Hard disk devices are designed to hold large volumes of data and programs. Although the disk is divided into tracks (or cylinders) and sectors, it isn't very helpful to know that the data you are looking for is stored on surface two, cylinder seven, sectors 15, 16, 17, and 18. Instead, you want to assign some easy-to-remember name to the data. For this reason, data and programs are given filenames, either by the program or the user creating them. In chapter 3, "Filenames And Directories," the rules for filenames will be described in detail. For now, all you need to know is that both programs and data are considered as files by the operating system and are saved accordingly.

There are two methods for storing and retrieving files from disk: *sequential storage* and *random storage*.

With sequential storage, the entire contents of the file are written to the disk onto adjacent sectors within a given track. If one track is insufficient for all the data in the file, the head moves to the next track and continues writing data.

Sequential storage requires that there be enough empty consecutive tracks and sectors to hold the entire file. Because this isn't always the case, sequential file storage normally isn't used. Instead, files are stored randomly.

Random storage, as its name implies, means that files are stored randomly on the disk according to the availability of sectors. Sectors are grouped together into clusters, and will be explained in chapter 3.

For example, assume you are creating a marketing proposal using your favorite word processor. When you are done entering data, the document is 27K in length. When you save the file, your word processor gives the job of saving the file to DOS.

At that moment, the read/write head happens to be positioned over cylinder 6, sector 9. DOS investigates surface 0 and finds data stored in this sector, so it moves on to surface 1. On this surface, sector 9 is empty, so DOS places the first 2K of the file into this and the subsequent adjacent sectors. However, the next available cluster on surface 1, cylinder 6, is full, so DOS moves down to surface 2. If this cluster and the corresponding cluster on surface 3 are both full, then DOS will move the access arm over the next cylinder looking for an empty cluster, where it stores the next 2K of data. This process continues until all 27K of the file have found a home.

Obviously, all this searching for empty sectors takes time. As you might expect, random storage and retrieval is slower than sequential storage and retrieval. Retrieval times are typically twice as fast for sequential files as for random files. Unfortunately, random storage is dictated by the random sizes of the files stored on disk.

You might realize that sequential storage can only be employed when copying the entire contents of one disk onto another. Then the operating system has a chance to work with a fresh disk and can write the files sequentially, one after another, onto the new disk.

One final note on random and sequential storage: these terms refer to the file storage method, not the contents of the files themselves. In programming, it is possible to create either *sequential access* or *random access* data files. Random and sequential access refer to the way individual records are stored within the data file itself. A sequential access data file will normally be stored randomly on the disk, although it might be stored sequentially if it is copied onto a new disk.

SUMMARY

This chapter has provided you with an overview of disk storage. Most experienced computer users are familiar with the concepts and terms included in this chapter. However, there are many more technical details pertaining to disk formats and file storage that you must be aware of when working with hard disks.

2
Preparing Hard Disks

PREPARING HARD DISKS for use involves three separate procedures: *partitioning,* *formatting,* and *sysgening.* Usually, one or more of these steps are performed by the hard disk manufacturer or your computer dealer prior to sale. If you've been using your hard disk for some time and these three terms are still unfamiliar to you, the chances are that your hard disk was prepared for you. In this case, you might wonder why you should bother reading this chapter.

Unfortunately, nothing in the world of microcomputers is static. (Unless you rub your feet on the carpet and touch your computer's metal case.) Both computer technology and your individual needs will change, often more rapidly than you expect. Because of changing software needs, the addition of a network, or merely as a result of your increased sophistication, you might find that the original setup of your hard disk is no longer appropriate.

In this chapter, you'll learn how to partition, format, and install the operating system (DOS) on your hard disk for initial use. You'll also learn how to repartition and reformat your hard disk, as well as install different versions of DOS on your hard disk to accommodate your changing software and computing needs. Each of these operations are explained in detail. However, before proceeding with specific instructions, the difference between logical and physical disk formats needs to be explained.

LOGICAL VERSUS PHYSICAL FORMATTING

Disks must be formatted prior to use. This is true regardless of the size or type of disk; even hard disks must be formatted.

DOS disk formats actually consist of more than just the tracks and sectors laid down on the surface of the disk. In addition to *physical* data addresses, a DOS disk format includes what's considered *logical* information. This information includes technical details regarding the disk format, as well as two work areas: the *directory* and the *File Allocation Table*, or FAT. (You'll learn more about these two features of a disk's format in chapter 3, "Filenames And Directories.")

The processes of physical and logical formatting are often performed independently with hard disks. These two formats are sometimes referred to as the disk's *low-level format* and *high-level format*. Before reading about these two components of a hard disk's format, follow the process of formatting a floppy diskette, where physical formatting and logical formatting are done at the same time.

The Format Operation

The DOS command to format a diskette is FORMAT. (It's actually a file on disk, FORMAT.COM, therefore it's considered an external DOS command.) FORMAT is typed at the DOS prompt and followed by the letter of the drive containing a diskette to be formatted. As is always the case, the drive letter is followed by a colon.

For example, to format a diskette in drive B, type the following FORMAT command:

```
A>FORMAT B:
```

You've probably done this dozens of times to format floppy diskettes. You might also recall that it's possible to format a diskette so that it can be used as a *system* (DOS, or bootable) diskette by including the /S option:

```
A>FORMAT B:/S
```

This and other formatting options will be explained in greater detail later in this chapter.

The Physical Format

When you enter the FORMAT command, DOS prompts you to insert a diskette in drive B (or whichever drive you've specified) and press any key when ready. Once the go-ahead is given, DOS formats the diskette.

The formatting process consists of several steps for floppy disks. First, DOS lays down the magnetic tracks and sectors on the diskette's surface, starting with the outermost track. As each track is formatted, the individual sectors within the track are established. The number of tracks per surface and the number of sectors per track are dictated by the version of DOS you are using. Also, DOS knows certain characteristics of the disk drive containing the diskette you're formatting. It will always attempt to format the highest capacity diskette for that drive, unless you direct it to do otherwise using FORMAT's optional switches. The tracks and sectors created by this initial step constitute the diskette's physical format.

In the case of floppy diskettes, DOS *initializes* each sector as it is created by filling in the individual bytes with dummy data. The actual value used by DOS is the decimal number 246, or F6 in hexadecimal. This initialization process is intrinsic to the process of physical formatting and cannot be circumvented. It's possible to reuse a diskette that has been used in a different type of computer, or which has been used with the same computer but for a different purpose, however any data originally stored on the diskette will be overwritten. Initializing the diskette ensures that no prior data or machine code remain from the diskette's former life. (Alas, there's no such thing as reincarnation with floppy diskettes.)

Formatting a previously used diskette can be both beneficial and destructive. It's beneficial if you really want to reuse the diskette for some new purpose. However, it can be devastating if you mistakenly format a diskette that has important information or a valuable program. Unfortunately, formatting a floppy diskette physically replaces the old data with new (dummy) data, and the process is irreversible.

The Logical Format

After the physical formatting is complete, DOS proceeds with the logical formatting of the diskette. Logical formatting establishes the work areas on the diskette. These work areas are used to control how and where files will be stored. The logical format of a disk, be it hard or floppy, consists of three separate work areas. The first of these is the *boot record*.

The boot record is stored in the first sector on the diskette and is quite brief. In fact, it occupies less than the full 512 bytes allocated for it. The primary function of the boot record is to assist DOS in *booting*, or loading the operating system on computer startup. (This function of the boot record will be discussed later in this chapter.)

Another purpose of the boot record is to serve as an ID record of the diskette's characteristics. These include the version of DOS used to format the disk and the details of the disk's physical format, such as the number of tracks per side and sectors per track. Additional information pertains to the diskette's other work areas: the directory and the File Allocation Table. Finally, the boot record contains a special two-byte ID code which DOS uses to indicate the type of disk format employed on the diskette, as shown in *Fig. 2-1*.

The special information contained in the boot record assists DOS in determining the diskette's physical format and in locating and reading files stored on the diskette. You can think of the boot record as the diskette's "dog tags." For example, *Table 2-1* describes some of the details about the boot record illustrated in *Fig. 2-1*. (The values listed are in base 16, hexadecimal):

Offset (in hexadecimal)

```
      00 01 02 03 04 05 06 07-08 09 0A 0B 0C 0D 0E 0F
000   EB 34 90 49 42 4D 20 20-33 2E 33 00 02 02 01 00    .4.IBM  3.3.....
010   02 70 00 D0 02 FD 02 00-09 00 02 00 00 00 00 00    .p..............
020   00 00 00 00 00 00 00 00-00 00 00 00 00 00 00 12    ................
030   00 00 00 00 01 00 FA 33-C0 8E D0 BC 00 7C 16 07    .......3.....|..
040   BB 78 00 36 C5 37 1E 56-16 53 BF 2B 7C B9 0B 00    .x.6.7.V.S.+|...
050   FC AC 26 80 3D 00 74 03-26 8A 05 AA 8A C4 E2 F1    ..&.=.t.&.......
060   06 1F 89 47 02 C7 07 2B-7C FB CD 13 72 67 A0 10    ...G...+|...rg..
070   7C 98 F7 26 16 7C 03 06-1C 7C 03 06 0E 7C A3 3F    |..&.|...|...|.?
080   7C A3 37 7C B8 20 00 F7-26 11 7C 8B 1E 0B 7C 03    |.7|. ..&.|...|.
090   C3 48 F7 F3 01 06 37 7C-BB 00 05 A1 3F 7C E8 9F    .H....7|....?|..
0A0   00 B8 01 02 E8 B3 00 72-19 8B FB B9 0B 00 BE D6    .......r........
0B0   7D F3 A6 75 0D 8D 7F 20-BE E1 7D B9 0B 00 F3 A6    }..u... ..}.....
0C0   74 18 BE 77 7D E8 6A 00-32 E4 CD 16 5E 1F 8F 04    t..w}.j.2...^...
0D0   8F 44 02 CD 19 BE C0 7D-EB EB A1 1C 05 33 D2 F7    .D.....}.....3..
0E0   36 0B 7C FE C0 A2 3C 7C-A1 37 7C A3 3D 7C BB 00    6.|...<|.7|.=|..
0F0   07 A1 37 7C E8 49 00 A1-18 7C 2A 06 3B 7C 40 38    ..7|.I...|*.;|@8
100   06 3C 7C 73 03 A0 3C 7C-50 E8 4E 00 58 72 C6 28    .<|s..<|P.N.Xr.(
110   06 3C 7C 74 0C 01 06 37-7C F7 26 0B 7C 03 D8 EB    .<|t...7|.&.|...
120   D0 8A 2E 15 7C 8A 16 FD-7D 8B 1E 3D 7C EA 00 00    ....|...}..=|...
130   70 00 AC 0A C0 74 22 B4-0E BB 07 00 CD 10 EB F2    p....t".........
140   33 D2 F7 36 18 7C FE C2-88 16 3B 7C 33 D2 F7 36    3..6.|....;|3..6
150   1A 7C 88 16 2A 7C A3 39-7C C3 B4 02 8B 16 39 7C    .|..*|.9|.....9|
160   B1 06 D2 E6 0A 36 3B 7C-8B CA 86 E9 8A 16 FD 7D    .....6;|.....}
170   8A 36 2A 7C CD 13 C3 0D-0A 4E 6F 6E 2D 53 79 73    .6*|.....Non-Sys
180   74 65 6D 20 64 69 73 6B-20 6F 72 20 64 69 73 6B    tem disk or disk
190   20 65 72 72 6F 72 0D 0A-52 65 70 6C 61 63 65 20    error..Replace
1A0   61 6E 64 20 73 74 72 69-6B 65 20 61 6E 79 20 6B    and strike any k
1B0   65 79 20 77 68 65 6E 20-72 65 61 64 79 0D 0A 00    ey when ready...
1C0   0D 0A 44 69 73 6B 20 42-6F 6F 74 20 66 61 69 6C    ..Disk Boot fail
1D0   75 72 65 0D 0A 00 49 42-4D 42 49 4F 20 20 43 4F    ure...IBMBIO  CO
1E0   4D 49 42 4D 44 4F 53 20-20 43 4F 4D 00 00 00 00    MIBMDOS  COM....
1F0   00 00 00 00 00 00 00 00-00 00 00 00 00 00 55 AA    ..............U.
```

Fig. 2-1. Information held in a 360K floppy diskette, formatted using PC-DOS 3.3, is shown here.

Table 2-1. Boot Record Details.

Offset	Value	Meaning
003	"IBM 3.3"	It's a PC-DOS 3.3 formatted diskette
00B	200	Bytes per sector; 200 hexadecimal is 512
011	70	Maximum files in the root directory; 70 hex is 112 decimal
015	FD	Type of media; FD is a 360K, 5^1/$_2$-inch diskette
018	9	Sectors per track
01A	2	Number of read/write heads (it's a double-sided disk drive)
01E	n/a	Boot loader program

The boot loader program, at offset 1E hex, would load the DOS routines on a system diskette. However, on this nonsystem diskette, the loader routine will probably display one of the messages seen in *Fig. 2-1*, starting at offset 177 hex.

Immediately following the boot record on the diskette is its *File Allocation Table* (there are two of them, actually). This table is a special work area reserved for keeping track of the physical location of the various files stored on the disk. This work area is established and initialized during the second, or logical, phase of the formatting procedure.

Adjacent to the File Allocation Table is the diskette's *root directory*. The root directory is a special file that contains entries for each individual file stored on the disk. As with the File Allocation Table, the directory is initially full of dummy data. Entries to the root directory are made when files are added to the diskette.

Although the boot record is always located in the first sector, the size and resulting locations of the File Allocation Table and the root directory vary according to the type of format used on the diskette. These two size characteristics are part of the diskette's format information and are recorded in the boot record. With this information, DOS determines where the data portion of the diskette is located. The data portion of the diskette is the area allocated for actual file storage, and it consists of most of the diskette's storage space.

Floppy Versus Hard Disk Formatting Procedures

When formatting floppy diskettes, DOS performs both physical and logical formatting at the same time. However, most hard disks come preformatted. This means that the physical format (i.e., the tracks and sectors) is established on the disk by technicians at the factory.

The physical format, or *low-level format* as it's sometimes called, is usually a permanent feature of the disk. However, it's possible for the format of the hard disk to become damaged, just as it's possible to damage a floppy diskette's format. For this reason, you should be familiar with reestablishing the physical format of your hard disk. A procedure for low-level formatting of a hard disk is included at the end of this chapter.

Drive Designators

Normally, you will only be required to establish a hard disk's logical, or *high-level*, format. Surprisingly, the same DOS FORMAT command is used to perform a high-level format. DOS is able to distinguish between your computer's hard disk and floppy drive(s). To understand how DOS recognizes a disk drive as either hard or floppy, you need to be familiar with *drive designators*.

Most microcomputers have at least two disk drives, although the original IBM PC came stocked with only one floppy drive. Many users add additional hard and floppy drives to their computers for various reasons. Each physical drive is assigned a *logical device designator*, which is a letter followed by a colon. Logical drive designators enable DOS to identify which drive a specific command is intended for. The number of logical device designators is determined by the version of DOS you are using. For example, DOS 3.3 allows up to 26 logical devices, one for each letter of the alphabet.

Traditionally, the designators A: and B: are used for the first two floppy drives, with the remaining alphabetical designators assigned to hard drives and other storage devices. You can even assign a drive designator to a portion of your RAM, and treat your memory like a disk drive. (You'll learn how to create "RAM disks," as they're called, in chapter 18, "Disk Access Optimization.")

The floppy drive on computers with one hard and one floppy drive can be referred to as either A: or B:. The hard drive is assigned the C: drive designator. Note that the single floppy drive, though physically drive A, can be logically referred to as either or A or B. When you enter a command for drive B, DOS will ask you to insert a diskette for drive B, and press a key to continue. When accessing drive A, the same question is asked for drive A. Internally, DOS keeps track of the logical drives B and A, although only one physical drive exists. *Table 2-2* shows designators and their devices.

Table 2-2. Device Drive Designators.

Drive Designator	Device
A	First/only floppy drive
B	Second floppy drive/logical second floppy drive
C	First hard drive
D	Second hard drive/other device/partitioned drive
E	Third hard drive/other device/partitioned drive
...	
Z	Twenty-fourth hard drive/other device/partitioned drive

When you type the FORMAT command, you have to include the designator for the drive containing the disk to be formatted. DOS then checks a table of drive designators for your computer. This table is stored in the computer's ROM BIOS, which is a special read-only memory chip installed by the computer's manufacturer. This table determines the type of disk to be formatted, and DOS proceeds accordingly.

On a hard disk, the DOS FORMAT command dispenses with the physical formatting process and only performs the logical, or high-level, formatting tasks. There are three tasks, covered in the previous section:

(1) Writing the boot record
(2) Establishing the File Allocation Tables (FATs)
(3) Installing the empty root directory

Contrary to floppy diskette formatting, DOS does not initialize the data area of a hard disk during formatting. Data stored on the hard disk is not actually destroyed during reformatting, but access to the data is removed because the root directory and File Allocation Tables are rewritten. However, there are special utility programs that will help you reconstruct the original root directory and File Allocation Tables.

PREPARING A HARD DISK

As soon as you understand the difference between physical and logical formats, you can put the process of hard disk preparation into a sequence of four individual operations:

(1) The physical (low-level) format
(2) Establishing any partitions
(3) The high-level format
(4) Copying the operating system

The first step in preparing a hard disk is physically formatting the surface of the disk. (Remember from chapter 1 that there can be several platters involved.) The physical format is usually written to the disk at the factory, and the disk is said to be preformatted, or low-level formatted. (This might not always be the case.)

The next step in hard disk preparation is to divide the hard disk into separate *partitions*. Partitions separate different file storage areas on the disk. There are a number of reasons why you would want separate file storage areas. One reason for partitions might be to create individual environments for different operating systems. Another reason could be to separate networking files from an individual user's files on a hard disk that is acting as a network file server. The third, and most common reason, is that DOS (up to version 4.0) can only deal with hard disks up to 32M in size. Larger hard disks must be partitioned into 32M segments so DOS can access the extra storage. Most hard disks, however, are prepared with a single partition in which all files are stored. This is probably the way your hard disk is currently set up if it's already in use.

After the hard disk is partitioned, each individual partition must receive a high-level format. The details of high-level formats vary from one operating system to another. This book deals only with DOS. If you plan to utilize one or more partitions on your hard disk to run other operating systems, such as the UNIX/Xenix, AIX, or CP/M 86, you'll need to follow the specific instructions for formatting hard disks included with those systems' manuals. Remember that these format routines will only perform logical formatting within the hard disk partition allocated to them.

The final step in preparing a hard disk is transferring a copy of the operating system to the disk. This procedure is sometimes called *sysgening* because it generates a copy of the operating system on the disk. As you will see, DOS consists of three separate system files, two of which are hidden from view. Once the operating system has been installed, the computer can be booted from the hard disk. This means the computer will start up and load the operating system directly from the hard disk without requiring a system disk in drive A.

Partitioning a Hard Disk

Assuming the hard disk has been physically formatted, the first thing you need to do when preparing a new hard disk is to partition it. Even if you only intend to operate your computer as a stand-alone DOS computer, you will have to perform this operation. However, you might want to check with your computer dealer, who might have performed this step as a service to you before delivering your computer. If so, you can skip this section and proceed to the section titled "Formatting a Hard Disk."

Hard disk partitions are created using the FDISK command. This command invokes a special program that prompts you for certain information and then uses this information to create a *partition table* on the disk. This partition table is written to the first sector of the hard disk and contains information on the number, size, and location of all the partitions.

Although the partition table is created with the FDISK command, the information contained in the table is accessible to other operating systems as well, to allow you to format separate partitions under different operating systems. You can think of partitioning as dividing your hard disk into several smaller hard disks, each with its own operating system and format. Without the partition table created by FDISK, programs or data from one operating system might attempt to read or write over programs and data from another operating system. The result would be chaos, a condition in computing we assiduously try to avoid.

For whatever purpose you have in mind, the FDISK command allows you to establish up to four partitions on your hard disk. One of the partitions established is considered to be the *active* partition. This is the partition DOS looks to when booting the computer, and it is the partition where programs and data will be stored and retrieved. Any one of the partitions can be made active, and you can change the active partition at any time. The instructions for the FDISK command are included in your DOS manual under the chapter on preparing your fixed disk; however they will be summarized here.

Using FDISK

To use the FDISK command, place the DOS diskette in the first floppy drive and turn your computer on. After the A prompt is displayed, enter:

```
A > FDISK
```

After DOS loads the FDISK program, the FDISK Options menu appears on your screen, as shown in *Fig. 2-2.* This menu displays the ID number of the current fixed drive

```
IBM Personal Computer
Fixed Disk Setup Program Version 3.30
(C)Copyright IBM Corp. 1983,1987

FDISK Options

Current Fixed Disk Drive: 1

Choose one of the following:

        1. Create DOS partition
        2. Change Active Partition
        3. Delete DOS partition
        4. Display Partition Information



        Enter choice: [1]



        Press ESC to return to DOS
```

Fig. 2-2. The FDISK Options menu.

and four options. If you have multiple hard drives, they will be numbered in correspondence to the letters "C," "D," etc., with drive C identified as drive number 1.

As you can see from the Options menu, you can only create and delete DOS partitions. Partitions for other operating systems must be created with their own programs. However, you can make a nonDOS partition active with the FDISK program choice 2. (Choice 3, "Delete DOS Partition," will be described later in the chapter in the section labeled "Changing The Hard Disk Setup.")

To create a new DOS partition, use choice 1, "Create DOS Partition," as shown in *Fig. 2-3*. A new screen displays three options for partitioning information:

(1) Create Primary DOS partition
(2) Create Extended DOS partition
(3) Create logical DOS drive(s) in the Extended DOS partition

```
Create DOS Partition

Current Fixed Disk Drive: 1


    1. Create Primary DOS partition
    2. Crate Extended DOS partition
    3. Create logical DOS drive(s) in
       the Extended DOS partition




Enter choice: [1]




Press ESC to return to FDISK Options
```

Fig. 2-3. The "Create DOS Partition" entry screen.

The first choice is used to make the entire drive usable by DOS. Options two and three are used to divide the disk up into other Extended (nonprimary) partitions, some capable of using DOS and others available for other operating systems. However, FDISK is designed to split up a very large hard drive into other logical drives, each in a separate partition or several in one large partition.

For example, suppose you have a 60M hard drive. You can't directly use all of that storage under DOS 3.3, but you can partition it into chunks DOS can deal with, each under 32 megabytes in size. So you can have two 30M partitions, three 20M partitions, or however you feel would best serve your needs. One of the partitions will be set aside as the primary DOS partition. The rest will be data partitions, each given drive letters D, E, and so on.

To partition a 60M hard drive, first choose option 1, to create the primary DOS partition. FDISK will then ask you to enter the starting and ending cylinder numbers for the partition. (These values will vary depending on your hard drive's size.) Your next step is to create a partition for the rest of the hard drive, dividing it into data disks. For that you choose option 2 and assign the rest of the cylinders on the hard drive to a data disk. Finally, choose option 3 to divide the Extended partition into logical drives D, E, and so forth, divvying up the remaining cylinders to each drive according to the size you want each drive to be.

If your hard drive is under 32M in size, dividing it up into partitions isn't really necessary—though you can do it if you want. A 22M primary DOS partition (drive C) with a 10M logical data (drive D) is a nice setup (23 + 10 = 32). You can use FDISK to partition the hard drive in that manner, or in some other combination, or just let the whole thing be a giant primary DOS partition, drive C.

Besides splitting up the hard disk into partitions for logical data drives, you can use FDISK to set aside partitions for other operating systems or networks. The specifics for those partitions can be obtained from the other operating system's or network's manuals. However, FDISK does have the facilities to do it by itself. (But without those other operating systems, networks, or their manuals, it's pretty pointless to proceed with it.)

If you're thinking ahead, and assuming that eventually you might want to try some of those operating systems, don't let partitioning bother you now. Just configure your hard drive for DOS. Worry about other operating systems after you have researched them, and are ready to make the move. Normally, they'll come with ample instructions for converting a DOS-only computer to the new operating system. Also, there might be telephone support to assist you through the conversion process. For now, just worry about FDISK and DOS partitions.

Before leaving the FDISK Options menu, you might want to view the "Display Partition Data" option by selecting number 4. This will give you information about all the partitions on your hard disk. At this point, you should have only one partition, which by default becomes the active partition. Options 2 and 3 from the FDISK Options menu are used in modifying the structure of the hard disk and will be discussed in a later section of this chapter.

Because it is possible to have more than one partition on the hard disk, each partition must have its own boot record, which gets created when the partition is high-level formatted. In addition, there is a special boot record for the entire hard disk. This boot record uses the information in the partition table to determine which partition is active. It then transfers control to the boot record stored in the first sector of that partition.

If you're just messing around with FDISK, examining your hard disk's partitioning information, then press ESC to return to DOS. However, if you've just setup or changed partition information on your hard disk, FDISK will reset your computer when you exit. (This is to load the new partition information, along with DOS, into low memory locations in your computer.)

With the advent of DOS 4, FDISK and DOS can now deal with hard drives of incredible sizes. The entire hard drive can be divided into one giant primary DOS partition, or you can create other Extended partitions for logical drives or other operating systems. Another addition with DOS 4's version of FDISK is that it allows you to set the size of your partitions as a percentage value or by size in megabytes. This is a bit more convenient than using cryptic cylinder values.

Formatting a DOS Partition

As was mentioned earlier, each partition on the hard disk must receive a high-level format. Recall that the high-level format is only a logical format, not a physical format. As a result, it does not alter the sector data already stored on the disk. Instead, the high-level format writes the DOS records and tables onto the partition that enables the partition to act as a separate DOS disk. These include the boot record, the File Allocation Table, and the root directory.

The logical formatting of a hard disk is done using the same FORMAT command you use to format floppy diskettes. Remember that DOS is able to distinguish between hard drives and floppy drives and will perform the appropriate formatting tasks accordingly.

Ordinarily when you initially format a hard disk partition, you want to transfer the operating system files onto the hard disk as well. This is accomplished by including the /S option with the FORMAT command. There are three files that need to be included on any *bootable* system disk: COMMAND.COM, IBMBIO.COM, and IBMDOS.COM. (With MS-DOS the files are COMMAND.COM, IO.SYS, and MSDOS.SYS.) Two of the files, IBMBIO.COM and IBMDOS.COM are *hidden*. That means they are not displayed in a disk's directory by the DIR command. All three files are required for both floppy and hard disks if they're to be used as boot disks.

A *boot disk* is a disk that can load the disk operating system into memory on computer startup, enabling the computer to function as a DOS computer. You've probably seen the message:

Non-System disk or disk error
Replace and strike any key when ready

This message appears when you attempt to start up your computer with a nonbootable disk.

How the Computer Boots

Investigating how a DOS computer locates these three files is worth some time. The process is essentially the same whether the computer is set up to boot off a floppy or a hard drive. In this case, assume the computer has one floppy and one hard drive, with the system files installed in a DOS partition on the hard drive.

When the power is turned on, a special program stored in the computer's BIOS ROM is activated. This program directs the computer to check drive A (the first floppy drive) for a disk. If a disk is present, the boot record is checked for the presence of the two system files, IBMBIO.COM and IBMDOS.COM. If these files are present, they are loaded into RAM and control is passed to them.

If there is no disk in drive A, the computer checks for a hard drive. The master boot record on the hard disk is checked to see where the active partition is located. Then the boot record in the active partition is investigated to locate the two system files. Again, if these files are present they are loaded into RAM. The end result is that you are presented with a system prompt, which will be either an A> or C> prompt, depending on which disk the computer booted.

Most systems are set up to boot off the hard disk, but not all. This is because DOS itself only recognizes certain device configurations, and not all manufacturers conform to them. If you cannot boot off the hard disk, then a system disk must be initially inserted in the floppy drive on startup. Once the computer has booted, the hard drive can be made the current drive. (Changing the current drive is described in more detail in chapter 3.) Hard disks that require a floppy to boot shouldn't be formatted with the /S option.

The Format Operation

To format a DOS partition, load the FORMAT program off your DOS diskette. If you've just completed establishing the DOS partition with the FDISK program, this diskette will still be in drive A. The command to format the active DOS partition and transfer the system files is:

A>FORMAT C:/S

After entering this command, you will be presented with the following message:

WARNING, ALL DATA ON NON-REMOVABLE DISK
DRIVE C: WILL BE LOST!
Proceed with Format (Y/N)?

You should type Y to this ominous message. DOS then continues formatting the disk cylinder by cylinder, surface by surface. You can follow the progress of the formatting as the cylinders and heads (surfaces) are clocked off on the screen. Note that some versions of DOS merely record the tracks as they are formatted. This is because early versions of DOS were designed to format mainly floppy diskettes, for which cylinders and heads have no meaning.

DOS 4 displays the disk being formatted as a percentage value. This gives you a good indication of the formatting progress, but is vague as far as information about the cylinders and heads being formatted.

In any case, after the entire disk has been formatted, the message

Format complete
System transferred

will be displayed along with information about your disk, such as the following:

xxxxxx bytes total disk space
 xxxxx bytes used by system
xxxxxx bytes available on disk

You will also be asked if you want to format another disk, to which you should respond with an N.

Format Options and the LABEL Command

The FORMAT command includes several optional switches in addition to the /S system option. There are options that allow you to control the number of sides a diskette should be formatted on and the number of sectors that should be formatted per track. These options are used when formatting floppy diskettes, and you shouldn't bother with them when formatting hard disks.

One very useful FORMAT option is the /V, volume option. This option allows you to specify an identifying volume label which will be written to the disk at the conclusion of the formatting process. Volume labels are especially useful in identifying floppy diskettes. Volume labels are also useful for keeping track of multiple partitions. Starting with DOS 3.3, the FORMAT command asks you to enter a hard drive's volume label before a hard disk, adding an extra level of security against accidentally formatting (and erasing) the data on the disk. For these reasons, most users add a volume label when formatting hard disks as well as when floppy diskettes.

The volume option is invoked by adding a /V to the FORMAT command as follows:

A > FORMAT C:/V

When you specify the /V option, you'll be prompted to enter a volume label at the conclusion of formatting. Volume labels follow the rules for filenames, except that they may contain up to 11 characters and spaces.

The LABEL command may be used to add a label to an unlabeled disk, or to change or delete an existing label after the disk has been formatted. To use the LABEL command you must specify the drive you wish to label. For example, to add a label to a previously unlabeled disk, enter the LABEL command followed by a C:, and the volume label you wish to use. To add the label DOSPART1 to your hard disk, you would enter:

A > LABEL C: DOSPART1

To change or delete an existing volume label, enter the label command followed by the drive letter and a colon. DOS will respond with the disk's current label and prompt you for a new one. You can either enter a new volume label or press Enter to delete the existing label. In case you do not really want to delete the old label, DOS prompts you with a confirmation message, to which you would type Y to delete the label or N if you pressed Enter by mistake.

Preparing a Hard Disk Under DOS 3.3

DOS 3.3 has provided a special command, SELECT, that you can use to format your DOS partition, copy the DOS system files onto the newly formatted disk, and create special startup files. SELECT also allows you to specify a keyboard routine and a country code. The keyboard routines and country codes provided in DOS 3.3 enable you to configure your computer's keyboard to represent foreign characters, such as the " ~ " over the "n" in Spanish, and to alter the date, time, and currency formats to conform to different national standards.

The SELECT command is described in detail in the Disk Operating System manual, which accompanies DOS 3.3. Unless you have a special need for foreign characters or alternate date, time, and currency formats, you can use the FORMAT/S command, then follow along with this book and you'll be set to go in no time.

ALTERING THE STRUCTURE OF THE HARD DISK

The number and location of disk partitions, the format of these partitions, and the type and version of operating system installed on the partitions all constitute what can be referred to as the disk's *structure*. This structure is not permanent, and can be changed in a variety of ways. Probably the most common change required involves updating DOS as new versions are released. However, it is possible to reallocate the space on the hard disk using the FDISK command.

Normally, after your hard disk has been partitioned and formatted, you can forget about the FDISK and FORMAT C: commands. But FDISK also can be used to add additional partitions or remove unwanted partitions from your hard disk.

Refer back to the FDISK Options menu in *Fig. 2-2*. Note that the "Create DOS Partition" option can be used to add an additional DOS partition. Although this is not normally done, such action may be required to accommodate disks with more than 32M of storage. You also can add other, nonDOS partitions to your hard disk. Such partitions are required if you intend to run programs written for different operating systems from your hard disk.

Whether you are adding a DOS or a nonDOS partition, you must remove the existing partition(s) from the disk before adding new ones. Unfortunately, the process of removing old partitions can be time consuming: it involves backing up the files stored on the old partition onto floppy diskettes (or some other medium). The techniques for backing up data stored on a hard disk are covered in chapters 12 and 13. For now, be aware that deleting an existing partition will cause the data stored to be lost, and necessitate the need for a backup.

If you have only one DOS partition on your disk and you want to add another, non-DOS partition, follow these steps:

(1) Back up all files on the disk
(2) Use FDISK Option 3 to delete the existing DOS partition
(3) Install a new, smaller DOS partition, leaving space for the additional partition
(4) Reformat the DOS partition
(5) Restore the files into the recreated DOS partition
(6) Create the nonDOS partition and format it according to the instructions provided by the software company
(7) Install the software into the nonDOS partition

When working with multiple partitions on a hard disk, you need to identify the partition you want to work with. This can be done using FDISK Option 2, "Change Active Partition." Selecting this option causes a screen such as *Fig. 2-4* to be displayed.

```
Change Active Partition

Current Fixed Disk Dirve: 1

Partition Status    Type  Start  End Size
   C: 1       A    PRI DOS     0  384  385
      2       N    non DOS   385 1021  637
```

Fig. 2-4. The "Change Active Partition" entry screen.

Note that the DOS partition is listed as "A" under the Status column. This means that the DOS partition is currently the active partition. You can change to another partition by entering the desired partition number at the prompt. The selected partition then becomes the new active partition, and the status is written to the partition table. When the computer is rebooted, control will be passed to the operating system stored in that partition.

If you repartition a hard disk, you will have to reformat the DOS partition. Follow the instructions indicated in the section on "Preparing a Hard Disk." Be sure to include the /S option; otherwise the system files won't be transferred to the hard disk, and you'll have to boot off the floppy drive. An optional volume label is highly recommended.

An important point to keep in mind when using the FDISK command: if the active partition is a nonDOS partition, you will need to boot up your computer with a DOS system diskette in drive A, then use FDISK to change back to the DOS partition. After a nonDOS partition has been made active, the only way to access DOS is to boot on a DOS system diskette in the floppy drive. However, some operating systems might incorporate their own versions of an FDISK-like utility, allowing you to change partitions and avoiding the floppy disk boot routine.

You should also be aware that, even though FDISK can be used to select an established nonDOS partition, it cannot be used to create or delete nonDOS partitions. The only way to remove nonDOS partitions is either by the nonDOS operating system itself or by reestablishing the low-level format on the disk.

Before accepting any hard disk, especially one which has had previous data stored on it, use FDISK Option 4 to view the partitions stored on the disk. If there are any unwanted nonDOS partitions, be sure to have them removed for you. Otherwise you'll be stuck with partitions that you can't remove short of physically reformatting the entire disk.

INSTALLING NEW VERSIONS OF DOS

Everything changes in the world of personal computers, even operating systems. The authors of DOS are continually adding enhancements and refinements to the basic operating system of your computer. Although this can result in increased ease of use and greater utility, it often means extra work and greater confusion when new versions of DOS are released.

To date, there have been four generations of DOS, coupled with various minor revision numbers within a major version. Such is the case with DOS versions 2.1, 3.0, 3.1, 3.2, 3.3, and 4.0 (and on and on).

The original DOS 1.1 was superseded fairly quickly by version 2.xx, and it's not used today. However, there are still quite a few DOS 2.xx versions floating around. As of the publication date of this book, DOS versions 3.3 is the most popular, but DOS 4.01 is the most current. Where will it all end?

The presence of multiple versions of DOS has important ramifications for hard disk users. One important consideration is that, as new versions of DOS are released, you might want to upgrade the version of DOS installed on your hard disk. Then again, after thinking about some of the hassles involved, you might not want to.

As a general rule of thumb, update DOS only when absolutely necessary. This happens under two circumstances:

- The new version fixes bugs present in the version you're using, bugs which prevent you from getting the most out of your system
- The new version offers features that you feel will make you more productive.

Bear in mind that you don't need to incrementally upgrade DOS. For example, there's nothing wrong with moving from DOS 2.1 or 3.1 up to DOS 3.3, or even up to DOS 4.0. Make the move when you feel it will benefit you the most.

Transferring the System Files

DOS consists of three files. These files form the core of the operating system, and they're absolutely necessary to boot a disk. As previously mentioned, the files have different names depending on which version of DOS you use.

Two of the files, IBMBIO.COM and IBMDOS.COM are hidden files, and don't show up on your directory. (For more information on these hidden files, see chapter 3.) Because hidden files cannot be copied with the COPY command, DOS provides an external command, SYS, which copies these hidden files from a DOS disk onto a target disk. Some versions of DOS, depending on the manufacturer, require you to manually use the COPY command to transfer a copy of COMMAND.COM onto the target disk. However, other versions' SYS command copies COMMAND.COM as well (especially when SYS-ing a hard disk). In any event, check the disk before booting a disk and getting a "Command interpreter not found" error.

Normally, you shouldn't have to use the SYS command. Specifying the /S option with the FORMAT command accomplishes the same thing, and it copies COMMAND.COM to the target diskette, negating the need for checking it personally.

A former peculiarity of the SYS command was that it would only work if there was enough room for all the system files at the beginning of the root directory. Simply put, the SYS command only worked if a disk was recently formatted, or if room was reserved on the disk to accommodate the system files. (FORMAT's /B switch saves room just for that purpose.) In fact, one function of the SYS command is to transfer the system files onto applications programs diskettes that are sold without the operating system installed.

Starting with DOS 3.3, however, SYS will transfer system files to a disk even when there isn't enough room. DOS version 4 goes so far as to move files out of the way to make room for the system files. But, if you ask the experts, they all recommend the same thing: Better to let those files have dibbies on the first two spots on a disk than to take chances. Therefore, assume SYS doesn't move files around. Nor is SYS forgiving; start with a blank diskette.

To use the SYS command to update the DOS system files on your hard disk, start your system with the new DOS system diskette in your floppy drive and enter the following:

A > SYS C:

The completion of this operation will be indicated by the message:

System transferred

After this command has been executed, make sure to copy a version of the updated COMMAND.COM onto your hard disk as well by entering the command:

A > COPY COMMAND.COM C:

To update the DOS files on your diskette, use the REPLACE command. REPLACE will search out all files on the hard disk that match the filenames of those found on drive A—your new DOS disk. The newer files will then be copied to the hard disk, locating the old DOS files and replacing them with the new versions. Type the following:

```
A>REPLACE A: \ *.* C: \ /R/S
```

This command directs DOS to search the hard disk (via the /S switch) for all files on drive A that also exist on drive C. The /R switch even allows REPLACE to replace files that are read-only, which some DOS files might be as a form of extra protection against accidental erasure. After SYS and REPLACE, your hard disk will be updated with the latest version of DOS and you'll be ready to go.

Incompatible System Sizes

The SYS command cannot always be used to update your hard disk whenever a new version of DOS is released. The problem is that the size of the system files might change with new versions of DOS. For example, if you attempted to use the SYS command to update from version 3.2 of DOS to version 3.3, you will likely see the following message:

Incompatible system size

In such cases, the only way to update your hard disk is to reformat and begin from scratch with the new DOS system diskette. Make sure you backup your files before performing this operation! You should BACKUP and RESTORE using the new version of DOS. Boot the new DOS diskette in drive A and then backup the hard disk. After installing the newest version of DOS, you can use RESTORE to bring your files back.

The DOS 4 INSTALL Program

Along with its many benefits and improvements, DOS 4.0 comes with a sophisticated and easy-to-use installation program called INSTALL. It combines FDISK, FORMAT, SYS, COPY, and even builds a few startup files (CONFIG.SYS and AUTOEXEC.BAT). Even if you're an advanced DOS user (or consider yourself one), the best way to update to DOS 4.0 is to use the INSTALL program. For novices and new computer owners, INSTALL is a gift from the gods.

DOS 4.0 comes on five 5^1/$_4$-inch or two 3^1/$_2$-inch diskettes. Additionally, you'll need several blank diskettes: anywhere from one 1.44M 3^1/$_2$-inch diskette to four 360K 5^1/$_4$-inch diskettes, depending on the size of your disk drive. The "Getting Started" manual is very clear on the subject and contains good, easy-to-understand information on the entire installation and setup process.

DOS 4.0 can be installed on either a new system or a system with DOS already installed. It handles all the details of partitioning and preparing the hard disk, or updating older versions of DOS. Just follow the instructions both on the screen and in the manual and you'll be up and running in no time. Advanced users note: When DOS 4.0 says it needs a blank diskette, it means it. Don't try to skirt around that procedure!

The INSTALL program can do any of these things:

- Put DOS 4.0 on a floppy-only system
- Put DOS 4.0 on a hard disk system
- Update DOS 4.0 on a hard disk system
- Add DOS 4.0 to a hard disk system, coexisting with another operating system

To start DOS 4.0 installation, insert the INSTALL diskette into drive A, close the drive door, and turn on the computer. Or, if the computer is already on, put the INSTALL diskette in Drive A and reset by pressing the Reset button or Control-Alt-Delete.

The boot process might take some time to start, and you might be asked to insert a second diskette. Eventually, the opening screen is displayed, as in *Fig. 2-5*.

Press Enter to continue and continue answering the questions. You will be asked several questions, all depending on how you're installing DOS 4.0. Each screen is carefully

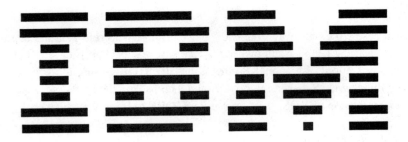

```
              DOS SELECT
              DOS 4.00
```

(C) Copyright IBM Corp. 1988.
All rights reserved.

Press Enter (◄─┘) to continue or Esc to Cancel

Fig. 2-5. PC-DOS 4.0's INSTALL program's opening screen.

laid out and help is always available by pressing the F1 key. Pressing Esc cancels any operation, and pressing Enter continues the operation.

If you're updating an older version of DOS, DOS 4.0's INSTALL program will create sample AUTOEXEC.BAT and CONFIG.SYS files for you, named AUTOEXEC.400 and CONFIG.400. You might want to examine these files by using a text editor (or EDLIN, covered in chapter 9), and incorporate some of their features into your own, custom AUTOEXEC.BAT and CONFIG.SYS files.

After INSTALL is done, reset your computer with Control-Alt-Delete and you'll be up and running with the latest version of DOS. If this trend of simplified, step-by-step installation programs continues, it might spell the end of confusing DOS setup procedures. Hopefully, if there are future releases of DOS, they too will incorporate INSTALL programs. (After all, most major software applications have been doing so for years—why not DOS?)

PERFORMING A LOW-LEVEL FORMAT

Performing a low-level format on a hard disk drive is a drastic action. All the data contained on the hard disk will be irrevocably lost. Remember, the low-level formatting process overwrites every data byte on the disk with dummy data.

You shouldn't need to perform a low-level format on your hard disk, which is why you won't find the instructions for low-level formatting in your DOS Operations Manual. (It's actually a function of the hard drive controller ROM inside your computer, which can differ between computers.) The DOS FORMAT command will usually be sufficient for reformatting your hard disk should the need arise.

When to Perform a Low-Level Format

There are certain instances when a high-level format will not suffice, and you will need to low-level format the hard drive. One situation that requires a low-level format is to remove non-DOS partitions. Suppose you have inherited a hard drive and the former user had established one or more non-DOS partitions. Unless you have access to the operating system software used to establish these partitions, the only way you can remove them and recover the storage areas they isolated is to perform a low-level format.

Another reason for performing a low-level format is if magnetic or physical damage has occurred to your hard disk and this damage is affecting the use of the boot record, File Allocation Table, or the root directory. If you get many "Boot Failure" error messages when you attempt to start your computer from your hard disk, or if you get messages like:

Directory not found

when you try to read your root directory, then you might need to perform a low-level format. Of course, you should always try to perform a high-level format first in hopes that this will correct the problem.

Because low-level formatting permanently overwrites any data stored on your hard drive, the procedure should only be used as a last resort. Of course, if you need to remove nonDOS partitions, or if your hard drive is not booting properly, you really have nothing to loose. If at all possible, be sure to backup all the data stored on your hard disk before formatting.

Using DEBUG to Perform a Low-Level Format

The process of low-level formatting is actually performed by your *hard disk controller*. This is a special set of circuits, or chips, that are either located on the hard disk itself, or more likely, on a special circuit board known as the *hard disk controller card*. The instructions for operating the hard disk controller are normally stored in the hard disk controller ROM chip. The address of this ROM chip is located in bank C of DOS memory. (Note: DOS actually can access memory above the 640K limit, but this memory is normally reserved for video display, special ROM memory such as the hard disk controller ROM, and the ROM BIOS.)

To access the instructions stored in the hard disk controller ROM, use the special DOS tool called DEBUG. A copy of DEBUG.COM is located on your DOS Supplemental Programs diskette. To use DEBUG, place a working copy of this diskette into drive A. Enter the DEBUG program by typing the following:

A > DEBUG

DEBUG will load and display its own prompt, which is the cryptic "-," the hyphen. (Okay, so "A >" is cryptic too.) To view the contents of the hard disk controller ROM, which is located at hexadecimal address 800 in bank C of memory, type the following command:

-dc800:0

After pressing Enter, about half a screen of data is displayed. On the right hand of the screen, you might see a description of your hard disk controller or the manufacturer's name. (See *Fig. 2-6.*)

From DEBUG, you can instruct your hard disk controller to perform a low-level format. The instructions for the format are located at offset 5 from address C800 with the Western Digital Controller in *Fig. 2-6.* (Other controllers will use different locations, such as c800:ccc.) To tell the hard disk controller to proceed, or "go," enter the following DEBUG command:

-g = c800:5

```
-dc800:0
C800:0000   55 AA 10 EB 7C E9 28 05-28 43 29 20 43 6F 70 79   U...|.(.(C) Copy
C800:0010   72 69 67 68 74 20 31 39-38 34 20 57 65 73 74 65   right 1984 Weste
C800:0020   72 6E 20 44 69 67 69 74-61 6C 20 43 6F 72 70 6F   rn Digital Corpo
C800:0030   72 61 74 69 6F 6E CF 02-25 02 08 2A FF 50 F6 19   ration..%..*.P..
C800:0040   04 64 02 04 65 02 65 02-0B 05 00 00 00 00 00 00   .d..e.e.........
C800:0050   00 64 02 02 80 00 80 00-0B 05 00 00 00 00 00 00   .d..............
C800:0060   00 64 02 04 65 02 80 00-0B 05 00 00 00 00 00 00   .d..e...........
C800:0070   00 32 01 04 32 01 00 00-0B 05 00 00 00 00 00 00   .2..2...........
```

Fig. 2-6. Sample screen displaying information pertaining to a hard disk as a result of the DEBUG command dc800:0.

This command will produce one of two results: The hard disk controller might go right ahead and reformat your hard disk, or it might display a menu offering you a variety of options. The action taken by the hard disk controller depends upon the manufacturer. Actually, a third possible result is that the hard disk controller will do nothing at all. This will occur only if you have a nonstandard hard disk controller which does not conform to the normal DOS memory assignments.

If your hard disk controller displays a menu or prompts you for the relative disk head number, head count, number of platters, interleave factor, etc., refer to the hard disk drive owner's manual. These numbers might need to be entered by setting specific microprocessor registers with DEBUG. If this is too daunting a task for you to face, you might want to take your computer into the shop and have a professional perform this procedure for you. Otherwise, between the manual and the instructions on the screen, you should be able to go ahead with no problem. Typically, the choices already offered (if there are default values) will be fine.

Remember, the worst you can do at this point is reformat your hard disk, which is exactly what you want to do. You can't do any physical damage to your drive.

If the above procedure doesn't work, you might need to use a special program provided on a diskette which came with the hard drive unit. Typical names for programs that perform a low-level format are HSECT, DTCFMT, and LFORMAT. These programs perform the low-level format either as a convenience to the user or on certain brands of hard drives which require nonstandard controllers. In most cases, however, you can use the DEBUG command, g=c800:5 to perform a low-level format.

SUMMARY

This concludes the discussion on hard disk preparation. At this point, you are ready to begin using your hard disk system. The first thing you'll need to do is install your application software onto your hard disk. So, you will need to understand the concepts of filenames and directories. The next chapter provides a thorough treatment of these two subjects, and teaches you the DOS commands for setting up work areas on your hard disk to store programs and data.

3
Filenames and Directories

BY FAR the most frequently used DOS command is the directory command, DIR. This command provides you with a list of the files stored on a disk as well as other useful information about the disk. You're probably already familiar with this command. But there's more to the DIR command than meets the eye, as this chapter will reveal.

You can use the directory command to obtain an alphabetically sorted listing of the files on your disk, or to obtain a partial listing of just your Lotus spreadsheets. You also can print out your directory listings for reference purposes. These and other handy techniques are explained in this chapter.

FILENAMES AND WILDCARDS

To get the most from the directory command, you need to understand the rules for filenames and wildcards.

DOS filenames consist of two components. The first part of the filename is used to describe the file's contents and is often referred to as the *descriptive* name. DOS limits descriptive filenames to eight characters, although you can use fewer than eight characters if you wish.

In addition, a filename may include an optional *extension*. Extensions are used to classify files according to the type of data or programs they contain. File extensions are separated from the descriptive component of the filename by a period and may consist of from one to three characters. Certain application programs automatically assign file extensions to the files they create. For example, some word processors tack a DOC onto the end of a filename. DOS itself uses the file extensions shown in *Table 3-1*.

Extension	Type of file
COM	A command file (program file)
EXE	An executable file (program file)
BAT	A batch file
SYS	A driver file
CPI	Code Page Information file

Table 3-1. File Extensions for DOS.

Rules for Filenames

Not all keyboard characters are allowed in filenames. Acceptable characters include the letters and the digits (0 through 9). Lowercase letters are converted to uppercase when the file is saved. (To avoid confusing filenames with text, filenames will appear in upper case throughout this book.)

Filenames also can contain most symbols available on the keyboard, except the following:

. " / \ [ ] : * ¦ < > + = ; , ?

Filenames can begin with any character (other than those above) and may not include spaces. Putting spaces in a filename is probably the most innocent mistake made by novice computer users.

If you use any of the disallowed characters in a filename, or if you do not correctly follow the rules for filenames, DOS will display an error message like the following:

Invalid character in filename
File not found

Some valid filenames include:

LETTER
LETTER1
LETTER.NEW
LETTER.OLD
MY_FILE
YOUR-FIL.84

Table 3-2 represents examples of invalid filenames, along with reasons why they won't work.

Table 3-2. Invalid Filenames.

Invalid Filename	Mistake made
YOUR_FILE	Filename too long
LONG.FILE	Extension too long
01/86.DAT	Filename contains the offending / character
LETR 2.MOM	Filename contains a space
86+87.DAT	Filename contains the offending + character

Wildcards

Wildcards are special characters that may be substituted for one or more characters in a filename, just like the card game Crazy Eights. In that game, the 8 card of any suit can represent any card or suit in the deck. This representation holds true with special symbols used by DOS. Those symbols can represent any single or group of characters in a filename for matching purposes.

The two DOS wildcards are the "?" and the "*" characters. You can think of these two characters as variables.

?. The ? wildcard is a variable that represents any single character. For example, the filename:

LESSON?

may be used to refer to:

LESSON1
LESSON2
LESSON3
LESSONA
LESSONB

and so on. . .

In fact, the filename LESSON? actually refers to all of those files at once. In this case, the use of the ? saves you from typing each filename.

You may include more than one ? in a filename. For example, suppose you had more than nine lesson files. In order to include all lesson files, you would need two ?'s:

LESSON??

This wildcard example encompasses filenames like LESSON12 as well as the single digit lesson files.

The ? wildcard may be used in file extensions as well. Suppose you had a series of financial statements that were labeled P&L.78 through P&L.99. Imagine you want to refer jointly to all the P&L files from 1980 through 1989. What generic filename would you use? If your answer is P&L.8?, you are correct. (Your gold star is in the mail.)

*. The * wildcard is more versatile. It can take the place of multiple ? wildcards.

In the descriptive filename, an * replaces all characters up to the period. In file extensions, the * replaces the remaining characters in the extension.

To refer to all the lesson files in the previous example, you could use a single *:

LESSON*

In fact, you could have used:

LES*

In this case, it's unlikely that any nonlesson files will begin with the three letters LES.

One use for the * is to save unnecessary keystrokes. Be careful, though; it probably would not be a good idea to use L* to refer to the lesson files.

As with the ? wildcard, the * wildcard can be used in file extensions. The most common usage of the * in extensions is to refer to "any extension." For example, if you weren't sure what file extension you used, if any, when naming the lesson files, you could refer to them with:

LESSON*.*

In this example, there are two *'s: one before and one following the period. Although the * wildcard can stand for multiple characters, you must use a separate * in the descriptive filename and the extension.

Another common usage of the * wildcard is to represent "any file with a given extension." To include all .COM files, you use:

*.COM

From this example, a simple continuation by using two *'s refers to all files:

.

This special filename, pronounced "star dot star," is very powerful. Chapter 4 will discuss this combination for copying files from one disk to another.

DISK DIRECTORIES AND FILE ALLOCATION TABLES

A disk directory is a file containing information about the other files stored on the disk. There are two types of directories: the main, or *root* directory, and *subdirectories*.

Although disks can contain more than one directory, every disk contains at least one directory, the root directory. The root directory is stored in a specific location on the disk, so DOS always knows where to find it. DOS uses the information stored in the root directory to locate other files stored on the disk.

The root directory can be linked to other directories, called subdirectories. Subdirectories are not usually used with floppy disks but are commonly found, and are necessary, on hard disks. The subject of subdirectories will be covered in detail in chapter 5, "Subdirectories and Paths."

Disk directories consist of file entries containing important information about the files stored on the disk, such as filenames, sizes of files, dates and times when they were created or last updated, and where the files are physically located on the disk's surface.

Directory Entries

Each file on disk has its own directory entry, which consists of 32 bytes of data. A typical directory entry is shown in *Fig. 3-1*. *Table 3-3* describes the information found in the directory entry.

Think of the individual file entries as consisting of records in the directory file, which is very similar to a database. These records contain specific fields of information pertaining to each file recorded in the directory.

Offset (in hexadecimal)

```
     00 01 02 03 04 05 06 07 08 09 0A 0B 0C 0D 0E 0F

000  43 48 41 50 54 45 52 20-30 30 31 21 00 00 00 00   CHAPTER 001!....
010  00 00 00 00 00 00 75 A9-16 13 BF 00 76 D0 0A 00   ......u.....v...
```

Fig. 3-1. A typical directory entry as DOS stores it on disk.

**Offset
(in hex)   Contents**

Offset (in hex)	Contents
00	Filename
0B	File attribute
0C	Internal information
16	File time
18	File date
1A	Starting cluster (location on disk)
1C	File size

Table 3-3. Information for a Directory.

Of course, the file entry includes the file's eight-character descriptive name as well as its three-character extension. These constitute the first two fields of file information.

Following the file's name is a single-byte field called the *file attribute*. The file attribute is used to denote whether the file is hidden or read-only. (You'll learn more about these special file characteristics in chapter 15, "Hidden Files and Data Encryption.")

Next comes a secret field containing internal information used by DOS. That's followed by two 2-byte fields used to record the file's Date and Time stamp, which are the date and time the file was created or last updated. (You'll learn more about the DOS Date and Time commands in chapter 4, "Other Essential DOS Commands.")

After the date and time fields in the directory comes the location of the beginning of the file, called the *starting cluster address* (at offset 1A hexadecimal). This tells DOS where the first segment of the file is stored on the disk.

The final field in the directory record contains a 4-byte integer value equal to the file's physical size in bytes. Although no file will probably be as large as a 4-byte binary integer (several billion bytes), this is the amount of room set aside in the file entry.

The number of file entries a directory can hold depends upon the size of the directory file itself. Because each directory entry is 32 bytes long, 16 file entries can fit into one sector (512 / 32 = 16). In DOS 1.1, 4 sectors were allocated for the disk directory, which could contain up to 64 file entries. The standard, 360K diskette has 7 sectors set aside for the disk directory, resulting in a maximum of 112 file entries. The size of the directory on a hard disk varies. In the case of most 20M hard disk, the root directory consists of 32 sectors, allowing up to 512 directory entries.

File Allocation Tables

Files are not actually stored on a disk sector by sector. Instead they're stored in *clusters*, or groups of sectors. The size of a cluster varies from one disk format to another. On double-sided diskettes, clusters are only 2 sectors, but on hard drives, the cluster size depends on the size of the hard drive, as well as the version of DOS the hard drive was formatted under. DOS 3.1 was really sloppy with it's format, and would assign 16 sectors to each cluster. This meant each file stored on disk took up 8K of space at a minimum—even if it was a paltry 2-byte file. Later versions of DOS use a four sector cluster, allocating 2K per file. This number is about fair because most files are larger than 2K, or at least, 2K and wastes little disk space.

Large files are stored in multiple clusters. For example, a 100K file requires 50 2K clusters. If a file does not fit exactly into some multiple of the cluster size, then an additional cluster is used. Although the cluster might only be partially full, the remaining empty sectors cannot be used by another file. In the preceding example, if the file were 99K, it would still require 50 clusters.

Chapter 1 discussed the differences between random and sequential file storage. Whether random or sequential storage is used, a file will occupy multiple clusters on the disk unless it is smaller than the cluster size. Piecing this file together would be extremely difficult without the aid of the *File Allocation Table*.

The File Allocation Table, or FAT as it's known in DOS circles, works in conjunction with the disk directory to keep track of where files are located on the disk.

Like the directory, the FAT is another file on the disk. In it are a series of 2-byte addresses, one for each cluster on the disk. (Actually, the first two entries are used by DOS to record information about the disk—the first real cluster reference is found in entry two.) As was mentioned earlier, the directory stores the address of the starting cluster for each file. To find the next cluster, DOS looks up the entry in the FAT for the starting cluster. This entry gives the location for the next cluster. (See *Fig. 3-2.*)

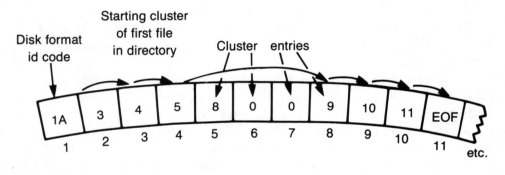

File   Allocation   Table

Fig. 3-2. Organization of the data entries in a sample File Allocation Table.

Following this procedure, DOS is able to locate the subsequent clusters that contain the complete file. When DOS checks the FAT for the reference value of the final cluster, it encounters a special control character indicating the end of the file has been encountered and there are no more clusters to be retrieved.

Essentially, the FAT contains a series of pointers DOS uses to chain together the various clusters into a complete file. All entries in the FAT are initialized at zero. The actual pointer values get entered into the FAT as files are written to the disk. A nonzero entry for a given cluster means the cluster is occupied.

The FAT also can be used to record that a cluster contains one or more bad sectors. Bad sectors are either physically or magnetically damaged and cannot be used to store data. If a cluster has been identified as containing bad sectors, a special code value is recorded in the FAT.

As you might imagine, a file's FAT is very important. Without it, the data stored in files on the disk would be unrecoverable. In fact, even if the disk directory becomes damaged, the directory can be rebuilt from the information contained in the FAT. (In chapter 12, "Backing Up Data and Programs," you will learn how to reconstruct disk directories using the DOS RECOVER command.)

Because the information in the FAT is so important, DOS actually stores a duplicate copy of it on the disk. If the original FAT becomes damaged, the backup copy can be used to recover the data stored on the disk.

THE DIRECTORY COMMAND

As you probably know, the directory command is entered at the DOS prompt as follows:

```
A > DIR
```

After pressing ENTER, DOS retrieves the filenames of all files stored in the root directory and displays them on the screen. In chapter 5, you'll learn about subdirectories and how to display directory listings for them as well. For the sake of simplicity, however, all examples in this chapter assume that the root directory is the only directory on the disk.

Information Contained in the Directory Listing

A sample directory listing is shown in *Fig. 3-3*. The filenames are listed vertically down the screen in the order they were retrieved from the root directory. Notice that the period between the descriptive filename and the file's extension is not displayed. In its place is a space. The file extensions are aligned in a separate column, beginning at column nine on the screen. Next to each filename is the size of the file in bytes, along with the date and time the file was created or updated.

In addition to information about individual files, the directory command provides you with two lines of information at the top of the listing. The first gives the volume name for the disk if any has been assigned. The next line gives the drive designator. In this case, the letter "A" followed by the colon refers to the A drive of the computer. The backslash character, " \ ," refers to the root directory. At the bottom of the listing, DOS indicates the number of files contained in the directory and the amount of space that is still available for storage.

The bottom line of information can be used as a quick check to determine how much room is left on the disk. Remember, you're limited not only by the amount of physical storage space available, but also by the amount of file entries in the root directory.

Changing the Current Drive

The directory command will display a listing of the *working directory* (for now, this means the root directory) on the currently logged disk drive. Most computers with hard drives are set up to boot off the hard disk, i.e., when the power is turned on, the computer's boot ROM tells the CPU (the computer's microprocessor) to check drive A (floppy

```
Volume in drive A has no label
Directory of  A:\

.                <DIR>        9-24-88   12:53a
..               <DIR>        9-24-88   12:53a
SETUPFIX COM       4865       4-07-88   10:36a
SHELL    EXE       8337       3-21-88    3:18p
DSA      EXE      22283       4-05-88    2:51p
HDSETUP  EXE      23661       4-05-88    2:32p
CONFIG   CFG       3783       3-29-88   10:30a
RAM      TST      10040       4-05-88    3:20p
VIDEO    TST      42838       4-05-88    3:20p
KEYBOARD TST      23306       4-05-88    3:20p
COPROC   TST       6417       4-05-88    3:20p
INTERNAL TST       6224       4-05-88    3:20p
PARALLEL TST       7838       4-06-88   10:51a
MODEM    TST       7543       4-05-88    3:20p
MOUSE    TST      12985       4-05-88    3:20p
SERIAL   TST       9868       4-05-88    3:20p
DISKETTE TST       9838       4-05-88    3:20p
HARDDISK TST      11751       4-05-88    3:20p
WDFMT    EXE      22150       8-12-86    2:24p
FMTREAD  ME         914       8-12-86    2:55p
        20 File(s)   133999 bytes free
```

Fig. 3-3. A sample directory listing.

drive) for the presence of a diskette. If a diskette isn't in the drive, the CPU next checks drive C (hard drive) to see if it can find the system files. If these files are present, they are loaded and drive C will become the current drive and the DOS prompt is displayed C>.

The directory command lists the current directory of the current drive. There are two ways to obtain a directory listing of a drive other than the current drive. The simplest way is to include the drive's designator as part of the directory command. For example, if drive C is the current drive, and you want a listing of the files on the diskette in drive A, type:

C>DIR A:

A second method to obtain a directory listing from a noncurrent drive is to make that drive the current drive. This method is about as easy as the first method, but it requires two separate DOS operations. Following the same example, first make the floppy drive current by entering its drive designator at the C prompt:

C>A:

DOS responds by displaying an A prompt instead of the C prompt. Then enter the directory command:

A > DIR

Directory Command Options

The standard directory command is fine when working with disks containing limited numbers of files. However, even with floppy diskettes, the number of files can quickly grow beyond the number that can appear on the screen at one time. With hard disks, the problem can become even more severe as the number of files can expand into the hundreds.

If there are more files in the directory than can be displayed on a single screen, the directory command scrolls off the top of the screen as it continues to list the files in vertical sequence. Unless you're particularly sharp, or your computer is particularly slow, you're apt to miss a filename that appears in the early part of the listing.

There are two ways to avoid this problem. The first is to use the *wide display* option when entering the directory command. The wide display option is activated using the /W switch after the directory command as follows:

A > DIR /W

The directory listing, as shown in *Fig. 3-4*, shows filenames displayed across the screen in five columns, allowing five times as many files to be displayed on a single screen. Of course, there's no such thing as a free lunch. In this case, DOS sacrifices the file size, as well as the Date and Time stamps for each file in favor of additional filenames.

```
Volume in drive A has no label
Directory of  A:\

.                   ..              SETUPFIX COM    SHELL    EXE    DSA      EXE
HDSETUP  EXE    CONFIG    CFG    RAM       TST    VIDEO    TST    KEYBOARD TST
COPROC   TST    INTERNAL  TST    PARALLEL  TST    MODEM    TST    MOUSE    TST
SERIAL   TST    DISKETTE  TST    HARDDISK  TST    WDFMT    EXE    FMTREAD  ME
         20 File(s)   133999 bytes free
```

Fig. 3-4. Directory listing obtained using the /W option.

If you need to view the file size or Date and Time stamps, or if you have even more files than can be displayed with the wide display option, you can use the Control-NumLock or Control-S key sequence to temporarily interrupt the scrolling process. The Pause or Hold key has the same effect, if your keyboard has them. Pressing any pause key sequence again causes the scrolling to resume.

If your fingers aren't nimble enough to master a pause key sequence, you can use the directory command with its pause option, /P. The pause option follows the directory command and can be used alone or in combination with the /W. There are two ways to use the pause option:

```
C > DIR /P
C > DIR /W/P
```

Whenever you add the pause option to the directory command, DOS displays as many files as will fit on the screen, and then displays the message:

Strike a key when ready . . .

at the bottom of the screen. You can view the contents of the screen as long as you like. When you wish to see the next screen, just press any key (the spacebar or Enter key will do nicely). This screen-by-screen display will continue, with you controlling the pace, until the entire directory has been displayed.

Printing Directory Listings

Sometimes, you might want to have a printed listing of the files stored on a disk. There are many specialized directory utilities that allow you to print a directory listing. A number of these utilities are available as public domain programs. (Chapter 19 contains a description of one such program.) However, you don't need any utilities at all to print a simple directory listing. Instead, you can make use of the DOS screen dump feature.

There is a special key on most keyboards labeled PrtSc, Print Scrn, or just Print. On some keyboards, this key is a stand alone, one function key. On other keyboards, notably the early PC/XT keyboards, you have to hold the Shift key down to activate the print screen. This combination is to prevent you from inadvertently performing the function by mistake.

Striking the PrtSc key causes DOS to send a copy of the screen's contents to the printer. (Actually, a copy of the video RAM is sent to the printer, but who wants to get technical?) PrtSc only gives you a copy of what's currently displayed on the screen. Also, the PrtSc key will only work if your printer is on, on-line, and connected to your computer. (You would be amazed how often people forget this simple feat.) If not, your computer might wait (and wait and wait) for the printer. Some smart PCs (depending on their BIOS) will note the printer isn't on and not bother waiting. (The only way to really find out is to try it.)

If your directory listings take up multiple screens, an alternate method to print the entire directory is the Control-PrtSc key combination. This combination will cause everything displayed on the screen to be sent to the printer until a second Control-PrtSc is entered. This is often referred to as *printer echo*. Everything displayed on the screen will be echoed to the printer.

On some versions of DOS and on some compatibles, the Control-P key combination works the same as Control-PrtSc. Try it with your PC or check the manual to see if it turns on printer echo.

Partial Directories

The directory command can also be used to determine if a certain file is on a given disk. You could issue the DIR command and scan the list to see if that file was present. This can be tedious, particularly if the listing runs to multiple screens. There is a simpler approach: type the filename after the DIR command. For example, if you want to see if LESSON1 is stored on drive A, you would enter:

```
C > DIR A:LESSON1
```

If it's there, DOS displays the filename and the size of the file, etc. If the file isn't present, DOS will respond with the message:

```
File not found
```

The directory command can be used with filenames containing wildcards as well. Sometimes you might only want a partial listing of the files on your disk. Usually you will want to view all files satisfying a certain condition, such as all spreadsheet files or all .COM files. To obtain a listing of all .COM files on the hard disk, you would enter:

```
C > DIR *.COM
```

After pressing Enter, DOS displays a directory listing including only those files with a COM extension. If there aren't any files satisfying this condition, the "File not found" message will be displayed.

Partial directory listings are a handy way of limiting the time required to determine the name, size, existence, etc., of a file if you don't remember its exact spelling. Imagine you are looking for a file you created last week. You're sure you called it something beginning with "INS" because it was an analysis of insurance policies held by your company. Rather than searching through the entire directory, you could enter:

```
C > DIR A:INS*
```

This would give you a listing of all files beginning with "INS." If the file were of a specific kind, say a Lotus 1-2-3 worksheet file, you could further narrow the search with:

```
C > DIR A:INS*.WK?
```

Chances are there will only be a few of these files. One word of advice: if several filenames are displayed and you still can't remember which one you want, jot all of them down on a piece of scratch paper or, better yet, use the PrtSc key to get a printed listing. It's amazingly difficult to remember more than two similar filenames without getting them confused.

FIND, MORE, AND SORT

As you have already noticed, either from the examples presented in this book or more likely from previous experience, the filenames in a directory listing are displayed in random order. This contributes to the difficulty when searching for a specific file in a long directory listing. Files are actually stored in the order they were created or copied to the disk.

You can have DOS sort the filenames for you before it displays them on the screen. You need two DOS tools: *filters* and *pipes*.

DOS filters are utility programs that alter the output of other DOS commands. There are three DOS filters: FIND, SORT, and MORE.

A DOS pipe simply passes, or pipes, the output of one DOS command or filter on to another DOS command or filter.

The SORT Filter

As the name implies, the SORT filter is used to arrange text into either ascending or descending order. When used with the directory command, the SORT filter takes the unsorted directory listing and sorts it alphabetically. To obtain a sorted directory listing, you must pipe the output of the directory command to the SORT filter.

The DOS pipe is the vertical bar character, " | ." This character hides in different locations on the keyboard depending on the model of computer you have. Some diligent searching will reveal its whereabouts. On the standard extended keyboard, it's located just above the Enter key (on the backslash key). The complete command is shown below:

```
C > DIR | SORT
```

As with the /P and /W directory options, the spacing between the DIR, the | , and the SORT is optional. Using the SORT filter on a diskette will result in a directory listing like the one shown in *Fig. 3-5*.

Notice how SORT sorted the entire directory listing. Not only are the files sorted by their names, but other information such as the number of files, directory name, and volume information, were also sorted. Generally, these items will always be placed at the top of the sorted list, so they don't interfere with the list of files, which are sorted in alphabetical order by filename.

```
      20 File(s)   133999 bytes free
   Directory of  A:\
   Volume in drive A has no label
   .            <DIR>        9-24-88   12:53a
   ..           <DIR>        9-24-88   12:53a
   CONFIG    CFG     3783    3-29-88   10:30a
   COPROC    TST     6417    4-05-88    3:20p
   DISKETTE  TST     9838    4-05-88    3:20p
   DSA       EXE    22283    4-05-88    2:51p
   FMTREAD   ME       914    8-12-86    2:55p
   HARDDISK  TST    11751    4-05-88    3:20p
   HDSETUP   EXE    23661    4-05-88    2:32p
   INTERNAL  TST     6224    4-05-88    3:20p
   KEYBOARD  TST    23306    4-05-88    3:20p
   MODEM     TST     7543    4-05-88    3:20p
   MOUSE     TST    12985    4-05-88    3:20p
   PARALLEL  TST     7838    4-06-88   10:51a
   RAM       TST    10040    4-05-88    3:20p
   SERIAL    TST     9868    4-05-88    3:20p
   SETUPFIX  COM     4865    4-07-88   10:36a
   SHELL     EXE     8337    3-21-88    3:18p
   VIDEO     TST    42838    4-05-88    3:20p
   WDFMT     EXE    22150    8-12-86    2:24p
```

Fig. 3-5. Directory listing obtained using the SORT filter.

The SORT filter includes two options: /R and /+. The /R option is used to reverse the order of the sort, resulting in listings from "Z" to "A." Although you are unlikely to need a reverse alphabetical listing, you might want to sort files numerically in descending order. For example, you might want to sort a directory according to the file size or date and time created. (This must be done using both of the SORT filter's switches.)

The /+ option allows you to specify which column of data should be used to sort the file. Unless /+ is specified and followed by a column number, SORT sorts by the first character in each line of the file.

As you might remember from the discussion at the beginning of this chapter, the root directory is actually a file containing individual file entries, or records. The information about each file is contained in various columns, with the descriptive filename occupying columns 1 through 8. The file size information begins consistently at column 14 in a directory listing. You can use this column to sort your directory listings according to the file size by entering the following command:

```
C>DIR ¦ SORT /R/+14
```

The MORE Filter

The SORT filter can be used in conjunction with the MORE filter when directory listings are long. The MORE filter works much like the /P directory command option. Information is filtered through the MORE filter one screenful at a time, pausing after each new screen and displaying the message:

—MORE—

at the bottom of the screen. Pressing the Enter key causes the next screenful of information to be displayed. Because the MORE filter controls the screen display, it is always the last filter to be included in a sequence of DOS commands. To use the MORE filter with SORT and DIR command, enter:

C>DIR ¦ SORT ¦ MORE

The result will be a sorted directory listing that pauses after each screenful of text.

The FIND Filter

The FIND filter is usually used to locate the occurrence of a word, phrase, or group of characters within a specified file. A group of characters are referred to as a *string* in computer terminology. Strings are indicated by appearing in quotes. To be designated as a string, as opposed to a command or filename, the phrase "HELLO THERE" would be entered as:

C>"HELLO THERE"

Because the directory is a file, the existence of a given filename can be verified within the directory by piping the output from the DIR command through the FIND filter. Note that the FIND filter searches for strings, so the filename (the string you're trying to locate) should be enclosed in quotes. To verify that the LESSON1 file is located on the diskette in drive A, you would enter:

C>DIR A: ¦ FIND "LESSON1"

The FIND filter also can check for partial strings. This concept is similar to the use of wildcards. For example, you could use the FIND command to list all the lesson files on the diskette by entering:

C>DIR A: ¦ FIND "LESSON"

Most people find wildcards simpler to work with and easier to enter than the FIND filter. However, the FIND filter can do some tricks that wildcards can't. For one, the FIND filter can be used to filter out unwanted filenames by adding the /V option. Consider you want to view all data files on a disk without including the program files. Entering the following command sequence would produce this result:

C>DIR A: ¦ FIND/V ".COM"

The FIND filter also can be used to determine which files were created or updated on a certain date:

C>DIR A: ¦ FIND "3-15-87"

Those Weird Filenames

Whenever you use a pipe to pass the output of one command or filter to another, DOS might create a temporary file on the disk. This is a scratch pad file and it might show up in directory listings displayed during the piping process. Such files might begin with "%PIPE" followed by some number and include the special DOS file extension $$$, such as %PIPE3.$$$. Other filters might create other, oddly named files. These temporary pipe files will be removed from disk at the conclusion of the piping process, so don't worry if they appear in your directories or other output from filter commands.

REDIRECTING DIRECTORY OUTPUT

Normally, the output of a directory listing is sent to the screen. This seems only reasonable, right? After all, where else would you want the directory listing to go? In fact, sometimes you might want to store a listing of a disk's directory in a data file for later reference. (This will become more apparent after you have read chapter 5, which describes subdirectories and paths.)

Excluding subdirectories, there is at least one valid reason for storing directory listings in a data file. This technique enables you to combine multiple disk directories into a single listing.

For example, suppose you have five floppy diskettes worth of word processing documents. You'd like to have a single listing of all the files on these five diskettes. You can create this listing by storing a copy of each diskette's directory into a data file. This data file can then be sorted or printed as needed.

Consider the problem of transferring a single directory listing into a data file. It's really quite simple. Merely redirect the output of the directory command to a disk file of your choosing, by using the ">" symbol and supplying a filename when entering the directory command. Suppose you wanted to save a copy of the directory listing in a data file named DIRLIST.DAT. You would enter:

```
C>DIR > DIRLIST.DAT
```

More to the point, assume you want to transfer a copy of the directory listings for each of the five word processing data disks mentioned earlier. In this example, the diskettes will be placed in drive A and the file DIRLIST.DAT will be stored on drive C. Place the first diskette into the drive A and issue the command:

```
C>DIR A: > DIRLIST.DAT
```

This will place a copy of the first diskette's directory listing in the DIRLIST.DAT file. If you were to repeat this process with the second disk, what do you think would happen?

If you guessed that the second directory listing would replace the first, you're right. But that's not what you want. To avoid this problem, use two > 's in all subsequent commands as follows:

```
C>DIR A: > > DIRLIST.DAT
```

The double > causes the additional directory listings to be appended to the original listing instead of overwriting it (and each other).

After the combined directory file has been compiled, it can be passed through the SORT filter to create a single, sorted listing of all the filenames. For this command, the DIRLIST.DAT file becomes the input, rather than the output, file. Use the " < " character to indicate an input file.

The following command will use the DIRLIST.DAT file as the input file for the SORT filter and place the sorted listing into the output file DIRSORT.DAT.

```
C>SORT < DIRLIST.DAT > DIRSORT.DAT
```

The contents of the DIRSORT.DAT file can be viewed on the screen with the TYPE command, or sent to the printer with the PRINT command.

SUMMARY

The directory command, DIR, is used to display a list of files stored on disk. The files are actually held in a special directory file that can be considered to be a database of sorts. The DIR command displays the information held in the directory file, allowing you to see which files are on disk and examine information about those files.

By using special options on the DIR command, you can view the files on disk either in a wide format, or in a special paged mode, one screen at a time. Additionally, you can use filters and the pipe to display the directory of files in a sorted or paged manner, or to find specific files in the directory. With redirection, you also can store the output of the DIR command in a file on disk for cataloging purposes.

4
Other Essential DOS Commands

USING A PERSONAL COMPUTER, especially one equipped with a hard disk, requires a number of different skills. Certainly, you need to know how to run the applications programs that enable you to do useful work. Before long you've added a word processing program, spreadsheet, database management, and maybe graphics or communications software to your repertoire. It's hard enough keeping track of all these programs and their commands. Besides the role of a computer "user," you wear another hat as well—that of computer "operator."

As your system's operator, you have the responsibility of maintaining the programs and data files stored on your hard disk, and of upholding the security of the system by creating duplicate copies of these files on floppy diskettes. File maintenance is an ongoing chore associated with using a personal computer, and the magnitude of this chore is directly proportional to the amount of disk storage on your system and the volume of data you process on a regular basis.

There are a number of DOS commands that enable you to perform the task of file management on your computer. These commands can copy files from one disk to another, delete and rename files, and view and compare the contents of files. There are also commands that allow you to check the status of your storage media. Still other DOS commands facilitate working with the operating system.

In this chapter, you'll learn the basic DOS commands you need to manage your files effectively. You probably know some of these commands already. However, the information in this chapter includes some tricks and suggestions you won't find in your DOS manual, so you might want to skim the sections on the commands you already know for these special gems. There is nothing quite so gratifying in the field of personal computing as knowing and using some clever little shortcut that the rest of the world hasn't heard of yet.

THE ROLE OF THE COMMAND PROCESSOR

In chapter 2, you read about the three system files, IBMDOS.COM, IBMBIO.COM, and COMMAND.COM. (Note: in MS-DOS, the first two files are named IO.SYS and MSDOS.SYS.) COMMAND.COM is the only system file that you can see in a disk's directory. This file is known as the *command processor*. This term refers to the program's function as an interpreter and performer of the DOS commands that you enter from the keyboard. COMMAND.COM intercepts anything you type at the system prompt, and attempts to process your command. This results in one of three possible outcomes.

(1) If the command you enter is a DOS command recognized by the command processor, it will execute that command directly.
(2) If your entry is not one of the basic DOS commands, the command processor will assume it is the name of a program file you wish to run. The command processor will then search the disk directory for the presence of that program and execute it.
(3) If the command processor doesn't recognize your entry as a DOS command, and can't find a program file on your disk by that name, it replies with the following error message:

Bad command or filename

RESIDENT VERSUS EXTERNAL COMMANDS

There are two types of commands in DOS, *resident* and *external*. Resident commands are commands that are directly executable by the command processor. These commands include COPY, RENAME, ERASE, and TYPE. When you're working at the system prompt, you have access to these commands. You can think of these commands as coming free with COMMAND.COM. Resident commands really are "commands" in the true sense of the word.

External commands, which are also DOS commands, are actually special programs designed to perform a DOS-related function. These short programs are usually referred to as *utilities*. The FORMAT utility is an example of an external DOS command. Because these commands can't be executed unless the program file with the command filename is present on the disk, they're said to be external, i.e., outside the command processor. External commands include FORMAT, FDISK, DISKCOPY, and CHKDSK, and many others. Your DOS manual identifies commands as either Internal (i.e., resident) or External.

The most commonly used external commands are stored on your DOS System diskette. Your copy of DOS also includes a second, Supplemental Programs diskette. This diskette contains files of interest to programmers and isn't normally copied to the hard disk. But everything else, all DOS's external commands, are copied to the hard drive so you'll always have access to them.

Resident Commands

The resident commands you'll use most often are COPY, RENAME, and ERASE. These commands are used with individual files, although each of them can be made to work with multiple files through the use of the wildcard characters, "?" and "*."

These commands are entered at the system prompt and are executed directly by the command processor. They can be used to affect files stored on the current disk, or on an alternate disk with the addition of a drive designator. Each of these commands will be discussed in turn. This book follows the conventions of your DOS manual in listing the format of DOS commands. The rules for languages and operating systems are often specified in terms of *format*. A command's format is a shorthand notation describing the rules, or syntax, for the command's use. The format for DOS command is somewhat cryptic if you are a computer novice. So a general, generic explanation is in order.

All words in capital letters pertain to the DOS command itself. This includes any command options (called *parameters* in your DOS manual). Words or letters in italics refer to the file or device on which the command is operating. A set of square brackets, [ ], imply that the word or characters within the brackets are optional. These format conventions will become obvious as you read the command descriptions included in this chapter.

The COPY Command. The COPY command is used to transfer files from one disk to another. The basic format of this command is:

COPY [d:]filename[.ext] [d:][filename][.ext]

The first filename (with optional extension) refers to the source file, while the second filename designates the *destination* file. The destination filename is optional. When copying a file from one disk to another, you don't have to include the filename a second time, unless you wish to rename the file on the destination disk.

Note also that drive designators are optional with the COPY command. If a drive designator is not provided, the current drive is used. If the file is present on the designated source disk, the file will be copied to the destination disk and a confirming message:

1 File(s) copied

appears on the screen.

But be warned: Unlike some applications that tell you if the destination file is already present on the target disk, COPY will cheerfully copy over an existing file, destroying its contents and replacing it with the version from the source disk. Although this replacement is often what you want to accomplish, such as transferring altered files to a backup disk, copying can occasionally result in the loss of important data. Know what is on your target disk before using the COPY command. For example, suppose you want to transfer a copy of the file FILE1.DOC from your hard disk to a diskette in drive A. You would enter:

```
C > COPY FILE1.DOC A:
```

No drive designator is used in front of FILE1.DOC because this file is stored on the current drive, C. Also, no filename is specified after the A: because the file is to keep the same name on the destination diskette.

If you want to transfer a copy of FILE1.DOC from the floppy drive to the hard drive, the command is now:

```
C > COPY A:FILE1.DOC
```

In this case, the drive designator precedes the source file. There is no need for a second drive designator, or even a second filename, because the hard disk is the current drive and the file will keep its name when it is copied.

You can copy the FILE1.DOC file from drive C to A with a new filename, such as FILE2.DOC. The command to do this would be:

```
C > COPY FILE1.DOC A:FILE2.DOC
```

One application of the COPY command is to create a backup of a file on the same disk. This can be handy if you are planning to modify a data file but you're not sure you'll like the results, or you're not sure if you'll be able to return the data to its original form.

You might want to make this kind of backup if you are planning to sort the data in a spreadsheet file. To make a duplicate copy of FILE1.DOC with the name FILE2.DOC, both stored on the hard disk, you would enter:

```
C > COPY FILE1.DOC FILE2.DOC
```

Notice that no drive designators are included in this command. Although it isn't necessary to include drive designators with the COPY command, forgetting to include them can lead to the error message:

```
File cannot be copied onto itself
```

This error message would be displayed with either of the following commands:

```
C>COPY FILE1.DOC FILE1.DOC
C>COPY FILE1.DOC
```

In the first command, the file is being copied from drive C onto itself because no drive designators were specified. Because the source and destination filenames are identical, the command is impossible to execute. Because both the optional drive designator and destination filename are absent in the second command, DOS is being told to copy the file onto itself.

Using Wildcards with the COPY Command. In chapter 3, you learned how to use DOS wildcard characters with the directory command to specify subsets of files stored on the disk. The wildcard characters also can be used with the COPY command to specify groups of files to be copied. For example, you could copy all the files with a DOC extension from drive C to drive A with the following command:

```
C>COPY *.DOC A:
```

The "*" wildcard also can be used on both sides of the period to copy all files on a diskette onto either another diskette or the hard disk. The following command can be used to copy all files from Drive A to the hard disk:

```
C>COPY A:*.* C:
```

The "?" wildcard may also be used in combination with the COPY command to substitute for individual characters in source filenames. Wildcards can be used in destination filenames as well. One practical application of this is to create backup files. Although some programs make backup files for you automatically, not all do. Keeping an extra copy of a file on the same disk but under a different name can be convenient. This extra copy provides you with quick access to the data in case the original file is damaged or destroyed due to program (or, more likely pilot) error. For example, you could periodically create backups of all your DOC files with the following command:

```
C>COPY *.DOC *.BAK
```

Each DOC file would be copied (duplicated, actually) to a file with the same descriptive filename but with the BAK extension.

Something to Look Out For. Be careful when including wildcards in the COPY command, you might be biting off more than you can chew. For example, consider what would happen if you entered the command:

```
C>COPY *.* A:
```

DOS would proceed diligently transferring all files on the hard disk onto the floppy diskette. At some point, the diskette would become full, and DOS would halt the operation, displaying the message:

Insufficient disk space

Sometimes this happens when copying files even without the global wildcards, *.*. If the source file is larger than the remaining space on the destination disk, you'll see this message displayed. At this point, every file but the final one (the one that caused the error) will be safely copied to the target diskette. All other files will not be copied. Also, DOS might stick some form of fragmented file on the diskette. This is a DOS "bug," and you can spot the offending file by its tell-tale 0K file size. Feel free to delete it with the ERASE command (covered in the next section).

Quick Copy. Here's a neat trick: The * wildcard can also be used as a shortcut when you want to copy single files. Suppose you wanted to copy the file FILE1.DOC from drive A to drive C. If you know there's only one file on the diskette beginning with the letter "F," you can use wildcards as follows:

C>COPY A:F*.*

This statement will get any file beginning with "F" and having any extension. Referring to the file as F*.* is much easier than entering FILE1.DOC. Of course, there is always the risk of copying more files than you bargained for if there is more than one file beginning with "F" on the diskette.

COPY's Options. The COPY command has four options, each of which helps customize its operations. The options are:

- The verify option, /V
- The combination/copy option, using the + symbol
- The /A, ASCII (text) copying option
- The /B, binary copying option

The Verify Option. The COPY command's verify option is /V, which stands for "verify" (duh). This parameter can be added to the COPY command whenever you want to ensure that the target medium is undamaged.

The /V parameter causes DOS to check the integrity of each sector where the source file is copied prior to transferring the data. This check gives you extra assurance that the file is transferred correctly. Of course, additional time is required to check each sector, which slows down the copying process.

An alternative to using the verify option with the COPY command is to check the integrity of the entire destination disk in advance with the CHKDSK command. (CHKDSK will be described later in this chapter.)

Combining Files with the COPY Command. As the term implies, combining files allows you to place the contents of several files into a single file. But don't get too excited. This option is primarily used with text files, combining several small text files into one big file. You can't combine program files, the result would be useless. Likewise, sticking data files together does nothing worth noting. The resulting file is useless to the program that created it—and to you. So if you combine files with COPY, stick to text files.

The most common reason for combining text files is to create a large print file. For example, you might want to combine CHAPT1, CHAPT2, CHAPT3, CHAPT4, and CHAPT5 into a file named PART1.PRN. This single file could then be printed out using only one print command from your word processing program, rather than printing each file separately. This technique can result in significant time savings. If you have a reliable tractor feed printer, you can submit the print job and take a coffee break (or wash the car) instead of attending to each file individually. A word of warning: Make sure that each file concludes with a page break command. Otherwise, the chapters will all run together.

To copy the five chapters into the single PART1.PRN file, the special + symbol is used:

```
C > COPY CHAPT1 + CHAPT2 + CHAPT3 + CHAPT4 + CHAPT5 PART1.PRN
```

The use of the "+" character causes the contents of each source file to be added to those of the preceding file, with the combined results stored in the destination file. This requires quite a lot of typing. Assuming that you only have the first five chapters on your disk, you could use the ? wildcard to accomplish the same thing with far fewer keystrokes using the following command:

```
C > COPY CHAPT? PART1.PRN
```

Think about what this command will do. Because of the ? wildcard, there are multiple source files specified, but only one destination file. All the chapter files will be copied into the single PART1.PRN file. In fact, it's possible to combine all the chapter files into the CHAPT1 file by eliminating the destination filename altogether. This process is known as *appending,* and is accomplished as follows:

```
C > COPY CHAPT1 + CHAPT2 + CHAPT3 + CHAPT4 + CHAPT5
```

This command can be simplified through the use of the ? wildcard. In this case, you have only to enter the brief command:

```
C > COPY CHAPT1 + CHAPT?
```

to accomplish the same thing.

Note that the command:

C > COPY CHAPT?

will not work as expected, but will result in a damaged CHAPT1 file and an error message such as:

Content of destination lost before copy

COPY's /A and /B Options. The /A and /B COPY parameters are used when working with binary files. These are usually either .COM or .EXE files containing machine code, or other data files.

Text files normally include a special control code, called *end-of-file*, which indicates the end of the file. When combining regular text files, as above, each file's end-of-file marker is included, so the data are separated from each other in the resultant file. However, combining several binary files into a single file with only one end-of-file marker is possible by specifying the /B parameter.

In effect, the /B parameter indicates to DOS that the file is to be copied without the inclusion of its end-of-file marker. The /A parameter, on the other hand, indicates that an end-of-file marker is to be included. The /B parameter affects all files following the file it's attached to, as does the /A parameter.

The standard format for combining binary files is to use the /B parameter with the first file and to include the /A parameter after the last file in the list (including an end-of-file marker in the resultant file).

For example, to combine files PROG1.BAS, PROG2.BAS, and PROG3.BAS into a single file PROGRAM.BAS with only one end-of-file marker, you would enter:

C > COPY PROG1.BAS/B + PROG2.BAS + PROG3.BAS/A PROGRAM.BAS

Copying Files Between Devices. When copying files from one disk to another, you are actually copying files between devices. Each disk drive is considered to be a device by DOS. There are a number of different devices in your computer system which include the disk drives, the screen and keyboard, the printer outputs (called ports), and any communications ports. Each of these devices has a special *device name* that is recognized by DOS. These devices are displayed in *Table 4-1*.

The disk drives are named A:, B:, C:, etc. The combination of the keyboard and screen is known as the *console*, and has the device name CON:.

Parallel printer ports are given the device names LPT1:, LPT2:, and LPT3:. If you have a printer hooked up to your computer system, it will most likely be a parallel printer attached to LPT1:. This printer output has another commonly used device name, PRN:.

Device name	Device
A:	First floppy drive
B:	Second (or logical) floppy drive
C:	First hard drive
CON:	Keyboard and screen
LPT1:	First printer
LPT2:	Second printer
LPT3:	Third printer
PRN:	Standard printer output
COM1:	First serial port
COM2:	Second serial port

Table 4-1. Device Designators.

Communications ports use the device names COM1:, and COM2:. (Note:, it is not necessary to include the colon (:) with the CON, LPTx, PRN, or COMx device names, but they have been included in this text for consistency.)

You can copy files to or from any of these devices following the standard COPY command format and substituting the device name you wish for the optional drive designator, [d:].

The most frequent application of copying between devices is to create short text files directly from the keyboard without entering a word processing program. You also can copy files directly to the printer for output, but a better technique is the TYPE command (as you'll see later).

To create a text file from the console using the COPY command, specify the CON: device as the source device and the filename you want as the destination. Then type in the text you wish to store in the file, ending each line with the Enter key (sorry, no word wrap here).

When you are done, conclude the file with the special end-of-file marker, Control-Z. You may either enter Control-Z, or press the F6 key. The end-of-file marker must also be followed by Enter.

To see how easy this really is, try creating a simple text file following these directions. Press Enter at the end of each line:

```
C>COPY CON: FLATTERY
HELLO THERE,
YOU HANDSOME DEVIL
[F6]
```

(That's the F6 key on the last line; remember to press Enter.)

If you followed the instructions, you should have seen your disk drive light pop on when you hit the final Enter, and the confirming message:

1 file(s) copied

appear on your screen. You have just successfully created a text file.

To view the results of your handiwork, simply reverse the sequence of the COPY command as follows:

C>COPY FLATTERY CON:

You'll see the text appear on the screen followed again by the confirmation message telling you that 1 file has been copied.

Although the preceding exercise might seem trivial, this technique provides a quick-and-dirty method for creating special text files called *batch files*. Batch files can be used to automate certain repetitive sequences of DOS commands. (You'll learn more about batch files in chapter 6, "Batch File Programming.")

The ERASE Command. From time to time, you will need to remove files from storage media, especially on fixed disks. Although 20 or 40M might seem like a lot of storage, you might one day encounter the dreaded "Insufficient disk space" error.

Normally, you wouldn't wait for that message to occur before removing files from your disk. Both the directory and the CHKDSK commands allow you to determine the amount of storage space left on your disk, so you can plan ahead.

The ERASE command can be used to remove single files from a disk, or it can be used in combination with wildcards to remove multiple files. Be careful when using wildcards with the ERASE command! You might accidentally remove files you didn't intend to erase. The format for this command is:

ERASE [d:]filename[.ext]

The rules for using wildcards with the ERASE command are the same as for the COPY command—with one exception. If you use the global wildcards, *.*, you'll be prompted with the following message:

Are you sure (Y/N)?

The purpose of this confirmation message is to ensure against inadvertently erasing all the files on a disk. Unfortunately, this message can't protect you against forgetting to include the floppy drive designator and deleting all files on the hard disk by mistake. This will occur if you enter the following command from drive C:

```
C>ERASE *.*
```

There is another version of the ERASE command that might be familiar to old hands in the microcomputer world. It's the DEL command, which is a hold-over from the ancient days of CP/M. The DEL command works just like ERASE; the only difference is that it's easier to type. For this reason, DEL will be used from now on in any examples that require files to be removed.

Here's something not everyone knows: When you erase a file, the file is not actually removed from the disk. This would require physically rewriting zeros in all the sectors which used to contain the file's data, as well as rewriting the directory entry—that's a lot of unnecessary DOS overhead.

Instead to totally obliterate a file from disk, the directory entry for the file receives a special marker that indicates the file has been "erased." The initial cluster entry in the FAT is also replaced with zeros, indicating the area on disk is available. However, nothing on disk has really changed.

Deleting files under DOS is somewhat like banishment. The file is still physically on the disk, but you can't see it in a directory listing, nor can you read the data stored in it. It is possible to remove this file marker and so recover the file.

The DEL and ERASE commands cannot be used to remove hidden or read-only files from a disk. Hidden files were discussed in chapter 2. Two hidden files are IBMDOS .COM and IBMBIO.COM. Read-only files have a special file attribute that denotes them as available for use, but not for copying or deleting. In chapter 15, you'll learn how to alter file attributes, which will allow you to create your own read-only files, and to change read-only files into read-write files.

The RENAME Command. The RENAME command is used to change the name of a file. You might wonder why you would ever want to change a file's name. After all, what's in a name, right?

"A file by any other name would have the same contents . . ."

Actually, there are several reasons for changing a file's name. One compelling reason is that you might have made an error when the filename was created the first time.

Another reason for changing filenames is dictated by some popular applications that make backup copies of files each time you change them. Some programs use the BAK extension to denote backup files. However, only one backup file is available for each filename. If you change a file a second time, the original backup is lost because the first altered version assumes the role of the backup file and the latest version gets the original filename. If you want to keep copies of all three versions, you need to give the original version a new name. Use the RENAME command to change the filename before the application replaces it.

You also can use the RENAME command to rename COM files, but only the descriptive name. If you change the extension, it is no longer a program in DOS's eyes.

For example, you can rename your dBASE program from DBASE.COM to DB.COM. The new name will save you three keystrokes each time you enter the dBASE program. (A drawback, however, is that it will confuse other dBASE users who access your computer.)

Another example for the RENAME command is with duplicate filenames. For example, two leading word processing programs, WordPerfect and MultiMate, both use the filename WP.EXE for their program files. Which one runs when you type WP at the DOS prompt? "This disk just ain't big enough for the both of us," is one way of looking at it. You can use the RENAME command to resolve this conflict. Rename one of the program files MM.COM (you figure out which one).

The format of the RENAME command is quite simple:

RENAME [d:]filename[.ext] [d:]filename[.ext]

Or, the way most DOS aficionados remember it:

RENAME oldname newname

Using a preceding example, here's how you'd rename WP.COM to MM.COM:

C>RENAME WP.COM MM.COM

You might recall that the COPY command also can be used to rename files. What do you suppose the difference between the preceding command and the following one is?

C>COPY WP.COM MM.COM

With the RENAME command, only one version of the file will be on the disk. With the COPY command, there will be two copies of the file on the disk, one with the original name and a duplicate with the new name.

However, the COPY command can be used to rename files as they are copied from one disk to another. If you want to copy the WP.COM file from the original program diskette to the hard disk with the new filename MM.COM, the following COPY command would be faster than copying and then renaming:

C>COPY A:WP.COM MM.COM

The TYPE Command. The TYPE command is used to view the contents of a file. In fact, TYPE will display the contents of any file on disk, but it only displays legible information when used with text files. If you use the TYPE command with program or data files, funny-looking characters will show up on the screen, and bells and whistles might go off in your computer.

TYPE might not work with some word processing documents. These programs store their documents in nonstandard formats, including special control characters to denote centering, underline, and other nontext formats. The results of using the TYPE command to view the contents of word processing files are somewhat disappointing. Nonetheless, the TYPE command will give you some idea of the contents of text files.

The format for the TYPE command is:

TYPE [d:]filename[.ext]

The contents of the file will be output to the screen in a continuously scrolling fashion until the entire file is displayed.

You can use the TYPE command with the MORE filter to view the contents of a file one screenful at a time. See chapter 3 for more on pipes and filters.

To view the contents of a file with the filename LETTER.DOC, you would enter:

C>TYPE LETTER.DOC

The output of the TYPE command is normally sent to the screen. However, output can be redirected to the printer. You can use either the PrtSc key to print a single screenful or the Control-PrtSc key to turn on printer echo. (These techniques were covered in chapter 3.)

To redirect the output to the printer without the PrtSc key, use the device name of the printer, LPT1: or PRN: in conjunction with the TYPE command, like the following:

C>TYPE LETTER.DOC > LPT1:

This command sends the output of the TYPE command to the device named LPT1:, which is the parallel printer port on most PCs. If this doesn't work, check to make sure that the printer is connected to the computer, the printer's power is on, and it is on-line or selected. If these checks fail to reveal the problem, try using LPT2: as the device name.

If you are having trouble reading the output from the TYPE command because it is scrolling too quickly, pipe the output through the MORE filter. This filter causes each screenful of text to remain on the screen until you press any key for the next screen. For example, to view the file LETTER.DOC one screen at a time, you would enter:

C>TYPE LETTER.DOC ¦ MORE

Remember that MORE is an external utility and must be on your hard disk before you can use it with the TYPE or any other command.

In the preceding section on the COPY command, you learned how to create and view simple text files by designating the CON: device as either the source or the destination for the copy. Ordinarily, you would use the TYPE command to view the contents of such text files rather than the COPY command. To view the contents of your FLATTERY file, enter:

```
C>TYPE A:FLATTERY
```

The DATE and TIME Commands. The DATE and TIME commands are used to reset the system date and time. The DATE and TIME prompts appear at the beginning of any DOS session, allowing you to enter the current date and time from the keyboard, unless you have an AUTOEXEC.BAT file present in your root directory. If that is the case, the initial DATE and TIME prompts are skipped. (AUTOEXEC.BAT is covered in chapter 6, "Batch File Programming.")

Most novice computer users don't pay much attention to the date and time, and consider these prompts at system startup to be more of a nuisance than a convenience. However, the system date and time can be used quite effectively with a number of database programs to automatically place the current date into data records such as invoices, statements, and letterheads.

The system date and time are also used to *stamp* the directory entry of a file when it is created or updated. You can see these dates and times whenever you view the directory in the long form. This information can be quite helpful when determining which version of a file is the most current. However, the system date and time are only useful if they are correct.

With the introduction of the PC/AT, the date and time are automatically updated by a battery inside the computer. There's no need to enter the date and time manually each time you start. Also, most non-AT computers today are sold with internal clocks that keep the time (or until the battery runs low). With AT systems, you can get away with just pressing Enter at the initial date and time prompts. PC systems with internal clocks must run a special clock program that either came with the computer or else the clock software must be purchased. However, if you're totally lame and you bypass these prompts, you're stuck with the default value for the date and time, January 1, 1980 at midnight.

The DATE command allows you to enter the current date in one of several formats. The mm-dd-yy format is standard for the United States. (For more on alternate formats, see your DOS manual under COUNTRY and SELECT.)

When you enter the DATE command, you'll be presented with the current date and prompted to enter the new date with a display such as this:

```
C>DATE
```

Current date is Tue 10-08-1991
Enter new date (mm-dd-yy):

You can enter the current date separated by hyphens (-), slashes (/), or periods. Single digit months don't have to be preceded by zeros. If you make a mistake when entering the date, you'll receive the message:

Invalid date
Enter new date (mm-dd-yy):

The TIME command works much like the DATE command. You are given the current time and asked to provide the new time:

Current time is 21:03:29:66
Enter new time:

Computers use military time, up to one hundredth of a second (you don't have to enter the time to this level of accuracy). Normally, all you do is enter the hours and minutes. The seconds and hundredths of seconds will be set to zero by default. Units of time are separated by colons (:).

After the date and time have been set, either at system startup or through the use of the DATE and TIME prompts, the system will increment the time (and date if you work long hours) for you automatically until the computer is shut off. Again, if you have an internal, battery-powered clock, this incrementation will continue when the computer is off.

The CLS and PROMPT Commands. The DOS command processor appears to be quite limited in its user interface. All you see is a simple letter prompt. Also, past commands, and worse, error messages remain on the screen after a command has been executed, providing you embarrassment for all to see.

The sterile system prompt and cluttered screen can be annoying, especially to novice computer users. Fortunately, there are ways to alter the appearance of the DOS interface.

One simple yet underutilized command is CLS. CLS stands for CLear the Screen, and it does just that. If you enter this internal command at the system prompt, DOS will obligingly clear the screen for you. This is especially nice if you have just made an error and you don't want your boss looking over your shoulder at following DOS error message:

File destroyed due to operator incompetence

A more powerful command for altering the appearance of the screen is the PROMPT command. Basically, PROMPT lets you determine what the system prompt looks like. For example, you could alter the system prompt so that it displayed the following:

Today is Mon 1-01-86
The time is 09:00:00.00
Your wish is my command. . .

Doesn't this look better than the standard C>.

The PROMPT command allows you to insert your own text messages at the system prompt, as well as include the date, time, current drive, and other stats. After you enter the PROMPT information, it remains in effect until you restart your computer—or until you use the PROMPT command again.

Altering the standard system prompt is simple. All you do is enter the PROMPT command followed by the text message you wish displayed. For example, suppose you want the system prompt to read "Enter your command:." You can create this prompt by entering the following:

C>PROMPT Enter your command:

For the remainder of your working session, "Enter your command:" would be the new system prompt.

Besides giving you control over text messages, PROMPT also lets you include date and time information, skip lines, display the current drive letter, and other tricks. You can even include the familiar " > " symbol if you like. There are a number of parameters that can be included with the PROMPT command to embellish your customized system prompts. They are summarized in *Table 4-2*.

To use the parameters in *Table 4-2* with the PROMPT command, they must be preceded by a "$" character. PROMPT parameters may be included with text. For example, if you wanted the message:

Today is Sat 11-30-91

to appear in the prompt, you would enter:

C>PROMPT Today is $d

To display the prompt:

Today is Sat 11-30-91
The time is 18:30:01.99
Your wish is my command. . .

PROMPT

Command	Displays
t	The time
d	The date
v	The current DOS version number
n	The current drive letter
g	The " > " character
l	The " < " character
b	The " ¦ " character
q	The " = " character
—	A new line

Table 4-2. Parameters for the PROMPT Command.

you would enter:

C > PROMPT Today is d_The time is t_Your wish is my command. . .

You can even include the current drive letter with the $n parameter. In fact, you could recreate the basic DOS prompt by entering:

C > PROMPT ng

Of course, you can always return to the boring letter prompt by simply entering:

C > PROMPT

Because of DOS incompatibilities, having the booted version of DOS displayed as part of the system prompt can be helpful. This can be accomplished with the $v parameter. For example, you might want to have the following prompt displayed on your screen:

IBM Personal Computer DOS Version 3.3
C >

This prompt can be created with the command:

C > PROMPT $v4_$n$g

Creating customized system prompts is both fun and helpful. It can also be a great source of entertainment as you sneak around changing the prompts behind your co-workers' backs.

The VER Command. As you have probably gathered by now, there are a number of different DOS versions in existence. In addition to the two distinct versions, MS-DOS and PC-DOS, there are major releases, such as 3.0 and 4.0, plus minor revisions, as in 3.3 versus 4.01. These differences can be confusing, especially as certain DOS commands occur in some versions but not others. Other problems involving differing DOS versions include incompatibilities in disk formats and command processors.

One especially aggravating problem is that DOS versions 2.xx cannot recognize disks formatted with DOS versions 3.xx. The maxim here is that newer DOS's can read older DOS's, but not vice versa. If you boot the computer with one version of DOS, and then replace that disk with another containing a different version of DOS, you'll run into problems whenever you try to execute DOS commands from the system prompt. You will receive the agonizing message:

Incorrect DOS version

Keep all your program and data files on diskettes formatted with the same version as your hard disk, and you will avoid any problems. However, you might have collected programs and data over time. As new versions of DOS are released, you probably failed to copy your old programs and data onto newly formatted diskettes. That's understandable. At least you can tell which DOS version was used for formatting the disks because you wrote the version number on the bottom of the disk label as a reminder, right? You mean you forgot? So now what?

Luckily for you, the DOS command processor includes the VER command. This command will report on the version of DOS used to create the current disk or diskette. To obtain this information, just enter:

C>VER

DOS will respond with its version number, such as:

IBM Personal Computer DOS Version 3.30

MS-DOS 3.3 displays:

MS-DOS Version 3.30

PC DOS 4.0 renders:

IBM DOS Version 4.00

It's all the same tune, just different lyrics.

External Commands

Although the command processor contains many useful DOS commands, there are some DOS commands which require additional utility files. These utilities are actually separate programs and must be available on the current disk before you can employ them.

You might wonder why DOS puts some commands in the command processor and makes others external. The reason has to do with the limited amount of memory available on your PC. If all the DOS utilities were placed into the command processor, it would take up much more memory than you have available. Because many of the DOS utilities, such as DISKCOPY, are used infrequently, putting them into separate program files makes more sense. These programs are loaded into memory when needed. This limits the resident size of DOS, freeing your computer's memory for applications and data.

There are a number of external DOS utilities. The remainder of this chapter will discuss four very useful utilities: DISKCOPY, DISKCOMP, COMP, and CHKDSK. In order to use any of these utilities, you must first have access to them. This means that the file with the utility name and either a .COM or .EXE extension must be present on the hard disk (or a diskette in the floppy drive). If you followed the instructions in chapter 2 for copying the system files onto your hard disk, then you already have access to these utilities.

The DISKCOPY Utilities. The DISKCOPY utility is used to copy the entire contents of one diskette onto another. It usually is used to copy floppy diskettes. The format of the DISKCOPY command is:

DISKCOPY [d:] [d:]

Two disk drive designators are optional because you can use the DISKCOPY command with a single floppy drive. When copying diskettes on a single floppy system, just specify the designator of the one floppy drive. Unless you have an optional second floppy drive with your system, you'll have to copy diskettes in this manner.

To illustrate, if you have a computer with a hard drive and one floppy drive, you would enter:

C>DISKCOPY A:

The A: indicates the drive you want to use to copy diskettes. In a one-drive disk copy operation, you'll be prompted first to insert the source diskette into drive A, then to insert the target diskette into drive A, then the source diskette again, then the target diskette, etc., until the entire process is concluded (or until your arms grow really tired). The number of swaps you have to make will depend upon the amount of RAM available and the version of DOS you are using.

If you have two floppy drives with your system, you would enter:

C > DISKCOPY A: B:

You would then be prompted to insert your source diskette in drive A and your target diskette in drive B. The two-drive disk copy operation will proceed without requiring disk swapping. After the disk copy operation is completed, you'll be asked if you want to:

Copy another (Y/N)?

Responding with a Y will allow you to repeat the process with a different set of diskettes. An N response will terminate the DISKCOPY program and return you to the system prompt. You can make multiple copies of a single diskette by removing only the target diskette. (Professional software developers, however, use these huge mega-disk copying machines, rather than toil through DISKCOPY.)

If the target diskette has not been previously formatted, DISKCOPY will automatically format it for you. This feature is very convenient. DISKCOPY assumes the format of the source diskette should be used on unformatted disks. In fact, DISKCOPY can only transfer between diskettes of like format. If you tried to use DISKCOPY with a 1.2MB source diskette and a 360KB target diskette, you would get the following error message:

Drive types or
diskette types not compatible

To transfer files between diskettes of different formats, you need to use the COPY command.

Many computer users routinely rely on the DISKCOPY command to transfer files between floppy diskettes. Although this method works in the sense that all files are transferred, it is inefficient in the way files are stored on the target disk. What these users fail to realize is that the DISKCOPY command is not equivalent to the COPY *.* command.

How's that?

The DISKCOPY command transfers an exact duplicate of the source diskette onto the target diskette. During its use, the files stored on the source diskette might become fragmented. As you might recall from chapter 3, the clusters where a file is stored are not necessarily contiguous due to the nature of the random storage process. This means that disk access times when reading or loading fragmented files are increased. However, when files are copied to a freshly formatted disk with the COPY *.* command, they are copied one by one into contiguous clusters. The result is the files are stored more efficiently, thus decreasing disk access time to these files.

For this reason, you should periodically recopy data files onto newly formatted diskettes to reorganize them. This and other techniques for improving the storage efficiency of your hard disk will be explored in chapter 17, "Storage Optimization."

The COMP and DISKCOMP Utilities. The COMP and DISKCOMP commands let you compare files and diskettes to see if they are identical. The COMP command is used to compare single files or sets of files. The DISKCOMP command is used to compare entire diskettes.

You need to understand the distinction between these two utilities. The DISKCOMP utility *cannot* be used to compare hard disks. To compare files stored on hard disks with those stored on floppies, you must use the COMP command.

The format of the DISKCOMP command is similar to that of the DISKCOPY command:

```
DISKCOMP [d:] [d:][/1][/8]
```

Again, the drive designator(s) you use will depend upon the number of floppy drives you have. For a single drive disk comparison operation, you would use drive A and swap floppies as with the one-drive disk copy operation. With dual floppy systems, you can specify A as the source drive and B as the target drive.

The DISKCOMP command compares both the diskette formats and the contents of the two diskettes. If either the formats or the contents differ, you'll get a message informing you that an error occurred on a given side and a given track, such as:

```
Compare error on side 0, track 23
```

DISKCOMP compares disks on a track-by-track basis. It bases its format comparison on the format of the source diskette unless you include the single-sided parameter, "/1," or the 8 sectors only parameter, "/8."

If two diskettes are identical, DISKCOPY issues the message:

```
Compare OK
```

After completing the comparison process, DISKCOMP asks:

```
Compare more diskettes (Y/N)?
```

Respond to this question the same way you respond to the prompt to copy more diskettes with the DISKCOPY command.

Because there is no verify option with the DISKCOPY utility, using DISKCOMP is a handy way to ensure that a target diskette was copied accurately after a disk copy operation. Note, however, that just because two diskettes contain the same files does not necessarily mean that DISKCOPY will return a "Compare OK" message, because the files might be fragmented and stored in different clusters. If this is the case, the track-by-track comparison will indicate that the two diskettes are not identical.

Because DISKCOMP is really designed to compare diskettes rather than individual files, and because DISKCOMP cannot be used with hard disks, you must use the COMP utility when comparing files stored on your hard disk. This utility has the format:

COMP [d:]filename[.ext] [d:][filename][.ext]

The first filename is required and is called the *primary* filename. The second filename, referred to as the *secondary* filename, is optional. If a second filename is not provided, COMP will ask you for it. However, if you provide a drive designator but no secondary filename, COMP assumes you want to compare two files with the same name but on different drives. If there is no file on either the source or the target drive matching the specified filename for that drive, COMP will inform you and ask you again for the primary and secondary filenames.

The COMP command employs two techniques to determine if files are unequal. First, it checks the lengths of the two files. If the file lengths differ, then the files are not identical, and COMP immediately returns the message:

Files are different sizes

If the files are of the same length, then COMP proceeds with a byte-by-byte comparison of the two files. COMP will report the location of any mismatched bytes in terms of their location within their respective files. The offset values (how far into the files the error occurred) are hexadecimal values.

Normally, you would not be concerned with the location of the mismatch. The mere fact that a mismatch is encountered is sufficient. COMP reports on the mismatched bytes encountered up to a maximum of ten. If ten mismatches are encountered, COMP concludes the comparison and issues the message:

10 Mismatches—ending compare

If the files are equal in length and identical in content, COMP displays the message:

Files compare OK

For example, suppose you have two letter files, both named LETTER1.DOC. One is stored on your hard disk and the other on a floppy. You could check to see if they were identical by entering:

C>COMP LETTER1.DOC A:

The COMP command may be used in combination with wildcards to check groups of files. To compare all DOC files on drive A with those on drive C, you would enter:

C>COMP A:*.DOC C:

Note the sequence of the drives. A is the source drive in this case because there are likely to be DOC files on C that aren't on A. If you specified C as the source drive, you would be asking COMP to look for a lot of nonexistent files on drive A.

When using wildcards, COMP compares files in the order they occur in the source directory with the corresponding files on the target disk. If there is no secondary file matching a given primary file, COMP displays the names of the two files plus a message that the secondary file was not found, as in the following example:

A:LETTER2.DOC and C:LETTER2.DOC
C:LETTER2.DOC—File not found

The status of each comparison is reported until all files matching the wildcard file specification in the primary filename have been checked. At the conclusion of a COMP command, the "Compare more files (Y/N)?" message is displayed.

You also can compare all files on one disk with those on another disk with the *.* global wildcards. However, simply specifying the drive designators with no filenames will accomplish the same thing:

C>COMP A: C:

Two files can be equal in content without being physically identical. Some programs always store their data files in multiples of 128 bytes. Thus, the last few characters of two files might not be identical because of the extraneous characters stored in the final sectors of the two files. Because COMP compares all bytes included in a file, it will consider these two files to be unequal. However, because COMP also looks for the end-of-file marker as the last character in a file, it will display the message:

EOF not found

If you see this message, it is possible that the two files might in fact be equal.

The CHKDSK Utility. The CHKDSK utility is one of the most useful of the external DOS commands. You are probably aware that this command can be used to find out how much storage space remains on a disk. However, the command also can be used with several optional parameters to reveal important information about the way files are stored, or to recover lost sectors. These features are especially valuable when managing hard disks. As the owner of a hard disk system, you should familiarize yourself with this utility, and use it frequently to improve the performance of your system.

The general format of the CHKDSK command is:

CHKDSK [d:][filename][.ext][/f][/v]

As you can see, only the command itself is required. All other elements of the command are optional. With floppy drive systems, most DOS users only employ the basic command itself, and never learn the purpose or application of the filename, "/F," and "/V" options.

In its simplest form, the CHKDSK command will reveal the following information:

- The disk volume name
- The date the disk was initially formatted
- The total storage space on the disk
- The amount of storage used by and number of hidden files
- The amount of storage used by and number of subdirectories
- The amount of storage used by and number of files
- The number of bytes in any bad sectors on the disk
- The amount of available storage remaining on the disk
- The total amount of RAM
- The amount of RAM available after the system files and any RAM-resident programs are loaded.

To obtain a listing of these statistics, enter the CHKDSK command and press Enter. To check a disk other than the current disk, follow CHKDSK with the drive designator.

The basic command results in the status report shown in *Fig. 4-1.*

CHKDSK all by itself is not particularly useful, though some naive users attribute a lot of power to CHKDSK. However, when used with the optional filename, "/F," or "/V" features, this utility can provide important information about your hard disk.

One important service CHKDSK performs is informing you of the condition of your files. If you recall from chapter 2, files can be stored in contiguous clusters or in fragmented clusters. File fragmentation occurs as more and more files are added to a disk. After a disk has been in use for some time, chances decrease that there will be just the right number of contiguous clusters available to store a new file, or one which has been revised. This new file must then be stored wherever empty clusters are located on the disk. Of course, the addition of each new, fragmented file further aggravates the problem, even

```
Volume COMPUCARD    created Sep 24, 1988 5:03p

 33409024 bytes total disk space
    53248 bytes in 3 hidden files
    94208 bytes in 43 directories
 15579136 bytes in 804 user files
 17682432 bytes available on disk

   655328 bytes total memory
   520352 bytes free
```

Fig. 4-1. Sample status display of a hard disk produced by the DOS CHKDSK utility.

to the point where new files will be scattered throughout the disk like pieces in a jigsaw puzzle.

File fragmentation reduces the performance of your system. In order to read data or access program instructions from a fragmented file, the access drive's arm must move back and forth over the disk surface, searching out the various tracks where the various clusters are located. This additional access time slows down the apparent operation of your computer. Although CHKDSK cannot remedy this situation, it can at least report on it for you. (You will learn to use techniques described in chapter 17, "Storage Optimization," to reorganize your files into contiguous clusters.)

To obtain a report on a particular file, include its filename in the CHKDSK command. For example, to check the file, LETTER1.DOC, on drive A for fragmentation, you would enter:

C>CHKDSK A:LETTER1.DOC

If the specified file is stored in contiguous clusters, the following message will be returned:

All specified file(s) are contiguous

However, if the file is stored in two or more noncontiguous clusters, this message will be reported to you:

A: \ LETTER1.DOC
Contains *n* noncontiguous blocks

The value of *n* is the number of noncontiguous clusters involved. Note the backslash character, " \ ," included in the filename. This character refers to the file's *path*. If there is nothing between this character and the filename, then the file is stored in the disk's root directory and can be ignored. Paths become important when you have more than one directory on a disk. Additional directories are called *subdirectories*. Paths and subdirectories are the topic of the next chapter, "Subdirectories and Paths."

You may use wildcards in filenames with the CHKDSK command. If you do, the status of all the files matching the wildcard filename will be reported. One way to check on the overall degradation of your hard disk is to use the global wildcard combination *.* such as:

```
C>CHKDSK *.*
```

If you have recently formatted your hard disk and copied the DOS system files onto it, you might see the "All specified file(s) are contiguous" message. However, if your hard disk has been in use for some time, you probably will be surprised by the extent of file fragmentation that has taken place. If you are really concerned, skip ahead to chapter 17 to learn how to correct the situation.

CHKDSK's /V and /F Options. Two optional parameters, "/V" and "/F," may be included with the CHKDSK command as well. The first of these, "/V," displays all the files on the disk (regardless of whether they are stored in noncontiguous clusters) along with their paths. The purpose of this option will become apparent in the next chapter.

The "/F" option causes CHKDSK to check the File Allocation Table for missing sectors. (You might want to read the section on "Directories and File Allocation Tables" in chapter 3 if you have not already done so.) Normally, all sectors are recorded in the FAT. However, sometimes the pointers from one sector to another get lost. If this happens, any data contained in these sectors will be unavailable to you. You must fix the FAT with the CHKDSK /F command to recover the lost data.

When you include the "/F" option, CHKDSK first checks the FAT to see if there are any lost sectors. Usually there won't be any because this is a fairly uncommon occurrence. If CHKDSK does discover any lost sectors, it will ask if you want to recover the data which is stored in the clusters containing these sectors. The message looks something like this:

008 lost clusters found in 002 chains
Convert lost chains to files (Y/N)?

Unfortunately, CHKDSK cannot append these lost clusters to their original files. However, CHKDSK will place the rediscovered clusters into individual files so you can look at them. Each cluster restored by CHKDSK is placed into a file beginning with the filename FILExxxx.CHK. The first cluster is named FILE0000.CHK, the second cluster is named FILE0001.CHK, etc. If the data is important, you can use the application program that created the data to restore it to the appropriate file.

As you can see, CHKDSK is a powerful and versatile utility. Not only can it be used to improve the performance of your system, but it can help you recover lost data.

You should perform periodic disk and file checks using CHKDSK. Just prior to your weekly system backup is a good time to perform this utility. You'll learn how to back up your hard disk in chapter 12, "Backing Up Data and Programs."

DOS 4's CHKDSK. Version 4 of DOS adds a few more bells and whistles to CHKDSK's display. As with most DOS 4 commands, these extras offer you more information about your hard disk than previous versions of DOS commands. With CHKDSK, you also get to see information about clusters in the CHKDSK display.

The output of CHKDSK under DOS 4 (in *Fig. 4-2*) looks the same as other versions of DOS, with the addition of a middle section on allocation units. These units are actually clusters, the minimum number of bytes DOS assigns to each file it puts on disk. DOS 4's CHKDSK tells you the size of each cluster (allocation unit), how many total clusters are on the drive, and how many are available.

```
Volume COMPUCARD   created Sep 24, 1988 5:03p
Volume Serial Number is 2862-079C

33409024 bytes total disk space
   53248 bytes in 3 hidden files
   94208 bytes in 43 directories
15579136 bytes in 804 user files
17682432 bytes available on disk

    2048 bytes in each allocation unit
   16313 total allocation units on disk
    8634 available allocation units on disk

  655328 bytes total memory
  520352 bytes free
```

Fig. 4-2. DOS 4's CHKDSK output.

Note that the number of clusters on the drive is simply the value of "bytes of total disk space" divided by the "bytes in each allocation unit" value. The "available allocation units on disk" value is the "bytes available on disk" value divided by the allocation unit size.

Also, if you're really paying attention, you'll notice that CHKDSK under DOS 4 tells you the "volume serial number." This is a unique, random number that DOS 4 gives to each disk it formats. Other versions of DOS ignore this value, but DOS 4 uses it for security and other purposes. Differing serial numbers on two diskettes will not affect a DISKCOMP.

SUMMARY

This chapter has described some of the most frequently used DOS commands and utilities. The internal commands covered are: COPY, ERASE, RENAME, TYPE, DATE, TIME, CLS, PROMPT, and VER.

The external commands explained are: DISKCOPY, COMP, DISKCOMP, and CHKDSK.

You'll probably use these utilities on a daily or weekly basis. However, there are a number of other DOS commands and utilities you'll need to be familiar with in order to manage your hard disk system effectively. These commands and utilities will be introduced throughout the remainder of the book.

5
Subdirectories and Paths

THERE ARE TWO major managerial tasks involved with hard disks. One is the repetitive chore of backing up accumulating data. The need to perform periodic backups can be addressed in several ways, which will be discussed in chapters 12 and 13.

The other major managerial task involves the creation and maintenance of an organized system for storing and retrieving data and program files on the hard disk. The first step in creating such a system is to segregate the hard disk into separate work areas according to user and/or application.

This chapter covers hard disk organization using subdirectories. So far, you've seen disks referenced as an absolute storage device. But DOS is more organized than that. Rather than put every single file you have onto the disk (which is inherently sloppy and confusing), you can use subdirectories to organize your files, programs, and data. For hard disk users, subdirectories are vital necessities.

HARD DISK ORGANIZATION STRATEGIES

File organization becomes crucial when working with hard disk systems. The sheer number of files involved can prove overwhelming, especially to novice computer users. Hard disks provide enough storage to accommodate thousands of files (with over 1,000 being typical on the average hard drive). You can see the complexity of the problem.

For example, the techniques for displaying directory listings (described in chapter 3) are unsuitable for use with fully-populated hard disks. The directory listing for a fully-utilized 20M hard disk could easily run to twenty or more screens. Locating a given file under such circumstances can be a daunting task, even with the FIND and MORE filters.

Imagine the plight of the beginning computer user facing the task of locating an applications program, executing it, and then finding a data file from among several hundred such files. Scenarios such as this occur far too frequently in the world of personal computing. Yet, they don't have to.

Work Areas

There are a number of techniques used to organize files into a workable arrangement on the hard disk. The simplest of these is the use of *segregated work areas.*

Segregated work areas allow each computer user to keep track of their own files without having to worry, or even know about, the files of the other users. There are several advantages to these work areas: 1) Directory listings for each work area show only those files relevant to the user of that area; 2) separate users can use the same filenames for different files, thus avoiding collisions that occur when files of the same name overwrite each other; 3) when data files are segregated into separate work areas, access to confidential data can be limited through the use of passwords, giving data security. Specific techniques for ensuring data security through the use of passwords will be described in chapter 14, "Password Security."

Individual work areas, each with its own directory, enable you to extend the number of file entries beyond the limit imposed by the use of a single directory. (Recall the file limit imposed on the root directory by DOS, as covered in chapter 2.)

Even if you're the only user of your hard disk, the use of separate work areas will be advantageous. For one thing, you can separate your application programs into individual work areas. Locating data files created with various programs will be easier. Even as a single user, the DOS limitation of eight characters for filenames can lead to unanticipated duplications. These are less likely to be a problem when files are segregated by application.

Subdirectories

To separate a hard disk into separate work areas involves the creation of *subdirectories.* Subdirectories are just what the term implies: subgroups of files within a disk's root directory. Each subdirectory acts like a separate directory, nearly like a separate disk (though it's not such a straight across analogy). You might have as many subdirectories as you wish. Each subdirectory can contain more subdirectories.

There is no limit to the number of files you can place in a subdirectory—other than the space available on your disk. After a subdirectory is created, it serves as the organizing structure for a separate work area. You can store files there, make more subdirectories, and anything else you can normally do with files in DOS. But the files exist only in that subdirectory, separate from other files on the disk.

All the files stored in the subdirectory can be viewed with the directory command, and files can be created or deleted without concern for files stored in other subdirectories. The subdirectory effectively separates those files it contains with files from other subdirectories. However, you can transfer files from one subdirectory to another, and even access files stored in other subdirectories. Subdirectories are powerful because they provide separation without isolation.

Although there is no limit to the number of subdirectories you can have, nor to the number of files within a subdirectory, you should give some thought to the location and organization of programs and data files within a subdirectory scheme. For example, if you have several users all working with a spreadsheet program, you need not have three separate spreadsheet program subdirectories. One program subdirectory with individual subdirectories for each user will work well. On the other hand, a single user might require more than one subdirectory, depending upon the number of applications used.

The CompuCard Scenario

To see how subdirectories can organize a hard disk system, both by user and application, consider this scenario: A small business, CompuCards, Inc., which creates and markets computer-generated greeting cards, uses a PC with a 33M hard disk.

The secretary, Sue, uses the computer to do word processing and to enter data into the customer database. The bookkeeper, Bob, runs a computerized accounting program off the hard disk. Jack, the sales manager, uses the data entered by Sue to produce sales reports and to plan marketing strategy. Mary, the graphics artist, works with a graphics program. Because she is the creative type, Mary also likes to play computer games while waiting for inspiration. Finally, Linda, the owner, uses the computer for financial management and to organize her annual and five-year business plans. A simple organization chart for CompuCards is shown in *Fig. 5-1*.

Individual work areas for this company are needed to accommodate all of the users. One each is needed for Bob's accounting program, Mary's art work, Jack's customer database, and Sue's word processing files. In addition, Linda, Jack, and Bob all use Lotus 1-2-3 to maintain various files, which they wish to keep separate. Also, both Linda and Jack use WordStar to write business plans, marketing proposals, and memos. Linda also uses an outline processor to help organize her thoughts. She wants to keep these brainstorming files separate from her actual written documents.

Within the customer database work area, Jack, being somewhat of a swinger, maintains his own private records of personal contacts and unlisted phone numbers. Finally, Linda suspects that Mary might be spending too much time blasting M-R-oids from the moons of Uranus and not enough time pumping out greeting cards. She wants to keep track of Mary's time by segregating the games from the graphics program and using a time-keeping utility to log Mary's time in each work area.

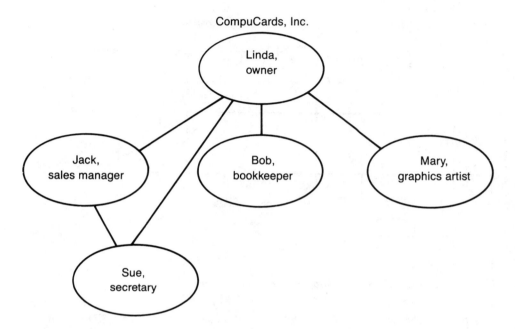

Fig. 5-1. Organizational chart for CompuCard, Inc.

One way to organize these work areas is to create three main subdirectories, named ADMIN, ACCT, and ART.

The ADMIN subdirectory is further divided into three subdirectories, WP, LOTUS, and DB3. Each of these subdirectories is divided by application and user. For example, the WP subdirectory might contain separate subdirectories for the three word processing applications, MM for MultiMate, WS for WordStar, and TT for ThinkTank. Under the WS subdirectory will be two user areas, LINDA and JACK. Similar user subdirectories can exist under the LOTUS and DB3 subdirectories. Finally, Mary's ART subdirectory will be subdivided into GAMES and GRAPHICS. The structure of the subdirectory system under this scheme is shown in *Fig. 5-2*.

Although this structure seems to be quite comprehensive, one very important aspect of the overall system has been neglected—the system files and utilities. These files should be separated from the rest of the application programs for convenience and simplicity. This separation requires the addition of a fourth main subdirectory, which can be labeled DOS. *Figure 5-3* illustrates the revised top level of the subdirectory structure.

Trees and Paths

Notice how the appearance of the subdirectory structure in *Fig. 5-2* resembles an inverted tree, with the root at the top. The system of the root directory and subdirectories

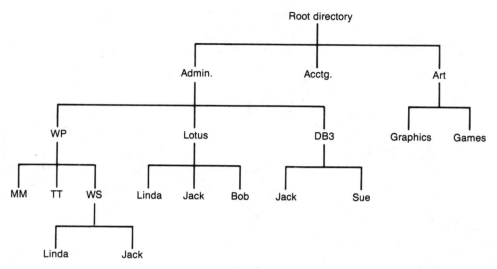

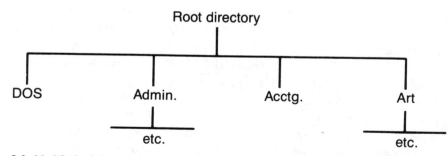

Fig. 5-2. *The structure of CompuCard's hard disk subdirectories.*

is often referred to as the *tree* structure of the disk. In fact, there is even a TREE utility you can use to display the various subdirectories and their relationships.

To access a subdirectory, you must follow the appropriate *path* to get to it. The subdirectory path is established when the subdirectory is created. This path might lead through several preceding subdirectories before arriving at the destination subdirectory.

Think of subdirectories in terms of levels in the tree structure. For the system outlined in *Fig. 5-3*, the root directory represents level 0, and the four subdirectories, ADMIN, ACCTG, ART, and DOS, constitute level 1.

Fig. 5-3. *Modified subdirectory system including a separate DOS subdirectory.*

Each level is preceded by the level prior to it. The root directory is indicated by a single backslash (\ ). Level 1 subdirectories are indicated by a backslash followed by the subdirectory name, such as \ ADMIN, and so on. The path to a given subdirectory consists of all the subdirectory names above that subdirectory. For example, to access files in Linda's Lotus work area you would follow this path:

\ ADMIN \ LOTUS \ LINDA

Paths allow you to specify any subdirectory or file in another subdirectory within the tree structure. For example, if Linda were working in her Lotus file subdirectory, she could call for a file named LETTER.DOC located in her WordStar file subdirectory by entering:

\ ADMIN \ WP \ WS \ LINDA \ LETTER.DOC

The inclusion of a file's path along with its drive designator and filename completes the path description (location) of that file. These three components, drive designator, path, and filename, are called a file's specification, or *filespec* for short. You'll see this term in your DOS manual, and it will be used in the remainder of this book.

Unless a subdirectory is protected through the use of passwords or some other form of security, you can access files contained within a subdirectory by including the path of those files in any DOS command.

SUBDIRECTORY COMMANDS

A disk's root directory is automatically created during the formatting process. Subdirectories, on the other hand, must be created manually. After a subdirectory has been created, it can be subdivided into additional subdirectories. After all subdirectories have been created, you can move among them and manipulate them using additional subdirectory commands. DOS has three commands to manipulate and work with subdirectories, and are internal commands. These commands are shown in *Table 5-1*.

	Command	Function
Table 5-1. Commands for Subdirectories.	MKDIR	Create (make) a subdirectory
	CHDIR	Change subdirectories
	RMDIR	Remove a subdirectory

Creating Subdirectories with MKDIR

The MKDIR command is used to establish a new subdirectory from either the root directory or another subdirectory. This command may be abbreviated as MD. The format of the MKDIR command is:

MKDIR [d:][path]subdirectory

Note that the drive designator and path are optional. If you omit the drive designator, the subdirectory is created on the currently logged drive. If you leave out the path, the subdirectory is created under the current directory or subdirectory. In this case, the current directory or subdirectory is said to be the *parent* of the new subdirectory.

All level 1 subdirectories have the root directory as their parent. If you include the optional path when making a new subdirectory, the subdirectory will be created under the appropriate parent directory (or subdirectory) according to the specified path. For example, suppose you are currently located in the LOTUS subdirectory. By entering the command:

C > MD LINDA

you would create a LINDA subdirectory under the LOTUS parent subdirectory. However, you could create the LINDA subdirectory under the WS parent subdirectory (or any other subdirectory on drive C) by entering the command:

C > MD ＼ADMIN＼WP＼WS＼LINDA

Be careful not to create subdirectories with the wrong parent. This is easy enough to do if you don't specify the correct path. Many hard disk users misunderstand the meaning of the " ＼ " character and assume it must be included before each subdirectory. If you were to include the backslash when attempting to create the LINDA subdirectory in the LOTUS subdirectory:

C > MD ＼LINDA

you would actually be creating a level 1 subdirectory under the root directory. Later in this chapter, you'll learn how to remove unwanted subdirectories, so don't worry if you've created one or more subdirectories with the wrong path.

Subdirectories are named just like files. They follow the same rules, an eight character descriptive name plus a three character extension separated by a period. (Most people elect not to use the extension on a subdirectory name.) Subdirectories can also use the same letters, numbers, and symbols as filenames, with the exception of the following characters:

. " / ＼ [ ] : * ¦ < > + = ; , ?

You can have more than one subdirectory on a hard disk with the same subdirectory name. For example, in *Fig. 5-3*, there are three separate subdirectories named JACK. But notice that these subdirectories each have different parents. This makes intuitive sense. You wouldn't name two of your kids Jack, but there might be a Jack living next door.

By the same logic, you can't have files and subdirectories with the same name under the same parent subdirectory. If you attempt to create a subdirectory under a parent subdirectory that already contains a file or subdirectory with the same name, the following message will be displayed:

Cannot create subdirectory

Moving Among Subdirectories with CHDIR

The CHDIR command is used to move between subdirectories. CHDIR may be abbreviated as CD. The format of this command is:

CHDIR [d:][path]

Note that the path is optional. Normally, you include the path to indicate which subdirectory you want. However, when omitted, CHDIR simply displays the current subdirectory. For example, if you were logged to the \ADMIN\WP subdirectory on CompuCards' computer, after entering CHDIR or CD you would see:

C:\ADMIN\WP

If you were logged to the root directory, you would see:

C:\

When used alone, DOS interprets CD as a request for help, "Where am I?" and responds with the current subdirectory. Once you know where you are, you can determine the appropriate path where you want to go.

However, CHDIR's main purpose is to change directories. You can move to the MM subdirectory by entering:

C>CD \ADMIN\WP\MM

The full path to a subdirectory is not always required. For example, if you are in a parent subdirectory, you need not include the parent's name in the path. In the preceding example, if you were already in the WP subdirectory, all you would have to enter is:

C>CD MM

Removing Subdirectories with RMDIR

You can delete unwanted subdirectories just like you can delete unwanted files. The command for this is RMDIR, abbreviated RD. The format of this command is:

RMDIR [d:]path

The path isn't optional with RMDIR, just as a filename isn't optional with ERASE or DEL. Why? Because you cannot remove the current subdirectory or the root directory, as the case (the default) would be if you didn't list a path.

Before a subdirectory can be removed, it must be empty. There can be no files or subdirectories within a subdirectory to be removed. This includes hidden files. If you attempt to remove a nonempty subdirectory, you'll be greeted with the message:

Invalid path, not directory,
or directory not empty

If this message occurs, you need to delete any files and subdirectories contained within the subdirectory you wish to remove. You can delete files with the global wildcard combination, *.*.

Assume the LINDA subdirectory under the LOTUS parent subdirectory is empty. You could remove this subdirectory by entering:

C > RD \ ADMIN \ LOTUS \ LINDA

Consider another example. In this case, the LOTUS subdirectory is to be removed. Assume in this example that the remaining subdirectories, JACK and BOB, contain files. To remove the LOTUS subdirectory, you must first remove the nonempty JACK and BOB subdirectories. This means deleting all the files contained within these two subdirectories. Then you could remove them from the LOTUS subdirectory. Finally, you would be able to remove the LOTUS subdirectory itself. This task requires the following sequence of commands:

C > DEL \ ADMIN \ LOTUS \ JACK *.*
C > DEL \ ADMIN \ LOTUS \ BOB *.*
C > RD \ ADMIN \ LOTUS \ JACK
C > RD \ ADMIN \ LOTUS \ BOB
C > RD \ ADMIN \ LOTUS

USING DOS COMMANDS WITH SUBDIRECTORIES

The presence of subdirectories on your hard disk alters the way you use and enter certain DOS commands. Specifically, the commands affecting files must include the path to the file as well as the filename and disk drive designator. For example, the complete format for the ERASE command is:

ERASE filespec

where the filespec is expressed as:

[d:][path]filename[.ext]

Paths allow you to enter DOS commands from any subdirectory to affect files in any other subdirectory. You must include the appropriate path. Otherwise, DOS assumes that you omitted the path on purpose. When no path is specified, DOS executes the command within the current subdirectory, just as it executes commands on the currently logged drive unless another drive is specified.

Copying Files Between Subdirectories

Copying files from one subdirectory to another requires that you pay particular attention to the paths of both the source and target files. The general format of the COPY command is:

COPY filespec filespec

The drive designator or path for either the source or the target file is optional. This option allows you to be in either the source or the target subdirectory when copying files between two subdirectories on the same disk. You also can be in the root directory of the hard disk when copying files from floppy diskettes into subdirectories on the hard disk. Finally, you can be logged onto the floppy disk drive directly and still copy files into a subdirectory on the hard disk.

While working with several subdirectories on the hard disk, you might find that you want to transfer files from one subdirectory to another. In such cases, the paths of both the source and the target files need to be considered. However, you don't necessarily have to include both paths in the actual COPY command.

If you're already located in the subdirectory which you want to copy the file from, you don't need to specify the path for this file. Similarly, if you are already in the subdirectory that you want to copy the file to, you don't need to include its path in the COPY command.

Consider the following three examples. In each case, Linda wants to transfer a file, LETTER.DOC from her WordStar subdirectory into her Lotus subdirectory. (You might want to refer back to *Fig. 5-3* to refresh your memory of CompuCard's hard disk tree structure.)

In the first example, assume that Linda is already in the LINDA work area of the WS subdirectory. To transfer the LETTER.DOC file into her Lotus work area, she would enter:

C > COPY LETTER.DOC \ ADMIN \ \ LOTUS \ LINDA

This command would copy the LETTER.DOC file from the current subdirectory, \ ADMIN \ WP \ WS \ LINDA, into the specified target subdirectory.

In the second example, assume that Linda is in her Lotus work area. In this case, the target subdirectory is the current subdirectory, and it is the source subdirectory path which must be specified in the COPY command:

C > COPY \ ADMIN \ WP \ WS \ LINDA \ LETTER.DOC

Because the target subdirectory is the current subdirectory and the filename doesn't change in the transfer process, the complete filespec for the target file is omitted.

In the final example, Linda is not currently in either of the subdirectories involved in the COPY command, but is in the root directory instead. She could still transfer the LETTER.DOC file from her WordStar work area into her Lotus work area by entering:

C > COPY ADMIN \ WP \ WS \ LINDA \ LETTER.DOC ADMIN \ LOTUS \ LINDA

In this command, the initial backslash is omitted from both the source and target paths because the first backslash refers to the root directory, which in this case is the current directory.

In conclusion, the current subdirectory path does not have to be included in the COPY command. With this in mind, what command do you think Linda would enter to transfer a copy of the BUDGET.WKS file from Jack's Lotus work area into her own if she is already located in the LOTUS subdirectory?

If you answered:

C > COPY JACK \ BUDGET LINDA

then you've got the right idea and should have no problem copying files between subdirectories.

You also can copy files from a floppy diskette's directory into subdirectories on the hard disk. This copy process does not require you to specify any path for the source files.

You rarely find diskettes that have been divided up into subdirectories. Although DOS allows you to use the MKDIR and CHDIR commands with floppy diskettes, there is really little call for subdirectories on floppies because the amount of storage space is so small.

You can copy files from a floppy diskette using the hard disk as the current drive, or you can log onto the floppy drive to perform the copy process. Both options will be illustrated later in this chapter.

Files in Subdirectories

When you create a subdirectory with the MKDIR command, you're actually creating a special file entry in the parent directory. The parent directory can be either the root directory or another subdirectory. Subdirectories act like the root directory because they include entries for each of the files they contain. These file entries record the filename, date and time stamp, file size, and beginning cluster number in the File Allocation Table.

There is one difference between subdirectories and the root directory: The root directory is physically stored in a specific location on the disk, immediately following the FAT, and is fixed in length.

The size of the root directory limits the number of file entries it can hold. For example, on a 20M hard disk, the size of the root directory is 32 sectors, which allows up to 512 file entries.

Subdirectories, on the other hand, are stored in the data section of the hard disk and can be any length. As a result, they can hold as many file entries as there is room on the disk.

As was mentioned earlier, if you have subdirectories created from the root directory, they will show up in a directory listing with the notation < DIR > next to them instead of a file size. *Table 5-2* shows a listing for the root directory of CompuCard's hard disk.

The four level 1 subdirectories are indicated with the < DIR > notation. Notice that COMMAND.COM is the only other file displayed in the directory. Individual files should be kept out of the root directory and placed in subdirectories instead. This organization keeps the root directory simple and easy to view, allowing you to focus on the overall structure of the subdirectory system rather than getting muddled by a lot of file entries.

Table 5-2. Directory Listing of CompuCard's Root Directory.

```
Volume in drive C is COMPUCARD
Directory of  C:\

COMMAND   COM     25307    3-17-87   12:00p
ADMIN         <DIR>        9-24-88    6:16p
DOS           <DIR>        9-25-88   11:26a
ART           <DIR>        9-28-88   11:37p
ACCT          <DIR>        9-24-88   12:49a
        5 File(s)   17680384 bytes free
```

Using the Directory Command with Subdirectories

The DIR command works within subdirectories just as it works with the root directory. You can use any of the directory options or filters described in chapter 3. However, when you view a directory listing of a subdirectory, you'll see two additional entries at the top of the listing: "." and ". ." (dot and dot-dot). For example, *Table 5-3* shows a listing obtained from the DOS subdirectory of CompuCard's hard disk.

The first two entries in this listing are followed by the <DIR> notation, so you know they refer to subdirectories. The . and . . are sometimes referred to as subdirectory *markers*. The . marker indicates the current subdirectory, the name displayed at the beginning of the directory listing. The . . marker refers to the parent directory; the directory that contains the current subdirectory's file entry.

For the DOS subdirectory, the parent directory is the root directory, \. Although the name of the parent directory is not displayed, the . . notation is used to represent the parent directory. You can specify ". ." instead of entering the parent directory's name. The utility of this abbreviation will become apparent later in this chapter in the discussion of subdirectory paths and tree structures.

Table 5-3. Directory Listing of CompuCard's DOS Subdirectory.

```
Volume in drive C is COMPUCARD
Directory of  C:\DOS

.                    <DIR>        9-24-88   12:49a
..                   <DIR>        9-24-88   12:49a
ANSI       SYS        1678        3-17-87   12:00p
COUNTRY    SYS       11285        3-17-87   12:00p
DISPLAY    SYS       11290        3-17-87   12:00p
DRIVER     SYS        1196        3-17-87   12:00p
FASTOPEN   EXE        3919        3-17-87   12:00p
FDISK      COM       48216        3-18-87   12:00p
FORMAT     COM       11616        3-18-87   12:00p
KEYB       COM        9056        3-17-87   12:00p
KEYBOARD   SYS       19766        3-17-87   12:00p
MODE       COM       15487        3-17-87   12:00p
NLSFUNC    EXE        3060        3-17-87   12:00p
PRINTER    SYS       13590        3-17-87   12:00p
REPLACE    EXE       11775        3-17-87   12:00p
SELECT     COM        4163        3-17-87   12:00p
SYS        COM        4766        3-17-87   12:00p
VDISK      SYS        3455        3-17-87   12:00p
XCOPY      EXE       11247        3-17-87   12:00p
EGA        CPI       49065        3-18-87   12:00p
```

```
LCD        CPI     10752   3-17-87   12:00p
4201       CPI     17089   3-18-87   12:00p
5202       CPI       459   3-17-87   12:00p
APPEND     EXE      5825   3-17-87   12:00p
ASSIGN     COM      1561   3-17-87   12:00p
ATTRIB     EXE      9529   3-17-87   12:00p
BACKUP     COM     31913   3-18-87   12:00p
CHKDSK     COM      9850   3-18-87   12:00p
COMP       COM      4214   3-17-87   12:00p
DEBUG      COM     15897   3-17-87   12:00p
DISKCOMP   COM      5879   3-17-87   12:00p
DISKCOPY   COM      6295   3-17-87   12:00p
EDLIN      COM      7526   3-17-87   12:00p
FIND       EXE      6434   3-17-87   12:00p
GRAFTABL   COM      6128   3-17-87   12:00p
GRAPHICS   COM      3300   3-17-87   12:00p
JOIN       EXE      8969   3-17-87   12:00p
LABEL      COM      2377   3-17-87   12:00p
MORE       COM       313   3-17-87   12:00p
PRINT      COM      9026   3-17-87   12:00p
RECOVER    COM      4299   3-18-87   12:00p
RESTORE    COM     34643   3-17-87   12:00p
SHARE      EXE      8608   3-17-87   12:00p
SORT       EXE      1977   3-17-87   12:00p
SUBST      EXE      9909   3-17-87   12:00p
TREE       COM      3571   3-17-87   12:00p
       46 File(s)   17680384 bytes free
```

Using DIR with the FIND Filter

The directory command can be used with the FIND filter to display only the files in the subdirectory without including the . and . . or other subdirectory entries. To accomplish this listing, pipe the output of the directory command through the FIND filter and request all entries that include the notation <DIR> be suppressed:

```
C>DIR ¦ FIND /V "<"
```

The optional parameter, /V, suppresses any entry including the character "<". Because this character occurs only in the <DIR> notation, all subdirectories, including the . and . . markers will be suppressed.

On the other hand, picking out the subdirectory entries from within a directory listing can be useful. You also can use the FIND filter to perform this task. In this case, you want to see all the entries with the <DIR> notation except the two subdirectory marker entries. The following command:

```
C>DIR ¦ FIND "<" /V "."
```

will produce the desired output. All entries including the "<" character are displayed except for the entries that also include a period. Because the only entries that include a period are the two subdirectory markers, these two entries are suppressed.

Transferring the System Utilities into the DOS Subdirectory

To see how easy working with subdirectories is, consider the task of creating a DOS subdirectory and copying the system utilities into it. In chapter 2, you learned how to format your hard disk and copy the DOS system files onto it by using REPLACE. However, if you have a new hard disk system, REPLACE won't do you any good—there's nothing to replace. You'll need to build your own DOS subdirectory and use COPY to put the DOS utilities into it.

Remember, the only files required to be in the root directory are the three system files. The remaining DOS utility files are only occasionally used and would be better stored in a special subdirectory set aside for that purpose, and they won't clutter up the root directory.

The first step in establishing the DOS utilities in their own subdirectory is to create a DOS subdirectory in the root directory. This subdirectory is created with the MKDIR command followed by the subdirectory name, in this case "DOS." The command would be entered as follows:

```
C>MD DOS
```

You can see the result of this command by asking for a directory listing of the root directory. You'll see the DOS subdirectory listed with the characters <DIR> alongside it. On a well-organized hard disk, the root directory will consist of nothing but subdirectory listings along with COMMAND.COM (and the two hidden system files, IBMDOS.COM and IBMBIO.COM, which you can't see anyway).

After the DOS subdirectory has been created, you can move into the subdirectory with the CHDIR command followed by the subdirectory name. This command, abbreviated with CD, is entered:

```
C>CD DOS
```

Creating a subdirectory does not automatically place you into that subdirectory. Remember that! You must always enter a subdirectory through the CHDIR command prior to working in it.

If you issue the DIR command after entering the new subdirectory, all you'll see are the two subdirectory markers because the newly-created DOS subdirectory is currently empty. Your next job is to copy the DOS utility files into it.

There are several ways to copy the DOS utility files into the DOS subdirectory. One method would be to enter the subdirectory and copy the files from the DOS System diskette. A second approach would be to log onto drive A and copy the files to the DOS subdirectory.

Because you're already in the DOS subdirectory, place the DOS System diskette in the floppy drive and use the COPY command as if you were in the root directory:

```
C > COPY A:*.*
```

This command will copy the DOS system files from the floppy diskette in drive A into the DOS subdirectory on drive C.

This process also could have been accomplished directly from the root directory. You wouldn't have had to move into the DOS subdirectory with the CHDIR command. Instead, specify the subdirectory you want the files to be copied into by including its path from the root directory:

```
C > COPY A:*.* \DOS
```

Alternatively, you could copy the DOS system files into the DOS subdirectory by logging onto the floppy drive with the following commands:

```
C > A:
A > COPY *.* C:\DOS
```

If you have followed one of these methods for copying the DOS system files into the DOS subdirectory, you can now move into this subdirectory (if you haven't already done so) and obtain a directory listing of the files stored there.

Notice that the DOS subdirectory contains the COMMAND.COM file. This file isn't needed because it is already in the root directory. You can use the ERASE or DEL commands to remove it. Whenever copying files into subdirectories, be sure to use the directory command when you're finished to check the results of the COPY command. Always remove unnecessary files, such as COMMAND.COM, that hitched along for the ride.

You now have the beginning of an organized subdirectory system. Your root directory consists of the three DOS system files and a single subdirectory containing all the DOS utility files. Now you can proceed to create other subdirectories and copy the appropriate files into them as needed. Make sure you change to the correct directory before copying files, or you might end up copying files into the wrong subdirectory, or worse, the root directory.

Using CHKDSK with Subdirectories

As you recall from chapter 4, the CHKDSK command provides you with information regarding the status of the specified disk and any files stored on it.

If you enter the CHKDSK command without including any optional parameters or filenames, you'll get a display of the disk's status. With DOS versions 3.2 and higher, this display includes the number of subdirectories included on the disk. For example, the result of running CHKDSK on CompuCard's hard disk results in the display shown in *Table 5-4*.

Table 5-4. Status of CompuCards' Hard Disk Produced by CHKDSK.

```
Volume COMPUCARD    created Sep 24, 1988 5:03p

 33409024 bytes total disk space
    53248 bytes in 3 hidden files
    94208 bytes in 43 directories
 15579136 bytes in 804 user files
 17682432 bytes available on disk

   655328 bytes total memory
   520352 bytes free
```

The CHKDSK command can be used with the optional /V parameter to reveal a much more detailed picture of the subdirectory and file structure of a hard disk. With /V parameter, CHKDSK examines the disk and displays a listing of all the files in the level 0 directory (i.e., the root directory), then all the subdirectories in this directory. It then steps down one level and displays all the files in each of the level 1 subdirectories, and all of the subdirectories under each of the level 1 subdirectories.

CHKDSK proceeds through each of the levels of the disk's tree structure, displaying the files and subdirectories at each level, until the final level has been reached.

Table 5-5 shows the output obtained by running CHKDSK with the /V option on CompuCard's hard disk. At this point, the complete tree structure has been established and the DOS utility files have been copied into the DOS subdirectory, but no user files have been created.

Table 5-5. Additional Information Provided by the CHKDSK /V Option.

```
Directory C:\
        C:\IBMBIO.COM
        C:\IBMDOS.COM
        C:\COMMAND.COM
Directory C:\DOS
        C:\DOS\ASSIGN.COM
```

```
                    C:\DOS\ATTRIB.EXE
                    C:\DOS\BACKUP.COM
                    C:\DOS\CHKDSK.COM
                    C:\DOS\COMMAND.COM
                    C:\DOS\COMP.COM
                    C:\DOS\DISKCOMP.COM
                    C:\DOS\DISKCOPY.COM
                    C:\DOS\EDLIN.COM
                    C:\DOS\FDISK.COM
                    C:\DOS\LABEL.COM
                    C:\DOS\MODE.COM
                    C:\DOS\MORE.COM
                    C:\DOS\PRINT.COM
                    C:\DOS\RECOVER.COM
                    C:\DOS\REPLACE.EXE
                    C:\DOS\RESTORE.COM
                    C:\DOS\SELECT.COM
                    C:\DOS\SHARE.EXE
                    C:\DOS\SORT.EXE
                    C:\DOS\TREE.COM
                    C:\DOS\XCOPY.EXE
          Directory C:\ADMIN
          Directory C:\ADMIN\WP
          Directory C:\ADMIN\WP\MM
          Directory C:\ADMIN\WP\TT
          Directory C:\ADMIN\WP\WS
          Directory C:\ADMIN\WP\WS\LINDA
          Directory C:\ADMIN\WP\WS\JACK
          Directory C:\ADMIN\LOTUS
          Directory C:\ADMIN\LOTUS\LINDA
          Directory C:\ADMIN\LOTUS\JACK
          Directory C:\ADMIN\DB3
          Directory C:\ADMIN\DB3\JACK
          Directory C:\ADMIN\DB3\SUE
          Directory C:\ACCTG
          Directory C:\ART
          Directory C:\ART\GRAPHICS
          Directory C:\ART\GAMES
          Directory C:\BOB

       21204992 bytes total disk space
          45056 bytes in 2 hidden files
          20480 bytes in 19 directories
         277504 bytes in 30 user files
```

Table 5-5. Continued.

```
20861952 bytes available on disk

  655360 bytes total memory
  609184 bytes free
```

As you can see, the output from the CHKDSK command can be quite lengthy. Imagine how long the output would be if all the user files were included. If you just want to get an overview of a hard disk's tree structure, you will be better off using the TREE command described later in this chapter.

Including Subdirectory Paths in the System Prompt

In chapter 4, you learned how to alter the system prompt using the PROMPT command. This command allows you to include special messages and other optional information, such as the system date and time, in your system prompt.

One of the options available with the PROMPT command is the $p parameter. You can include this parameter in combination with any of the other parameters or text messages to display the current drive and subdirectory path in the system prompt. For example, you could create a customized prompt that displayed the date, time, logged drive, and current subdirectory, such as:

Today is Fri 08-23-1991
Time is 18:04:30.50
Current disk is C
Current subdirectory is C: \ ADMIN \ LOTUS \ LINDA

Although the display reveals a lot of information, the above prompt is rather wordy and takes up four lines on the screen to boot. A simpler but useful prompt might be:

C: \ ADMIN \ LOTUS \ LINDA >

To create this prompt, you would enter:

C > PROMPT PG

Customizing the system prompt to include the current subdirectory is a simple yet powerful technique to facilitate working with your hard disk. You should definitely include it in your bag of tricks.

The PATH and TREE Commands

The advantage of subdirectories is that they allow you to divide user files and application programs into separate work areas. But there are disadvantages as well.

One critical limitation of subdirectories is the difficulty to access programs stored in another subdirectory. You must use the program's entire pathname each time you access it. Also, some programs require that they be started in the subdirectory they're in (possibly to give them access to other, supplemental programs also stored in that subdirectory). Although this isn't usually a problem, as you'll normally move into the appropriate subdirectory before using the desired program anyway, there might be times when you'll want to run programs stored in one subdirectory from another subdirectory.

This is analogous to a household with several rooms, each with a different function. Suppose you're in the den watching a football game, and you decide you want to make a Dagwood sandwich. Unfortunately for you, the sandwich makings are in the kitchen. To make the sandwich, you have to leave the football game and go to the kitchen. This is, to say the least, inconvenient. On the other hand, would you want to live in a house with all the appliances and furniture (not to mention kids) in a single, large room?

A similar situation arises when working with subdirectories on a hard disk. For example, if you were in the LOTUS subdirectory and you ran the CHKDSK program, which is in the DOS subdirectory, you would get the error message:

Bad command or filename

You can get around this problem by telling DOS where the program is located by including the path to the program in the command:

C> \ DOS \ CHKDSK

But isn't that too much to ask? After all, the program is on the disk. "Why can't DOS find it?" Or, a more logical question to ask (remember, it's a computer and, therefore, logical), is "How can I tell DOS where to look for the programs I want to run?"

The PATH Command. Fortunately there is a convenient solution. The DOS PATH command allows you to specify subdirectories from which programs can be run. PATH is an internal command and may be entered from any subdirectory. As soon as the PATH command is in effect, programs from any of the specified subdirectories can be executed from any other subdirectory. The format of the PATH command is:

PATH [path][;path][;path][;etc.]

The PATH command can be followed by one or more paths. The individual paths are separated by semicolons; if only one path is indicated, the semicolon is omitted.

Each path specified in the PATH command identifies a valid subdirectory to be searched whenever a program filename is entered at the system prompt. In fact, the PATH command is referred to in the DOS User's Manual as the "Set Search Directory Command."

The PATH command functions as follows: The individual paths specified by the PATH command are retained in memory. Whenever a filename is entered at the system prompt, DOS first checks if it's an internal command. If not, DOS checks the current subdirectory for a file with that filename and a COM, EXE, or BAT extension. If none is found, DOS next checks the first subdirectory specified by the PATH command. If the file isn't located in this subdirectory, DOS proceeds to check each subsequent subdirectory specified by the PATH command until the program is located or all subdirectories have been investigated. If the program is found, it is executed. If the program isn't located in either the current subdirectory or in any of the subdirectories specified in the PATH command, the "Bad command or filename" message is displayed.

To see how multiple paths can be established using the PATH command, consider the following scenario: Linda wants to use WordStar to write her annual report. She wants to be able to access ThinkTank, though, to help outline her ideas. Also, she wants to have access to the DOS utilities in case she needs to format a floppy diskette to store a backup copy of the finished document. In order to have access to the TT and DOS subdirectories from the WS subdirectory, she would enter the following command:

C > PATH C: \ ADMIN \ WP \ TT;C: \ DOS

The PATH command remains in effect until the computer is turned off or rebooted, or until you specify a new PATH.

Although your computer will remember the paths you established at the beginning of a long session, you yourself might forget. To refresh your memory, you can enter the PATH command with no parameters. For example, if Linda were to enter the command:

C > PATH

she would see the following displayed on the screen:

PATH = C: \ ADMIN \ WP \ TT;C: \ DOS

If any of the specified paths don't exist, DOS will simply ignore them when it searches the specified paths looking for a program file. This means you must specify subdirectory paths correctly. DOS will not catch your errors for you.

To remove all subdirectories from the PATH, enter the PATH command with only a semicolon:

C > PATH;

The TREE Command. Unless the tree structure of your hard disk is very simple, you might find yourself forgetting how the various subdirectories were created and where files are stored. Also, a new user won't be familiar with the organization of subdirectories and files on an existing hard disk.

One way to determine where files are stored is ask for a listing of the root directory to determine which subdirectories are stored there. You could then move into each subdirectory and obtain a listing of each one, and so on through each level of subdirectories stored on the disk. But doesn't that sound tedious? Could you possibly keep track of that information in your head?

Wouldn't it be nice if there were a simple command which would produce a listing of all the subdirectories on the hard disk, and the paths to each one? Fortunately, the DOS TREE command performs just this service. The format of the TREE command is:

TREE [d:][/F]

The TREE command has a single, optional files parameter, /F. Without the files parameter, TREE simply lists all the subdirectories on the disk according to levels, with the level 1 subdirectories listed first. *Table 5-6* details the output TREE command applied to the CompuCard tree structure.

Table 5-6. TREE Command as Applied to CompuCard's Tree Structure.

```
DIRECTORY PATH LISTING
Path: \DOS
Sub-directories:   None

Path: \ADMIN
Sub-directories:   WP
                   LOTUS
                   DB3

Path: \ADMIN\WP
Sub-directories:   MM
                   TT
                   WS
Path: \ADMIN\WP\MM
Sub-directories:   None
```

Table 5-6. Continued.

```
Path: \ADMIN\WP\TT
Sub-directories:   None
Path: \ADMIN\WP\WS
Sub-directories:   LINDA
                   JACK
Path: \ADMIN\WP\WS\LINDA
Sub-directories:   None
Path: \ADMIN\WP\WS\JACK
Sub-directories:   None

Path: \ADMIN\LOTUS
Sub-directories:   LINDA
                   JACK
Path: \ADMIN\LOTUS\LINDA
Sub-directories:   None
Path: \ADMIN\LOTUS\JACK
Sub-directories:   None

Path: \ADMIN\DB3
Sub-directories:   JACK
                   SUE
Path: \ADMIN\DB3\JACK
Sub-directories:   None
Path: \ADMIN\DB3\SUE
Sub-directories:   None

Path: \ACCTG
Sub-directories:   None

Path: \ART
Sub-directories:   GRAPHICS
                   GAMES
Path: \ART\GRAPHICS
Sub-directories:   None
Path: \ART\GAMES
Sub-directories:   None
```

The optional files parameter, /F, may be appended to include all the files stored in the subdirectories as well. In this case, the output will be substantially longer. For example, a partial TREE listing for CompuCard's hard disk including the DOS subdirectory files is shown in *Table 5-7*.

If your tree structure is fairly complex, the resulting output will scroll by quite quickly. You can freeze the scrolling with Control-NumLock, but a better alternative is to

Table 5-7. A Partial TREE Listing.

```
DIRECTORY PATH LISTING
Files:              COMMAND .COM
Path: \DOS
Sub-directories:    None
Files:              ASSIGN   .COM
                    ATTRIB   .EXE
                    BACKUP   .COM
                    BASIC    .COM
                    BASICA   .COM
                    CHKDSK   .COM
                    COMMAND  .COM
                    COMP     .COM
                    DISKCOMP.COM
                    DISKCOPY.COM
                    EDLIN    .COM
                    FDISK    .COM
                    FIND     .EXE
                    FORMAT   .COM
                    GRAFTABL.COM
                    GRAPHICS.COM
                    JOIN     .EXE
                    LABEL    .COM
                    MODE     .COM
                    MORE     .COM
                    PRINT    .COM
                    RECOVER  .COM
                    REPLACE  .EXE
                    RESTORE  .COM
                    SELECT   .COM
                    SHARE    .EXE
                    SORT     .EXE
                    TREE     .COM
                    XCOPY    .EXE

Path: \ADMIN
Sub-directories:    WP
                    LOTUS
                    DB3
Files:              None
Path: \ADMIN\WP
Sub-directories:    MM
                    TT
```

Table 5-7. Continued.

```
                         WS
Files:                   None

Path: \ADMIN\WP\MM
Sub-directories:  None
Files:            None

Path: \ADMIN\WP\TT
Sub-directories:  None
Files:            None
```

pipe the output through the MORE filter:

```
C>TREE \F ¦ MORE
```

Another option is to redirect the output to the printer with the command:

```
C>TREE \F >PRN
```

You can then keep this printout as a reference to the tree structure and file location of your hard disk. Remember to print out a new copy whenever you revise the structure of your hard disk.

DOS 4's TREE command vastly improves upon earlier versions. Primarily, it uses the special graphics characters to display the TREE. *Table 5-8* shows the output of DOS 4's TREE command on a 20M hard disk.

Table 5-8. Output from DOS 4's TREE Command.

```
Directory PATH listing for Volume DOS400
Volume Serial Number is 2620-07C9
C:.
├───SKPLUS
├───SYSTEM
│   ├───DOS
│   ├───HSG
│   ├───UTIL
│   └───INTEL
└───MAGELLAN
    └───VARIOUS
```

TREE under DOS 4 also has an extra option that provides compatibility with systems that don't have the line drawing graphics character set installed. (These could be systems used in other countries that have their CODEPAGEs set to display the special characters found in that country's alphabet.)

The /A option is used to display standard characters, such as -, ¦ , and +, instead of the line drawing characters in a tree listing. *Table 5-9* is the same TREE listing, but with the /A switch specified.

Table 5-9. DOS 4's TREE Output with the /A Option Specified.

```
Directory PATH listing for Volume DOS400
Volume Serial Number is 2620-07C9
C:.
+---SKPLUS
+---SYSTEM
|    +---DOS
|    +---UTIL
|    \---INTEL
\---MAGELLAN
     \---VARIOUS
```

Note how the line drawing characters used in *Table 5-8* were substituted with common keyboard replacements. This ensures a proper output on systems that might be used in foreign countries, computers that don't have access to the line drawing characters.

SUMMARY

In this chapter, you've learned how to create and work with subdirectories on your hard disk. This involves a new set of DOS commands and special techniques. Some of these commands, such as MKDIR and TREE, will only be used periodically. However, other commands, such as CHDIR, PROMPT, and PATH, must be used every time you operate your computer. Because these commands can be quite lengthy to enter, especially on a repetitive basis, it would be nice if there were some way to retain them for reuse each time the computer is turned on.

In fact, there is a technique for entering repetitive commands through the command processor without having to key them in each time you need them. This technique involves creating special DOS command files called *batch* files. You will learn how to develop and enter your own customized batch files in the next chapter.

6
Batch File Programming

IN THE LAST CHAPTER, you learned how to place program and data files into separate subdirectories and how to move into these subdirectories to access files within them. You also learned how to customize the DOS system prompt to include the current subdirectory.

Although all the tricks you've learned are useful, these and other DOS-related activities require you to enter a series of simple, yet repetitive, commands every time you start up your computer. But isn't a computer supposedly the master of the simple yet repetitive task? Why should you have to do all the work?

Fortunately, DOS provides you with a way to automate these repetitive command sequences by placing them into special command files called *batch* files. This chapter covers batch files, what they are, how to create them, and what types of things you can do with them.

WHAT ARE BATCH FILES?

Batch files contain readable, ASCII text and are identified by the special extension, BAT. Each line of text in a batch file represents a DOS command or special batch file instruction. When the command processor sees a file with this extension, it executes the individual lines included in the file as DOS commands, almost as if you'd typed those commands at the prompt yourself.

Batch files can be quite simple or very elaborate. Most simple batch files are used to automate repetitive processes, such as setting the system prompt or changing the current subdirectory and starting a program.

On the other hand, large, powerful batch files can be used to drive complete, menu-driven hard disk management systems. Such files can display specially designed menu screens, accept user input, and perform complex system-related tasks involving decision-making and looping. These sophisticated batch files are literally computer programs, and the techniques for creating them rightly deserve to be considered under the heading "Batch File Programming."

HOW BATCH FILES WORK

When you make an entry at the system prompt, the command processor first determines whether the entry is actually an internal command. If not, it next checks the current directory to see if there is a COM or a EXE file corresponding to the command you entered. If there is no file, the command processor checks to see if there is a BAT file matching what you typed. If such a file is found, the commands stored in the file are then executed by the command processor.

Because of the sequence the command processor follows in attempting to execute commands entered from the system prompt, you should be careful with what you name your batch files. For example, a batch file that sets the system prompt shouldn't be called PROMPT.BAT. Why? Because PROMPT is an internal DOS command. When you type PROMPT, DOS will first check for the internal PROMPT command—PROMPT.BAT will never be executed.

DOS MACROS

Anyone can learn how to create and execute fairly simple batch files. For example, you might want to set up a special batch file to change the system prompt, to save you from entering the PROMPT command every time you start up your computer. This batch file would include the PROMPT command plus the specialized text and parameters needed to customize your system prompt. You could assign a short, easily entered filename to this batch file. By entering this filename at the DOS prompt, you cause DOS to execute this file and change the system prompt for you automatically.

Batch files serve a useful, but limited function. They allow you to store either single or multiple DOS commands in a file for execution at a later time. To execute the stored command(s), all you have to do is enter the name of the batch file. Because a number of commands can be stored in a single batch file, the result of typing a single batch filename at the system prompt is greater than a single command entry. Batch files with multiple commands are commonly called DOS *macros*.

You might have heard of macros in a slightly different context. Many application programs include macro capabilities among their features. Perhaps the most popular application program to include macros is Lotus 1-2-3.

When used in reference to application programs, the term macro means a stored sequence of program commands. For example, a Lotus 1-2-3 user could create a macro to automatically load and update a summary spreadsheet from each of several detail spreadsheets on a regular basis.

Some word processing programs include macro capabilities, primarily to simplify entering complex commands and cut down on typing time. For example, a WordPerfect macro was written to convert this text from WordPerfect format into ASCII for the publisher.

Creating and Running Batch Files

Continuing with the system prompt example, suppose you want to create a batch file to have your prompt display the current subdirectory as well as the current drive (as described in chapter 5). To refresh your memory, the system prompt might look like this:

C: \ ADMIN \ LOTUS \ LINDA >

The following command changes the standard system prompt to display the current subdirectory:

C > PROMPT PG

You might decide to name the batch file PRMPT.BAT. You can create this file by placing this command into an ASCII text file using your word processor. Be careful, many word processors, such as WordStar and WordPerfect, do not automatically create ASCII text files—although documents created with these programs can be converted to ASCII files.

An easier and faster way to create PRMPT.BAT is to enter it directly from the console at the system prompt by following a few simple steps. Remember to press Enter after each line:

```
C > COPY CON: PRMPT.BAT
PROMPT $P$G
^Z
```

(^Z is entered either by pressing the F6 function key or Control-Z.)

When you press the final Enter, you should see the confirming "1 file(s) copied" message. (If not, reread the instructions and try again.)

You now have a simple batch file to change the system prompt. To execute this batch file, enter the descriptive filename at the C prompt:

C > PRMPT

The command processor will search the current subdirectory, and will find and execute the command contained within the PRMPT.BAT file for you. That really cuts down on your typing.

Want to cut down on it even more? Use the RENAME command to rename the file to P.BAT. Now, just type a P to change your system prompt.

A Batch File to Set the PATH

Another routine operation, often performed at system startup, is to set the path to certain commonly used subdirectories.

In the CompuCard hard disk tree structure, all the DOS utilities are stored in the DOS subdirectory. In order to run any of these utilities, a path to this subdirectory should be established. The PRMPT.BAT file could be modified to include this step as well. In this case, PRMPT.BAT would include two commands as shown below:

```
PROMPT.BAT

PROMPT $P$G
PATH \ DOS
```

To modify an existing batch file, you can use either your word processor (if it can work with ASCII files) or the DOS text editor, EDLIN.

EDLIN is described in Appendix B. However, for simple batch files such as PRMPT.BAT, deleting and starting over is just as easy. For example, to delete the old PRMPT.BAT file and create a new one, follow these steps:

```
C > DEL PRMPT.BAT
C > COPY CON: PRMPT.BAT
PROMPT $P$G
PATH \ DOS
^Z
```

Now PRMPT.BAT will set your prompt and your path. But is PRMPT still an appropriate name? How about renaming it to SETUP? That would be descriptive, as well as easy to remember.

Batch Files that Load Application Programs

Batch files can include either DOS commands or special batch file program instructions.

Batch file instructions can be combined with DOS commands in a single macro. Consider the recurring need to change subdirectories and run applications. For example, every

time Linda wants to use WordStar to create a document, she must execute the following
sequence of commands:

```
C>CD \ADMIN\WP\WS
C>PATH \ADMIN\WP\WS
C>WS
```

Linda might also want to have access to the ThinkTank program, so she needs to
include a second path, \ADMIN\WP\TT. Any new PATH command destroys previously established paths, such as the \DOS path created by the PRMPT.BAT file. The
\DOS path must be added as well. So the final path she can use is as follows:

```
PATH \ADMIN\WP\WS;\ADMIN\WP\TT;\DOS
```

All this involves quite a lot of typing just for Linda to get into her work area and load
the WordStar program. Is that an example of a computer making your life easier?

Clearly, it would be simpler to place Linda's sequence of commands into a batch file
named WSLINDA.BAT. This file could be created as follows:

```
C>COPY CON: WSLINDA.BAT
CD \ADMIN\WP\WS
PATH \ADMIN\WP\WS;\ADMIN\WP\TT;\DOS
WS
^Z
```

After the file, WSLINDA.BAT, has been saved, all Linda has to do to begin using
WordStar is enter the batch filename, WSLINDA, at the prompt. Similar batch files can be
created for each of the users and their specific applications.

The current WSLINDA batch file leaves Linda in her WordStar work area after she
exits from WordStar. An improved version of the WSLINDA.BAT file changes the current
subdirectory back to the root directory, and resets the path to \DOS after WordStar has
been run.

```
CD \ADMIN\WP\WS
PATH \ADMIN\WP\WS;\ADMIN\WP\TT;\DOS
WS
CD \
PATH \DOS
```

An important aspect of batch files is illustrated by the above example. Quoting a common expression, "It ain't over 'til it's over." A batch file that contains subsequent com-

mands after running a program will continue to execute even after the program is concluded.

The conclusion of the batch file is indicated by the special end-of-file marker, ^Z. Including an end-of-file marker when creating batch files from the console, or CON: device is very important. Word processors and text editors automatically place an end-of-file marker at the end of their text files, so you don't have to worry about this step if you are using such a program to create your batch files.

Batch Files to Simplify DOS Commands

Many people want to use their computers without having to learn much about them. To such users, the computer is a productivity tool and nothing more. Although these users might be willing to learn the commands necessary to create documents with their word processor, or build worksheets with their spreadsheet program, they are not interested in learning the details of DOS. Unfortunately, such users do have to put on the system operator's hat from time to time, even if only to perform such necessary tasks as formatting diskettes or copying files.

As the old saying goes, "A little knowledge is a dangerous thing." A computer user who knows a little DOS is potentially more harmful than one who knows nothing about DOS at all. The classic blunder made by DOS proselytes is formatting the hard disk when attempting to format a floppy disk. Oops! Perhaps this has even happened to you.

One application of batch files is to facilitate the use of DOS commands. In the remainder of this chapter, you'll learn various techniques that will enable you to create special batch files to simplify such DOS commands as COPY, ERASE, and FORMAT. In fact, you've already learned how to create a batch file which simplifies the PROMPT command.

A Disk-Formatting Batch File

Inadvertently formatting the hard disk when attempting to format a diskette can be a major problem. You can prevent this from occurring by creating a special batch file called FORMAT.BAT which formats a floppy diskette by including the A: drive designator in the FORMAT command. Then, whenever a user entered FORMAT at the system prompt, the batch file would ensure that the floppy drive was used instead of the hard drive.

You're probably wondering how there can be a batch file, FORMAT.BAT, with the same descriptive filename as FORMAT.COM. However, as long as FORMAT.COM isn't in the current subdirectory, the batch file will be executed.

In CompuCard's tree structure, FORMAT.COM is located in the DOS subdirectory. If the FORMAT.BAT file is stored in the root directory, then it will have precedence whenever the root directory is the current directory. You can ensure this will be the case by entering all application programs with the use of batch files like WSLINDA that return you to the root directory when they are done.

Before creating the FORMAT.BAT file, you might want to determine the necessary commands you need. When planning a DOS macro, pretend you're entering each of the commands in the macro individually from the system prompt. First, move into the DOS subdirectory. Next, enter the FORMAT A: command. (You could include the optional /s parameter if you wanted to copy the DOS system files after formatting.) Finally, change back to the root directory.

The complete FORMAT.BAT file should look like this:

```
CD \ DOS
FORMAT A:
CD \
```

To execute this batch file from the root directory, enter the descriptive filename, FORMAT, at the system prompt. DOS responds with the message:

Insert new diskette in drive A
and strike any key to continue

even though the drive designator, A:, was not included in the command. If the drive designator is included, it will be ignored, meaning that the user could even enter:

C > FORMAT C:

with no adverse effects.

Infinite Loops

You might have realized that you can use the PATH command to gain access to the FORMAT.COM utility in the \ DOS subdirectory. You might think that the commands:

PATH \ DOS
FORMAT A:

will accomplish the same thing as the preceding batch file. However, if you enter the above commands into a file called FORMAT.BAT and try to run it, you will be surprised at the result.

Instead of following the \ DOS path to run the FORMAT.COM file, the FORMAT A command will execute the FORMAT.BAT file located in the current, or root, directory. This problem is a case of a batch file running itself. Each time the FORMAT.BAT file encounters the command FORMAT A:, it will run itself again and again and again, also called an *infinite loop*. The only way to break out of an infinite loop is by using the key sequence Control-Break, or Control-C. Infinite loops are a common occurrence in batch file programming. You'll learn more about infinite loops and how to avoid them later in this chapter.

Terminating a Batch File

You can terminate a batch file in the middle of execution by pressing Control-Break. If your computer keyboard lacks a Break key, use the Control-C key sequence instead. Pressing Control-Break causes the following message to appear on the screen:

Terminate batch file (Y/N)?

You must respond with either a "Y" or an "N" with obvious results.

Although Control-Break can be used to terminate an unwanted batch file, you should be aware that Control-Break will not halt a DOS command after it is started. For example, if the formatting process has started before pressing Control-Break, the batch file will not be terminated until the process is completed.

AUTOMATIC STARTUP BATCH FILES

Even though the PRMPT.BAT file simplifies setting the system prompt and establishing the path to the DOS utilities, it still must be entered manually each time you start your computer. Think about how many times your computer is turned on in a month and then multiply this number times 5 (the number of characters in "PRMPT"). In some sense, these keystrokes represent wasted effort. The PRMPT entry really belongs under the heading of an operating system entry. On the other hand, you are more interested in working with the computer as a tool.

One function of batch files limits or even eliminates the need for you to deal with the operating system. DOS has established a special batch filename, AUTOEXEC.BAT, that is recognized and executed automatically when the system is booted.

You can assign the name AUTOEXEC.BAT to any batch file you wish. After a batch file has been created in the root directory and given the filename AUTOEXEC.BAT, that file will be executed at startup without having to enter it by name.

The AUTOEXEC.BAT file must be present in the root directory. DOS won't look elsewhere for it. If an AUTOEXEC.BAT file is not present, DOS proceeds with the standard startup procedure, which consists of prompting for the system date and time.

Automatic Date and Time Stamping

If you don't include the commands DATE and TIME in your AUTOEXEC batch file, these prompts will not be displayed at startup. Without an opportunity to set the date and time, any new or modified files will be stamped with the system's original date and time. If your computer doesn't have an internal clock, the PRMPT.BAT file should be renamed to AUTOEXEC.BAT and amended as follows:

```
DATE
TIME
PROMPT $P$G
PATH \DOS
```

You can delete the old PRMPT.BAT file and create a new file under the name AUTOEXEC.BAT, or use your word processing program to edit and rename it.

In the last example, the AUTOEXEC batch file includes the DATE and TIME commands if the computer that uses this file doesn't have an internal clock. However, if your system does have an internal clock installed, the last thing you want is to have to manually enter the date and time every time you start your computer. After all, that's why you installed the clock in the first place, to eliminate those extra steps. If you have an internal clock, leave out the DATE and TIME commands from your AUTOEXEC.BAT file.

Automatic System Modification

Your system might have other special hardware features, such as a special video adapter or a serial printer. In such cases, you might need to set certain system parameters at system startup using the DOS MODE utility.

The MODE utility lets you change the system defaults. For example, programs ordinarily send output to the printer via the LPT1: device. This logical device is assigned to your computer's first parallel printer port. If you have a serial printer, however, you want the output to go to the serial port instead. This port is usually identified as COM1: (or COM2: if you have more than one serial port). To reassign the printer output to the serial port, use the MODE command as follows:

```
C>MODE LPT1:=COM1:
```

Rather than entering this command every time you start up your computer, place it into your AUTOEXEC.BAT file. The MODE command also can be used to change the character pitch and line spacing on your printer as well as set the video parameters of your monitor.

Checking the AUTOEXEC.BAT File

If you've added any special hardware components to your system, such as an internal clock or a RAMDISK, the chances are good that your hard disk already has an

AUTOEXEC.BAT file located in the root directory. This AUTOEXEC file was either placed on your disk by the technician who installed the add-on device, or you were told to run an installation program which placed this file into your root directory for you. Before creating an AUTOEXEC file of your own, you should check for an existing file.

If there is already an AUTOEXEC.BAT file present in your root directory, you have two options. You can print out a copy of the existing AUTOEXEC file with the following command:

```
C>TYPE AUTOEXEC.BAT >PRN
```

After you have a hard copy of the commands contained in the original AUTOEXEC file, you can delete it and create a new one that contains all the original commands plus any extra commands you wish to include.

A second option is to use your word processing program or EDLIN to edit the original AUTOEXEC.BAT file. This process might necessitate copying the AUTOEXEC.BAT file into the subdirectory containing your word processor or EDLIN. Don't forget to copy it back to the root directory when you are finished.

MESSAGES, PROMPTS, AND VARIABLES

Simple DOS macros such as PRMPT.BAT or FORMAT.BAT are useful for automating repetitive tasks and easing the use of DOS. However, batch files such as these are quite limited. All they can do is perform a series of predetermined DOS commands, which could have been entered directly from the system prompt. You can create batch files that can accomplish far more than the simple examples illustrated so far.

By including messages and prompts to the user in your batch files, you can guide the user through a series of steps. Further, with the inclusion of batch file variables, you can devise general purpose batch files to perform a variety of tasks. These "generic" batch files can be made to perform specific functions by replacing the variables with actual values at the time of execution.

Including Messages in Batch Files

If you've executed any of the batch files described so far in this chapter, you've probably noticed that DOS echoes each of the commands in the batch file as it is executed. For example, consider the screen display as the PRMPT.BAT file is executed:

```
C> DATE
Current date is Tue 1-01-1980
Enter new date (mm-dd-yy): 10-19-91
```

```
C> TIME
Current time is 0:01:56.00
Enter new time: 15:33

C> PROMPT $P$G
C: \ >PATH \DOS

C: \ >
C: \ >
```

As you can see, each of the commands in the file is displayed next to the system prompt as if you had entered them yourself.

The ECHO Subcommand

Displaying commands during the execution of a batch file can be confusing. For this reason, echoing can be turned off with the ECHO OFF *subcommand*. (The DOS manual uses the term subcommand to refer to commands which are only used in batch files.)

If ECHO OFF is placed at the top of a batch file, the remaining commands will not be echoed to the screen. Unfortunately, the ECHO OFF command itself is still echoed. However, this can be taken care of by including a CLS command immediately after the ECHO OFF.

Echoing can be turned back on again with the ECHO ON subcommand, though it is rarely used.

ECHO also can be used to display messages on the screen, even after issuing ECHO OFF, by placing the text you want echoed after the ECHO subcommand. For example, to echo the phrase, "Happy computing!", you would include the subcommand:

ECHO Happy computing!

With ECHO subcommands, the FORMAT.BAT file might look like this:

```
ECHO OFF
CLS
ECHO This batch file only formats floppy diskettes.
ECHO To format the hard disk,
ECHO place the DOS System diskette in drive A
ECHO and follow the instructions in the DOS manual
ECHO for formatting the hard disk.
ECHO To abort this batch file
ECHO press Control-Break.
FORMAT A:
ECHO ON
```

In the preceding example, the messages included in the ECHO entries will be displayed to the screen and will remain there because the next command, FORMAT A:, requires an action on the part of the user. This command causes the message:

Insert new diskette for drive A:
and strike ENTER when ready

to be displayed on the screen and pauses until the user complies.

The @ Subcommand

Starting with version 3.3, DOS uses the "@" (at) symbol with batch files. Any line starting with an @ is suppressed (not displayed on the screen), regardless of whether or not ECHO is ON or OFF. This includes the initial ECHO OFF. For example, to suppress the first ECHO OFF with the previous batch file, you can change these lines:

ECHO OFF
CLS

to this:

@ECHO OFF

The initial "ECHO OFF" won't be displayed, and neither will any other commands in the file.

You also can use @ to suppress every line in a batch file from being displayed, neglecting the need for having an initial ECHO off at all. For example, the AUTOEXEC.BAT might look like:

@DATE
@TIME
@PROMPT PG
@PATH \ DOS

Not a single line in this AUTOEXEC.BAT file will be displayed on the screen. The @ subcommand suppresses each of them.

The PAUSE Option

You can halt the execution of a batch file temporarily to allow the user to read the screen or perform some task. This stopping is accomplished by including a special command in the batch file at the point where the file is to be temporarily interrupted. The PAUSE command halts the execution of the batch file and displays the message:

Strike a key when ready . . .

PAUSE waits for you to press any key, after which the next line in the batch file is executed.

For example, suppose Linda wants to have a batch file automatically backup her WordStar documents onto a floppy diskette. This special batch file, WSLINBU.BAT, could be run by Sue on a weekly basis to back up all the documents in Linda's WordStar work area. Linda wants to make sure that the files get stored on a special diskette reserved for this purpose.

Linda can accomplish this by including a prompt instructing Sue to insert the diskette labeled "Linda's WordStar Backup" into the floppy drive. The PAUSE command can be used in the batch file, as shown in the WSLINBU.BAT batch file:

```
@ECHO OFF
CLS
CD \ ADMIN \ WP \ WS \ LINDA
DEL *.BAK
ECHO Place Linda's WordStar Backup diskette in drive A
PAUSE
COPY *.* A:
```

When this batch file is executed, the screen will be cleared and the following message is displayed:

Place Linda's WordStar Files diskette in drive A
Strike any key when ready . . .

The execution of the COPY command will be held up until Sue has a chance to place the appropriate diskette in the proper drive. When Sue has performed this task, she indicates she's ready to continue by pressing any key. At this point, the batch file will resume and the COPY command will be executed.

REPLACEABLE PARAMETERS

You can customize the execution of DOS commands by including your own messages and prompts. Still, all the commands contained in the batch files introduced so far have been predetermined, which means that each batch file will only perform a specific function.

Suppose you have several different but related tasks that you want to automate. Rather than creating a separate batch file for each task, you can develop a general purpose batch file, and then identify the specific task you want performed at the time of execution.

DOS gives you this flexibility by allowing you to include *replaceable parameters* in your batch files. Replaceable parameters serve as variables, and are included with the individual commands in a batch file. They can take the place of filenames, paths, and even DOS commands. The actual filename, path, or command is provided by the user at the time the batch file is executed.

Replaceable parameters are indicated by the percent character, %, followed by a digit, 0 through 9. In a DOS command line, each word in the line is assigned to a replaceable parameter, beginning with the parameter %0. For example, consider the following command line:

    C > COPY LETTER.DOC \ LINDA

The first command, COPY, is assigned to the variable %0. The filename, LETTER-.DOC, is assigned the variable %1. Finally, the path name, \ LINDA, is given to variable %2.

DOS remembers the replaceable parameter assignments until the next command line is entered. If the value %2 is referred to, it will stand for \ LINDA in the previous example. If the following command was issued:

    C > COPY LETTER.DOC \ SUE

the value of %2 would be \ SUE.

A Batch File with a Parameter

Consider the WSLINBU batch file. This file changes the directory to Linda's Word-Star work area, and then prompts the user to insert Linda's WordStar Files diskette in drive A. After the user has acknowledged the completion of this task, the batch file copies all the files in this area onto the floppy diskette. A similar backup batch file could be created for Bob and Jack's files as well. However, one batch file, WSBACKUP.BAT, could be made to serve all three users through the inclusion of a replaceable parameter as follows:

```
@ECHO OFF
CLS
CD \ ADMIN \ WP \ WS \ %1
DEL *.BAK
ECHO Place %1's WordStar Backup diskette in drive A
PAUSE
COPY *.* A:
```

To execute this batch file, the user would supply the actual value for the replaceable parameter when entering the batch filename. For example, to backup Jack's files, the entry would be:

C > WSBACKUP JACK

At execution, every occurrence of the %1 parameter would be replaced with the entered value, JACK. The CD command would change the directory to the \ ADMIN \ WP \ WS \ JACK subdirectory. The ECHO and PAUSE commands would instruct the user to:

Place JACK's WordStar Files diskette in drive A
Strike a key when ready . . .

You can include up to ten different replaceable parameters in a single batch file by using the variables %0 through %9. The use of multiple parameters is illustrated in the next section.

The MOVE Batch File

Consider the useful but missing DOS command, MOVE. Such a command would move a file from one disk or diskette to another. The COPY command only transfers a copy of a file from one disk to another, leaving the original file on the source disk. You can create a batch file, MOVE.BAT, which will copy a file from the source disk to the target disk and then delete the file from the original disk. The MOVE.BAT file incorporates two replaceable parameters, one for the source filespec and one for the target filespec:

@ECHO OFF
COPY %1 %2
DEL %1

To execute this batch file, you must supply both parameters. For example, to move the file, LETTER.DOC, from its current location on the hard disk to a floppy in drive A, you would enter:

C > MOVE LETTER.DOC A:

After entering the command, LETTER.DOC would be substituted for %1 and A: would be substituted for %2 in the COPY and DEL commands. Executing this batch file will have the effect of copying the LETTER.DOC file from drive C to drive A, and then deleting the file from drive C.

SUMMARY

This chapter has shown you how to create simple DOS macros through the use of batch file techniques. However, there's much more to batch files than simply stringing DOS commands together. In the next chapter, you'll learn how to use the techniques of sequential execution, looping, conditional testing, and chaining to create fairly elaborate batch file programs.

Although these techniques are powerful in their own right, the real power of batch file programming comes in allowing you to take control of your hard disk. You will learn how to combine batch file programming with your knowledge of DOS to create complete, menu-driven systems of batch files for accomplishing all the tasks of loading application programs, managing your system, and backing up your data files.

7

More Batch Files

IN THE PRECEDING CHAPTER, you learned how to include DOS commands in special files called batch files. These batch files allow you to execute a series of DOS commands without having to enter them individually. The batch file essentially stores them up for later execution. You also learned some special subcommands, such as ECHO and PAUSE, which are used to enhance batch files and make them more user friendly.

Although the batch file techniques learned in the preceding chapter extend the power of your system significantly, they are still rather limited in their range of applications. In order to gain further control over the operation of your hard disk, you'll need batch files that can perform repetitive tasks, make decisions, and use the functions in other batch files.

This chapter covers batch file subcommands which belong under the heading of "Programming Techniques." These subcommands include GOTO, FOR, and IF. Before discussing each of these subcommands in turn, the basic concepts involved in programming will be discussed so you will better understand how each subcommand is used.

PROGRAMMING TECHNIQUES

Programming in any computer language is nothing more than the collection of individual commands put into an executable file. Some commands used in a computer program can be executed directly, such as a command to print out the results of a computation, and others are used to control the execution of the program itself.

There are four ways that commands in a program can be executed:

- Sequentially
- Looping
- Conditionally
- Chaining

The simplest way to execute commands in a program is *sequential* execution. Sequentially executed program commands are executed one after the other from beginning to end. All the batch files covered so far operate sequentially. This execution of commands is the simplest programming technique.

Not all programming tasks can be accomplished sequentially, however. Certain repetitive processes are best handled by a technique known as *looping*.

Looping applies a sequence of commands to a series of different values. It is accomplished through the use of variables, or, in the case of batch files, replaceable parameters. The variables are used in the commands within the loop and are replaced with actual values each time the loop is executed. Program loops must be properly controlled or they might continue indefinitely, called an *infinite loop*. The following spurious dictionary entry is an example of an infinite loop:

REDUNDANT: See "REDUNDANT"

Sequential execution and looping are two important programming techniques. However, in each case, the execution of the commands involved is predetermined and therefore limited. You are able to select one command from a number of options with the use of *conditional* statements.

Conditional statements typically begin with the word "if." You deal with conditional situations every day: If the traffic light is green, you keep driving; if it's red, you stop; if it's yellow, you drive like hell because it's about to turn red.

Similar conditional situations can occur in programming. If you have ever used a menu-driven program, you are familiar with the results of conditional programming: If you select "1," you get option one; if you select "2," you get option two; etc.

Another way to execute program commands is by *chaining*. Chaining is a technique that involves linking various groups of commands together. These individual groups of commands are each designed to perform some specific task. In the BASIC programming language, these groups are referred to as *subroutines*, other languages might call them *modules* or *functions*.

A number of different subroutines can be chained together within a single batch file using the special IF and GOTO batch file commands. In addition, separate batch files can be chained together to form a complex, sophisticated network of batch files capable of monitoring and controlling your computer. The goal of this book is to teach you how to develop just such a system of batch files specifically designed to meet the needs of your system.

Looping In Batch Files

Certain tasks in computing are repetitive. Rather than reissue the same sequence of commands over and over again, they can be included in a loop. For example, the same type of processing often needs to be performed on all the records in a database file. Suppose you want to print mailing labels for each of over 1,000 names and addresses stored in the file.

The application uses a programming language to print the labels. Using that language, you could create the sequence of commands necessary to print a single label. For example, suppose the commands to print the first label are:

```
GO TO RECORD 1
PRINT LABEL
```

These commands could be placed into a loop. The loop commands would cause the computer to move to the next record in the data file, print out the mailing label, and proceed until all the records are completed. For example:

```
GO TO RECORD 1
REPEAT 1000 TIMES:
    PRINT LABEL
    GO TO THE NEXT RECORD
```

PRINT LABEL and GO TO THE NEXT RECORD are in the loop. The loop is defined by the REPEAT 1000 TIMES command.

The Batch File GOTO Command. Simple looping in batch files is accomplished by the use of the GOTO subcommand. This looping is similar to looping in BASIC. The GOTO subcommand redirects the flow of commands in a batch file, skipping all subsequent commands until the specified point in the batch file is reached.

GOTO alone is insufficient because DOS won't know where to go to unless you tell it. Imagine responding to a lost tourist's request for directions with the single phrase, "Go to." Pretty uninformative.

The Label. In order for the GOTO subcommand to work, it must be used in conjunction with a *label*. Labels in batch files act like place markers or street signs. Just as you might say to the traveller, "Go to Maple Street and turn left," you can include a GOTO subcommand, such as GOTO DONE, in a batch file.

Labels are preceded by a colon and are placed on a line by themselves, such as:

:MAPLESTREET

Labels can be as long as you like, but only the first eight characters are recognized by DOS. After labels have been inserted into a batch file at appropriate locations, they can be used in GOTO subcommands to alter the order in which the commands of the batch file are executed.

You can redirect the flow of statements in a batch file, as in the following nonsensical batch file, NONSENSE.BAT:

```
@ECHO OFF
ECHO This batch file is
GOTO WORTHLESS
ECHO a wonderful batch file
ECHO full of useful commands.
:WORTHLESS
ECHO worthless!
PAUSE
```

When executed, the above batch file displays the following on the screen:

```
This batch file is
worthless!
Strike a key when ready . . .
```

Do you see the lines, "a wonderful batch file" and "full of useful commands"? Instead of being executed, these two ECHO commands are skipped over by the GOTO statement. The next line to be executed after the "ECHO This batch file" statement is the "ECHO worthless!" statement. Note that the :WORTHLESS label itself is ignored.

GOTO Backwards. The preceding example illustrated the use of the GOTO subcommand to execute a forward jump in the batch file. You also can use GOTO to jump backward as well. However, after you go backward, you must proceed forward through commands already executed. This will continue until the backward GOTO command is encountered, when the process will repeat itself again. A backward GOTO can be used to create a circle of commands, or loop, within a batch file.

Often times, an individual must create multiple copies of a series of worksheet files for distribution within a large organization. Assume these files have already been placed into a special subdirectory on the hard disk. The path to this subdirectory is \ LOTUS \ DISTRIB.

A batch file could be created to repeatedly transfer all the files stored in this subdirectory onto separate floppy disks. This will happen until the individual running the batch file halts it with a Control-C. A DISTRIB batch file is shown here:

```
@ECHO OFF
CD \LOTUS\DISTRIB
:AGAIN
CLS
ECHO Place the target diskette in drive A.
PAUSE
COPY *.* A:
ECHO Copying completed.
ECHO To conclude this activity, enter Control-C.
ECHO To copy another diskette,
PAUSE
GOTO AGAIN
```

This batch file turns off the echo feature and moves into the \LOTUS\DISTRIB subdirectory. The :AGAIN label is ignored and the loop processing commences by clearing the screen. The user is then instructed to place a diskette into drive A and strike any key when ready. After this is done, the batch file transfers all files stored in the \LOTUS\DISTRIB subdirectory onto the diskette in drive A.

When the copying is completed, a confirmation message is displayed, and the user is instructed to enter a Control-C to conclude the operation or proceed by striking any key. Unless a Control-C is entered at this point, the control of the batch file is transferred back to the :AGAIN label, and repeats itself.

The DISTRIB.BAT file is an example of an infinite loop. The file will repeat itself unless the user stops it by pressing Control-C (or a Control-Break).

Infinite loops are a quick-and-dirty programming technique for accomplishing repetitive tasks. Batch files employing infinite loops rely upon a certain competence on the part of the user. A rank beginner might respond to the prompt to enter a Control-C by literally typing in the letters "Control-C." (It's been known to happen.) That won't work. Press and hold the Control key and type a C. Release both keys.

FOR and Conditional Loops

To avoid infinite loops, two other looping strategies are used: *FOR* loops and *conditional* loops.

FOR loops proceed through a specified sequence of parameters, performing the same processing on each parameter. Conditional loops involve the use of special *error codes*. An error code indicates a condition that can be used to control the looping process.

FOR Loops. The DOS FOR subcommand allows you to specify a group of similar parameters to be substituted into a command until each member of the group has been processed. Because the command does not have to be repeated for each element in the parameter list, the FOR subcommand can save you considerable typing. The format of the FOR subcommand is:

FOR %%variable IN (parameter list) DO command

A *variable* is a single letter code that takes on each of the specific words in the parameter list. You worked with variables back in your high school algebra days. In algebra, the variables, like X and Y, were used to represent unknown numbers. As such, they could be used to represent any number. The same is true with DOS variables. They can be used to represent any of the individual parameters within the parameter list. DOS variables are preceded by two percent symbols, %%.

The use of variables and parameters in the FOR command can be clarified by the following example. Suppose you want to backup the dBASE III database files in a given subdirectory. In dBASE III, in addition to the database files themselves, which have a DBF extension, there are memo files that have MEM extensions, and index files that have NDX extensions.

Ordinarily, to copy all of the files with each of these extensions would require three separate COPY commands. However, by including these three extensions in a parameter list, you can use a single COPY command in a FOR loop as follows:

FOR %%F IN (*.DBF *.MEM *.DBF) DO COPY %%F A:

The above FOR loop uses the variable, %%F, as a dummy in the command "COPY %%F A:". In fact, %%F itself never gets copied to A:. Instead, %%F is used to represent each of the parameters in the parameter list. In this case, the parameter list contains three parameters, *.DBF, *.MEM, and *.NDX. First, *.DBF is substituted for %%F, and the command COPY *.DBF A: is executed. Next, *.MEM is substituted for %%F, and the command COPY *.MEM A: is executed. Finally, the COPY command is executed with the *.NDX command.

Conditional Loops. FOR loops execute their commands as many times as there are parameters. Conditional loops, on the other hand, continue until their condition has been met or the user cancels them.

A conditional loop usually performs some sort of test to determine whether or not it is to continue executing. This testing is done with the use of the IF subcommand. Although the IF subcommand has other applications to batch file programming, its use is the key to creating conditional loops. The format of the IF subcommand is:

IF condition outcome

Statements involving the IF subcommand are called *conditional statements* because they involve testing for a given condition to see whether a specified outcome will result.

You're already familiar with conditional statements—they are a part of our reasoning and vocabulary. For example, you might think to yourself, "If that cinder block hits me in the face, it will doubtless be painful." The condition to be tested is whether the cinder block will hit you in the face. The outcome is painful. Note that it will only be painful if the cinder block does hit you in the face, that is, if the condition is true.

The problem with this example is that it is hard to determine exactly what painful is: A direct hit, scrape, close call? Conditions in DOS must be specific, usually as simple as true or false.

The ERRORLEVEL Condition. For conditional loops, one condition to be tested is the value of a special variable, ERRORLEVEL. ERRORLEVEL is called an *exit code* in DOS terminology, and can be used to test a variety of conditions. When a program quits, it returns to DOS with an optional value between zero and 255. Certain programs and DOS utilities use the ERRORLEVEL value to communicate what functions were performed, or, as the name implies, if any errors occurred. Not every program will return an ERRORLEVEL value, but some do. With those programs, you can use the ERRORLEVEL value to test for various conditions.

A good example of using ERRORLEVEL is found in a common utility program, ASK.COM, which has been provided for you on the accompanying diskette. ASK displays a message on the screen and then checks the user's answer according to which key was pressed. If the user enters a "Y," then ERRORLEVEL is set to 0; if the user enters an "N," ERRORLEVEL is set to 1.

In order to use the ASK command in your batch files, it must be in either the current subdirectory or in a subdirectory specified by the PATH command. To see how a conditional loop using the ASK/IF ERRORLEVEL combination works, consider the modified DISTRIB.BAT file shown below:

```
@ECHO OFF
CD \ LOTUS \ DISTRIB
:AGAIN
CLS
ECHO Place the target diskette in drive A.
PAUSE
COPY *.* A:
ECHO Copying completed.
ASK Do you wish to copy another diskette (Y/N)?
IF ERRORLEVEL 0 GOTO AGAIN
```

In this version of the batch file, the loop is controlled by the final statement, IF ERRORLEVEL 0 GOTO AGAIN. As long as the value of ERRORLEVEL is 0, the loop will repeat another time. The value of ERRORLEVEL is determined by the user's response to the preceding ASK statement. This statement displays the message:

Do you wish to copy another diskette (Y/N)?

and then awaits the user's response. After the user answers, the response is used to set the value of ERRORLEVEL.

Conditional loops involving ASK and IF ERRORLEVEL are much more user-friendly than infinite loops, which must be aborted using Control-C. Remember to keep the skill level of the intended user in mind when designing batch files to automate repetitive processes. Also, if you're planning to ask the user to respond to a question, be sure to indicate the appropriate responses by including "(Y/N)" at the end of the prompt. Your fellow computer users will appreciate these special touches. If nothing else, conditional loops are more professional looking than infinite loops.

Conditional Branching. The IF subcommand can do more than control conditional loops. It also can be used to allow your batch files to make decisions about what action to take based on a given condition. This ability allows you to truly program your batch files to perform a variety of different tasks depending on the specific conditions encountered when they are executed.

The three conditional tests that IF is able to perform are:

- EXIST
- ==
- ERRORLEVEL

You've already seen how ERRORLEVEL is tested in the preceding discussion of conditional loops. In the next section, you will learn how to use the ERRORLEVEL test in other applications as well.

The EXIST Conditional Test. The EXIST conditional test is used to check for the presence of a given file in the specified subdirectory. The EXIST condition follows the IF subcommand and precedes the filespec of the file being tested. The format of the IF subcommand when testing for the EXIST condition is:

IF EXIST filespec outcome

The following example shows how you would use the EXIST test in a simple batch file called WSLOAD.BAT. This file allows the user to specify a filename as part of the batch file call and have WordStar automatically open that file, placing the user directly into the Editing Menu at execution. However, if the file is not present, the batch file will inform the user that the file is not available and will simply load WordStar and leave the user at the Opening Menu instead:

```
@ECHO OFF
IF EXIST %1 GOTO LOAD
ECHO %1 is not available.
PAUSE
WS
GOTO QUIT
:LOAD
WS %1
:QUIT
ECHO ON
```

This batch file is executed by entering the descriptive filename, WSLOAD, followed by the name of the file to be opened. For example, to open the file LETTER, you would enter:

```
C>WSLOAD LETTER
```

The filename, LETTER, would be substituted for the %1 replaceable parameter in the batch file.

If you follow the logic of this batch file, you'll see that there are two possible outcomes, depending on the result of the EXIST test. If the file specified by the %1 replaceable parameter is present on the disk, then the WS %1 command following the :LOAD label will be executed. Otherwise, the next command, WS, will be executed and the WS %1 command will be skipped over because of the GOTO QUIT statement.

The beauty of this batch file is: If no filename is specified after WSLOAD, the batch file will default to the WS command, which is what you want anyway.

The Equality Conditional Test. The IF subcommand also can be used to test for the equality of two items. The equality conditional test requires two equals symbols (==) to represent equality. This test allows you to create batch files that perform a variety of different tasks depending upon the parameter(s) supplied with the batch file call.

Look at the batch file, LOAD.BAT, which loads either WordStar or Lotus 1-2-3 depending upon whether the user specifies WS or LOTUS after the initial LOAD:

```
@ECHO OFF
IF %1 == WS GOTO WSLAND
IF %1 == LOTUS GOTO LOTUSLAND
GOTO QUIT
:WSLAND
WS
```

```
GOTO QUIT
:LOTUSLAND
LOTUS
:QUIT
```

If the user specifies LOAD WS, then the batch file will match %1 with "WS," and control will be transferred to the :WSLAND label. On the other hand, if the user enters LOAD LOTUS, control will be transferred to the :LOTUSLAND label instead.

There are several important points to note in the LOAD batch file. First, you should realize that there are really three possible outcomes. The batch file will either load Word-Star, load Lotus, or terminate. In the first case, after the program has been loaded, the subsequent GOTO command transfers control of the batch file to the final :QUIT label. Can you see why this is necessary? If the GOTO QUIT command were omitted here, the batch file would proceed to load the Lotus 1-2-3 program after the user had exited from WordStar.

Second, the case of the characters being tested is also important. In this batch file, the user must enter the WordStar call letters in capitals. If the user entered the command in lowercase, "load ws," the test for "WS" would fail, and WordStar would not be loaded. Of course, you could circumvent this by including a separate test for lowercase "ws" as well:

```
IF %1 = = WS GOTO WSLAND
IF %1 = = ws GOTO WSLAND
```

The ERRORLEVEL Conditional Test. You've already seen one application of the ERRORLEVEL conditional test in controlling the exit from a conditional loop. The initial purpose of the exit code was intended to allow programmers to check the way in which certain applications and utilities quit. For example, if a utility for backing up the hard disk onto floppies successfully backed up all sectors in the FAT, ERRORLEVEL would be set to 0. The value of ERRORLEVEL could then be tested with an IF ERRORLEVEL 0 test.

For simple batch file programming, however, the value of the IF ERRORLEVEL test lies in its use with the ASK utility described previously. This utility has the capability of setting ERRORLEVEL according to a user's response to a question. As you saw in the discussion on conditional loops, a "Y" response sets ERRORLEVEL to 0, and an "N" response sets it to 1.

The resulting ERRORLEVEL value can then be tested in an IF ERRORLEVEL conditional test to determine what action should be taken. The outcome will usually be a GOTO subcommand redirecting the flow of the program to a set of statements elsewhere in the batch file. In conditional loops, the flow goes back to the beginning of the loop for another pass through the loop procedure.

There are other applications for the ASK command besides exiting from a loop. You can use ASK to determine whether the user wishes to proceed with a course of action. For example, the WSLINBU.BAT file assumes that the diskette labeled "Linda's WordStar Backup" is available. Unless the user knows enough to press Control-C to abort, the batch file will remain in limbo until the user places a diskette in the drive.

You might ask the user if the required diskette is available before executing the rest of the batch file. This can be accomplished with the following set of statements:

```
ECHO This procedure transfers copies
ECHO of Linda's WordStar files onto the diskette
ECHO labeled "Linda's WordStar Backup"
ASK Is this diskette presently in drive A (Y/N)?
```

The user's response to the ASK statement can then be tested with an IF ERRORLEVEL statement. If the response is "N," a GOTO command can be used to terminate the batch file.

The ASK. . .IF ERRORLEVEL combination can be used in batch files whenever you want to check with the user before proceeding with a sequence of commands. Prompts can take any of the following forms:

```
ASK Do you wish to proceed (Y/N)?
ASK Would you like to continue (Y/N)?
ASK Is this correct (Y/N)?
ASK Would you like to try again (Y/N)?
```

One last example will show how an ERRORLEVEL conditional test can be used to provide an *error trap* for an incorrectly entered filename. This test involves a modification of the WSLOAD.BAT file. The modified version tests for the existence of the filename entered as the replaceable parameter %2. Parameter %1 is used to represent a work area.

If the specified file %2 isn't present, the user is informed and asked if she wishes to view a directory listing. This version of WSLOAD.BAT employs several conditional branches. See if you can follow the logic of the various GOTO's:

```
@ECHO OFF
CD \ %1
PATH \ ADMIN \ WP \ WS
IF EXIST %2 GOTO OPEN
ECHO %2 not found.
ASK Do you wish to see a list of files available (Y/N)?
IF ERRORLEVEL 1 GOTO DONE
DIR /W
```

```
GOTO DONE
:OPEN
WS %2
:DONE
CD \
PATH \DOS
```

The NOT Option. Sometimes you'll be more interested in testing the opposite of a condition rather than the condition itself. For example, in WSLOAD.BAT, the real purpose of the IF EXIST test was to determine if the file was unavailable. Otherwise, the batch file would have caused WordStar to open a new file, which isn't what the user intends. The absence of the file can be tested directly by including the word NOT before the EXIST conditional test:

```
IF NOT EXIST %2 GOTO. . .
```

Of course, a NOT in the conditional test changes the logic of the batch file, and different labels are required. Here's how the WSLOAD.BAT file would look using NOT:

```
@ECHO OFF
CD \ %1
PATH \ADMIN\WP\WS
IF NOT EXIST %2 GOTO NOFIND
WS %2
GOTO DONE
:NOFIND
ECHO %2 not found.
ASK Do you wish to see a list of files available (Y/N)?
IF ERRORLEVEL 1 GOTO DONE
DIR /W
:DONE
CD \
PATH \DOS
```

You also can use NOT with the = = and ERRORLEVEL conditional tests. Note that the word NOT always precedes the conditional test. This might seem intuitively obvious for the EXIST and = = tests, but many beginners make the mistake of writing:

```
IF ERRORLEVEL NOT 0. . .
```

which sounds better than:

IF NOT ERRORLEVEL 0. . .

Testing the opposite of a condition with NOT is called testing the *converse*. Using the converse of a conditional test often results in batch files that are easier to follow and understand.

CHAINING

So far, you've seen how batch files can be used to issue a series of DOS commands and load applications. You are also able to execute one batch file from another by including the descriptive filename of the batch file you want to execute in the first batch file. Using one batch file to run another is known as *chaining*. There is no limit to the number of batch files that can be chained together.

For example, suppose you have an AUTOEXEC.BAT file that sets your system configuration at system startup. At the conclusion of this batch file, you want to load Word-Star. You can call WordStar by including the WSLOAD batch file call as the final line of the AUTOEXEC batch file. The resulting AUTOEXEC.BAT file would look like this:

```
@ECHO OFF
CLS
DATE
TIME
PATH \ DOS
PROMPT $P$G
WSLOAD
```

Although this version of AUTOEXEC.BAT saves the trouble of having to execute the WSLOAD.BAT file separately, it has a number of drawbacks. For one thing, the WSLOAD batch file will automatically be executed whenever the computer is restarted. This result might not always be desirable. You can overcome this problem by including an ASK. . .IF ERRORLEVEL test in the AUTOEXEC file, such as the following:

```
@ECHO OFF
CLS
DATE
TIME
PATH \ DOS
PROMPT $P$G
ASK Do you want to load WordStar (Y/N)?
```

```
IF ERRORLEVEL 1 GOTO DONE:
WSLOAD
:DONE
```

This revised version of the AUTOEXEC.BAT file permits the user to bypass the WSLOAD call by entering "N" at the prompt. However, this version still has several shortcomings.

Remember that AUTOEXEC.BAT files load automatically at system startup. This means that there is no opportunity for the user to supply values for any replaceable parameters. The latest version of WSLOAD.BAT presented in this chapter employs two replaceable parameters, one for the work area and one for the file to be opened. Because AUTOEXEC.BAT can't accept user-supplied values, any batch file called from an AUTOEXEC batch file can't take advantage of this feature.

The only way to get around this limitation is to rename the AUTOEXEC.BAT file, such as STARTUP.BAT. This batch file can then be executed from the system prompt along with any user-supplied values. To open the LETTER document file in Linda's WordStar work area, she would enter:

```
C>STARTUP LINDA LETTER
```

Although the STARTUP batch file makes no reference to replaceable parameters, the WSLOAD.BAT file does. The two user-supplied values, LINDA and LETTER, will be transferred, or *passed*, to the WSLOAD batch file when it is executed from STARTUP-.BAT.

Even with this problem overcome, there's one final limitation to the method of chaining batch files. Even though application programs return control to the calling batch file when they terminate, called batch files do not.

After a new batch file is called from the original batch file, control passes to the new batch file. When that batch file concludes, the user is returned to the system prompt.

In the STARTUP.BAT example, the consequences are rather minor, because there's nothing, no final line, to execute. However, you might have batch files that need to reset certain system parameters, or move back into the root directory at their conclusion. With the method of chaining described thus far, resetting parameters can only be accomplished by chaining WSLOAD.BAT to a concluding batch file, which makes a clumsy solution at best.

THE CALL SUBCOMMAND

Fortunately, DOS provides a solution to this problem with the use of the CALL subcommand. (DOS versions prior to 3.3 used COMMAND/C instead of CALL.) The

CALL subcommand allows you to call a batch file, have that batch file executed, and return control to the original batch file after the second file terminates. Batch files called using the CALL subcommand are sometimes referred to as *subroutines.*

The use of chained subroutines in batch file programming has several advantages. Obviously, greater control is allowed over the execution of the calling batch file. Also, this technique permits a modular approach to batch file programming. A large programming task can be divided into a series of smaller tasks, each of which can be handled easily. Further, the same subroutine can be used, or called, by a number of different batch files, reducing the amount of programming involved in large projects.

For example, in chapter 12, you will find a batch file, SHUTDOWN.BAT, which performs special tasks at system shutdown. This batch file could be called from a number of different batch files, eliminating the need to include the same commands in each of these batch files separately. The format of the CALL subcommand is:

CALL filespec

The filespec following CALL refers to the batch file subroutine being called. This filespec may include paths and even drive designators.

The called batch file returns control to the first batch file when it is done. (Older versions of DOS using COMMAND/C required the batch file to end with an EXIT command.)

Consider the following example using two batch files, STARTUP.BAT and LOAD-.BAT:

STARTUP.BAT

```
@ECHO OFF
CLS
DATE
TIME
PATH \DOS
PROMPT $P$G
CALL LOAD %1
ECHO All done!
```

LOAD.BAT

```
@ECHO OFF
CLS
IF %1 == WS GOTO WSLAND
IF %1 == LOTUS GOTO LOTUSLAND
GOTO QUIT
```

```
:WSLAND
WS
GOTO QUIT
:LOTUSLAND
LOTUS
:QUIT
```

The STARTUP batch file sets the system parameters and then calls the LOAD subroutine batch file with the CALL LOAD statement. Any value %1 entered with the STARTUP batch file will be passed along to the LOAD.BAT file as %1. LOAD.BAT will determine if either WordStar or Lotus 1-2-3 should be loaded. If neither of these programs were specified (as WS or LOTUS respectively), LOAD.BAT will do nothing. Whatever the outcome, at its conclusion, LOAD.BAT returns control to the STARTUP batch file when it's done, and STARTUP concludes by displaying "All done!"

You might have noticed that the LOAD.BAT file begins with an @ECHO OFF. This subcommand doesn't need to be repeated in the subroutine batch file because the ECHO state, ON or OFF, is retained by all CALLed batch files. ECHO OFF is included in case the user wants to run LOAD.BAT separately.

SUMMARY

In this chapter you learned about the extended power of batch files. Not only can batch files setup certain conditions for you in DOS and load applications, but they can make decisions and evaluate conditions. This power, provided by such commands as GOTO, FOR, IF, and CALL, allows you to build creative batch files capable of doing interesting things on your system, as well as saving you valuable time.

Incidentally, if you're interested in pursuing the concept of batch file programming further, you should check out TAB BOOKS' batch file programming texts. *MS-DOS Batch File Programming* by Ronny Richardson and *Advanced MS-DOS Batch File Programming* by Dan Gookin are available if you're interested in pursuing the subject further.

The next chapter takes the knowledge you've gained from learning about DOS and batch file programming one notch further. With batch files, you'll construct a unique and powerful menu system under which you can run your hard disk system.

8
Batch File Menu Systems

IF YOU have spent any time working with personal computers, you have probably been exposed to some form of menu-driven software. Any program that displays a list of choices or options and allows you to select from among them utilizes menus. When program commands or options are selected from a menu, the program is said to be *menu-driven*.

This chapter expands on what you have learned about batch files and shows how to create a menu system for running applications on your hard disk. It's not as hard as it seems. In fact, you already know more than enough to get the job done. You need to become familiar with assembling the proper pieces in the right order. And you'll know how to do that by the end of this chapter. (Be prepared to amaze yourself!)

SOFTWARE MENUS

As with restaurant menus, software menus can take many forms, ranging from one-line menus to elaborate, full-screen graphic menu systems.

Some programs reserve a portion of the screen for displaying command options. These menus are called *screen menus*. You usually select the option you want by entering the code letter(s) or number corresponding to your choice in response to a prompt on the screen. The WordStar Editing Menu is an example of a screen menu.

Other programs place command options in a single line. These one-line menus are often referred to as *menu bars*. To select a choice from a menu bar, you normally use the left and right cursor control keys (or the Tab key) to move back and forth across the menu bar. Command selection is accomplished by highlighting the desired command or option and pressing the Enter key. Lotus 1-2-3's menu works this way.

Some menu-driven programs provide brief descriptions for each of the choices included in the menu. Still others provide optional on-screen help which can be selected by pressing a special *help key*. Sometimes a single menu is insufficient for displaying all the command choices or program options. In these cases, the programs rely upon additional *submenus* for displaying additional commands. These commands are usually grouped together in some logical fashion.

The collection of menus, submenus, prompts, and attendant help screens that are used to guide a user through a program is called a *menu system*. You can create customized menu systems for controlling access to files and programs stored on your hard disk. These menu systems might consist of simple, single-screen menus or elaborate systems complete with submenus and optional help screens.

WHY USE MENUS?

Menu-driven hard disk management systems have numerous advantages. The most obvious is that a well-organized menu system makes using the hard disk on a computer easier for both the novice and advanced user.

Menus allow the user to enter short codes to load programs and locate files, which saves typing. Also, menus take the memory and guess work out of working with complex, tree-structured subdirectory systems. Menus and submenus that correspond to a hard disk's tree structure also help users from inadvertently interfering with each other's work areas.

Another reason for using menu systems to control access to the hard disk is security. There are several security considerations that can be addressed with the use of menu-driven hard disk management systems.

DOS commands can be made part of a special DOS submenu. Within this submenu, one choice could be "Format a diskette." This choice would be tied to a batch file such as the one described in chapter 6. By forcing the user to select DOS commands from a menu, you eliminate the possibility of incorrectly entering commands, such as formatting the hard drive and wiping out all the data stored there.

Other security considerations include limiting access to programs and data files. Password security can be added to ensure that only authorized individuals are allowed access to programs and data in menus. The techniques for including passwords as part of your menu system are covered in chapter 14, "Password Security."

Ease of use, convenience, and security are three reasons for developing a menu-driven hard disk management system. With only the techniques described so far in this book, and a little help from your word processing program (or DOS's text editor EDLIN), you can develop your own customized, menu-driven system for loading programs, accessing data files, and executing DOS commands. No prior programming experience is necessary.

DEVELOPING A SIMPLE MENU SYSTEM

Developing your own menu system is easy, creative, and fun. Most users get a kick out of designing and implementing their own menus. Also, customized menu systems are easily modified as your system requirements change. Whether your hard disk system is intended for a single user or several different users, and no matter what the skill level of the individuals using the computer, a set of customized menus will make your computer more efficient and easier to use. Menus also will add a more polished and professional appearance to your hard disk system.

In this section, you'll learn how to create a single-screen menu system. This simple menu system includes the menu screen itself, as well as the batch files to execute the various menu selections. Later in this chapter, you'll see how you can add submenus and help screens to your menu system.

For the initial menu system, a simplified version of the CompuCard tree structure is used. The tree structure consists of one word processing subdirectory, \ WP, one spreadsheet subdirectory, \ LOTUS, one database subdirectory, \ DB, an accounting subdirectory, \ ACCT, and a subdirectory containing the DOS utilities, \ DOS, as shown in *Fig. 8-1*.

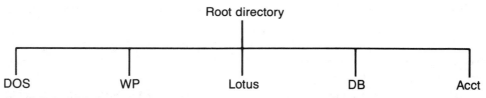

Fig. 8-1. Simplified tree structure for the CompuCard hard disk.

The root directory will be used to hold the system files, the AUTOEXEC.BAT file, the menu screen text file, and the various batch files needed to execute the menu choices. Later, this example will be expanded to accommodate the complete CompuCard tree structure described in chapter 4.

Creating Menu Screens

Menu screens are nothing more than text files designed to display a series of commands or options. To create your menu screens, you can use any word processor capable of generating ASCII text files. For example, you could use WordStar's nondocument mode, or DOS's EDLIN text processor.

```
             CompuCard Main Menu

W   WordStar              A   Accounting
D   dBASE III             F   Format diskette
L   Lotus 1-2-3           S   Show files on diskette

                  Q   Quit
```

Fig. 8-2. Sample menu created using WordStar's nondocument mode.

Look at the simple menu screen shown in Fig. 8-2. This screen was created in Word-Star using the nondocument mode. Centering was accomplished with WordStar's "Onscreen Center" command. The menu was saved as a text file named MAIN-MENU.TXT. If this file is located in the root directory of CompuCard's hard disk, you can display the file on the screen with the command:

```
C>TYPE \ MAINMENU.TXT
```

Even better, this command can be included as part of the AUTOEXEC.BAT file as follows:

```
@ECHO OFF
CLS
DATE
TIME
CLS
TYPE \ MAINMENU.TXT
```

After this AUTOEXEC.BAT file has been created, the menu screen will appear each time the computer starts or is restarted. On the line following this menu, the regular DOS prompt will be displayed, as shown in *Fig. 8-3*.

```
             CompuCard Main Menu

W   WordStar              A   Accounting
D   dBASE III             F   Format diskette
L   Lotus 1-2-3           S   Show files on diskette

C>                 Q   Quit
```

Fig. 8-3. Menu displayed with the TYPE command. Note the DOS prompt that appears below the last line of the menu.

Adding User Prompts

Although this menu might appear obvious to someone familiar to personal computers, the use of the menu can be improved with the addition of a prompt, such as:

Enter the letter corresponding to your choice:

Your first inclination might be to include this prompt as part of the menu screen. The problem with this prompt is that the DOS prompt will still appear on the next line. This intrusion of DOS into the menu screen can be distracting, especially to novice users.

So why not change the DOS prompt? A PROMPT command in the AUTOEXEC.BAT file will change the DOS prompt as follows:

```
@ECHO OFF
CLS
DATE
TIME
CLS
TYPE \MAINMENU.TXT
PROMPT Enter the letter corresponding to your choice:
```

Now, when the AUTOEXEC batch file is executed, the DOS prompt, which is the last line that appears on the screen, will display like a prompt to the user to enter one of the letters appearing on the menu. *Figure 8-4* shows this prompt. Clever, isn't it?

```
              CompuCard Main Menu

W   WordStar             A   Accounting
D   dBASE III            F   Format diskette
L   Lotus 1-2-3          S   Show files on diskette

                 Q   Quit
Enter the letter corresponding to your choice
```

Fig. 8-4. *Modifying the DOS prompt results in a more meaningful prompt.*

Although this version of the AUTOEXEC.BAT file takes care of all the details needed to display the menu and user prompt on the screen, the last two commands should be placed into a separate batch file, MAINMENU.BAT, and call this file from the AUTO-EXEC.BAT file:

AUTOEXEC.BAT

```
@ECHO OFF
CLS
DATE
TIME
MAINMENU
```

MAINMENU.BAT

```
@ECHO OFF
CLS
TYPE \ MAINMENU.TXT
PROMPT Enter the letter corresponding to your choice:
```

The TYPE and PROMPT commands should be placed in a separate batch file named MAINMENU.BAT so the batch file can be called from any other batch file that needs it.

Batch Files to Complete the System

After the menu text file has been created, and the AUTOEXEC.BAT and MAIN-MENU.BAT files have been established to display the menu on the screen, all that remains is to write the batch files needed to run the system.

In this simple case, seven batch files are required. These batch files should be named: W.BAT, D.BAT, L.BAT, A.BAT, F.BAT, S.BAT, and Q.BAT respectively. Each of these batch files must be located in the root directory along with the AUTOEXEC.BAT and MAINMENU.TXT files.

Three of these files will be shown below to illustrate how the menu choices are used to load programs and execute DOS commands:

W.BAT

```
@ECHO OFF
CLS
CD \ WP
WS
CD \
MAINMENU
```

F.BAT

```
@ECHO OFF
CLS
CD \ DOS
FORMAT A:
```

```
CD \
MAINMENU
```

S.BAT

```
@ECHO OFF
CLS
CD \DOS
DIR A: | SORT | MORE
CD \
MAINMENU
```

Notice that each of these batch files causes DOS to move into the appropriate subdirectory before loading the application program or executing the DOS command. Each batch file concludes by returning to the root directory and redisplaying the menu and user prompt by calling the MAINMENU batch file. You can see why it is necessary to have a separate MAINMENU.BAT file rather than including the commands to display the menu and prompt in the AUTOEXEC.BAT file.

The remaining batch files for loading dBASE, Lotus 1-2-3, and the accounting program are similar to W.BAT. You can create them by modifying W.BAT, specifying the appropriate subdirectory instead of \WP, and replacing WS with the name of the fitting application.

The final batch file, Q.BAT, consists of special commands for backing up the hard disk and shutting down the system. This batch file can be patterned after the SHUT-DOWN.BAT file described in chapter 12. For now, you can have a simple file that resets the system prompt and ends the menu session. The Q.BAT file should suffice for now:

```
@ECHO OFF
CLS
CD \
PATH \DOS
PROMPT $P$G
ECHO Type MAINMENU to restart the menu system
```

SUBMENUS AND HELP SCREENS

The preceding example showed how you can create a menu screen with your word processor, and use this screen in conjunction with the DOS prompt to instruct the user to run one of several batch files that load programs or execute DOS commands. For simple hard disk tree structures, a single-screen menu system such as this might be sufficient. However, many hard disk tree structures are much more complicated than this simple example. They might contain many different application programs or multiple work areas for each application program.

The complete tree structure for the CompuCard system has many application programs and multiple work area. (You might want to refer back to *Fig. 5-2*, which provides a schematic diagram of the CompuCard tree structure.) In this tree structure, there are three different word processing programs. Also, the WordStar, Lotus 1-2-3, and dBASE application programs are shared by several users, each of whom has his or her own work area for storing data files.

In order to have a separate choice for each user's work area in each of the applications available on the CompuCard hard disk, a single-screen menu would have to contain at least twelve different options, not including options for DOS commands and the Quit option. The resulting menu screen would appear cluttered because the user has too many options to choose from. Instead, a better approach has the main menu containing fewer than eight options. The main menu then calls for submenus containing specific options for each work area.

Submenu Systems

Look at the menu screen illustrated in *Fig. 8-5*. In this menu, the choices are indicated by multiple letters rather than single characters because the overall system will contain numerous choices, and there aren't enough single-letter choices to go around. For example, both DOS and dBASE begin with the letter "D."

```
            CompuCard Main Menu

   WP      WordStar         ACCT    Accounting
   DB      dBASE III        ART     Graphics
   LOTUS   Lotus 1-2-3      DOS     DOS Commands


                  Q   Quit
```

Fig. 8-5. Modified menu for CompuCard's hard disk.

As your menu systems become more involved, you'll find that single-letter options become unworkable. Of course, the prompt message will have to be changed slightly to indicate that the user should enter the complete option. A prompt such as the following should suffice:

Enter your choice (WP, DB, etc.):

Notice that the WP and DOS options are general in nature. They don't refer to a specific application program or command. Instead, these options refer to categories. Selecting either of these options should cause a separate submenu to appear.

For example, *Fig. 8-6* shows the Word Processing Menu. This menu contains four choices for working with the various word processing programs available on the disk, plus an option for returning to the main menu.

```
Word Processing Menu

LIN    Linda's WordStar Files      MM   Multimate
JACK   Jack's WordStar Files       TT   ThinkTank

             E  Exit to Main Menu
```
Fig. 8-6. *The word processing submenu.*

As with the Main Menu, this menu screen could be created using your word processing program and saved as a text file, WPMENU.TXT. This menu would be called from the Main Menu by the batch file, WP.BAT:

```
@ECHO OFF
CLS
TYPE \ WPMENU.TXT
PROMPT Enter your choice (LIN, JACK, etc.):
```

The various options from within the Word Processing Menu would be executed by batch files named LIN.BAT, JACK.BAT, MM.BAT, and TT.BAT respectively. These batch files are straightforward and need no explanation. The Exit option batch file, E.BAT, is shown below:

```
@ECHO OFF
CLS
MAINMENU
```

The other options from CompuCard's Main Menu should produce similar submenu screens like the Lotus Menu in *Fig. 8-7.*

Does anything seem amiss to you? Although on the surface this menu appears to present no problems, it contains two options that will produce undesirable results. What will happen when the user selects the LIN or JACK options? The LIN.BAT or JACK.BAT files will load the WordStar program, not Lotus 1-2-3.

There are two ways to avoid these conflicts. The easy way is to use different option codes, such as LINDA and JAC, for the Lotus Menu. This is a poor solution. You want to

```
              Lotus 1-2-3 Menu

        LIN    Linda´s Lotus Worksheets
        JACK   Jack´s Lotus Worksheets
        BOB    Bob´s Lotus Worksheets


              E   Exit to Main Menu
```

Fig. 8-7. The Lotus submenu.

maintain a consistent "look and feel" to your menu screens. So how do you keep the codes LIN and JACK in each of your submenus?

The answer is to use subdirectories for each of your submenus. This solution results in a more orderly and systematic approach to developing a coordinated menu system. It also keeps the root directory from becoming cluttered up with submenu text files, and little batch files to execute each of the submenu options.

This solution might appear to require the creation of additional subdirectories for each of the submenus, but this really isn't the case. Remember, there are already subdirectories in the tree structure for each of the options in CompuCard's Main Menu. The submenu text files and batch files can be located in these subdirectories. For example, the WPMENU.TXT file and attendant batch files, LIN.BAT, JACK.BAT, MM.BAT, TT.BAT, and E.BAT, can be placed in the \ ADMIN \ WP subdirectory.

Only two additional changes are needed to implement this setup. First, the WP.BAT file located in the root directory needs to be modified to reflect the new location of the WPMENU.TXT file:

```
@ECHO OFF
CLS
CD \ ADMIN \ WP
TYPE WPMENU.TXT
PROMPT Enter your choice (LIN, JACK, etc.):
```

Also, the E.BAT file, now located in the \ ADMIN \ WP subdirectory, must be altered to move back to the root directory before executing the MAINMENU batch file call:

```
@ECHO OFF
CLS
CD \
MAINMENU
```

Adding Help Screens to Your Menu System

Submenus add to the overall "user-friendly" feel of a menu system. However, the use of a main menu and submenus requires the user to make certain generalizations. Although the choices in the main menu might be obvious to the person creating the menu system, a new user can have some trouble figuring out how the menu system works.

One way to overcome this problem is to provide individualized training for each user sharing the system. Sometimes, however, this isn't practical. In such cases, special help screens can be added to the system.

Help screens provide extra information to explain how the menu system works, and where specific applications or work areas are located within the menu system. Often, a single help screen, accessed from the main menu, is all that is required. The help feature can be included as an option within the main menu itself.

Figure 8-8 shows a modified version of CompuCard's Main Menu that includes a Help option. Another technique is to include instructions for obtaining help within the prompt itself, such as:

Enter your choice (WP, DB, etc.) or H for Help:

Help screens are nothing more than text files describing the functions of the menu from which they are accessed.

```
           CompuCard Main Menu

WP       WordStar          ACCT   Accounting
DB       dBASE III         ART    Graphics
LOTUS    Lotus 1-2-3       DOS    DOS Commands


     H   Help                  Q   Quit
```

Fig. 8-8. Modified main menu including Help option.

Figure 8-9 gives an example of a help screen to accompany CompuCard's Main Menu. This screen was created using WordStar's nondocument mode, and saved under the filename MAINHELP.TXT. Assume that this help screen is accessed through the batch file, H.BAT. This batch file contains the following statements:

```
@ECHO OFF
CLS
TYPE \ MAINHELP.TXT
PAUSE
MAINMENU
```

```
     Help for Main Menu

The following options are available from
the Main Menu:

Word Processing - allows you to access
                  WordStar, Multimate
                  and ThinkTank

dBASE III - allows you to access the
            customer database

Lotus 1-2-3 - allows you to access worksheets

Accounting - Accounts Receivable, Accounts
Payable, General Ledger, Payroll

Art - allows you to access graphics designs

DOS - allows you to perform DOS operations
      such as formatting diskettes, copying
      files, etc.
```

Fig. 8-9. A sample help screen.

As you can see, the H.BAT file displays the text of the file MAINHELP.TXT and then pauses, waiting until the user strikes a key.

Note that the prompt, "Strike a key to continue . . . ," will be displayed at the bottom of the help screen as a result of the PAUSE subcommand. After the user has had the opportunity to read the screen, pressing any key causes the MAINMENU batch file to be executed, returning the user to the Main Menu.

Help screens can be provided for each of the submenus as well. However, avoid overwhelming the user with too much help. All levels of users feel intimidated by too much information on the screen. Keep your screens simple. If necessary, divide the information into several screens. A good rule of thumb is to limit your help screens to fifteen or so lines. Also, vertical and horizontal centering, indentation, and blank lines help draw the user's attention to the critical information you are trying to convey.

SUMMARY

You've progressed from simple batch file programs of the previous chapter to complete menu-driven systems in this one. Congratulations! Did you ever think you would be a systems programmer? Actually, you've only just begun. Throughout the remainder of this book, you'll continue to learn more DOS programming tricks and techniques for improving your menu-driven system.

Although you might feel justifiably proud of the menus you have created in this chapter, the appearance of these menus is limited by the power of your word processor. The following chapters will continue work on the menu system, adding snazzy menu screens, complete with special borders and multiple colors.

9

The EDLIN Utility

IN THE PRECEDING CHAPTER, you learned how to create simple menu screens using your word processor, and assumed that your word processor could save text files in ASCII format. Even though your word processor might be able to save documents as ASCII files, it might not provide access to the extended ASCII character set.

For either reason, you might find you need to use the EDLIN utility to create your menu screens. Although EDLIN offers only limited editing functions, it does provide access to the special graphics characters which you can use to enhance your menus.

This chapter is about EDLIN, DOS's text editor. Usually, EDLIN is overlooked by everyone who uses a PC, save for two types: Book authors who need an extra chapter to fill, and computer science teachers, who have an extra week to kill. Seriously, EDLIN is put down a lot but it does have positive points. The most important of those being that everyone who has a copy of DOS has access to EDLIN; it's common ground.

WHAT IS EDLIN?

EDLIN is a DOS utility. It is a *text editor* you can use to create ASCII or text files.

EDLIN is located on your DOS disk under the filename EDLIN.COM. In order to use EDLIN, this file must be available to you. If you've placed the DOS files into a special subdirectory on your hard disk, such as \ DOS, you must be in this subdirectory or initiate a path to it with the command:

```
C > PATH \ DOS
```

Before using EDLIN, you should weigh its advantages and disadvantages. EDLIN has three advantages:

- It produces ASCII text files
- It can give you access to the IBM extended character set
- It's free

The disadvantages are: It is difficult to use and has only limited editing capabilities. That's why most people shun it. Still, knowing EDLIN means that you can use it on any DOS computer anywhere, rather than having to second guess some obscure text editing program found on some obscure user's obscure PC.

Advantages of EDLIN

You might be forced to use EDLIN if your word processor can't create ASCII text files, or if there's nothing familiar around to use. And even though your word processor is capable of producing ASCII files, it might require a conversion procedure that's more trouble than it's worth for short batch files.

For these reasons, you might find EDLIN to be a convenient way to create batch files. Of course, there's also the COPY CON: method. However, this method provides no editing capabilities. If you make a single mistake, you must delete the entire file and begin from scratch. The editing commands of EDLIN can be used to edit text as you are entering it, and to edit existing text files at a later time.

A second advantage is that EDLIN gives you access to the IBM extended character set. This set is a collection of special characters that can be displayed by the IBM family of personal computers, and can be printed on IBM compatible graphics printers. You can use these special characters in your menu screens to enhance their appearance. (In the next chapter, you'll be shown how to create simple borders using EDLIN. You can experiment with other characters on your own.)

The final advantage needs no elaboration. One thing you've got to agree with: you can't beat the price!

Disadvantages of EDLIN

The main disadvantage of EDLIN is that it is a text editor, not a word processor. EDLIN doesn't have many of the features found in word processors. In fact, you wouldn't want to write business correspondence, much less long manuscripts, with EDLIN. It does have simple text editing capabilities, including move and search-and-replace commands. These editing capabilities are sufficient for creating batch files and single-screen menus.

A second disadvantage of EDLIN is that it is a *line editor*. With EDLIN, you can only work on one line at a time. You can't use the cursor control keys to move around the screen, editing at will. Instead, you must specify the line to be entered or edited in advance. This is done by entering line numbers. Each line in a file is assigned a line number by EDLIN. These line numbers are used to reference the lines to be edited, moved, displayed, etc.

WORKING WITH EDLIN

Despite these disadvantages, you might find that the availability from the root directory or the access to the extended character set makes EDLIN worth using for simple tasks such as batch file editing or screen generation.

To access the EDLIN program, enter the following:

C > EDLIN filespec [/B]

Note that the filespec is not optional. You must include it. The filespec may include a drive designator and path as well as the filename itself. (The optional /B parameter will be explained later.)

When you issue the command to load EDLIN, it looks on the specified drive and path to see if the file exists. If so, the file will be loaded into memory. (Actually, as much of the file that will fit into 75% of memory will be loaded, but for the purposes of batch file and menu editing, this isn't a consideration.) If the specified file isn't found, EDLIN assumes you intend to create one, and the filename will be used when you save any entered text.

As a result of the search and load procedure, one of two messages will be displayed on the screen. If the file exists and has been loaded into memory, the message will be:

End of input file
*

If, on the other hand, no file is found, the message will be:

New file
*

The asterisk following the displayed message is EDLIN's prompt. Note that, in the first message, EDLIN does not display the contents of the input file. To view the file, you must issue the proper EDLIN command.

In fact, in order to do anything in EDLIN, you must first enter a command. You can't even begin entering text without first entering the Insert command. In the following sections, the various EDLIN commands that you need are summarized.

Creating a New File

To create a new file, call up EDLIN and include the proposed name of the file you wish to create. For example, suppose you want to create a batch file named TEST.BAT. Enter the following:

```
C > EDLIN TEST.BAT
```

With most word processors, all you have to do to enter text is begin typing. Not so with EDLIN. Remember: you must begin by entering a command.

If you do start off typing, EDLIN will interpret your first keystroke as a command. This could be devastating, as many beginning EDLIN users have discovered. To begin entering text, issue the Insert Lines command (note: commands in EDLIN may be entered in either upper- or lowercase):

```
*I
```

Because this is a new file, EDLIN will start inserting lines at line number 1. You'll see line number 1 displayed on the screen waiting for you to enter text:

```
1:*
```

Note the asterisks to the right of the number 1. When the asterisk appears to the right of a line number, that line is the *current* line. (The meaning and use of the current line indicator will be explained later.)

After you're in the Insert Lines mode, enter text by typing it in and pressing the Enter key at the conclusion of each line.

Suppose you want the first line of TEST.BAT to include the command @ECHO OFF. Enter the following:

```
1:*@ECHO OFF
```

After pressing the Enter key, the next line would appear:

```
1:*@ECHO OFF
2:*
```

The asterisk appearing in line 2 indicates that this is now the new current line. (Line 1 is ancient history, which is why its asterisk still remains on the screen even though line 2 is now the current line.)

Continue entering text until there are no more lines to enter. The next display is how the screen will look after entering the five lines of TEST.BAT:

```
1:*@ECHO OFF
2:*CLS
3:*ECHO This is a test batch file
4:*PAUSE
5:*
```

Line 5 is awaiting additional input. However, in this case, the file is complete. To conclude input, enter Control-Break (or Control-C) at the beginning of the last line. Control-Break terminates the Insert Lines mode and takes you back to the * prompt.

To save a file created with EDLIN, enter the End Edit command. There's no need to specify a filename because it was entered when EDLIN was started. For example, to save the five lines you entered under the name TEST.BAT, you enter:

```
*E
```

EDLIN writes the lines you entered to the TEST.BAT file and returns you to the DOS prompt.

If you did not want to save the lines you entered, you can cancel your EDLIN session without saving using the Quit Edit command:

```
*Q
```

Which causes EDLIN to ask you for confirmation:

```
Abort edit (Y/N)?
```

To cancel the session, answer "Y."

Editing an Existing File

To edit a batch file located in the root directory of your hard drive named TEST.BAT, enter the command:

```
C>EDLIN \TEST.BAT
```

EDLIN locates the file, loads it into memory, and responds with the "End of input file" message.

The contents of the file will be stored in memory but not displayed on the screen. To view the file, enter the List Lines command:

    *L

The contents of the file would then be displayed as follows:

    1:*@ECHO OFF
    2: CLS
    3: ECHO This is a test batch file
    4: PAUSE

The asterisk in front of line 1 indicates that it is the current line. Most of EDLIN's commands require you to provide a line number. You can refer to a line by its unique number, or if you want to work with the current line, you can use a "." period. The use of the period is a helpful shortcut when referring to the current line.

Up to 23 lines of a file can be displayed at one time. In this example, the entire batch file can be displayed in fewer than 23 lines. Later, you'll learn how to work with text files that are longer than 23 lines.

Inserting Lines

You can insert lines by using the Insert Lines command.

When you want to insert an empty line between existing lines, you must include the line number that the inserted line will precede. Lines are inserted immediately before the specified line. To insert a new line between lines 3 and 4, the command would be:

    *4I

The following display appears on the screen:

    4:*

You can then type in the text of the new line and press the Enter key, causing the screen to look like this:

    4:*ECHO That doesn't do anything useful
    5:*

The number 5 on the next line indicates that you have another new line to work with (if you want). Assuming that you didn't want to add any more lines at this time, you could terminate the Insert Lines command with a Control-Break (or Control-C).

You can edit a line by entering that line number at the * prompt. This will cause the line to be displayed on the screen along with a second line displaying the same line number and the blinking cursor:

```
*3
    3: ECHO This is a test batch file
    3:
```

Editing is performed with the use of the function keys and the Ins (insert) and Del (delete) keys. For example, suppose you want to change the word "test" to read "sample." You would need to delete the characters "t," "e," "s," and "t," and insert the characters "s," "a," "m," "p," "l," and "e." (See? It's primitive.)

This change can be accomplished with the following sequence of steps. First, move along the line as far as the "t" in "test." This much of the line you can reuse. To display a portion of the line up to a given character, press the F2 key and then enter that character. Type F2 then "t." In this case, you would see:

```
    3: ECHO This is a test batch file
    3: ECHO This is a
```

The cursor will blink under the "t" of the first line in the two-line display. Now delete the four characters, "t," "e," "s," and "t" by pressing the Del key four times. Don't be concerned if you try this, nothing happens on the screen at this time. However, these four characters have been deleted from the computer's memory. (Picture it in your head.)

At this point, you want to insert the characters "s," "a," "m," "p," "l," and "e." However you can't simply type them in. You must first press the Ins key to let EDLIN know you want to insert some characters. After pressing Ins and typing "sample" (don't press Enter yet), the screen will look like:

```
    3: ECHO This is a test batch file
    3: ECHO This is a sample
```

Finally, you have to ask EDLIN to complete the line by pressing the F3 function key. The remainder of the line will be added and your screen should look like the following:

```
    3: ECHO This is a test batch file
    3: ECHO This is a sample batch file
```

To save the changes to line 3, press the Enter key.

From the time you place the cursor under the "t" of "test" using the F2 key, until you complete the line with the F3 key, you do not press the Enter key. Pressing Enter accepts any changes made to that point and returns you to the * prompt.

If you make a mistake and want to cancel the changes, you can press Control-Break to return to the * prompt. Now you can edit the line again by reentering the number 3 at the prompt.

To end the session and save all changes, including the added line and the alterations to line 3, enter the End Edit command:

```
*E
```

This command will cause the changes stored in your computer's memory to be written to the disk, and you are returned to the system prompt.

A SUMMARY OF EDLIN's COMMANDS

There are many EDLIN commands, each of which is described in detail in your DOS manual. However, the manual is an instance of too much information being worse than too little. If you're like many computer users, you've probably avoided EDLIN because of its abundant description in the DOS manual. It does seem intimidating.

Actually, you only need to know a limited number of EDLIN's commands to use the program effectively. These commands are summarized in Appendix B. This appendix lists each command, parameters necessary for the command, and its function.

The most commonly used commands are:

* Insert Lines
* Edit Line
* List Lines
* Replace Text
* End Edit

You've already seen how the Insert Lines, Edit Line, List Lines, End Edit, and Quit Edit commands are used. However, for ease of reference, each of the commands in Appendix B will be described briefly in this chapter.

The Insert Lines Command

The Insert Lines command is used to add extra lines to a file. Lines can be added at the beginning, in the middle, or at the end of a file. The Insert Lines command may include an optional parameter. This parameter can be a line number, a period (.), or the number symbol (#).

After you enter the Insert Lines mode, you will be provided with new lines until you terminate the command. The Insert Lines command is terminated by entering Control-Break at the beginning of a new line. All lines moved down by the Insert Lines command are automatically renumbered.

To add lines at the beginning of the file, enter the command:

```
*I
```

To insert lines into the middle of a file, you enter the Insert Lines command with the line number where you want the insertion to take place. Lines are inserted above the specified line number.

For example, if you wanted to insert one or more lines before line 5, you would enter:

```
*5I
```

To insert lines above the current line, you would enter:

```
*.I
```

To insert lines at the end of the file, you use the number symbol (#):

```
*#I
```

The Edit Line Command

The Edit Line command is used to edit a single line in a file. This command is by far the most difficult EDLIN command to master. It is clumsy and difficult to use. In fact, it's often easier to retype a short line than to edit it because line editing is performed in memory rather than on the screen. You can't always see what you are doing until after it's been done.

The general technique for editing a line is as follows: First, use the F2 key and type a character to bring up onto the screen all the text up to the point where that character first appears; second, make the desired changes with the Del and Ins keys, or by typing over existing text; finally, bring up the remainder of the text with the F3 key.

To edit a line, enter the line number of the line to be edited. For example, to edit line 4, you would enter:

```
*4
```

The Edit Line command uses a two-line display. The first line shows the complete text of the line being edited. The second line is used as a work line. For example, suppose you entered the above command to edit line 4 of the revised file, TEST.BAT. You would see the following display:

        4: ECHO That doesn't do anything useful
        4:

You use the second line to make your changes. The F2 key and a letter are used to place text on the line up to the point where you want your changes to occur. The text will be displayed up to the character you entered. This process can be repeated as needed until the desired point is reached.

For example, suppose you want to change the word "anything." To move up to this word, you should enter:

        4: ECHO That doesn't do anything useful
        4: [F2][a]

EDLIN will display the text of line 4 up to the "a" of "That":

        4: ECHO That doesn't do anything useful
        4: ECHO Th

Because this location isn't where you want to be, repeat the F2 command followed by another "a." This time, the text up to "anything" will appear on the work line:

        4: ECHO That doesn't do anything useful
        4: ECHO That doesn't do

After the cursor is positioned under the text to be edited, you can use the Del key to remove as many characters as you wish. Each time you press Del, another character will be removed. Unfortunately, EDLIN doesn't show the characters that have been removed.

To insert new characters, press the Ins key once, and then enter the required characters. You also can enter characters in the overstrike mode by typing them without pressing the Ins key. To change "anything" to "something," press the Del key three times, press the Ins key once, and enter "some." Now press F3 to go to the end of the line and strike Enter.

One trap to avoid is pressing the Enter key after making the changes. This mistake will cause the line to be concluded at that point. However, the line is not yet complete. Normally, the Enter key is only pressed after the editing process is completed.

If further editorial changes are required, you can continue editing the line by pressing the F5 key.

You also can use the Edit Line command to retype a line from scratch. However, instead of using the F2 and F3 function keys, simply type the new line in place of the old one and press Enter when you are done.

The List Lines Command

The List Lines command is used to view one or more lines of a file. List Lines can be used in conjunction with two optional parameters to view a single line, a group of lines, or the entire file (up to 23 lines).

Both parameters are used to view a block of lines. For example, to view lines 4 through 10, the command would be:

```
*4,10L
```

To view the entire file (up to 23 lines worth), enter the List Lines command with no parameters:

```
*L
```

The List Lines command is plural, that is, it's used to list lines. You might think that you could view a single line by including that line number before the List Lines command. However, if you enter the command:

```
*8L
```

you'll see the remainder of the file, beginning with line 8. To view a single line, you must enter the line number twice, separated by a comma:

```
*8,8L
```

To view the current line, just use the period (.):

```
*.,.L
```

The Delete Lines Command

The Delete Lines command is used to remove one or more unwanted lines from a file. Delete Lines may include one or two optional parameters. To remove several lines at once,

enter the beginning line number, a comma, the ending line number, and the letter "D."
For example, to delete lines 6 through 10, you would enter:

*6,10D

To delete a single line, you only provide the line number of the line to be deleted. To
delete only line 6, the command would be:

*6D

If no line number is specified for either the first or the second line number parameter,
the current line is used by default. For example, to delete from the current line through
line 10, the command would be:

*,10D

After the lines are deleted, EDLIN renumbers the remaining lines to keep them in
sequence.

The Replace Text Command

The Replace Text command is used to replace one string of characters with another.
The replacement made by the Replace Text command can take place in a single line, a
range of lines, or throughout the entire file. Optionally, the Replace Text command can be
used to delete a specified character string by omitting the replacement string from the
command.

This command can be used for normal editing to correct errors or make changes to the
text of a file. However, the real power of this command is the provision of a shortcut for
text entry.

For example, suppose you were creating a batch file that used a number of ECHO
statements. Instead of typing "ECHO" at the beginning of each statement, you could type
a single character, such as "$." When the text entry was complete, you could use the
Replace Text command to replace all occurrences of "$" with "ECHO." (As you'll see in
the next chapter, this technique also can be used to facilitate the use of the extended character set.)

The Replace Text command usually is used with two line parameters. These parameters specify the lines to be included in the text replacement process. Following the two line
parameters is the "R" of the Replace Text command. Next comes the two strings. These
are separated by a Control-Z (you can use the F6 key to enter a Control-Z). The command
is concluded by pressing Enter.

Suppose you had entered the TEST.BAT file as follows:

    1:*@# OFF
    2:*CLS
    3:*# This is a test batch file
    4:*# That doesn't do anything useful
    5:*PAUSE

You can replace every occurrence of "#" with "ECHO" by entering the following command:

    *1,5R#^ZECHO

When EDLIN performs the replacements, it echoes each line to the screen. Lines that require no alteration are not echoed. In the previous example, the following lines will be displayed:

    1:*@ECHO OFF
    3: ECHO This is a test batch file
    4: ECHO That doesn't do anything useful

Each occurrence of the string to be replaced constitutes a separate replacement action. If EDLIN performs several replacements in a single line, that line will be echoed each time a replacement takes place. (As you'll see in the next chapter, this can be rather time consuming when replacing keyboard characters with line drawing characters to produce borders for your menus.)

As mentioned, the Replace Text command also can be used to delete character strings by omitting the second string from the command. To delete the string "ECHO" from the TEST.BAT file, the command would be:

    *1,6RECHO^Z

One more thing to note: The Replace Text command is *case sensitive*, meaning you must type in the text exactly as it appears in the file or Replace won't find it. When that happens, EDLIN reports a "Not found" error, and returns you the * prompt. Try again using the proper upper- and lowercase characters.

The End Edit and Quit Edit Commands

The End Edit command is used to save any changes to the file being edited. After the changes are written to the disk, EDLIN is terminated and you're returned to DOS. The

End Edit command requires no parameters.

You might find times when you would rather not save your editing changes, especially when you are first learning how to use EDLIN. To leave EDLIN without saving, use the Quit Edit command. This prevents the changes in memory from being written to the disk.

After typing "Q" at the * prompt, EDLIN will display a confirming message:

Abort edit (Y/N)?

To confirm, enter "Y."

The Quit Edit command can be a lifesaver. You can make mistakes while using the Edit Line or Delete Lines commands that would be time consuming to correct. The best strategy in these cases is to quit the editing session with the Quit Edit command. Although you will be returned to DOS and will have to reload EDLIN, this method might be faster than trying to correct the mistake.

SUMMARY

This chapter was a brief, but deep, dive into EDLIN, DOS's text editing program. There are positive and negative points about using EDLIN, with its strength lying in its common ground as a free (with DOS) text editor. Its weaknesses are many, but overall it's a capable text editor, especially for writing or patching up quick batch files.

The next chapter, however, will show you some real horsepower behind EDLIN. Using the knowledge you gained in this chapter, combined with what you've learned about menu systems from the previous chapter, you're about to embark upon an interesting journey. With your skills at making menus and knowing EDLIN, you can now teach your PC some truly amazing tricks—all the time making your hard disk system easier to use.

10
Building Up the Menu

NOW THAT YOU have a functioning, menu-driven system for accessing programs and data on your hard disk (thanks to chapter 8), you might feel your system is complete. But in fact, there are a number of enhancements you can add to your system. Although the systems described so far are functional, admittedly they aren't very exciting. The screen displays consist of a simple list of options and a prompt telling the user to select from one of the choices. Yawn.

You can use your PC's full range of color, special graphics characters, and screen features like inverse video to jazz up your displays. You also can perform some magic that will allow you to use the ten function keys to call up applications programs instead of entering in a batch filename. Your menu system will be simplified significantly because you'll be able to select options by pressing a single key.

This chapter presents a variety of techniques for enhancing your screen displays and simplifying the use of your menu system. The basic tool here is EDLIN, which, as was promised in the previous chapter, really has some interesting tricks to making all these fancy menus possible.

IMPROVING YOUR MENU SCREENS

To take full advantage of the graphics capabilities of your computer, you will need to have access to the *extended ASCII character set*.

ASCII files contain only printable characters. Most word processors add additional control characters to denote end of lines, end of paragraphs, special indentations, bold face, underscore, italics, etc. These control characters can produce unexpected results in a batch file, or when TYPEd to the screen.

The standard ASCII defined character set consists of printable characters, those available on the standard keyboard; the letters, digits, and characters like "*" and "#." On most PC's, however, an additional character set also exists. These Extended ASCII characters (not really defined in the ASCII standard) include a number of special characters such as Greek letters, tiny hearts, smiling faces, arrowheads, and characters for producing single- and double-line border graphics.

Most word processors don't give you access to those special characters. They use them instead to control the format or appearance of the documents they produce, which means you can't have access to them to create special graphics effects. This is true of WordStar, for example.

Some word processors, including WordPerfect and MicroSoft Word, do allow you to work with Extended ASCII characters. You can use these programs to create fancy screen displays. However, these screen displays can only be TYPEd by DOS as long as you save them as ASCII files.

The screen in *Fig. 10-1* was created with WordPerfect using the extended character set to draw the solid menu border and the double line border around the menu heading.

The highlighting around the prompt message, "Enter your selection," was accomplished with the use of special screen controls. On a color system, controls for changing

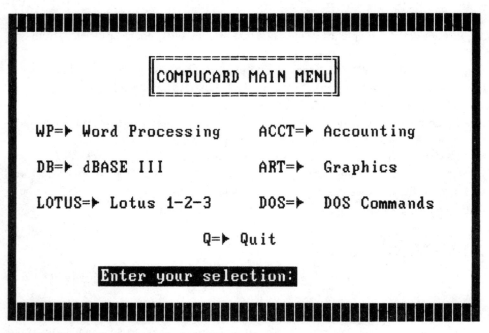

Fig. 10-1. Improved main menu including border lines.

foreground and background colors can be added as well. These screen controls also are available in the PROMPT command. The techniques for drawing borders and controlling the screen will be described later in the chapter.

Adding Borders to Your Menus with EDLIN

As mentioned in the previous chapter, EDLIN gives you access to the Extended ASCII character set available on most PCs. This character set provides special drawing symbols that can be used for producing single- and double-line borders. You might have seen such borders used in commercially available programs. *Figure 10-2* shows a simple border added to the CompuCard Main Menu. This menu screen was created using EDLIN.

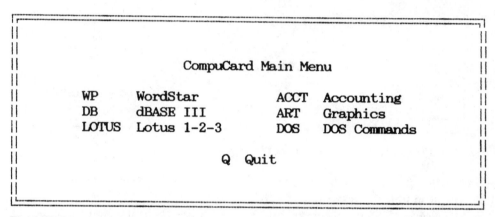

Fig. 10-2. *Menu screen created in EDLIN.*

Working with the Extended ASCII Character Set

The border in *Fig. 10-2* was created using six special characters from the extended character set. These are the four double-line corner characters, the horizontal double-line character, and the vertical double-line character. These and other drawing characters are shown in *Fig. 10-3*.

In Appendix B, you'll find a table displaying the complete extended ASCII character set. Although these characters can be displayed on the screen, they can only be printed on special, IBM compatible dot-matrix printers. Check your printer's manual to determine if it's capable of printing the IBM character set.

Notice that each drawing character is referenced by a number. These numbers are the Extended ASCII code values that represent the characters. Every character has a corresponding decimal code value. For example, the character "A" has the decimal value 65.

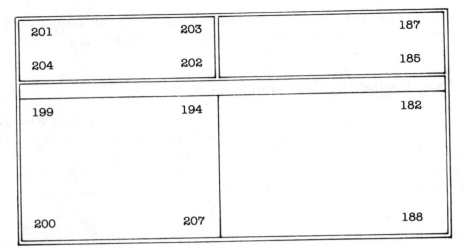

Fig. 10-3. The Extended ASCII line drawing characters and their character values are shown here.

Fortunately, you don't have to enter code values for the normal characters. Instead, you can type them from the keyboard.

The problem with the characters in the extended ASCII character set is the lack of symbols for them on the keyboard. The only way to get these special characters is by entering their decimal codes.

To enter the decimal code value for an ASCII character, hold down the Alt key and simultaneously type the decimal code. Note: you must use the numbers on the numeric keypad. The numbers across the top of the keyboard won't work.

Not all word processors are able to access the extended character set. MicroSoft Word and WordPerfect will allow you to work with the drawing symbols and other special characters directly on the screen. Later in this chapter, you will see how WordPerfect can be used to draw some rather fancy borders and add other enhancements to your menu screens.

If your word processor doesn't allow you to work with the extended character set, you'll need to use EDLIN to draw borders around your menu screens. EDLIN allows you to enter special characters by using the Alt key.

For example, to enter the upper left double-line corner symbol, hold down the Alt key and type the number 201 from the numeric keypad. This will produce the corner symbol on the screen. Although entering numeric sequences from the numeric keypad is time consuming, you can at least get the characters on the screen. In the following section, you will see how to use the Replace Text command to shorten the process.

A Sample Menu Screen

Before actually entering the text and border characters for a given menu screen, you should plan out the screen's appearance in advance. For example, notice that the border is centered in the middle of the screen in *Fig. 10-2*. Also, notice the placement of the text within the borders. Finally, notice the margin between the top of the screen and the top border line. Keep these spacing factors in mind when creating your menu screens.

To create the menu screen in *Fig. 10-2*, you create a file using EDLIN. Start off by calling this file MENU1. (Later you can rename it to MAINMENU.) You might not get this screen right the first time, and it would be a shame to overwrite the existing MAIN-MENU screen until you're satisfied with the new one. You create this file with the command:

```
C > EDLIN MENU1
```

At EDLIN's asterisk prompt, enter the Insert Lines command, I. Skip three lines by pressing Enter at line numbers 1, 2, and 3.

On line 4, enter the characters to produce the top border line with the following 4 steps.

(1) Enter 15 spaces.
(2) Hold down the Alt key and enter 201 from the numeric keypad. The upper left double-line corner symbol will appear on the screen.
(3) Enter 48 asterisks. These will be replaced by the horizontal double-line symbol later.
(4) Enter the upper right double-line corner by holding down the Alt key and entering 187.

Your screen should look like *Fig. 10-4* at this point.

On line 5, enter 15 spaces, Alt-186, 48 spaces, and Alt-186 again. On line 6, enter the 15 spaces, Alt-186, 14 spaces, the text "CompuCard Main Menu," 15 more spaces, and another Alt-186. Continue with this process until you come to line 14.

Line 14 is similar to line 4 except that you use the lower left corner, Alt-200, and the lower right corner, Alt-188. At this point, your screen should resemble *Fig. 10-5*.

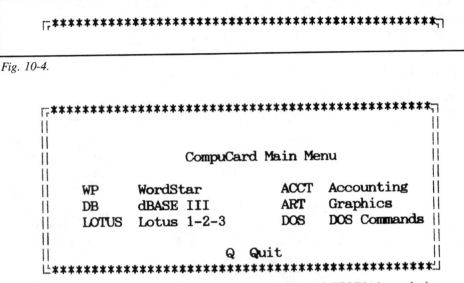

Fig. 10-4.

Fig. 10-5. *The CompuCard Main Menu takes form slowly, but with EDLIN it's nearly done.*

You are now ready to use the Replace Text command to substitute the horizontal double-line symbol for the asterisks you entered in lines 4 and 14. The command is:

4,14R^ZAlt-205

(Remember that ^Z is entered by typing Control-Z. "Alt-205" is holding the Alt key and typing 205 on the numeric keypad. This sequence will produce the horizontal double-line character.)

EDLIN will proceed to make the necessary replacements. Each time EDLIN replaces an asterisk with a horizontal double-line symbol, the line where the replacement takes place will be echoed to the screen. A total of 96 replacements are made in this operation, so be prepared to wait while the process is completed.

After the file has been altered to include the horizontal double-line symbols, you can view the file with the List Lines command, L. If the screen is to your liking, you can save it with the End Edit command, E.

To be sure you really like the screen, try it out using the TYPE command:

C>TYPE MENU1

The screen is now available for use in your MAINMENU batch file. Make sure you rename it to MAINMENU first.

FANCY MENU SCREENS WITH WORDPERFECT

The CompuCard Main Menu screen created in the last section is a big improvement over the version developed in chapter 8. The addition of a border really enhances the menu, giving it an identity of its own and a professional edge. Unfortunately, using EDLIN to create screens is tedious and time-consuming. If you have access to a contemporary word processing program, such as WordPerfect or MicroSoft Word, you can use these programs to create menu screens in a fraction of the time it takes with EDLIN.

WordPerfect, for example, not only allows access to the extended character set, but provides you with special commands for drawing on the screen. To draw a border in WordPerfect, select the drawing character you wish to use, say a solid block, and then use the cursor keys to draw the border. Using WordPerfect to draw borders is somewhat like working with the old Etch-a-Sketch boards. (You were a kid once too, weren't you?)

Using the Extended Character Set in WordPerfect

In addition to special commands for drawing borders, WordPerfect allows you to insert any of the extended characters directly into your text. For example, if you want to create a pointer, you can use a horizontal double-line character followed by an arrowhead. (Refer to *Fig. 10-1* to see how these symbols have been combined.)

To work with any of the special characters, hold down the Alt key and type in the decimal code for the character on the numeric keypad. The character appears wherever the cursor is located. For example, to create the pointer following the WP choice in the CompuCard Main Menu screen, the cursor was located after the "P." The horizontal double-line character was produced by pressing Alt-205. Then the arrowhead was added with Alt-16.

Instead of trying to remember the decimal codes for all the special characters, refer to WordPerfect's built-in reference chart. *Figure 10-6* is a reproduction of this chart.

To view the chart, use the WordPerfect Screen Key (Ctrl-F3) which will produce a list of options at the bottom of the screen. From this list of options, select option 3 for Ctrl/Alt keys.

WordPerfect 5.0 shows the chart in the help screen. To access the characters, type Control-V. To see the chart, type F3 then Control-V.

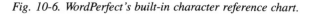

Fig. 10-6. WordPerfect's built-in character reference chart.

To read the chart, locate the character you are interested in. Find the row value of this character on the left. This value will be a three digit number ranging from 0 to 250. Add the column value of the character found at the top of the chart to this number. These numbers range from 0 to 49.

For example, find the code value for the solid block character. This character might be difficult to locate because it's connected to two other solid characters that form a solid (though off-center) U shape in the next-to-the-last row.

Got it? To determine this character's code value, take the row number, 200, and add to it the column number, 19. The resulting value is 219. Enter Alt-219 to use the character.

Line Drawing in WordPerfect

WordPerfect provides a useful tool for creating borders. This tool is the Line Draw option, option number 2, which is accessed by pressing the Screen Key, (Ctrl-F3).

When you select the Line Draw option, you are presented with several choices for drawing, erasing, or moving lines, as shown in *Fig. 10-7*. The first three choices let you draw lines using either the single- or the double-line character. The third choice displays an asterisk as the drawing character. However, you can change this character to any other character you wish—including the entire range of extended characters.

1 ‖ ; 2 ‖ ; 3 *; 4 Change; 5 Erase; 6 Move: 1   Ln 1   Pos 10

Fig. 10-7. WordPerfect's line drawing menu.

To draw a border, place the cursor at one of the corners of the border rectangle. To use either the single- or double-line character, select the appropriate option (1 or 2). Then use the cursor keys to move left, right, up, or down as desired. As you press the cursor keys, a line is drawn in the direction you specify. If you change directions by 90 degrees, WordPerfect automatically inserts the correct corner character for you. For example, to draw a double-line border extending 40 characters across, 10 characters down, and centered on the screen, do the following eight steps:

(1) Place your cursor on line 4, position 25.
(2) Press the Screen Key (F3) and select option 2, Line Draw.
(3) Enter option 2 for the Line Draw command, which will activate the double-line character.
(4) Use the right arrow key to extend the double-line 40 characters to the right, or press the repeat key, ESC, type 40, and then press the right arrow key.

(5) Use the down arrow key to draw a vertical line from line 4 to line 14. WordPerfect will automatically turn the corner for you. (You also can use ESC: Press ESC, then type 10, then press the down arrow key.)

(6) Use the left arrow key to move back to position 25, completing the third side of the border.

(7) Use the up arrow key to draw the remaining side of the border.

(8) To get out of the Line Draw mode, type the Exit Key (F7).

As you are drawing, your border lines might not meet up as you planned. Determining exactly where to turn the corner (like the Etch-a-Sketch) can be difficult. If you make a mistake when drawing lines in WordPerfect, use option 5 to Erase. When this option is selected, any movement using the cursor keys will cause the line to be rubbed out in the direction of the arrow key you're using.

To draw lines using any of the other extended characters, substitute that character for the asterisk in option 3 by choosing option 4, Change. This option, shown in *Fig. 10-8*, displays a list of eight drawing options consisting of various sizes and shades of drawing characters.

1 ▨; 2 ▨; 3 ▨; 4 ■; 5 ▬; 6 ▌; 7 ▐; 8 ▀; 9 Other: 0

Fig. 10-8. WordPerfect's other line drawing characters.

You can select from one of these, or choose option 9, Other. If you select this option, you will see a message:

Solid character:

displayed at the bottom of your screen. At this point, you can enter the Alt-number sequence for the character you want. (Remember, you can look up the code value using the Ctrl/Alt keys option of the Screen Key.) The character you select through this process becomes the new drawing character.

After you've drawn your border, you can insert the text of your menu. Be careful to use the Typeover mode, or you'll break up the vertical lines. After they are drawn, borders are affected by any editorial changes you make. If you insert additional characters or lines, the borders will be broken up by the insertion, just as any other characters would be. If you inadvertently break up your borders, you can bring the border lines back into alignment by deleting empty spaces to the left of them or removing extra blank lines.

One way to avoid possible damage to your borders during screen editing is to enter the text of your menu before drawing your borders. After the text is in place, use the Screen

Key to draw borders around it. Be careful here as well: Make sure you're in the Typeover mode, or your text will get moved around in strange and mysterious ways.

Saving WordPerfect Menu Screens as ASCII Files

After the menu screen is complete, you can save it in two forms. First, save the screen as a regular WordPerfect document by using the Save Key (F10). You'll also want to save the menu screen as an ASCII file.

Like many word processors, WordPerfect places hidden control characters into its files. Although you don't normally see these characters when working in WordPerfect, they show up when TYPEd from DOS. Fortunately, WordPerfect provides a conversion command that can remove these control characters from the file and create a displayable ASCII file.

To save a document as an ASCII file, use the Text In/Out Key (Ctrl-F5). This key provides you with several choices. Option 1 will save the document in ASCII format as it appears on the screen. Be careful because WordPerfect will suggest the same name that you used to save the file as a WordPerfect document. If you accept this name, WordPerfect will replace the WordPerfect version with the ASCII version. You should use separate names for your WordPerfect and ASCII versions of your menu screens.

The reason for maintaining two versions of your menu screens is to make editorial changes to the menu easily. This editing is accomplished by bringing up the WordPerfect version of the menu. This version can be edited using any of the WordPerfect commands, including moving or erasing border lines. The border lines in the ASCII versions cannot be easily edited. After making any changes, be sure to resave the file as both a WordPerfect document and as an ASCII file.

CONTROLLING THE SCREEN CHARACTERISTICS

Borders and graphics characters are only one way to increase the impact of your menu screens. You also can use a number of video tricks to draw attention to your menus and any special messages or prompts to the user.

DOS provides access to a wide variety of video display features, including bold and inverse video, blinking, underscore, and color, if you have a color display card and monitor (you can't get blood from a turnip). The remainder of this chapter tells how you can further spice up your menus and prompts using some secret tricks.

The Power of ANSI.SYS

To take advantage of your computer's special display modes, you must be able to manipulate the special DOS display driver, ANSI.SYS. ANSI.SYS is a file on your DOS diskette. It allows you to control the screen display (also the keyboard) in ways that you can't otherwise do. With ANSI.SYS, you can control the location of the cursor, change video modes on monochrome systems, and alter the foreground and background colors on color systems. ANSI.SYS also enables you to redefine the keyboard functions.

In order to work with ANSI.SYS, your system must be set up to recognize its commands. DOS does this through a file named CONFIG.SYS. This file might already be in your root directory. If not, you can put it there using COPY CON:, your word processor (in the text mode), or EDLIN.

CONFIG.SYS is a user-created file. You won't find it on your DOS diskette. If you find a file by this name in your root directory, it was probably placed there by the individual who set up your system. The CONFIG.SYS file can be created or modified at any time using a text editor, but note that you need to reboot your system for any changes to take effect.

If CONFIG.SYS already exists in your root directory, all you need to do is add the following command:

```
DEVICE = ANSI.SYS
```

Don't worry if there are other lines saying DEVICE= something else. You can have more than one DEVICE= line in your CONFIG.SYS file.

If you don't already have a CONFIG.SYS file in your root directory, you need to make one. Use EDLIN to create a new file named CONFIG.SYS. It should consist of the single line, DEVICE=ANSI.SYS.

If you're smart and have put ANSI.SYS into your \ DOS subdirectory (and, in fact, it might already be there), then remember to specify its full filespec:

```
DEVICE = C: \ DOS \ ANSI.SYS
```

When DOS is booted, it checks to see if the file CONFIG.SYS is in the root directory. If so, DOS reads the contents of CONFIG.SYS to see if any special drivers are to be installed. In this case, the *device* driver, ANSI.SYS, is to be installed.

ANSI.SYS will control the console device. Because the console consists of the screen and the keyboard, ANSI.SYS will control the way these two components of your system work. Of course, unless you take advantage of ANSI.SYS, the screen and the keyboard will work the way they normally do. You won't notice anything different unless you tap ANSI.SYS's power.

To make ANSI.SYS do its stuff, you must make *calls* to it. A call to ANSI.SYS is like saying, "Hey, yo, ANSI.SYS!" and then specifying what screen or keyboard attribute you want to alter.

Calls to ANSI.SYS are made by sending DOS an *escape sequence*. An escape sequence is just an Escape character (generated by the ESC key) followed by a bracket, [, and one or more special numbers or characters. Unfortunately, these escape sequences cannot be sent directly from the system prompt. Why not? Just try pressing the ESC key to enter the Escape character and see what happens.

However, where there's a will, there's a way. In this case, the way is the PROMPT command itself. Believe it or not, you can enter the Escape character for batch files using EDLIN. (See, I told you it would come in handy.) Not even grand WordPerfect will let you do that!

Using PROMPT to Call ANSI.SYS

Although you can't send escape sequences directly to DOS from the system prompt, the PROMPT command has a way of sending them.

In the discussion of the PROMPT command in chapter 4, you'll recall that PROMPT includes a number of optional parameters, such as $n, $p, $g, etc. One of these parameters not introduced was $e, which sends an Escape code to DOS. (Ta da!) This Escape code can be teamed up with the ANSI.SYS control codes to make calls to the device driver.

The *DOS Technical Reference Manual* refers to ANSI.SYS escape sequences and what they can do by categories: cursor functions, erasing, graphics modes, and keyboard reassignment. Each of these functions will be discussed in the following sections. Some of the more interesting escape codes are listed in *Table 10-1*.

To send an escape sequence to ANSI.SYS via the PROMPT command, include the PROMPT Escape code ($e) followed by a bracket, [, and whatever ANSI.SYS control code you wish to transmit. For example, the escape sequence to clear the screen and home the cursor (the DOS subcommand, CLS) is ESC[2J. In PROMPT command talk that's $e[2J. Note that the "J" must be uppercase. ANSI.SYS is fussy about those things.

The escape sequence for clearing the screen and homing the cursor to ANSI.SYS would be:

```
PROMPT $e[2J
```

Don't type that in, however! You can, sure, and nothing will happen—except that your screen will clear after each DOS command to display your new "prompt." That doesn't make for very good directory reading. If you did type in that PROMPT string, change it back to your default prompt by entering PROMPT on the command line.

Escape sequences can be strung together and included with messages to the user. This method is the most effective way to incorporate ANSI.SYS into your system prompt. The

Table 10-1. Escape Codes for ANSI.SYS Screen Functions.

ESC [Pl ; Pc H	Moves cursor to line 1; column c.
ESC [1 A	Moves cursor up 1 line.
ESC [1 B	Moves cursor down 1 line.
ESC [c F	Moves cursor right c columns.
ESC [c D	Moves cursor left d columns.
ESC [s	Saves current cursor position.
ESC [u	Restores cursor to previous position.
ESC [2 J	Clears screen and homes cursor.
ESC [k	Erase from current position to end of line.
ESC [0 m	Normal text.
ESC [1 m	High-intensity.
ESC [4 m	Underscore.
ESC [5 m	Blinking.
ESC [7 m	Inverse video.
ESC [8 m	Invisible.
ESC [30 m	Black foreground.
ESC [34 m	Blue foreground.
ESC [32 m	Green foreground.
ESC [36 m	Cyan foreground.
ESC [31 m	Red foreground.
ESC [35 m	Magenta foreground.
ESC [33 m	Brown foreground.
ESC [37 m	White foreground.
ESC [40 m	Black background.
ESC [44 m	Blue background.
ESC [42 m	Green background.
ESC [46 m	Cyan background.
ESC [41 m	Red background.
ESC [45 m	Magenta background.
ESC [44 m	Brown background.
ESC [47 m	White background.

inverse video escape sequence (ESC[7m) and the message "Enter your command:" can be used as follows:

```
PROMPT $e[7m Enter your command:$e[0m
```

The ESC[0m (that's a zero-m) is used to change back to normal video. You can omit it if you like the inverse display. Also, feel free to experiment with color options. The following PROMPT command creates the popular bright white characters on blue background screen that many users strive for:

```
PROMPT $e[1m$e[37m$e[44m$p$g
```

Cursor and Erase Functions

ANSI.SYS allows you to position the cursor anywhere you want. You can move the cursor up a line, down a line, forward or backward across a line, or to a specific position on the screen. ANSI.SYS also allows you to save the cursor position in memory, report on the cursor position, and restore the cursor to its former position.

The most useful of the cursor functions is the cursor position function. This function uses the escape sequence:

```
ESC[pl;pcH
```

The pl and pc values are the line and column parameters. For example, to position the cursor on line 14, column 20, the sequence would be:

```
Esc[14;20H
```

You might have wondered how the prompt in the menu screen displayed in *Fig. 10-1* was located within the menu itself. This display was accomplished with the use of the CUP function in the PROMPT command:

```
PROMPT $e[14;20H Enter the letters corresponding to your choice
```

Note in this case that the line and column parameters, as well as the letter "H," are not separated by spaces in the interest of keeping the PROMPT command as compact as possible.

Keyboard Reassignment Functions

Another feature of ANSI.SYS reassigns the function of any key on the keyboard. This includes the function keys, F1 through F10.

Although ANSI.SYS is limited in the number of reassignments it can accommodate at any one time, it is still a useful feature. On the other hand, if you have a full-featured keyboard macro processor, such as ProKey or SuperKey, you'll be better off using that program to make keyboard reassignments.

Most computer users accept their keyboards at face value. Did you think that, when you entered an "A," the ASCII code for the letter "A" was actually sent to your computer?

A special *scan code* is sent to the computer. In the case of the "A" key, the scan code is 30. There are also scan codes for the shift keys, so the computer can tell whether you are entering a lowercase or uppercase "A."

The scan code for the letter you type is translated into the corresponding ASCII code by the computer's BIOS ROM chip. This ASCII value will then be sent to the screen for display. However, the ANSI.SYS device driver can intercept the ASCII codes before they get to the screen. ANSI.SYS will then generate its own ASCII code, sending it to the screen. In fact, ANSI.SYS can send an entire sequence of characters, and a single key can be reassigned to represent a complete sentence.

The ability to reassign letter keys is not especially useful. After all, you ordinarily want an "A" to be an "A" and not a "B." (You might want to try some simple key reassignments on your friend's computer, though. This makes a great, if unappreciated, practical joke!) On the other hand, reassigning the values of the function keys can simplify the use of your menus. Consider the menu screen displayed in *Fig. 10-9*.

Figure 10-9 refers to the function keys F1 through F8 for selecting the options displayed on the screen. The use of function keys to represent menu choices is often preferable to letter choices. For one thing, pressing F1 is faster than typing "WS" and pressing the Enter key. Also, the function keys are easier for novices to find.

For these reasons, you might want to build your menus around function keys rather than letter choices. You can use ANSI.SYS to reassign the values of these function keys. Remember one thing: If you use ANSI.SYS to reassign the function keys, you won't be

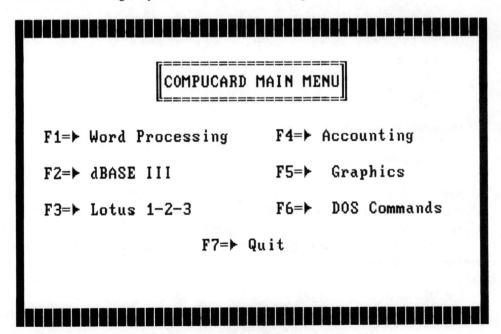

Fig. 10-9. *Menu screen relying on function keys for selecting choices.*

able to use these keys in their normal capacity as editing keys for EDLIN. Of course, if your system is fully menu-driven from power on to shutoff, you won't be using EDLIN anyway.

Keyboard reassignments are not returned to their default even if another PROMPT command is issued. The only way to get the default key assignments back is to reboot the computer. If the keyboard reassignments are part of a PROMPT command contained in the AUTOEXEC.BAT file, you'll have to reboot off the floppy drive.

The escape sequence for keyboard reassignment consists of the Escape key, the bracket, the ASCII code of the key being reassigned, a semicolon, and the new string value assigned to the key. A little "p" ends the command. For example, to reassign the function key F1 to assume the string "WS," you would use the following escape sequence:

ESC[0;59;"WS"p

The first two values, 0 and 59, are the extended ASCII code for the F1 function key. The final "p" is the ANSI.SYS keyboard reassignment function parameter.

To include this escape sequence in a PROMPT command, you would enter:

PROMPT $e[0;59;"WS"p

After this reassignment is effected with the PROMPT command, pressing the F1 key will cause the letters "WS" to be displayed on the screen. The only problem with this reassignment is that the user must still press the Enter key. Even this task can be reassigned to the F1 key by including the ASCII code for a carriage return, 13, as part of the escape sequence:

ESC[0;59;"WS";13p

The corresponding PROMPT command would be:

PROMPT $e[0:59;"WS";13p

Now, whenever the user presses the F1 key, the WS batch file will be automatically called up, simplifying the use of the menu system considerably.

The extended ASCII codes for the ten function keys are listed in *Table 10-2*.

One recommendation for reassigning function keys: Reassign each function key to its digit character and a return. For example, the key reassignment for the F1 key would be:

PROMPT $e[0:59;"1";13p

F1	059	
F2	060	
F3	061	
F4	062	
F5	063	*Table 10-2. Scan Codes for the Ten Function Keys.*
F6	064	
F7	065	
F8	066	
F9	067	
F10	068	

With this reassignment, when the F1 key is pressed, the "1" character will be sent (along with Enter). Of course, the WS.BAT file must be renamed to 1.BAT.

Digit characters are used so you don't have to reassign function keys every time you modify your menu. Instead, all you have to do is change the name of the batch file to match choice 1, 2, etc., on your modified menu.

An even better approach keeps a set of batch files labeled 1.BAT, 2.BAT, etc., in your root directory. Each of these batch files would contain a line which calls the batch file for each of the choices in the menu.

Using *Fig. 10-9* as an example, the 1.BAT file would consist of the following lines:

```
@ECHO OFF
CLS
WS
```

With this batch file, the only changes that need to be made when modifying the system are to edit the menu screen and change the batch file call in the numbered batch file. Suppose you want to change from Lotus 1-2-3 to SuperCalc4. Edit your menu screen and substitute "SuperCalc4" for "Lotus." You could also substitute the batch call SC for LOTUS in the batch file labeled 3.BAT.

A Menu System Based on Function Keys

You can combine multiple key reassignments in a single PROMPT command. For example, the following PROMPT command will reassign the eight function keys, F1 through F8, to the batch calls, "1" through "8," respectively:

```
PROMPT $e[0;59;49;13p $e[0;60;50;13p $e[0;61;51;13p $e[0;62;52;13p
$e[0;63;53;13p $e[0;64;54;13p $e[0;65;55;13p $e[0;66;56;13p
```

This PROMPT command could be included at the beginning of the AUTOEXEC-.BAT file. Then, whenever the computer is started, the function keys will be reassigned automatically. These eight function keys can then be used to call up the eight menu choices displayed in Fig. 10-9. These choices relate to the batch files 1.BAT through 8.BAT. These batch files correspond to the batch files, WP.BAT, LOTUS.BAT, Q.BAT, etc.

Although some of these batch files execute commands or load programs directly, such as 4.BAT or 8.BAT, others cause submenus to be displayed. Consider the 6.BAT file, which is executed when the F6 function key is pressed:

```
@ECHO OFF
CLS
CD \DOS
TYPE DOSMENU
PROMPT $e[14,20H Press the function key corresponding to your choice
```

The DOSMENU screen is shown in *Fig. 10-10*.

As you can see, the function keys are used to select choices from this menu as well, which poses no problem. The function keys retain their reassigned values. The only difference is that, in the DOS subdirectory, the batch files 1.BAT through 8.BAT contain different commands.

For example, the 2.BAT file corresponds to the FORMAT.BAT file described in chapter 6. Pressing the F8 key returns the user to the Main Menu. The 8.BAT file contains the

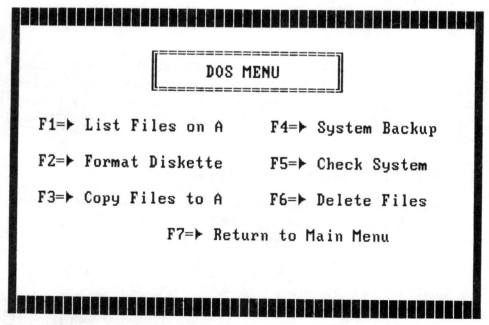

Fig. 10-10. DOS menu using function keys.

necessary commands to return the user to the root directory, and then call the MAIN-MENU batch file to redisplay the Main Menu.

SUMMARY

Using the menu strategy covered in this chapter, you can create a complete menu system including submenus, help screens, etc., all using function keys. When combined with borders, colors, and special video effects, your menus will rival those of professional programs.

Most of the magic here is done via the PC's built-in graphics character set and ANSI.SYS. To use the graphics characters, which are part of the Extended ASCII characters, you need a word processor that allows you to enter their values using the Alt-keypad trick—or EDLIN. To make calls to the powerful functions of ANSI.SYS, you need to install that file in your computer's CONFIG.SYS file located in your root directory.

There is a special feeling that comes from creating your own, customized applications. If you have ever written a simple Lotus macro or dBASE command file, you have experienced this feeling. Just think how proud you'll be to show off your slick, integrated menu system. Your computing buddies will be impressed!

11
DOS Shells

NOW THAT YOU'VE learned how the disk structure of your computer is organized and have developed your own menu system, you can consider some really serious applications. In other words, welcome to the "big time."

Ever since DOS reared its ugly head in 1981, enterprising individuals have sought to improve it. These improvements vary in approach. Some alterations are menu systems to replace DOS, very similar to what you've worked on in the past few chapters, and others use graphics to hide DOS's homely face. But all of the applications have one goal in mind: Making the computer easier to use, and the hard disk easier to manage.

This chapter looks at two different, but related, topics. First, you'll learn about *menu generators*. These programs help you create fancy menu systems in a fraction of the time of doing them yourself, giving you that professional-look without sacrificing your input. Second, you'll discover how DOS *shells*, programs that insulate you from the harsh operating system, can revolutionize your use of DOS.

ORDERING FROM THE MENU

In the last three chapters, you learned how to use the techniques of batch file programming to develop a professional-looking menu system for accessing programs and executing DOS commands. As you can imagine, menu-driven hard disk systems, especially ones using function keys, are quick, efficient, and easy to use. Also, fully menu-driven systems loaded automatically at system startup keep the user out of DOS.

As you have seen, menu-driven hard disk management systems can range from the simple to the elaborate. A well designed menu system includes attractive, eye-catching menu screens, submenus, and help screens to assist the user working with the system. A menu system designed to be used by novice computer users should contain one or more DOS submenus to automate those few DOS commands the user will need. In addition, password security might be a consideration when several users will be sharing the system.

So far, the advantages of menu-driven systems have been highlighted without consideration for the disadvantages. However, the only real disadvantage to menu-driven systems is that they are time-consuming to create.

Unless you have a word processor capable of drawing graphics characters and saving text files in ASCII format, you need to create menus and borders with EDLIN. Also, reconfiguring the function keys with the PROMPT command is tedious. Wouldn't it be nice if there were a program designed to create menus for you?

MENU GENERATORS

A menu generator is a program capable of making (generating) a menu system for you. You tell the generator what you want, and it designs the menus for you, or gives you the tools to easily do so yourself. Additionally, these programs come with options and features that make them more powerful than anything you could do with EDLIN on a good day.

There are several menu generator programs available. One of these, AUTOMENU, is a shareware program that is provided on the supplemental programs diskette offered with this book.

AUTOMENU, and programs like it, helps you draw menu screens, set up batch files for changing directories and loading programs, and have their own keyboard reconfiguration schemes. Many menu generator programs also include password security, which allows you to restrict access to programs or data.

Menu generator programs take much of the drudgery out of setting up menu-driven systems. AUTOMENU is so easy to use, you might wonder why you had to wade through the last three chapters on batch file programming. Actually, a menu generator assumes some understanding of DOS and batch files. Although you don't have to write the batch file programs yourself, you're actually programming when you use a menu generator.

Closely related to menu generators are programs that simplify the use of DOS. These programs sit between you and DOS and provide menus or simplified versions of the DOS commands you need to manage your disks and files. Such program shells are sometimes called DOS *front ends*.

DOS shells use a *user interface* that is easy to work with. The interface enables the user to load programs, delete and rename files, and move between subdirectories and disks by pointing at the file or subdirectory and then pointing at the desired function. Examples of several commercial DOS shells are listed near the end of this chapter. In fact, one of the most useful DOS shells, DOSSHELL, comes free with DOS version 4.

AUTOMENU

The AutoMenu program, from Magee Enterprises, is a powerful, easy-to-use menu generator. Besides the menu generating capability, the package includes several other features, including password security and data encryption. (Discussion of these two features will be deferred until chapters 14 and 15, which cover password security and data encryption in detail.)

AutoMenu paints your menu screens for you, making menu-creation easy. However, you must adhere to AutoMenu's menu format.

AutoMenu allows up to eight selections per menu. These menu selections are labeled 1 through 8 (logically), and are displayed vertically in a full-screen menu. When building menu screens with AutoMenu, you can add a menu title and optional display information for each of your menu choices. In addition, AutoMenu adds supplemental information to your menu screens, including the date, time, status of special keys (Caps Lock, Num Lock, etc.), and available memory. Finally, AutoMenu provides on-line help describing how to make selections from the menu. The various components of a sample menu screen are shown in *Fig. 11-1*.

```
|-------------------------------------------------------------------------|
|| ===================== COMPUCARD MAIN MENU ===================== ||
|| ||
|| ||
||           -> 1 - Word Processing                               ||
|| ||
||              2 - dBASE III                                     ||
|| ||
||              3 - Lotus 1-2-3                                   ||
|| ||
||              4 - Accounting                                    ||
|| ||
||              5 - Art                                           ||
|| ||
||              6 - DOS Commands                                  ||
|| ||
||              7 - Quit                                          ||
|| ||
|| ||
|| ||
||          For WordStar, Multimate, and ThinkTank                ||
|| =============================================================== ||
|| June 2, 1988 11:40:30 am              SHIFT    Memory: 562 K   ||
|-------------------------------------------------------------------------|
                          Press H for Help
```

Fig. 11-1. Sample menu created with AUTOMENU.

Menu selections are made in one of several ways. The fastest selection is to type the number (not the function key) corresponding to the desired choice. Alternatively, the Up and Down arrow keys can be used to move the pointer to the desired selection. Pressing

Enter causes that numbered choice to be selected. Finally, the space bar can be used to highlight individual selections. Each time the space bar is pressed, the subsequent selection is highlighted. Highlighted options are selected by pressing Enter.

The full-screen, eight-selection, vertical format of AutoMenu's menu screens cannot be altered. However, you can customize the foreground and background colors and intensities. Also, you can create a series of menus, each containing up to eight individual selections. A menu series is not the same as submenus. Instead, it is a set of linked menus accessed by using the PgUp and PgDn keys to move from menu to menu.

Each menu in the series is numbered, and this number is displayed in the upper right corner of the menu screen. With a series of menus, you can provide the user with more than eight selections for a given application or work area.

AutoMenu also supports submenus. Submenus are called as selections from a parent menu. For example, selecting option 1 from the CompuCard Main Menu shown in *Fig. 11-1* displays the Word Processing Menu, which is shown in *Fig. 11-2*. Submenus are accessed from main or parent menus and are used to segregate the various programs and work areas on the disk. Submenus should always contain an option that returns the user to the main or parent menu. In a way, submenus help guide the user through the tree structure of the disk.

The AutoMenu diskette includes a fairly large DOC file which explains many of its features. However, certain important steps in the program are unclear. You'll find the fol-

```
+-------------------------------------------------------------------------+
|| WORD PROCESSING MENU                                                  ||
||=====================================================================  ||
||                                                                       ||
||                  -> 1 - WordStar                                      ||
||                                                                       ||
||                     2 - Multimate                                     ||
||                                                                       ||
||                     3 - ThinkTank                                     ||
||                                                                       ||
||                     4 - Return to Main Menu                           ||
||                                                                       ||
||                                                                       ||
||                                                                       ||
||                                                                       ||
||                                                                       ||
||                                                                       ||
||                                                                       ||
||                     Load WordStar Program                             ||
||=====================================================================  ||
|| June 2, 1988 11:40:31 am                          Memory:  562 K  ||
+-------------------------------------------------------------------------+
```
                        Press H for Help

Fig. 11-2. Submenu created with AUTOMENU.

lowing discussion helpful if you plan to use AutoMenu. The AutoMenu diskette also provides you with a set of sample menus and submenus. The samples can be used to demonstrate the use of AutoMenu. You also can use the files that produce these menus as guides for developing your own menu screens.

Installing AutoMenu

The instructions for installing AutoMenu are quite simple. Installation is accomplished with the use of an installation batch file, INSTALL.BAT. There are a few, self-explanatory questions to answer. You'll be asked to select a name for the subdirectory where the AutoMenu files will be stored. You don't have to create this subdirectory; Auto-Menu will perform this task for you. You also will be asked to enter the name of the subdirectory where your DOS files are located. Next, you'll be asked if your AUTOEX-EC.BAT file creates a path to your DOS subdirectory. Finally, you will be asked if you want AutoMenu loaded automatically at system startup. You should probably answer "No" to this question. Installation takes a few minutes, so be patient.

When you run INSTALL.BAT, AutoMenu copies all the files on the AutoMenu diskette onto your hard disk. Many of these are for illustrative purposes only. After you have the AutoMenu program up and running, you won't need these files. Instead, you can use the following procedure to provide a more streamlined approach to using AutoMenu. Place the AUTOMENU.COM and AUTOTEMP.BAT files into your root directory.

- Place your main menu file (say, MAINMENU.MDF) into the root directory as well.
- Modify your AUTOEXEC.BAT file to include, as its last call, the command AUTOMENU MAINMENU.MDF (or whatever you call your main menu file).
- Place your other submenu files (files with MDF extensions) in the subdirectories that they refer to.
- Finally, remove the original \ AUTOMENU subdirectory from your hard disk.

This procedure will allow you to run AutoMenu without taking up unnecessary disk space. If you need to modify existing menus later, you can run the AUTOMAKE.EXE or AUTOCUST.COM files from your floppy drive. Such modifications should only be necessary on an infrequent basis.

Running AutoMenu

The AutoMenu system uses a program, AUTOMENU.COM, to call up menu screens generated by the AUTOMAKE.EXE program. These menu screens are described in Menu Definition Files, indicated with an MDF extension. The appearance of these screens is dictated by the AUTOMENU.COM program, but certain screen attributes can be altered with the use of the AUTOCUST.COM program. When you install AutoMenu, you are presented with a set of sample MDF files, one of which is called AUTO-MENU.MDF. You also are given an AUTO.BAT file that automatically runs AutoMenu. All you have to do is enter:

```
C > AUTO
```

The AUTOMENU.MDF and other MDF files provide you with a sample menu system to practice with. You also can view the contents of these files to learn how to create your own MDF files.

Play with the sample menus to get a feel for how AutoMenu works. AutoMenu lives up to the documentation claims for an intuitive interface. Selecting menu items is so simple it requires no explanation. Note, however, that the sample menus might contain choices which you won't be able to execute on your computer. The 4.0 version, for example, provides a word processing choice which calls up the IBM Personal Editor. Obviously this choice won't work if you don't have this program installed on your system.

Certain menu choices provide you with a text message at the bottom of the screen. These messages are used to clarify a menu selection. Still other menu choices will prompt you for additional information. For example, the Move choice in the DOS menu asks for the name of the file to move and the location of the move. You will learn how these messages and prompts are implemented in the next section.

One thing to note when working with the sample menus is the menu number in the upper right corner of the screen. The first menu will appear as:

Menu 1 of #

where # is the number of menus in the series. Remember, a menu series does not refer to submenus. Instead, the series is really one large menu broken into a series of screens so no one screen overwhelms the user with too many choices. To move on to the next menu, you use the F10, the PgDn, or the Right Arrow keys. To move backward through the menu series, use the F9, PgUp, or Left Arrow keys. Home selects the first menu in a series, and End selects the last menu.

AutoMenu features a screen *blackout* feature that automatically blanks the screen after a specified period of disuse. Blacking out the screen can prevent your monitor from becoming permanently burned from the menu display. The delay before blackout can be customized to your specifications with AUTOCUST.COM. When the screen is blacked out, a message is displayed on the screen telling the user how to return to the menu. This message also can be customized or disabled entirely.

Designing Your Own AutoMenu Screens

At the heart of the AutoMenu program is a combination menu generator and batch file *engine*. The menu generator draws the menu screens, including the borders, menu title, selections, and descriptions that have been specified by the user. The batch file engine creates the batch files necessary to execute the various menu choices. The menu selections and commands necessary to execute the files are stored in a special MDF file. MDF files are created using the AUTOMAKE facility that comes with AutoMenu.

AutoMenu uses special symbols to indicate the various functions within an MDF file. For example, a * is used to indicate a menu selection. Each entry in the MDF file is preceded by one of the special symbols. *Figure 11-3* shows a typical screen from the AUTO-MAKE utility. This screen includes a portion of the MAINMENU.MDF file used to create the Main Menu (illustrated in *Fig. 11-1*).

Use the AUTOMAKE facility to create your own MDF file. You can access this facility in one of two ways. If you have installed the complete AutoMenu system on your hard disk, use the AUTOMAKE facility by selecting this option from the sample AutoMenu menu that is installed on your hard disk. Just run the AUTO.BAT file to call up this menu and select option 2, "AutoMenu Building Facility."

Alternatively, you can run AUTOMAKE directly from your hard disk or floppy drive. For example, you may not want to keep a copy of the AUTOMAKE.EXE file on your hard disk. In this case, you can insert the AutoMenu diskette in drive A and call up AUTO-MAKE as follows:

```
C > A:AUTOMAKE
```

AUTOMAKE offers three options: create or modify menus, print MDF files, and exit from the program. To create a new MDF file, choose option 1, "Modify an old or start a new Menu Definition File." You will be prompted to enter the name of the file to work with. You can use any filename you want, but you must specify the MDF extension. Path names and drive specifications are permitted. If the MDF file you specify is already present on the disk, the file will be loaded for modification. If the file is not found, AUTOMAKE will assume that you want to create a new file.

The AUTOMAKE program is used like a word processor. It is extremely intuitive. The only feature that might not be obvious is the Insert function.

To insert characters or new lines, the Insert function must be turned on. As you might suspect, this function is toggled on and off with the use of the Ins key. The various special symbols used by AutoMenu are displayed in the bottom of the AUTOMAKE entry screen. As you enter one of these symbols at the beginning of each line, AUTOMAKE displays the function to the left. This display helps you make sure that you are entering the correct symbol for the function you wish to accomplish with that entry.

MDF Information

Functions		
Comment	.	: Set Up CompuCard Main Menu
Title	%	: COMPUCARD MAIN MENU
Selection	*	: Word Processing
Descript	?	: For WordStar, Multimate, and ThinkTank
Load a MDF	@	: WP.MDF
Selection	*	: dBASE III
Password	<	: dbase
Output Msg	>	: Enter name of dbase program to execute
Input	<	
Batch-Res	!	: cd dbase
Batch-Res	!	: dbase %1
Selection	*	: Lotus 1-2-3
Batch-Res	!	: cd lotus

```
===================== MDF Functions =====================
. = Comment      < = Password      + = Batch-NRes    > = Output Msg
% = Title        [ = Time Start    ! = Batch-Res     < = Input
* = Selection    @ = Load a MDF    - = Direct
? = Description                    = = Direct/P       # = End of MDF
=========================================================
```

F1 = Toggle Help ON/OFF   F3 = Insert line   F4 = Delete line   ESC = QUIT

Fig. 11-3. A screen from AUTOMAKE showing entries and special symbols used to create a menu display.

Screen Functions

The special symbols are described in the AutoMenu documentation that comes with the program; however, some additional explanations might serve to clarify certain symbols. The Title symbol (AutoMenu) for example, is more complex than you might think. This symbol can be used more than once in a given MDF file. Each time this symbol is used, it indicates a new menu screen within a series of menu screens.

Remember that you can only have eight menu selections in a single screen. This does not mean that you are limited to eight selections in a single MDF file. Instead, you can define up to eight menu screens in an MDF file, each indicated by a new Title symbol. Each of these menu screens can include up to eight menu selections. This gives you up to 64 menu selections within a single MDF file.

Each time you enter the Title symbol, AutoMenu generates a new menu screen and assigns it a menu number. The menu number is displayed in the upper right as "Menu X of Y," where X is the menu number and Y is the total number of menus in the series. As mentioned in the preceding section, you can move between menu screens by using the PgUp or PgDn keys.

The Selection (*) and Description (?) symbols need little extra explanation. The text that you enter after an * is displayed as one of your menu selections. Again, you can have up to eight selections within a single menu screen. For each menu selection, you can include an optional description by including an entry preceded by a ?. Description entries are displayed at the bottom of the screen and serve to clarify the selection by providing additional explanatory information or instructions.

Command Functions

The commands to execute a particular menu choice follow directly after the Selection entry for that choice. There are five different ways to implement menu selections: Direct (-), Direct/P (=), Batch-Res (!), Batch-NRes (+), and Load a MDF (DOS). Each of these implementations functions differently and has its own advantages and disadvantages.

The Direct and Direct/P functions can only be used to implement a single DOS command, program call, or batch file call for the menu selection where they are linked. At first, this seems extremely limiting, and you might wonder why AutoMenu includes these two options. Actually, these two options are the fastest way to implement menu selections.

As you will see, the Batch options take time to create batch files from the commands included in the MDF file. However, when you implement a menu option with either of the Direct options, the DOS command or program call is executed directly with the Auto-Menu command processor. This execution is useful for loading programs or performing a DOS function, such as deleting or copying a file.

The Direct/P function includes a PAUSE command that asks the user to press a key before returning to the menu that called the DOS command. This option provides a way for information, such as a directory listing, to remain on the screen until the user has had an opportunity to read it.

The two Batch options are used to implement a series of commands by placing them into a batch file. The batch symbols, ! and +, cannot be combined. To implement a given menu selection, you must use an ! or +. The elegance of the AutoMenu program is that it doesn't require a separate batch file for every menu selection. Instead, it creates the necessary batch file to implement a menu item only when that item is selected by the user.

Remember that every batch file takes up space on your hard disk (up to 8K depending upon your DOS and hard disk size). A menu system with a total of 20 menu choices would require 20 batch files using the techniques described in chapter 7. With AutoMenu, you only need one batch file. Of course, AutoMenu must create a batch file each time one is needed. However, this procedure takes almost no time at all.

AutoMenu always uses the same filename for its batch files to ensure that it doesn't clutter up your hard disk with lots of little batch files. AutoMenu calls this file AUTO-TEMP.BAT. This file needs to be available to AUTOMENU.COM, so be sure to include it in the same directory that you run AutoMenu from.

There is a difference between the Batch-Res and the Batch-NRes implementations. In the Batch-Res option, AutoMenu remains resident in memory. When a menu selection is implemented using an !, the user will be returned to the menu where the item was selected.

For example, if an ! is used to move into the LOTUS subdirectory and load Lotus 1-2-3, the user will be returned to the AutoMenu menu when she exits from the Lotus option. Menu selections implemented with a +, on the other hand, returns the user to DOS when the selection is concluded.

The Load a MDF symbol (DOS) is used to call another MDF file. Load a MDF entries call up a submenu defined by the MDF file named in the entry. This file is a Menu Definition File in its own right, and can employ up to eight menu screens each containing up to eight menu items. With the use of Load a MDF options, you can create a virtually unlimited menu system.

Note: If you want to be able to return to the calling menu, be sure to include a "Return to XXX menu" selection in your submenu. This submenu selection should be followed by a Load a MDF call to the calling menu in your MDF file.

Dialog Functions

You can display a series of instructions to the user and accept user input with the use of the Output Msg and Input functions. Text following the Output Msg symbol (>) is displayed on a clear screen. You can have multiple lines of text, and you can skip lines by including >'s with no text after them.

User input can be captured in one of two ways. You can include a set of input options after the Input symbol (<). For example, suppose you want the user to select from one of three drive designators. You could include an Output Msg and an Input function as follows:

> >Please enter the drive you want to use:
> <A:,B:,C:

The three options would be displayed under the output message. The first option, A:, would be highlighted. To select a different option, the user would use the left and right arrow keys to move the cursor onto the appropriate choice. After the desired choice has been highlighted, the user presses Enter to conclude the selection process.

Alternately, the Input function can be used to record user input directly by including a < symbol with no options. Then, whatever the user enters from the keyboard is treated as input. An example of this type of Input function is illustrated below:

> >Please enter the name of the file to delete:
> <

The Input function captures user input and places it into one of the replaceable parameters. For example, if the last two Output/Input implementations were combined with a Direct command, you would have the following sequence:

> >Please enter the drive you want to use:
> <A:,B:,C:
> >Please enter the name of the file to delete:
> <
> -del AutoMenu1 AutoMenu2

This command sequence would prompt the user for the drive to use and place the user's selection into AutoMenu1. Next, the user would be prompted for the name of the file to be deleted. The filename would be placed into AutoMenu2. Finally, the Direct function would execute the DOS command to delete the file from the specified drive.

Figure 11-4 is a listing of the complete MAINMENU.MDF file used to display and implement the CompuCard Main Menu shown in *Fig. 11-2*. Although the menu is elementary, it serves to illustrate all the features of the AutoMenu program. You might find this example helpful in designing your own MDF files.

The first entry is a comment. Comments are used to describe what you are doing. The next entry is the title for the menu. AutoMenu claims that the title will be centered automatically, but this was not the case in version 4.0. Instead, the title had to be centered manually.

The next three entries pertain to the first menu option. The entry, *Word Processing displays the selection "Word Processing" as option 1 in the menu and the entry, ?For

A listing of MAINMENU.MDF printed on 03-18-1987.

```
.Set up CompuCard Main Menu
%                    COMPUCARD MAIN MENU
    *Word Processing
    ?For WordStar, Multimate, and ThinkTank
       @WP.MDF
    *dBASE III
    ^dbase
       >Enter name of dbase program to execute:
       <
       !cd dbase
       !dbase %1
    *Lotus 1-2-3
       !cd lotus
       !lotus
    *Accounting
    ?Run GL, AP, AR, Payroll
       >Enter module to use:
       <GL,AR,AP,PR
       !cd acct
       !bpi %1
    *Art
    ?To access graphics programs and games.
       @ARTMENU.MDF
    *DOS Commands
    ?Directory, Format, Check Disk, etc.
       @DOSMENU.MDF
    *Quit
    ?Backup all altered files and park hard disk.
       +q
 #End of Main Menu
```
Fig. 11-4. Listing of the MAINMENU.MDF file.

WordStar, Multimate, and ThinkTank, displays the description "For WordStar, Multi-mate, and ThinkTank" at the bottom of the menu screen when option 1 is highlighted. The entry, DOS \ WP \ WPMENU.MDF causes the WPMENU.MDF file, located in the WP subdirectory, to be loaded and displayed if option 1 is selected from the CompuCard Main Menu.

The *dBASE III selection displays "dBASE III" as menu option 2. If this option is selected, the user will be prompted to enter a password. This password must match the password, "dbase", in the Password entry indicated by the ^ symbol. If the user passes password check, he will be prompted to "Enter name of dbase program to execute:." The user's input will be captured and stored in AutoMenu1. Then, the DBASE subdirectory will be accessed. Finally, the dBASE III program will be loaded and an optional dBASE command file will be executed by the !dbase AutoMenu1 entry. (Remember, the ! entries will first be assembled into a batch file.)

The *Lotus 1-2-3 selection needs no explanation. The *Accounting selection includes an optional Descript function, ?Run GL, AP, AR, Payroll. This description will be displayed at the bottom of the screen whenever option 4 is highlighted. If option 4 is selected, the user will be prompted to select the module to use: GL, AR, AP, or PR. This selection will be stored in the replaceable parameter AutoMenu1. The ACCT submenu will be accessed and the accounting program, BPI will be executed with the optional module indicator stored in AutoMenu1 (Note: This is for illustrative purposes only. Check your BPI manual if you plan to use this program for any accounting needs.)

The *Art and *DOS command selections function much like the *Word Processing selection because they both load submenu MDF files. The *Quit selection places the descriptive message, "Backup all altered files and park hard disk," and then runs the Q.BAT file. This selection is implemented with the Batch-NRes function (+), rather than the Batch-Res function (!), because you don't want to return to the CompuCard Main Menu after executing this batch file.

The final entry in the MAINMENU.MDF file is the #End of Main Menu line. Make sure you conclude your menus with an End (#) entry.

Password Security and File Encryption

One useful feature of AutoMenu is the password protection feature. Strategies and justifications for the use of password security will be discussed generally in chapter 14, "Password Security." For now, the focus will be on the mechanics of password utilization in AutoMenu. As you read in the preceding section, you can use the Password function (^) to program passwords into your menus. AutoMenu also allows you to issue passwords to your MDF files as well.

Password protection for your MDF files serves two purposes. First, you might not want other individuals to be able to alter your menus after they have been created. Second, if you have included passwords as part of the MDF file, they aren't secure as long as anyone can view the MDF file and read the passwords stored in it.

When you save a newly created MDF file, AUTOMAKE asks you if you wish to protect it with a password. If you supply a password, you will be asked to reenter the password for verification.

Note: Be sure to write your passwords down! Otherwise, you will not be able to get back to your menus to modify them later. After the MDF file is saved with the password you supply, the password must be entered to edit or print the MDF file. The password can be changed by viewing the file and then saving it again with a different password.

AutoMenu menu uses the password you supply to *encrypt* the MDF file as well as lock it. Data encryption is covered in detail in chapter 15, "Hidden Files and Data Encryption." For now, think of encryption as converting the file to a secret code that only AutoMenu can read. After the file has been encrypted, you can't view it with the DOS TYPE command. In fact, the only way you can see the contents of a password protected file is by the use of the AUTOMAKE facility, which requires you to provide the password before decrypting the MDF file.

Installing Your Own Menus

AutoMenu menu defaults to the AUTOMENU.MDF menu file whenever it is run. In order to use your own MDF files, you will have to establish one of them as the parent menu. In the example used in this chapter, the *parent* menu has been the MAIN-MENU.MDF file.

The MDF file can contain entries to load other MDF files. These *child* MDF files provide you with access to submenus and can contain entries to load still other MDF files. Each child MDF file should contain an entry that returns the user to the preceding level, so there is always a path back to the parent menu. The parent menu might or might not contain an option to return the user to DOS, depending on the way you want your users to access the computer system.

After your system of MDF files has been established, you can move the children MDF files to their appropriate subdirectories. Again, the only files you need to retain in your root directory are the AUTOMENU.COM file, the AUTOTEMP.BAT file, and your parent MDF file. To run your parent MDF file, enter the call for AutoMenu followed by the filename of the parent menu (be sure to include the MDF extension). For example, to run the MAINMENU.MDF file, the command would be:

```
C>AUTOMENU MAINMENU.MDF
```

You can include this command as part of your AUTOEXEC.BAT file. Now, whenever the computer is turned on or rebooted, your menu will be loaded automatically. If you have not included menu options that return the user to DOS, loading the parent menu from system startup effectively locks the user into the menu system. This result might be desirable, especially if password protection has been implemented to lock out users from certain applications or work areas.

Of course, the AUTOEXEC batch file can always be circumvented by booting off one of the computer's floppy drives. There are ways of hiding what's on the hard disk, however, so that this trick does the unknowing user little, if any good.

DOS SHELLS AND FRONT ENDS

For many years, personal computer users had to deal with their computers' operating systems much the way users on large systems did. Personal computer operating systems mimicked the command structure of mini and mainframe computers. DOS is a descendant of an earlier microcomputer operating system, CP/M, which itself has antecedents in the larger computer world.

Operating systems that rely on single character prompts, terse commands, and cryptic error messages in computerese might be fine for macho computing types (who read assembly language programs with their Cap'n Crunch at breakfast), but what about the rest of us?

Apple Computer recognized that not everyone is as adventurous as those bold computer frontiersmen who stride forward to conquer the uncharted realms of DOS with nothing but their ten digits and a box of Ding Dongs to sustain them. In fact, the Apple Macintosh revolutionized the way personal computer users looked at computing. The *user interface* took on an entirely different meaning. No longer did users have to struggle with DEL *.*'s, COPY PROG.BAS B:/V's, and "Invalid command or file not found" 's. Instead, users can look at cute little pictures on the screen, play with friendly mice, and point at what they want.

Actually, the *icon*-based interface popularized by the Macintosh was developed as a large computer interface by a research team at XEROX. However, the prevailing reaction to such a "cutesy" interface was: "*Real* men don't use icons!" And so the project languished until it was revived by the Apple Lisa. DOS users were quick to jump on the user-friendly bandwagon, and a host of products designed to simplify DOS were released. Most of these fell into one of two categories: shells and front ends.

DOS shells actually sit on top of DOS. They display their own, easy to use interface. When the user indicates the command to be executed, the shell program performs the steps necessary to accomplish the command. Usually, this involves passing parameters down to DOS and having DOS do the actual work.

Windows, a program by Microsoft (who ironically gave us DOS), is an example of a DOS shell. Windows uses graphics and windows on the screen, and employs cute icons and friendly dialog boxes to represent operating system activities such as deleting files. With the addition of an optional mouse, this user-friendly program converts your PC into something suspiciously resembling an Apple Macintosh. Digital Research's GEM operating shell provided an even more similar environment.

DOS front ends, on the other hand, are little more than window dressing for the DOS operating system itself. User commands are handled directly by DOS; only the interface has been changed to protect the naive. Front ends make DOS easier to use without disguising the basic nature of the operating system itself. Files are still represented by their filenames, extensions and all, and commands retain their DOS nomenclature (COPY is still Copy, etc.).

Although the subject of windows, icons, and mice is an interesting one, and something you might consider looking into, it's not really a practical way to go. For one, computers must be equipped with top notch graphics displays to make everything look good. The standard graphics adapters make those fancy windows and icons look like mush. Also, without the mouse, using these programs is even more clumsy than using DOS. Sure, it's a cute picture on the screen. But cute doesn't help get the job done if you still have to explain details to the person using the computer.

Commercial DOS shells are better than Window applications. These are professional packages that lie somewhere between AutoMenu and that ugly DOS prompt we've been avoiding all chapter.

New commercial shell programs come out just about every week. The proliferator is usually some person in a data processing department who's sick of making the rounds, reexplaining DOS commands. They come up with their own easy-to-use menu scheme and try to sell it. Without knocking the multitudes who have done this (and trust us, I looked at a lot of this software before deciding on four winners), most of their DOS shells are similar. And they're boring.

Basically, the bottom line is making the computer easier to use. This process is usually done in a DOS shell by displaying a menu of applications or categories. Submenus usually contain the programs to run. The better DOS shells also have their own utilities, including some fancy file rescue utilities that might come in handy. Also included are methods for tracking computer usage, password protection, and the facilities for redesigning or creating your own custom menus.

For this book, we've chosen three such DOS shells that you might be interested in:

- Direct Access
- The Norton Commands
- DOSSHELL

These programs were chosen from the crowd because of their interesting methods of accomplishing jobs, features, presentation, ability for a DOS guru such as yourself to use them, ability for a nonDOS guru to use them, and their longevity. With the exception of DOSSHELL, each of the programs has been around for a time and will, doubtless, be around even when this book hits middle age. Because DOSSHELL is included free with DOS version 4, it will be around for sometime to come as well.

Direct Access

Direct Access is one of the oldest DOS shell/menu programs around. Not only is it one of the oldest (a program named 1DIR is older), it is consistently a best seller for years. There's a reason for this, Direct Access does the job and does it well.

```
        W E L C O M E    T O    T H E    M A I N    M E N U

            Good Afternoon...Please Enter Your Selection

            ┌──────────────────────────────────────────┐
            │                                            │
            │         A) Spreadsheet & Graphics          │
            │         B) Word Processing                 │
            │         C) Data Base Management            │
            │         D) DOS Utilities                   │
            │         E) Programming                     │
            │         F) Miscellaneous                   │
            │                                            │
            └──────────────────────────────────────────┘


            F1 Menu Maintenance           F10 Exit To DOS

        ═ Firday  August 30, 1991 ═══════════ 1:55:08 pm ═
```

Fig. 11-5. Direct Access's main menu uses a simple, easy-to-follow design.

Direct Access is low on the frills department. There are no graphics, no poppity-zippity sounds, and no exploding windows. You just see a menu with options, as in *Fig. 11-5*.

You have to build your own main menu and connecting submenus. But this isn't a problem. The menu creation screens are logically laid out and easy to follow. What you see when you're done is a clean screen, perhaps with some hints of colors (very tastefully done), and your menu options. Novices pick up on the procedure very quickly. In fact, Direct Access is the preferred choice of many educational institution's computer labs, as well as software stores for running demos.

Direct Access also offers password protection for certain menu items, as well as time usage tracking. Password protection comes in handy on computers used by multiple users, as demonstration, or lab computers. The usage tracking can be used on single computers used by multiple users to determine how much time is being used by whom and for what. On computers used by one person, usage tracking can be used for billing purposes and, for curiosity's sake, just to see what you do on your computer.

The only major ticket item lacking from Direct Access is any file manipulation utilities. However, this isn't a drawback. You can add any utility on your hard drive to a Direct Access submenu. Overall, Direct Access is a very competent and clean DOS shell.

Direct Access
Delta Technology International
P.O. Box 1104
Eau Claire, WI 54702

The Norton Commander

Where Direct Access is simple, elegant, and uncomplicated, the Norton Commander's strength lies in its kitchen-sinkness. The program is definitely for utility lovers, as well as hard disk manipulator types. True, its a DOS shell, but the shell part is hard to see through the fancy displays, the many commands, options, and various utilities tossed into the program. No, it's not really messy. But it's not for the DOS fainters either.

The strength of the Norton Commander lies in its 747 cockpit approach to working with your hard disk. You have at your disposal the DOS prompt for entering commands, a pull-down menu system at the top of the display, a left or right (or both) panel system for displaying files or information about files, and a row of function key options at the bottom of the screen. (The screen is depicted in *Fig. 11-6*.) If you have a mouse, the Norton Commander will sense its presence and even let you use it to manipulate the commands.

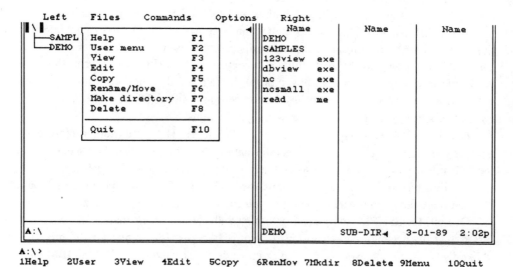

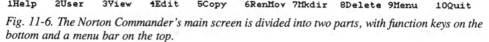

Fig. 11-6. The Norton Commander's main screen is divided into two parts, with function keys on the bottom and a menu bar on the top.

A few beginning users will probably shy away from the Norton Commander because of its complexities. This is too bad. Yes, you really do need to read the manual to find out what's going on. But, contrary to what's popular in the field of computer manuals, this one is pretty good—even funny in spots. So you can get out of the program whatever you like. It is even customizable, allowing you to install your own programs and options.

The bottom line on the Norton Commander is that it is a utility lover's DOS shell. If you're into having a handful of interesting programs, features, and options always available as you run your computer, then the Norton Commander is worth looking into—especially if you feel a simple menu program such as Direct Access doesn't do enough for you. (They're actually at opposite ends of the DOS shell spectrum.)

The Norton Commander
Peter Norton Computing
2210 Wilshire Blvd., Ste 186
Santa Monica, CA 90403

DOS 4's DOSSHELL

Because DOS 4 is a new version of DOS, IBM really had to make a splash to lure PC users to the new operating system. DOS 4 offers the use of expanded memory, hard disk partitions of unlimited size, customizable menu setup and installation, and a free, graphic user shell, DOSSHELL. It's much better than anything you could create with batch files, but it still has a way to go to compete with some of the other shells out there.

DOSSHELL is a graphics-based shell using windows and menus to display information, although on monochrome and nonIBM displays it is used in the character mode only (in fact, so far it only works well with and recognizes official IBM equipment, though it can be tweaked to work with a nonIBM mouse). It offers a full set of shell features, including DOS utilities, and password protection on certain options. DOSSHELL also is customizable, letting you enter your own menus and options.

Figure 11-7 shows a typical display in DOSSHELL. There are graphic representations of your disk's tree structures, plus information about files on disk. The menu on top the screen is used to activate options and help is always available via the F1 key.

Applications, or batch files, can be installed in DOSSHELL's main menu as a group. You can run them from the main menu, or you can choose them from the graphic display.

Overall, DOSSHELL is interesting to play with. However, its major detracting feature is that it's not intuitive—even for PC pros. There just isn't a feel for the program, unlike Direct Access or even the Norton Commander. Also, unless you have an IBM computer, IBM display, IBM printer, and IBM mouse, it's not friendly to your hardware. Later, hopefully, some developers will come out with drivers for popular displays (such as Hercules) and printers. Until then, DOSSHELL is an IBM-only program. Hopefully (if they keep making DOS), better versions of it will come out in the future.

SUMMARY

This concludes this chapter, as well as Part I of *Hard Disk Management with MS-DOS and PC-DOS*. By now, you should be comfortable with the terms and concepts of hard disks and file organization. You've learned a number of DOS commands related specifically to hard disk management, and you've seen how you can use the techniques of batch file programming to control access to your programs and data files.

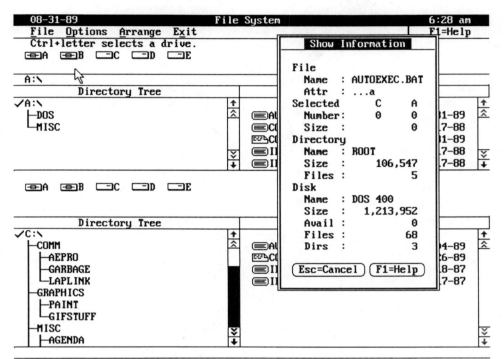

Fig. 11-7. DOSSHELL uses graphics to display information, such as the two disk listings and file information shown here.

Throughout this and the last few chapters, you've been shown several methods for creating customized, professional-looking menu screens for guiding yourself and others through the intricacies of your hard disk tree structure. Finally, you have read about commercially available alternatives to DOS for managing your programs and files.

Unfortunately, there is more to hard disk management than the tasks of organizing and accessing programs and data. There are two other important issues of concern to owners of hard disk owners: hard disk security, which includes data backup security, file access security, password protection, data encryption, and other topics related to the security of your data; and hard disk optimization, which is the methods and practices that will extend the performance, reliability, and life of your computer system.

PART TWO
Hard Disk Security

HARD DISK SECURITY isn't all passwords, secret codes, locking out prying eyes, and tossing a bundle of backup diskettes into a fire safe every night at five o'clock. It is a software (as well as hardware) solution to maintaining the integrity of your data. After all, you've worked hard and put a lot of effort into the information stored on your system. This part of the book will show you how to sleep sounder at night knowing that information is safely kept.

12

Backing Up Data and Programs

BY NOW YOU should have your hard disk set up just the way you want. You've learned about DOS commands, subdirectories, batch files, shells, and the menu programs. You're probably enjoying the comfort, speed, and efficiency of your hard drive every day. Everything works fine. You couldn't be more happy. Until . . .

It's that "until" you should worry about. Hard disks perform so flawlessly that most of the time you can just forget about them. And with the advances in technology, hard drives have become much more reliable than in past years. Still problems might occasionally happen.

When a problem does pop up, you need to be prepared for it. You shouldn't try to fix your hard drive yourself. However, there are several things you can do in case something does go wrong.

In this chapter preventive maintenance is introduced, which includes steps you can take to better prepare yourself for a potential mishap. DOS provides two programs for this, BACKUP and RESTORE. The RESTORE command is used in conjunction with BACKUP as part of that "just in case."

Also discussed in this chapter are two other DOS programs hard disk owners might find invaluable, XCOPY and REPLACE. Finally, numerous hard disk manufacturers include a program called PARK with their hard disk. This program adds a defensive level to hard disk protection, dealing with problems other programs do not touch.

PREVENTIVE MAINTENANCE

There are several reasons for backing up important data. For one, it is valuable. Whether your data consists of numbers in a spreadsheet, names and addresses in a mailing list or customer database, or important word processing documents, time was spent to enter the data.

Although some of the information on your hard disk could be reentered into the computer, at a tremendous loss of time and money, a greater amount is probably original and irreplaceable data. Like most valuables you own, you should have an insurance policy to protect your data just in case. The BACKUP program is that insurance policy.

BACKUP provides a safety copy of your data by transferring the information on your hard disk to floppy diskettes. BACKUP makes efficient use of the floppies, filling each to capacity, not wasting one byte of space on the disk. After the operation is complete, you have an extra copy—an exact duplicate—of the data already on the hard drive. If anything should happen to the hard drive now, say a hardware failure or disk crash, you still have a copy of your valuable data.

To new computer users, backing up a hard disk might seem like a frivolous task to do. After all, the data is already stored on the hard disk, why waste time making a duplicate? Backing up takes time and requires someone to manually insert floppy disks during the backup procedure. With all the benefits of having a duplicate copy of your data, you might think every hard disk owner would regularly perform backups. But that's not the case.

The importance of making backups cannot be overemphasized. If you don't back up your data, you are taking an unwise and unnecessary risk. After all, if (the big IF) something happens, you'd feel much better about sitting there, wasting your time and 50 diskettes backing up the hard drive.

General rules to follow when backing up your data are:

- Backup files used each day at the end of the day
- At the end of the week, back up the entire hard disk

As an example of the first rule, consider Jack at CompuCard. Each day he updates his customer data base. At the end of the day, he'll back up all the customer files to diskette for safekeeping. Because these files are in their own subdirectory, this operation is relatively easy to perform (yet another advantage of having subdirectories).

Friday afternoon, as CompuCard is wrapping up the week, the designated BACKUP employee (probably Sue) sits down and backs up the entire hard disk. This way, changes, additions, or modifications to any file on the hard disk are saved.

At CompuCard, each employee is responsible for making backups of their work every day. At the end of the week, the entire hard disk is backed up. This same approach to backing up should be followed by anyone using a hard disk.

Now consider a hard disk crash. Recalling from chapter 1, a hard disk crash happens when the disk's read/write head literally crashes into the surface of the disk. The resulting collision scratches the surface of the disk, rendering it unusable.

If the hard disk ups and dies early on Monday, the data backed up from Friday will provide a full replacement. Because the entire disk was backed up, nothing new was added and nothing needs to be replaced. After the problem is fixed, the backed up data is simply restored back to the hard disk. The only time that is lost is when the computer is *down*.

If a hard disk crash occurred on Wednesday, the problem still isn't that bad. First, there's the complete backup made on Friday. Second, individual employees should have made their own backups on Monday and Tuesday. If this were the computer in the order entry department, and backups of all orders taken the first two days of the week were made, a full replacement of the hard disk should be available. (Combine the two daily backups with the full backup from Friday.) Only information that wasn't backed up Monday and Tuesday, say a memo or the high score of a game played during lunch break, would be lost.

THE BACKUP COMMAND

The purpose of the BACKUP command is to copy all information from the hard drive (or a large volume disk) onto floppy diskettes. BACKUP can be a specific program, all files from the hard drive, or just those files you choose. BACKUP could be by subdirectory, date and time of last backup, or files modified since the last backup. BACKUP copies files to floppy diskettes for archiving. When one diskette fills up, the BACKUP program asks you to insert another. The procedure is repeated until all the files you've specified have been backed up.

Note: BACKUP is not the same as COPY.

BACKUP deals with *archiving* files—storing them "just in case." The files on a BACKUP disk are neatly packed into a special file format. That format is readable only by DOS's RESTORE program. The backed up files are there, but to allow them to be restored to the same location on disk, plus to allow for files to be backed up and restored by date and time, extra information is stored with each file. This procedure makes them different from files copied to diskettes using the COPY command. The format of the BACKUP command is:

BACKUP d:path[filename][.ext] d: [/S][/M][/A][/D:][/T:][/F][L:filespec]

(DOS 3.3 adds the last three options. Earlier versions of DOS used only the first four switches, /S through /D:. Some versions of MS-DOS use a /P switch, which is briefly covered later in this chapter.)

The first item listed after the BACKUP command is the disk drive you're backing up, followed by a path designator. This drive is referred to as the *source* drive. The second item is the disk drive where you're backing up, or the *target* drive. The source can be a single file, group of files, a subdirectory, or the entire tree structure of the hard drive. The target will always be a single drive, which is normally your A drive, although B drive also can be used if you have one.

The source drive cannot be write protected, otherwise the backup will fail. Also, if your computer is part of a networked system, BACKUP will not archive programs you don't have access to. Refer to your network guide for more information.

An Example

The following command is used to back up files from the hard drive to a floppy diskette in drive A, assuming the diskette is formatted:

C>BACKUP C:\ *.* A:

The source drive is drive C, specifically all the files in the root directory of drive C. The target drive is drive A. The path doesn't need to be specified for the target drive, but is necessary for the source. After all, you need to tell BACKUP which files you want to back up. After pressing Enter, you'll see the following message displayed:

Insert backup diskette 01 in drive A:

Warning! Files in the target drive
A:\ root directory will be erased
Strike any key when ready

The computer will beep, warning you that any information already on the target disk will be erased. If you haven't already done so, insert a freshly formatted or reusable diskette into drive A and press the spacebar or Enter key. DOS then begins archiving all the files from the root directory of drive C to the floppy diskette in drive A. The following displayed on the screen:

*** Backing up files to drive A: ***
Diskette Number: 01

\ IBMBIO.COM
\ IBMDOS.COM
\ COMMAND.COM
\ CONFIG.SYS
\ AUTOEXEC.BAT

BACKUP always lets you know what it's doing. In the last list, BACKUP lets you know that it's backing up to the first diskette. Then, as it copies each file from the source, it lists that file's full pathname. If another diskette is required, BACKUP prompts you to insert it:

Insert backup diskette 02 in drive A:

Warning! Files in the target drive
A: \ root directory will be erased
Strike any key when ready

Note: BACKUP numbers the target diskettes sequentially. In fact, you should put the numbers on the diskette labels before you back up. (This assists you in the RESTORE operation, covered later in this chapter.)

One nice thing about the previous warning message is that it beeps at you. This way, you can be off doing something else and simply wait to hear the beep, then return to the computer and insert the next diskette. When the entire BACKUP is complete, you'll be returned to DOS.

Before you do your own backup, here are a few important tips to remember that apply to all backup situations. (The last example only backed up the root directory of the hard drive. Later you'll see how an entire hard disk is backed up):

- All files in the target drive's root directory are erased by the BACKUP command.
- The disks you back up to should be formatted before you start the BACKUP procedure (although there is a way around this, as you'll see later).
- If you don't specify a directory for the source drive, only the files in the current directory are backed up. BACKUP C: A: only backs up those files in the current directory on drive C.
- Backing up to 360K floppies requires a lot of diskettes. The multiplication factor is thirty 360K floppy diskettes for every ten megabytes of hard disk storage. That means 60 disks are required for a full 20M hard disk backup. The 1.2M drives are more space efficient. You'll generally use only one 1.2M diskette per megabyte of hard disk storage. The same holds for the 720K and 1.44M 3^1/$_2$-inch diskettes, although they're more expensive than the 5^1/$_4$-inch variety.
- You should number and date the diskettes you're using for the backup. Use them in order. When finished, keep them together with a rubber band and store them in a safe place.

What Happens Behind the Scenes

The BACKUP program is not like COPY. In fact, from the BACKUP example, the following is a directory listing of the files on the target diskette after the backup operation was completed:

```
Volume in drive A is BACKUP 001
Directory of A: \

BACKUP      001      53281     8-31-91     11:41p
CONTROL     001        345     8-31-91     11:41p
2 File(s)    1159680 bytes free
```

Yes, five files were backed up. And it's true, there are only two files on the backup diskette. In fact, that's the maximum number of files you'll always have on any backup diskette—no matter how many files were backed up to it. Remember, BACKUP stores all the source files in one large file, which is named BACKUP.001. Only the RESTORE program can pull those files out. (So you see, I wasn't kidding when I said BACKUP isn't the same thing as COPY!)

Behind the scenes, the first thing BACKUP does is erase every file from the root directory of the target drive. It then gives the diskette a new label, equivalent to the sequential number of the backup diskette. In the last example, the diskette was given the label, BACKUP 001 to help keep track of the diskette.

Next, BACKUP creates two files on the target diskette: BACKUP.XXX and CONTROL.XXX. XXX is the number of the backup diskette, the same number value that appears in the diskette's label.

The BACKUP.XXX file contains all the files to be backed up. Each file is copied into the single BACKUP.XXX file, one after the other. The locations of the files in BACKUP.XXX are kept in CONTROL.XXX. However, to the untrained eye, BACKUP.XXX is simply a long string of files chained together.

The CONTROL.XXX file contains information about all the files held in the BACKUP.XXX file. Information inside CONTROL.XXX includes the file's subdirectory (its original location on the source drive), name, location in the BACKUP.XXX file, and date and time of the backup. Also included is information on whether or not the file is split between two backup diskettes, which will happen when a file is too big to fit on one diskette.

By using these two files, BACKUP is overcoming the limitation on the number of files in a diskette's root directory. Normally, if BACKUP simply copied files to the target disk, after 112 files (on a 360K floppy) the diskette would be "full," even if tons of space remains. Two files will always fit on a diskette, with the BACKUP.XXX file expanding to fill the available space.

Note: The contents of these two files hold meaning only to the RESTORE program (covered later in this chapter). A user—even an advanced user—cannot extract the backed up programs and files from BACKUP.XXX. Also, this efficient BACKUP program (DOS version 3.3) is 100 percent incompatible with previous versions of BACKUP. Older

BACKUP programs cannot read DOS 3.3's BACKUP files, nor can DOS 3.3's BACKUP read older DOS's files. So, back up your hard disk with the same version of BACKUP as RESTORE. You can't cross DOS version numbers here.

Backing Up an Entire Disk

The previous example had some limitations. The biggest one is that only files in the root directory of the source drive were backed up. Normally, the entire contents of the hard disk are backed up. Use BACKUP's /S option, or "switch," to back up the entire hard drive.

```
C > BACKUP C: \ *.* A: /S
```

The /S switch tells BACKUP to back up all the files starting with the path specified as the source and including all subdirectories and files under it. In the above command, all files from drive C's root directory, and all files in any subdirectories under the root directory will be backed up to drive A. The command will perform a complete backup of the hard drive.

Before entering the command, you should prepare a stack of diskettes. These diskettes should be formatted and labeled with numbers indicating the order of the diskettes. After pressing Enter, follow the instructions on the screen, inserting each new diskette as BACKUP calls for it.

The /S switch doesn't necessarily have to be used with the entire hard drive. You can use it to back up any branch of your hard disk's tree structure. For example, suppose you have a subdirectory \ WP containing your word processor. Under \ WP you have several additional subdirectories, each containing various memos, letters, short stories, poems, and essays. To back up \ WP and all its subdirectories, use:

```
C > BACKUP C: \ WP \ *.* A: /S
```

Like the COPY command, wildcards can be used with BACKUP to archive only specific files. Suppose you have one, large subdirectory on your hard disk that contains all your Lotus 1-2-3 spreadsheets. To back up only the spreadsheets (with the WKS file extension), use:

```
C > BACKUP C: \ LOTUS \ *.WKS A:
```

In this example, only the files with the WKS extension are backed up. The /S switch is not needed in this case. If /S were included, all subdirectories under \ LOTUS and all files in those subdirectories would have been archived as well.

Backup's Switches

The /S switch is referred to as the subdirectory switch. This switch translates into "back up everything in the indicated directory, as well as any subdirectories in the directory."

BACKUP has several other switches to help simplify and tidy the backup process. With these switches, you can get specific about which files to back up. These switches can be used in any combination to make for an efficient backup system.

/M. The /M switch is used to back up only those files modified since the last backup. Every file on disk has a special bit associated with its directory entry called the *modify* bit. (This information is not displayed by the standard DIR command.) When a file is backed up, the BACKUP program sets this bit to 0. If the file is accessed or changed after the backup, DOS changes the modify bit to a 1.

When /M is specified, BACKUP archives only those files modified since the last backup:

    C > BACKUP C: \ *.* A: /M

The backup proceeds as before, directing you to insert backup diskettes as required until the process is completed.

    C > BACKUP C: \ LOTUS \ *.WKS A: /M

This /M switch makes a backup of only the files with the extension WKS that have been modified since the last backup. This is an example of a periodic or daily backup procedure. If a backup of the entire hard drive is made once a week, then this example could be used daily to back up only the modified files.

/A. The /A switch adds files to the backup disk. Normally, BACKUP erases all files on the root directory of the target disk. When the /A switch is used, the files backed up are added to the files already on the target disk.

    C > BACKUP C: \ MYBOOK \ CHAPT1?.* A: /A

This example backs up all files named CHAPT1?.* to the disk in drive A, adding those files to any files already found there. The disk in drive A must be the last (highest numbered) disk from any previous backup.

To start the backup, DOS prompts:

    Insert last backup diskette in drive A:
    Strike any key when ready

DOS adds the files specified on the source to those already on the target. Even if the files are of the same name, they are still appended to the BACKUP.XXX file on the target. (You can, however, pull out individual versions of the files using RESTORE.)

A good example of using the /A switch is when updating a single (or only a few) files at the end of a work day. For example, suppose you're working on a novel and presently stuck on chapter 12. After each day's work, you run the following batch file:

```
@ECHO OFF
ECHO Insert your backup disk into drive A
BACKUP CHAPT10 A: /A
ECHO Done!
```

The first day, the directory of the backup diskette might be:

```
Volume in drive A is BACKUP 001
Directory of A: \

BACKUP      001 53281    9-01-91    5:24a
CONTROL     001   345    9-01-91    5:24a
    2 File(s)    1159680 bytes free
```

The second day, after you've backed up using the /A switch, the directory might look like this:

```
Volume in drive A is BACKUP 001
Directory of A: \

BACKUP      001     106562   9-02-91    5:45a
CONTROL     001        551   9-02-91    5:45a
    2 File(s)    1105920 bytes free
```

Each day, the BACKUP.001 file gets bigger and bigger because you keep appending CHAP12 to it. The nice part about this scheme is that, with RESTORE, you can pull any of the individual chapters out of the BACKUP.001 file at any time, so you can see the way your work looked earlier in the week. (Under normal circumstances, when you don't want to resurrect a file like that, you need not use the /A switch.)

/D. The /D switch backs up only those files created or modified on or after a certain date. This option is not the same as the /M switch. Even if a file might have been backed up since the date listed, it will still be backed up when the /D switch is specified.

```
C>BACKUP C: \ DATABASE \ CUST*.DAT A: /D:10-19-91
```

Only the customer files (CUST*.DAT) created or modified after October 19th, 1991 are backed up to drive A. The /D switch looks at the date of the file (which is seen in the DIR listing). If that date is the same as or later than the date listed after /D, the file is backed up.

C > BACKUP C: \ *.* A: /S/D:9-04-91

BACKUP archives all files on the hard disk C: (because of the /S switch) dated on or after September 4th, 1991.

The /P, /T, /F, and /L Switches. The /P switch was used in older versions of MS-DOS only, not PC-DOS. This difference is one of the few subtle items that separate each of the brands of DOS. The /P option packed files on the backup diskette, and allowed more files to be added per diskette. The use of this option should be avoided because implementing it will make your system non-PC-DOS compatible.

The /T switch is used like the /D switch except that /T specifies a specific time on or after which files should be backed up. When using both /D and /T, you can get down to the minute when selecting files to back up.

C > BACKUP C: \ WORK \ PROJECTS \ *.* A: /S/T:10:54

This command will back up all files in the \ WORK \ PROJECTS subdirectory on drive C, and any files or subdirectories in it, that were created or modified on or after 10:54 in the morning. Because a date wasn't specified, BACKUP will back up any file created on or after that time, regardless of which day it was created on.

If you want to back up only those files created or modified since 3:15 this afternoon (if today is 11-30-91), you could use:

C > BACKUP C: \ *.* A: /S/D:11-30-91/T:15:15

Note: 24-hour military time is used to identify the time (15:00 hours).

The /F switch causes BACKUP to recognize an unformatted disk and immediately execute the FORMAT.COM program (providing you have it in a subdirectory on the PATH). BACKUP will format the disk, and ask if you need any others formatted before continuing with the backup.

Note: If you don't specify /F and encounter an unformatted diskette, or you run out of diskettes, you have to start the backup procedure all over again. (With DOS version 4, there is no /F switch; BACKUP will automatically format a diskette if it is unformatted.)

The /L switch is used to create a backup log file. /L is followed by a colon and the pathname for a file to contain information about the backup. If a filename isn't included, a file BACKUP.LOG is created in the root directory of the source drive.

A typical BACKUP.LOG file contains the following kind of information:

```
9-1-1991     5:59:35
001     \ BOOKS \ CHAPT1.DOC
001     \ BOOKS \ CHAPT2.DOC
001     \ BOOKS \ CHAPT3.DOC
001     \ BOOKS \ CHAPT4.DOC
001     \ BOOKS \ CHAPT5.DOC
```

The first entry shows the date and time of the backup. The remaining entries list the diskette number and the pathname of the files on that diskette. Each time you back up, new information is appended to the BACKUP.LOG file. You can use the log file created to keep track of the file's locations, or simply for verification purposes.

THE RESTORE COMMAND

After you've done a daily or weekly backup, you should store your diskettes in a safe place. Normally there is no need to use these diskettes—they're just there for insurance. Hard disks are fairly robust and perform flawlessly. However, if something does go wrong, or if you've accidentally deleted a file, you need to restore the archived file from your backup diskettes with the RESTORE command.

The format of the RESTORE command is:

RESTORE d: [d:][path]filename[.ext] [/P][/M][/S][/B][/A][/E][/L][/N]

The first item listed after RESTORE is the disk drive containing your backup diskettes. The second item tells RESTORE which files need to be restored. This file can be a single file, a group of files using a wildcard, a subdirectory, or the entire tree structure of a disk drive.

If your computer is part of a network system, the RESTORE program will not restore programs you currently do not have access to. Refer to your network guide for more information.

After you start RESTORE, it asks:

Insert backup diskette 01 in drive A:
Strike any key to continue

After pressing any key you'll see:

*** Files were backed up 09-01-1991 ***

*** Restoring files from drive A: ***
Diskette: 01

RESTORE scans each backup diskette for the files to be restored. RESTORE asks you to insert each diskette sequentially until the indicated files are all found and restored. For example:

C > RESTORE A: NOVEMBER.WKS

RESTORE searches the backup diskette in drive A for the file NOVEMBER.WKS. After it is found, RESTORE copies (unarchives) that file from the backup disk to the current disk drive/directory. If a file named NOVEMBER.WKS already exists, it is replaced, otherwise the file is created.

C > RESTORE A: C: \ ACCTING \ MARTIN \ *.WKS

This command restores all the files *.WKS from the backup diskette in drive A to the subdirectory MARTIN in the subdirectory ACCTING on drive C.

C > RESTORE A: C: \ *.*

This command might not do what you suspect. RESTORE restores all backed up files from drive A to the root directory on drive C. Only the files originally in the root directory are restored. Although this might seem odd, remember the BACKUP command BACKUP C: A: only backs up files from the root directory.

The /S Switch

To restore the entire hard disk, the /S switch is used. This switch is the same for RESTORE as it is for BACKUP:

C > RESTORE A: C: \ *.* /S

This command restores the entire hard drive from the backup diskettes in drive A. RESTORE recreates the original tree structure (if necessary) to place every file back in its original subdirectory.

After restoring the entire hard disk, the following message might appear:

System files restored
The target disk may not be bootable

After a two hour restore operation, this message might seem depressing. Usually, nothing is wrong. What the message is telling you is that the system files, IBMBIO.COM and IBMDOS.COM were restored from the backup disk. These programs might be older versions of DOS, and your disk will not boot. If you ever see this message, use the SYS command from your DOS master disk (the current version) to update the system files on your hard disk. Then copy COMMAND.COM from your DOS master diskette to the hard disk. (For more info on the SYS command, see chapter 2, "Preparing Hard Disks.")

The /S switch also can be used to reconstruct a smaller portion of the hard disk:

```
C > RESTORE A: C: \ ACCTING \ *.* /S
```

Only the files and the subdirectories of the \ ACCTING subdirectory are restored from the backup diskettes in drive A. If the files or subdirectories have been erased, RESTORE will recreate them. RESTORE will scan each backup diskette until it has found all files in all subdirectories under \ ACCTING.

The /P Switch

When the /P switch is specified, RESTORE checks each file on the backup diskette to see if it is *read-only*. (Read-only is discussed in chapter 15, "Hidden Files and Data Encryption.") If the file is read-only and the file already exists on the hard disk, RESTORE beeps and asks:

Warning! File *filename*
is a read only file
Replace the file (Y/N)?

To replace the version already on disk with the one on the backup disk, press Y. Pressing N leaves the file as it is—the previously backed up file is not restored.

The /P switch should always be specified when restoring an entire system disk. When RESTORE encounters the files IBMBIO.COM, IBMDOS.COM, and COMMAND .COM, it will not restore them when the /P option is specified. (And the "Target disk may not be bootable" message will not be displayed.)

The /N Switch

The /N switch is used to search out and restore files on the backup diskettes that no longer exist on the target disk. In other words, if you accidentally erased a file on your hard disk and want it back, you can use the RESTORE command with the /N switch. For example:

C > RESTORE A: C: \ WORK \ IMPORTNT \ *.DOC /N

After entering this command, RESTORE will direct you to insert your backup disk-ettes sequentially starting with the first one. It will scan each diskette for any files match-ing the target filespec above with all DOC files in your \ WORK \ IMPORTNT subdirectory on drive C. If any DOC files are found in the backup set that don't exist on the hard drive, they will be copied over. (This option should probably be /W, for "Whew!")

As long as you keep a recent backup around, you can rescue any accidentally deleted file or subdirectory with RESTORE and its /N switch.

RESTORE's Date and Time Switches

RESTORE has four interesting switches that allow you to restore files from a backup set based on their date and time. That is, the date and time of the files stored on the backup diskettes, not the time of the backup or the current time. For example, a file entry in a directory might look like this:

ADIR   TXT   362   9-01-91   5:45a

ADIR.TXT was created at 5:45 a.m. on Sunday, September 1, 1991. The dates and times used by RESTORE's special date and time switches refer to that date, not the date of the backup or the current date.

There are two sets of date and time commands for RESTORE: Switches to RESTORE files created or modified on or before a specific date or time, /B and /E; and switches to RESTORE files modified on or after a specific date or time, /A and /L.

	Date	Time
On or after:	/A	/L
On or before:	/B	/E

The /A switch RESTORES only files modified on or after the indicated date. For example:

C > RESTORE A: C: \ *.* /S/A:08-01-91

This command restores only the backup files to the hard drive that were modified or created on or after August 1, 1991. The following command will back up only the files modified on or before July 31, 1991:

```
C > RESTORE A: C: \ *.* /S/B:07-31-91
```

The time switches, /L and /E, work only by the time of day, just as BACKUP's /T switch works. To get specific with the time, you have to specify both a time and date switch with RESTORE.

Note: RESTORE doesn't like it if you use the /B, /A, and /N switches in any combination.

SOME FINAL NOTES ON BACKUP AND RESTORE

Backing up your hard disk is a must. Yet, RESTORE is a program rarely (and hopefully never) run. There's no real need to back up and then restore the hard disk unless something goes wrong with the hard drive. As a precautionary measure, you should do a complete backup before any of the following operations:

- When your computer is modified, either by yourself or a professional. This modification includes adding a memory card or other expansion option, second hard disk, or some other hardware modification.
- When you use a new hard disk controller card with the same hard disk you're presently using. Each controller card formats the drive differently, therefore when you use a new card, you'll need to back up, format, and then restore your files to the hard disk with the new controller.
- Before a major move involving the computer, including a move between offices, across town, or some long distance when the hard drive could be damaged.
- Always back up your hard disk before you take the computer into the shop (if possible). Even if they're fixing something unrelated, it's still a good idea.

THE XCOPY PROGRAM

Starting with DOS 3.2, the XCOPY program has provided a unique hybrid of the BACKUP and COPY programs. XCOPY made its debut with the IBM PC Convertible Laptop computer. This computer added 3$^1/_2$-inch disk drives capable of storing 720K on a disk.

XCOPY has many of the advantages of BACKUP, but acts more like COPY because the files are not stored in the archived format. XCOPY can be directed to copy entire subdirectories, or part of a tree structure, from one place to another. Finally, XCOPY makes the best use of the memory in your computer. Rather than copy one file at a time, XCOPY loads as many files as it can into memory before moving them. This makes XCOPY much faster than a simple COPY.

Unlike BACKUP, XCOPY will not ask you to insert a second floppy diskette if the first one runs out of room. If there isn't enough room on a diskette to copy all the indicated files, XCOPY displays an error message.

The format of the XCOPY command is:

XCOPY [d:][path][filename][.ext] [d:][path][filename][.ext]
[/A][/D][/E][/M][/P][/S][/V][/W]

XCOPY might look confusing at first, but it is really a powerful and flexible file copying program. The first item after XCOPY is the source filespec, the second the target. Both items can be a single file, group of files (with the wildcard), or a subdirectory. Where XCOPY differs from COPY is in its optional switches. Without any switches, XCOPY does a simple COPY:

C > XCOPY C: \ WP \ POEM*.* A:

XCOPY copies the files POEM*.* from the hard disk to drive A. After typing XCOPY, DOS displays:

Reading source file(s) . . .

XCOPY now reads as many files as it can into memory. Then it copies the files from memory to the target disk A, displaying the name of each file as it is copied. As with COPY, the names of the files are not changed (unless specified).

Many of XCOPY's optional switches are similar to those used by BACKUP and RESTORE. Some of the switches can be used in conjunction with others to vary the preciseness of the files XCOPY copies.

/S. The /S switch directs XCOPY to copy all files in all subdirectories under the current subdirectory. If the subdirectories do not exist on the target disk, they are created. This is the same as the /S switch for BACKUP and RESTORE.

/E. The /E switch can be used with the /S switch. /E creates subdirectories on the target disk even if the subdirectory is empty on the source disk. The /S switch alone will not copy empty subdirectories.

C > XCOPY \ WP \ *.* A: /S/E

This command copies all files and subdirectories in and under the \ WP directory to drive A. The subdirectory structure under \ WP will be duplicated on drive A, even empty subdirectories will be copied.

/M. The /M switch directs XCOPY to copy the files which have been modified or changed since the last backup (the same as BACKUP's /M switch). After XCOPY /M is performed, the files are considered by DOS to be backed up (their modify bit is reset as is done by the BACKUP program).

/A. The /A switch works exactly like the /M switch with one difference. /A does not reset the file's modify bit. According to DOS, the files copied still have been modified or changed since the last backup.

```
C > XCOPY \ WP \ BOOK1 \ *.* A: /M
```

This command copies files from the \ WP \ BOOK1 subdirectory to drive A. Only the files that have been modified since the last backup are copied.

```
C > XCOPY \ WP \ BOOK1 \ *.* A: /A
```

This command behaves the same as the previous example, copying only the files that have been modified since the last backup to drive A. However, those files' modify bit is left unchanged, which means DOS still considers the files to be modified or changed since the last backup.

/D. The /D switch is followed by a date. When specified, XCOPY only copies those files that have been created or updated since that date. The date XCOPY checks is the same date that appears in the directory listing.

```
C > XCOPY \ ADMIN \ LOTUS \ *.* A: /S/D:5-6-88
```

All files and subdirectories under \ ADMIN \ LOTUS which have a date of May 6th, 1988 or later are copied to drive A.

/P. When the /P switch is specified, XCOPY prompts (Y/N)? for each file listed. Pressing Y directs XCOPY to copy the program. If N is pressed, the file is not copied.

```
C > XCOPY \ WP \ NOVEL \ *.* A: /P
```

Files in the directory \ WP \ NOVEL are copied to drive A. As XCOPY displays the name of each file, you're asked whether or not you want that file copied by pressing Y or N:

```
CHAPT1 (Y/N)? y
CHAPT1.BAK (Y/N)? n
CHAPT2 (Y/N)? Y
CHAPT2.BAK (Y/N)? n
OUTLINE (Y/N)? y
    5 File(s) copied
```

/W. When the /W switch is specified, XCOPY displays the following message before it begins copying:

Press any key to begin copying file(s)

After any key is pressed, XCOPY proceeds with the copy operation.

/V. The /V switch turns on the verify option. This is the same for COPY /V and DOS's VERIFY command. When specified, XCOPY verifies (double checks) that the information copied is the same as the original. Because of this extra checking, XCOPY with the /V switch operates slower than a normal XCOPY.

THE REPLACE PROGRAM

The REPLACE program was introduced with DOS 3.2, and is briefly discussed in chapter 2, "Preparing Hard Disks." The REPLACE utility is a clever and long overdue blessing to hard disk owners. This utility selectively replaces files on the hard disk with newer versions of the files found on floppy. It upgrades the files without you having to individually search and update each file. The REPLACE program can scan the entire hard disk for a matching file and then replace it with latest version. This utility greatly simplifies the task of updating software on a hard disk.

REPLACE isn't a substitute for the RESTORE command, just as XCOPY isn't a replacement for BACKUP. Instead, REPLACE is a very specific tool with a variety of interesting uses.

For example, suppose you just received an upgrade to your accounting system. To update the files on the hard disk, place your upgrade diskette into the floppy drive and use the REPLACE program. REPLACE will find any files on the hard disk that match those on the floppy. Depending on which REPLACE options are specified, the old files will be replaced by the new ones, or the new files will be added to the hard disk.

The format of the REPLACE command is:

REPLACE [d:][path]filename[.ext] [d:][path] [/A][/P][/R][/S][/W]

The first item after REPLACE is the source filename, directory, or disk drive. The second item is the target drive or path specification. REPLACE searches the target drive or path for any filenames matching those found on the source. If a match is found, the file on the target is replaced.

C>REPLACE A:*.* C:

This command replaces any files in the current directory of drive C with matching files on drive A. If drive C is currently logged to the DOS subdirectory and drive A contains the latest upgrade of DOS, this command replaces all matching DOS files on drive C with the latest editions on drive A.

Many of REPLACE's switches are similar to those used by XCOPY. The /P, /S, and /W work exactly as described for XCOPY.

/A. The /A switch adds files not found on the destination. Not only will REPLACE update any matching files, but files not matching those on the destination are also copied. This switch cannot be used with the /S option.

```
C > REPLACE A: \ *.* C: \ DOS /A
```

This command copies all files from drive A to the DOS subdirectory on drive C. Any files in \ DOS matching those on drive A are replaced. Any files on drive A that are not already in \ DOS C are also copied.

/R. The /R switch is specified when the files on the destination disk are read-only. (See chapter 15 for information on read-only files.) DOS sets the read-only status only on special files. DOS does not allow read-only files to be changed, modified, or deleted. When the /R switch is specified, REPLACE ignores the read-only status and replaces the file anyway.

COMMERCIALLY AVAILABLE BACKUP PROGRAMS

Many private software developers have realized the limitations of DOS's BACKUP and RESTORE program—mainly that they are slow. Because computers are supposed to be time savers, any program that can do a job faster than another is worth looking into.

There is a subsoftware industry, under the utility branch that deals only with backup and restore software. These programs come and go almost as fast as they claim to do backups. A few of the popular holdouts are FastBack and COREfast, although these are old-timers in a crowded field.

Rather than describe what each of these programs does individually, this section will discuss what features to look for in a commercial backup program. Remember, BACKUP and RESTORE work. With DOS 3.3 and later, they work quite reliably. (DOS 3.2's RESTORE program was riddled with bugs.) The following sections highlight some of the reasons why you should or should not try to go with a commercial backup application.

Speed

Commercial backup programs are notably faster than DOS because there are more files packed on a diskette or special, high density (and non-DOS compatible) diskette formats are used. More time initially might be spent to format your backup diskettes under the special format, but in the long run, the backup will be quicker.

The Ability to Restore

DOS's RESTORE program works. Commercial backup software relies on speed as a selling point. They rarely will mention the speed of a restore—let alone the restore's efficiency. Can you restore single files, groups of files, or files by date and time just as DOS's RESTORE can? One popular program can restore only 256 programs from a backup set— that's it! Even if the backup contains more files than that, you can only grab 256 at a time. Is that efficient?

File Lists

Some backup software can back up files by subdirectory or by file group. A file group is a set of files or wildcard specs that you provide. The backup program will read through that list and back up only the files that match. If the application also has such a feature with its restore half, then it is all the better.

Compatibility

A good reason for not going with a commercial backup program is compatibility. BACKUP and RESTORE come with each version of DOS. They are a staple. Know them once and you don't have to learn them again on a new machine. And because they come with DOS, they will be on every DOS system you ever work with. Commercial backup programs are compatible with themselves, but they usually can't read other backup programs (or DOS's) formats.

EXTRA HARD DISK PRECAUTION: PARK

Most hard disks come with a special software disk. What's on this disk depends on the brand and model of your computer, the type of hard disk, or where you bought your hard disk. One program on this disk you should pay special attention to is called PARK. (It might also be called HEADPARK, HARDPARK, DISKPARK, SHIPDISK, SIT, or incorporate the name of the computer.)

What PARK does and how you use it are crucial to the longevity of your hard disk. Yet, the PARK program is really quite simple. Its sole job is to instruct the hard disk drive to "park" the read/write heads on the far outside of the hard disk.

If you recall from the earlier discussion of hard disks, the read/write heads are responsible for storing and retrieving information from the hard disk. This device sits only microns above the hard disk itself. If the read/write head comes in contact with the hard disk, irreparable damage can occur. With the hard disk spinning at 3,600 RPM, this contact is equivalent to a head-on collision at 60 MPH. Such hard disk collisions are known as *head crashes*.

The PARK program prevents a possible head crash. Because PARK moves the read/ write head to the far outside of the disk where no data is stored, any head crash will not interfere with your data.

You should PARK your hard disk just before turning the computer off, and especially before moving the computer. You might want to PARK the hard disk when leaving the computer unattended for a period longer than an hour.

Because of the variety of PARK and PARK-like programs, discussing how each is used here is impossible. However, you should note that for each brand of hard disk there is a unique PARK program. Your friend's PARK program might not work on your hard disk. (It might make your hard drive go nuts, but it won't mess up your data.) You should only use the PARK program that came with your hard disk, or one you know will work properly.

Also, all PARK programs behave differently. Some move the read/write heads to the outside of the disk and then return you to DOS. Others park the read/write head then lock up in a loop, instructing you to turn off your computer. Still others might sit and continually beep at you until you turn the computer off. Unfortunately, you have little choice over the result when you use your PARK program. The most important thing to remember is PARK can prevent a possible head crash.

A DAILY BACKUP BATCH FILE

A special batch file can be written to ensure that a daily backup of important data files is done. This batch file should be run at the end of each working day.

Just like the AUTOEXEC.BAT file is run when the computer is first booted, the SHUTDOWN.BAT file can be run just before the computer is turned off. However, unlike AUTOEXEC.BAT, which is automatic, you'll have to get into the habit of typing SHUT-DOWN at the end of each working day. One way to ensure that the SHUTDOWN batch file is run at the conclusion of each session is by including it as part of the Q.BAT file in your menu system.

A typical SHUTDOWN batch file would be:

```
@ECHO OFF
CLS
CD \ ADMIN \ LOTUS
ECHO Insert today's LOTUS backup disk into drive A:
BACKUP C: \ ADMIN \ LOTUS \ *.* /S/M
CLS
ECHO Backup completed. Bye!
PARK
```

The line, BACKUP C: \ ADMIN \ LOTUS \ *.* /S/M, makes a backup of all the files in all subdirectories under \ ADMIN \ LOTUS that have been modified since the last backup. In other words, a backup of only the work done today. Make sure a different set of disks are used everyday, with each day of the week's disks kept labeled and separate.

After the backup is completed, the computer waves goodbye and parks the recording heads on the hard drive with the PARK program. The computer can now safely be shut down.

SUMMARY

The programs discussed in this chapter all help make using a hard disk easier. BACKUP provides an insurance policy by archiving files from the hard disk to diskette. RESTORE, if needed, brings the archived files back. XCOPY and REPLACE are two nearly invaluable utility programs provided with DOS. PARK acts as preventive maintenance.

Although all these tools have been provided with DOS, other companies have seen their limitations. You can choose a commercial BACKUP program to archive files on the hard disk more quickly than DOS's BACKUP. Beyond this lies hardware solutions; tape backup, removable hard disks, and fault tolerant systems. These hardware solutions are discussed in the next chapter.

13
Tape, Removable Disk, and Fault Tolerant Systems

A COMPUTER'S HARD DISK is not the final word in mass storage. For example, the last chapter pointed out that although backing up data is important, it is time consuming. A secondary form of mass storage is tape backup. Because of the inefficiency of floppy diskette backup, several companies offer the convenience of backup onto tape.

Other, alternative forms of mass storage consist of physically removable hard disks. Keeping all your valuable information on a single hard disk can be risky from a mechanical point of view, as well as from a security standpoint. Nothing could be more secure than taking the hard disk out of the computer and locking it up in a safe. And some users might want to remove their hard disks and treat them just like floppies. For example, take them home or on a business trip.

This chapter describes the hardware alternatives for storing and backing up data. Tape drives are ideal for quickly backing up hard disks. Tape cassettes are more convenient to store than a stack of rubber-banded floppy disks. Some manufacturers are aware of the importance of valuable data and have implemented *fault tolerant* hard disk systems. These systems are two hard disks working in tandem, each containing a duplicate copy of information on the other. And finally, this chapter goes into the interesting subject of removable hard disks, including the amazing Bernoulli Box.

STREAMING TAPE SYSTEMS

The most popular alternative to backing up data on floppy disks is a *streaming tape* backup. The streaming tape drive is like a high quality cassette recorder. It copies all data from the hard disk in one, fell swoop, putting that information onto a special cassette tape. Because the primary purpose of the tape drive is to back up a hard disk, it is very fast.

Streaming tape drives can be installed either internally or externally. Internal models occupy the same size as a $1/2$-height disk drive, and might require an expansion board or plug into the floppy or hard disk controller. External models mount outside the computer. In most cases, the external tape drives use the computer's own power supply. However, some do require an external power supply, or have one available as an option. The external models generally operate off the 37-pin external drive connector on the back of the floppy disk controller and won't take up valuable slot space, or they come with their own controller card.

An advantage to external drives is that they can be shared by a number of computers. For example, an external tape backup system could be carted around to various computers in the office. Each user could connect their computer to the tape drive, perform the backup onto their own tape, and then roll the cart to the next user. As long as the external drive is a "plug-in" type, the expense of buying a tape drive for each computer system would be saved.

The entire backup operation from hard disk to cassette takes about 20 minutes for a full 20M hard drive. The multiplication factor is about one minute per megabyte used on the hard disk. Sure, it might not compare that well with the time required to back up a hard disk to floppies, but with a tape drive, you only need to use one tape. When the backup is done, the cassette cartridge can be put back into its box and stored away in a safe place.

Incidentally, tape drives were the original form of mass storage for computers, not hard disks. Information was and still is recorded and retrieved from reel-to-reel tapes. However, because the tape is one long, continuous surface, all data on the tape must be accessed serially, one file after another. The advantage disks have over tape is that they can use random access; any point on the disk can be read simply by moving the disk's read-write head to that spot. This saves time over searching through a reel-to-reel tape.

Information Storage on Tape

Information is stored on tape with one of two methods: *Start-stop* or *Streaming*. Start-stop refers to the way tapes were used in the "old days" for accessing data. Streaming is a continuous flow of tape, used primarily for backup. Some streaming drives are capable of start-stop data storage, but at a much slower speed than dedicated start-stop tape drives.

Streaming tapes are always moving. The information is written to the tape by a write head, and a few fractions of an inch away a read head reads back the data just written. This reread of a streaming tape drive detects write errors. When an error occurs, the write head rewrites the bad information, while the tape is still moving.

For example, suppose an error exists in a block numbered N. The read head catches the error while the write head is writing block N+1. The write head then attempts to rewrite block N, then N+1 again. If all is okay, the following blocks are written (N+2,

N+3, etc.) as the tape continues to move. On the tape, the block order would be:

N   N+1   N   N+1   N+2   N+3   N+4 . . .

The first N contained the error. Block N+1 was written before the error was detected, so the following block is a rewrite of block N again. With this error detection scheme, data can be written to the tape in one, continuous motion.

If an error occurs during a restore (when the tape is being read), the drive will back up and reread the bad block. Read errors aren't corrected the same as write errors. Instead, special information is stored on the tape along with the data. This information tells about the data, such as the block number, and includes a CRC (Cyclic Redundancy Check) error check. When the information is read from tape, another CRC is performed and the two CRCs are compared. If they aren't equal, the tape rewinds and the data is read again. If after a given number of attempts the data cannot be read, an error message is displayed, or depending on the type of tape software, the block might be ignored.

Tape Drive Buying Tips

Cost is the most important item when looking for a tape drive. These devices are expensive (sometimes as much as buying a second hard drive), and they are an extremely specific item for the computer. As with anything you buy for the computer, the cost should be weighed against the alternatives, in this case, backing up with floppies. For large volume disks where backups are crucial, tape drives are worth the price. For other systems, tape drives are more convenient than diskette backups. But cost-wise you should ask yourself if they are really worth it.

The next most important items to look for in a tape backup system are the formatted capacity of the tape, the data transfer rate, and the speed of the drive. The formatted capacity of the tape is important in relation to size of your hard disk. Unlike floppies, tape systems will not pause when the tape gets full and ask you to "Insert next tape." The tape backup must be smooth and contiguous. For a 20M hard drive, you'll need a 20M capacity tape drive and 20M tapes. (For specific tape systems, check to see the capacity of the drive and tape cartridge match that of your hard disk.)

Tapes also can be used to back up one small portion of a hard disk, such as a group of files or a subdirectory. Although the formatted capacity of the tape can be as large as your hard disk, you can put several backup "sessions" on a single tape. For example, if your company's order entry information takes only 1M of storage, you can back up each day's information using a single tape. (The tape keeps a directory of its information just like a disk does.)

The data transfer rate, the speed at which information is read from or written to the tape, is measured in kilobytes per second, Kbytes/sec. The higher the number of Kbytes/

sec, the faster information is transferred to and from the drive. Ninety to 100 Kbytes/sec is a good transfer rate for a tape drive.

The speed of the tape drive is measured in inches per second (IPS). The larger the formatted capacity of the tape and the faster the tape speed (IPS), the less time a tape backup will take. For example, a tape capable of holding 20M and records at 30 IPS will take approximately 12 minutes to do a full 20M backup. If the tape speed is tripled to 90 IPS, the backup takes only 4 minutes.

Final buying considerations might be the physical size of the drive and its interface. Some tape drives are fairly large and tend to be external. Others can occupy the space of the typical 1/2-height disk drive.

The interface on the drive should be PC bus, or one that uses the same size connector on the back of the floppy diskette controller. SCSI, Small Computer Serial Interface or "Scuzzy," tape drives can be used only if your computer is equipped with a SCSI controller card. These tape drives are high performance devices, often more efficient than PC bus tape drives. SCSI will doubtless be the wave of the future, but unless your computer sports a SCSI port you shouldn't mess with a SCSI tape drive.

One final note: Some tape drives are not considered a *logical* device. This means, you don't treat a tape drive as drive D: (or T:). You cannot load or execute programs from the tape drive, nor can you save directly to the tape drive with DOS. The tape drive is simply a device for storing backups. Only special software controls the action of the tape. As far as DOS is concerned, the tape drive does not exist.

For those interested, Archive Corporation of Costa Mesa, California offers a complete book on the subject of tape drives. The book is titled *Streaming*, and it retails for $14.95. It goes into detail about mass storage units, including the how's and why's of hard disks, floppy disks, and tape drives. Contact Archive for more information.

Archive Corporation
1650 Sunflower Avenue
Costa Mesa, CA 92626

The Irwin Tape Backup System

Irwin Magnetics is the leading manufacturer of tape backup systems for the IBM PC/ XT, AT, and compatibles. Irwin tape drives are not streamers, yet they provide a fast and space-saving method of backing up hard disks. The design of the tape drive and the method information is recorded on the tape allows Irwin to guarantee that data recorded on one Irwin drive can be read by another Irwin drive.

One case mentioned in Irwin's literature tells of a man whose computer, hard disk, and tape drive were stolen from his house. Fortunately, he made a backup of all his important information before the burglary. After purchasing another computer tape drive, the man was able to restore his entire system from his backup tape. This might not be possible with other tape backup systems.

Irwin tape drives come with everything you need, including the amazing EZTAPE backup software, on two disks. The INSTALL program copies all files to a directory on your hard disk. It's very simple and straightforward. Note: EZTAPE needs at least 512K of RAM in order to run.

The manual that comes with the Irwin Tape drive (the 420-XT, 20M External unit was tested for this book) is well written. It contains an abundance of information not only on the product, but backup procedures as well. The manual is hefty, yet the reading is easy and well paced. No computerese.

Installing the tape backup hardware is relatively simple. If you're not used to messing with a "naked" computer, you should have a qualified technician install the tape drive unit. Otherwise, anyone handy with a screwdriver can install the tape unit in a matter of minutes.

For PC/XT and compatible computers, the external tape drive plugs into the 37-pin connector on the back of the floppy disk controller. A power cable needs to be installed by using a Y-splitter cable between the floppy disk drive and the tape unit. Irwin provides the Y cable and a special backplate that attaches to the XT's rear panel.

On ATs and compatibles, the floppy disk controller is different than the XT's. A special expansion card is needed to operate the tape drive. This card plugs into a short slot on the motherboard. The Irwin drive then plugs into a 37-pin connector on the back of the card.

Internal tape drive units don't take up the desk space of the external units. The manual is very clear on internal (and external) installation, providing step by step procedures as well as photographs. However, if your technical skills are rusty, you should have a qualified person install the internal drive.

The EZTAPE software is impressive. It goes above and beyond the call of duty. Besides being tape backup utility software, EZTAPE is capable of hard disk organization: copying files, moving files, deleting files, and maintaining directories. All that plus EZTAPE is easy to use and has extensive on-line help information.

Included on the EZTAPE disk is a special program for performing backups at specific dates and times. EZSTART is a unique memory-resident utility that directs the EZTAPE backup software to perform a backup at a given date and time. For example, you could instruct the computer to back up one particular group of files at 5:30 p.m. on Monday, another group at 5:30 p.m. on Tuesday, and the whole hard disk at 3:00 a.m. Wednesday morning.

Before using a tape, it must be formatted or initialized. A tape should come with the unit ready for use. But eventually you will be purchasing other tapes (they're available at most computer dealers) or reusing old tapes.

To initialize a tape, choose the Initialize option from EZTAPE's Utility menu. If the tape already has any data, EZTAPE will let you know. The entire initialization process takes some time (31 minutes on the tape tested for this book), but fortunately it doesn't need to be done for each backup.

After the tape is initialized, the backup can proceed. Again, this is as easy as choosing an item from a menu. EZTAPE lets you back up files by the entire disk, selected subdirectories, or individual files. After everything is set, either the drive, subdirectories, or individual files are selected, the backup begins.

The software writes information to the start of the tape drive, like creating a directory. Then it starts reading files from disk and saving them to tape. It happens quickly and automatically. There's no need to sit and watch (although it is interesting to watch if you have nothing else to do). There's no disks to swap as with a floppy backup.

After the information is on tape, EZTAPE resets the status bits of all the files it backed up, informing DOS that a backup was made (refer to the last chapter on the Modify attribute). After the backup, a copy of those files, or the entire hard disk, is on one, compact tape the size of a deck of cards.

To restore the files is as easy as backing them up. Because EZTAPE keeps a directory on each tape backup, individual files, subdirectories, or entire disk drives can be restored with ease. EZTAPE asks a series of yes/no questions. After answering each of them to determine what type of restore you'd like, the program goes out to tape, retrieves the desired files, and places them back on the hard disk.

The nicest part of all this is the EZSTART program, combined with EZTAPE's backup and restore options, can make an excellent automatic and efficient backup system. In an office where the workers forget to make proper backups, or for the individual who wants automatic backups as a convenience, the combination of EZTAPE, EZSTART, and the Irwin tape backup system is hard to beat.

FAULT-TOLERANT SYSTEMS

The most elegant hard disk and hard disk backup alternative is a fault-tolerant system. Although not exactly a replacement for the hard disk, a fault-tolerant system involves using two hard disks in a *mirror* arrangement. Each disk contains a duplicate of the information on the other. When one disk fails or contains a bad sector, the information is instantaneously read from the second disk.

Before going on, note that a fault-tolerant system isn't for everyone, certainly not for the average computer user at home or the office. These systems normally appear in places such as hospitals, precision manufacturing plants, air traffic control computers, NASA, banking industries, the defense department, and organizations where the integrity and timeliness of computer data is crucial. Those types of users need accurate data and can't afford any downtime.

Fault-tolerant systems involve two or more identical computers or devices (not necessarily disk drives), each updated at the same time. If one system fails, the second immediately takes over. These systems are like having two computers, both with the identical data stored in them. When one fails, the second quickly moves in and continues a smooth, uninterrupted operation. Although these systems tend to be 2 to 3 times as expensive as a single system, the extra cost for industries relying upon critical data is worth the expense.

The fault-tolerant disk system involves two hard disks hooked into one fault-tolerant controller. Information stored on one hard disk is instantaneously updated on the second. Each hard disk is a mirror image of the other. The updating of the second disk takes place so quickly it goes unnoticed to the computer operator. (One interesting fault-tolerant system uses three hard disks: two as above and a third for comparison purposes only. It's a beast.)

With a fault-tolerant system, backups are done instantly. Errors are detected and recovered without any interruptions. The only drawback to fault-tolerant systems is the price. Because the hardware contains two (or sometimes three) of everything, the price can be double or triple what individual devices cost. Also, fault-tolerant systems are not for everyone. Only in critical situations do they come in handy. If the data is very sensitive and price is no object, then a fault-tolerant hard disk system should be considered.

REMOVABLE HARD DISKS

People who grew up as floppy drive users have an assortment of interesting questions regarding hard disks. For example, floppy users want to know why you can't take the disks out of a hard drive. The easily paranoid find it hard to believe data will stick to the hard disk even when the computer is off. They want that data on a disk in their hands, not in some hermetically sealed black box at the mercy of the wicked machine.

The reasons why hard disks are rigid, fixed media were discussed earlier in this book. The disk must spin at an extremely fast rate, and the read/write head is only microns away from the disk surface. As an interesting aside, you might have heard the term "flying head" when referring to the read/write head of a hard disk. This term is accurate because the read/write head is so close to the spinning disk, and it creates a physical phenomenon where it actually does "fly" over the surface of the disk.

The same performance could be obtained from a floppy diskette if it weren't for two problems. First, the diskette would have to spin at the same speed as the hard disk, upwards of 3,000 RPM or ten times faster than a floppy spins. At this speed, the flexible media flutters like a pinwheel, and does not make for good contact with the read/write head.

Secondly, the read/write head would need to be just as close to the surface of the disk as it would with a hard disk. The close distance of a hard disk enables more information to be stored on the surface. With the head so close and the speed of the drive so great, a head crash would be inevitable on a floppy.

The rigid media provides stability at high spin rates, and the hermetically sealed black box provides a safe, air-tight environment to prevent disk crashing.

Still, there are valid reasons for wanting a removable hard disk. Some of the oldest types of hard disks were called "packs." The entire pack of disk platters was removable from the system. The packs could be removed, cleaned, taken to another site, and stored away without damage to the media. Yet this form of removable hard disk would prove too costly for microcomputers.

The advantages of removing a hard disk are many, with security first among them. Nothing is safer than removing a hard disk from the computer and locking it up in a safe overnight, avoiding the potential problems of theft, vandalism, and even fire. No password system, lock and key or chain, is as good as removing the hard disk from the computer.

Removable hard disks are also handy. Taking work home from the office, or from one branch to another is as easy as slipping out the hard disk. If many users all use the same computer, each of them can have their own hard disk. They simply sit down, plug the disk into the slot, and use the computer. When they're done, they remove the hard disk media and let others use the computer.

Backups are relatively easy with removable hard disks. Because they can be treated like floppies, copying a removable hard disk is conceivably as simple as typing DISKCOPY C: D:. If the backed up disk is a system disk, then you have two working copies of your hard disk. Unlike other forms of backup (floppy and tape), a second copy of a removable hard disk is simply slid into the slot and you're ready to work.

Possibly the best advantage to removable hard disks is the potential limitless size of storage. Rather than buy yourself a second hard drive, you just buy a second removable disk, or a third or a fourth. Typically, the cost of the media is far less expensive than buying an entire hard disk.

Bernoulli Disk Drives

Daniel Bernoulli was an 18th century Swiss mathematician and inventer who discovered a number of interesting things, primarily dealing with the flow of fluids around certain, interesting objects (and air is considered a fluid). One of his theories states: "The pressure in a stream of fluid is reduced as the speed of the flow is increased." This theory is usually illustrated using an airplane wing; the pressures created by the airflow around the wing cause the wing to lift in the air. Because air takes longer to get around the top of the wing, the air pressure is greater than below the wing and the wing rises.

As Bernoulli was toying around with air pressure flow over certain objects, he discovered that if you spin a flexible disk fast enough, it will wobble like a pinwheel (not his words). He then discovered that if you spin that same flexible disk next to a flat, rigid surface, the disk stabilizes. The airflow causes the flexible disk to become as smooth as a solid disk. This principle causes the Bernoulli Box to operate.

In the early days of personal computing, the Bernoulli drive was an inexpensive alternative to a hard disk. For a comparative price, you got a faster (twice as fast as the original PC/XT's hard disk) disk drive. You also got removability. You could take the media out of the drive. Or, you could buy a lot of media and have as many megabytes of storage as you had removable disks.

The Bernoulli Box consists of an external or internal unit and the actual disk itself. The disk is a flexible floppy disk, contained in a hard plastic case. The disk spins next to a solid surface creating the Bernoulli Effect, and enables the Bernoulli Box to behave just like a hard disk.

The external Bernoulli Box comes in a variety of configurations. The most important thing to look for is whether or not the disk is bootable. A bootable Bernoulli disk means it is treated just like a hard disk; you start the computer and the computer looks at the Bernoulli drive just like a hard disk. Computers with nonbootable Bernoullis are booted from a floppy disk.

Like external hard disks or tape drives, the external Bernoulli Box needs to interface with the computer via an adapter card. The externals come in three sizes, 5, 10, and 20M, and one or two drives can fit into one unit. The Bernoulli Box Plus contains an 80M hard disk plus two 20M Bernoulli disks.

The internal Bernoulli drive is the same size as a $^1/_2$-height disk drive. It uses the SCSI interface to connect to the computer (so your computer must have a SCSI card installed). The Bernoulli drive sports a smaller removable cartridge than the external Bernoulli Boxes, roughly $5^1/_2$ inches square.

The cartridges for the external Bernoulli Boxes are about the size of a sheet of paper, 8 by 11 inches and about $^1/_2$-inch thick. They contain the flexible media and the rigid surface it spins next to. The cartridge doesn't need to be hermetically sealed. Because of another interesting aspect of the Bernoulli Effect, any foreign material that comes into contact with the disk does not cause a disk crash. In fact, a dust particle on the spinning disk creates a dimple. The dimple temporarily wrecks the Bernoulli effect, causing the disk to momentarily flutter. The flutter dislodges the dust and returns the disk back to normal. (It's incredible no one else ever thought of the Bernoulli Box before IOMEGA, pure genius.)

The speed of the Bernoulli drives is comparable to the best of hard disks. In terms of millisecond (m.s.) access time, Bernoulli drives average about 35 m.s. compared to $65-80$ m.s. for XT drives and 40 m.s. for AT drives. The error rate is also impressively low when compared to traditional, fixed disks.

The only drawback to the Bernoulli Box is the price. Hard disk prices have literally gone through the floor in recent years. Yet, the Bernoulli Box is comparatively expensive. Even with its advantages of removable media, easy backups, and speed, purchasing this system must be justifiable.

The payoff comes with the volume of information and security. When fixed disk sizes climb into the 100M range, the prices really shoot up. For less than half the cost of a 100M hard disk you can purchase a single Bernoulli Box and a number of 10M cartridges. Not only will you save some money, but you have the added bonus of security and quick backup protection, with a reliable removable disk system.

Other Removable Hard Disks

The announcement of Tandon Computer's Personal Data Pac has changed the way people think about portable computing. The Data Pac is a totally removable, high speed hard disk. It's about half the size of a brick, $7 \times 5 \times 3$ inches. Inside this compact shape is a 30M hard disk. The unit contains its own shock mounts and is fairly durable. The whole unit slides into a Data Pac subsystem on your computer and you're ready to compute.

The second half of the Data Pac removable hard disk is the hardware you plug it into, the Ad-PAC 2. (Tandon also sells an AT-compatible computer system based around the Data Pac, called the PAC 286.) The Ad-PAC 2 contains the disk controllers and receptacles for Data Pac removable hard disks. The external unit plugs into an expansion slot on your PC/AT or compatible.

The Data Pac is truly a removable hard disk. You simply eject the drive and go with it. Unlike the Bernoulli Box, it's a true, fixed disk. But like the Bernoulli Box, it offers the same security and flexibility that any removable disk system has. The only drawback is that it's only AT-compatible. The unit does not work with the PX/XT and compatibles. Other than that, the Tandon Ad-PAC 2 is a truly unique device.

SUMMARY

The most important point of this entire chapter is that you're not limited to a hard disk/floppy disk arrangement on your computer. Many hardware manufacturers offer interesting and productive options for hard disk storage. Some of these devices, like the Irwin Tape Backup System, provide a quick and easy alternative to BACKUP programs. Others, such as the Bernoulli Box and Tandon Ad-PAC 2, are complete removable disk systems. Each offers an alternative form of hard disk storage with its own advantages and disadvantages.

Although this chapter concentrated on physical (hardware) solutions for hard disk security, the next few chapters deal with software solutions—programs you can use and certain tricks that allow you to further protect your hard disk investment and the security of your files.

14
Password Security

IF YOUR COMPUTER is used by more than one person, you might want to look into a password security system. By adding password protection to your computer, you can selectively choose which users are allowed access to which areas of the computer.

Passwords are used on mainframe computers and public bulletin board systems (BBS's). Each of the system's users is assigned a unique password only he knows. The password positively identifies the user because only he knows what it is. After the password is entered, it acts like a key to unlock certain doors. The system can direct the user to the specific areas of the system he has access to. Not only will the password prevent the user from wandering around, but it prevents other users from getting into that user's area.

Adding password security to your hard disk is discussed in this chapter. DOS has no built-in methods or programs to establish password security. Therefore, password security must be done through either a commercial or public domain program, or by writing a batch file to check and verify passwords. Additional forms of security include an actual lock and key assembly on some computers, and special programs to further protect your machine.

A BATCH FILE TO CHECK FOR PASSWORDS

If you're the only person using your computer, you don't really need to have password protection. Nothing can be more frustrating than forgetting the password and being locked out of your own system. However, if more than one person uses a computer, a simple password system can be maintained with a batch file.

The following batch file tests for the password "lucky." If "lucky" isn't typed, the batch file displays "Invalid Password!" Create this batch file and name it PASSWORD .BAT. Either use EDLIN or the COPY CON command. You also can use whichever text editor or method you're used to. (Remember: If you are using DOS's COPY command, end the file by pressing F6 or typing Control-Z.)

```
@ECHO OFF
CLS
IF %1N==N GOTO NOPASS
IF %1==LUCKY GOTO OKAY
ECHO Invalid password!
GOTO END
:NOPASS
ECHO Try again, this time type your password after PASSWORD
GOTO END
:OKAY
ECHO Welcome aboard!
:END
```

This batch file is designed to check for the replaceable parameter, %1. After the batch file is run, and the screen is cleared (to prevent anyone else from seeing the password), the %1 parameter is compared with a possible password "LUCKY" (line 4). If the password matches, batch file execution branches to the :OKAY label and "Welcome aboard!" is displayed.

The third line of this batch file is specially designed to verify that a replaceable parameter was written. The statement tests to see if nothing is entered as the replaceable parameter. "N" is used as the test. If %1 isn't equal to anything, then "N" equals "N" and the IF statement will GOTO the :NOPASS label. If %1 is equal to something, meaning a password was specified, then whatever %1 is equal to is tacked onto the first "N," making the statement invalid.

If an incorrect password is entered, a special message is displayed (in line 5). Because no matches were found, the ECHO command displays "Invalid Password!" Execution then branches to the :END label.

To use this batch file, type PASSWORD followed by your password:

C>PASSWORD LUCKY

The PASSWORD batch file runs and if lucky is the correct password, "Welcome aboard!" is displayed. If an improper password is typed, "Invalid Password!" is displayed. If no password is typed, the special "N==N" test in the second line of the batch file causes the message:

> Try again, this time type your password after PASSWORD

Tests for multiple passwords should be added to the batch file after line 4. Passwords can be added by including them in lines with an IF %1==*test*.

```
@ECHO OFF
CLS
IF %1N==N GOTO NOPASS
IF %1==LUCKY GOTO OKAY
IF %1==BOSCO GOTO OKAY
IF %1==ROMEO GOTO OKAY
IF %1==SNOOPY GOTO OKAY
ECHO Invalid password!
GOTO END
:NOPASS
ECHO Try again, this time type your password after PASSWORD
GOTO END
:OKAY
ECHO Welcome aboard!
:END
```

This modified version of the PASSWORD.BAT file checks for the passwords BOSCO, ROMEO and SNOOPY after checking for LUCKY. Any number of passwords can be added, and any password can be as long as DOS will accept (although a good length for a password is 7 characters, plus or minus 2).

Remember, when using a batch file case is very important. Although both "lucky" and "LUCKY" are the same, according to DOS they are not. One is lowercase, the other is uppercase. Therefore they are not equal. Of course, this can be to an advantage. Consider the following line in the batch file:

> IF %1==lUcKy

Although lUcKy might be a bit harder to type quickly, it also will be a bit harder for someone to figure out.

On the same train of thought, keep your passwords simple, but not obvious! Too many people use their initials, their spouse's name, their children's name, etc., as a password. Be creative when it comes to passwords!

One ideal use for the PASSWORD.BAT program is in a department where more than one person uses the computer. Suppose Jack and Sue both need access to files in the DB3 subdirectory of CompuCard's computer. To add a level of password protection, the following batch file could be written:

```
@ECHO OFF
CLS
REM test passwords:
IF %1 = =JACK GOTO JACK
IF %1 = =SUE GOTO SUE
REM wrong password entered
ECHO Wrong password!
GOTO END
:JACK
PATH = C: \ ADMIN \ DB3;C: \ DOS
CD  \ ADMIN \ DB3 \ JACK
DBASE TICKLER
GOTO EXIT
:SUE
PATH = C: \ ADMIN \ DB3;C: \ DOS
CD  \ ADMIN \ DB3 \ SUE
DBASE FILER
:EXIT
PATH = C: \ DOS
:END
CLS
ECHO Type PASSWORD followed by your password below:
```

This batch file tests for two passwords, JACK and SUE. After the screen is cleared, the passwords are tested. If no match is found, the batch file echoes "Wrong Password!"

If a match is found, the batch file branches to the appropriate routine, either SUE or JACK. Both routines set the path to C: \ ADMIN \ DB3 and to C: \ DOS. Next the CD command is used to change JACK and SUE to their respective private subdirectories under \ ADMIN \ DB3. Because the path has been preset to \ ADMIN \ DB3, there is no need for them to be logged to that directory.

The batch file runs the appropriate program for either SUE or JACK. Finally, the batch file branches to the :EXIT routine, and the path is set to C: \ DOS (where it was originally). The screen is cleared and the message "Type PASSWORD followed by your password below:" is displayed. This last line resets the entire process. If other users of the same system had similar password protected routines set into the batch file, the final message would help them use the PASSWORD program.

Limits of Batch File Passwords

Anyone with a tiny knowledge of DOS can examine your PASSWORD.BAT file to check for passwords, which is the major drawback with password batch files. A sneaky way around this might be to make the PASSWORD.BAT file invisible, and will be discussed in detail in the next chapter.

Another way around the limitation of batch files is to use an "official" programming language to test for passwords. The program in Fig. 14-1 can be used to prevent anyone from accessing your system. It is written in the BASIC programming language. The program limits access to your system to those who know the system's password.

This program is included on the Supplemental Program Diskette. However, it can be typed in and saved in BASIC, which is available on all versions of PC-DOS and most versions of MS-DOS. The BASIC program is used to write other programs, including the password program listed below.

Enter BASIC by typing GWBASIC at the prompt. Note: BASIC, although the same language, might be called BASICA, BASIC, or MBASIC depending on the particular version you own. The BASIC program's first screen is displayed. You are now in the BASIC program interpreter where other programs for your computer can be written.

Carefully type in the program, including the line numbers. Double check your work to make certain you don't mistype anything (if you do, use the Backspace key to erase).

After you've typed the file in be sure to SAVE it before running it. Save the program (SAVE "C:\PASSWORD") before running it to prevent you from being prematurely locked out of your system. (The program is very efficient about preventing anyone from accessing your system.) Incidentally, you can save PASSWORD.BAS in any directory on disk. Just remember to include its full path when you run it.

The program reads a single password from a disk file called PASSWORD.DAT. In order to use your computer, you must successfully type in the password. If you type in the wrong password, the program locks up your computer. The computer cannot be reset using Control-Alt-Delete, nor can the program be stopped. To return to DOS from BASIC, type:

```
SYSTEM
```

The next step is to create the PASSWORD.DAT file in your system's root directory with the copy command:

```
C> COPY CON PASSWORD.DAT
BULLWINKLE
^Z
```

Remember to press F6 or Control-Z to complete the COPY command. The file PASSWORD.DAT now contains the single word BULLWINKLE. This is the password for your system. PASSWORD.DAT, like PASSWORD.BAS, need not be in your root directory. If you place PASSWORD.DAT in another directory, modify line 1170 of the BASIC program to read:

```
1170 OPEN " \ PATH \ password.dat" FOR INPUT AS 1
```

where PATH is the path to the file PASSWORD.DAT.

The PASSWORD.BAS program is set into effect by adding it to your AUTOEXEC .BAT file. Now, the first thing to come up on the computer screen is a question asking for the system's password. If "BULLWINKLE" (or whatever password is in PASSWORD .DAT) isn't entered, the user is denied access to your computer.

After the @ECHO OFF line, add:

```
C: \ DOS \ GWBASIC PASSWORD
```

If the PASSWORD file is in another directory, include the full path:

```
C: \ DOS \ GWBASIC \ DOS \ PASSWORD
```

This statement assumes the PASSWORD.BAS file is in the \ DOS subdirectory. Likewise, line 1170 of the program should be modified to indicate the full pathname for the PASSWORD.DAT file.

Now the AUTOEXEC.BAT file will run the GWBASIC program PASSWORD when the computer is booted. Your screen will clear and the following message is displayed:

Please enter your password:

The characters you type are not displayed on the screen. After typing BULL-WINKLE, or whatever your password might be, the word "Welcome" is displayed and your AUTOEXEC.BAT file continues. If you make a mistake typing the password, the program informs you:

Wrong! Try again from start of password.

Start over with the first letter of the password. If you make more than 3 mistakes, the PASSWORD program locks up your computer. You cannot press Control-Break, Control-Alt-Delete, or any other key to stop the computer. If the proper password is not entered after 3 tries, the computer displays:

** System Locked **

You must now turn your computer off, then on, to regain control. (If you attempt to press Control-Break, Control-C, or any other key to stop the program it displays a smart-alecky message.)

The BASIC PASSWORD program provides an almost foolproof way to keep unauthorized people out of your system. It does, however, have a few drawbacks.

First, there is only one password for the entire computer. This program was originally used in a computer store where the salespeople used the computer to demonstrate software. They didn't want any kids or other unauthorized people using the computer without their consent, so they added the PASSWORD program to their AUTOEXEC.BAT file. The salespeople only needed to know one password to get into the system, a password that the customers did not know. Because PASSWORD only uses one password for the entire system, it might not provide enough protection.

Second, as with any BATCH file, AUTOEXEC.BAT can be halted by pressing Control-C. If it is halted before the PASSWORD program is run, anyone can gain access to your system. Likewise, anyone who understands BASIC and DOS can TYPE the PASSWORD.DAT file to see what the password is.

Last, and perhaps most important, no matter how sophisticated the hard disk PASSWORD program is, it doesn't prevent someone from booting the computer with a floppy disk. No matter how much protection you add to your system, someone can still put a DOS system disk in drive A and start the computer.

To sum it up, no security system is entirely flawless. Even the PASSWORD program has a "back door" to it. Someone can still enter a system that uses the PASSWORD protection program just by pressing the tilde (~) key. As the old saying goes, this method of protection only helps keep the honest more honest.

```
= = = = = = = = = =
1010   'PASSWORD.BAS (From "Softalk", March, May & July, 1984)
1020   'minor mods and color added by P. Eskildsen, July 10, 1984
1030   'other mods and color removed by Dan Gookin, March 5th, 1987
1040   'Uses BASICA 2.0 key trapping to kill Ctrl-Alt-Del,
1050   'Ctrl-C, & Ctrl-Break — user cannot RESET
1060   '
1070   KEY OFF
1080   KEY 15,CHR$(12) + CHR$(83)          'CTRL-ALT-DEL
1090   KEY 16,CHR$(4) + CHR$(46)           'CTRL-C
```

Fig. 14-1. BASIC program with password security for a computer system.

```
1100   KEY 17,CHR$(4) + CHR$(70)                    'CTRL-BREAK
1110   ON KEY(15) GOSUB 1520 : KEY(15) ON
1120   ON KEY(16) GOSUB 1520 : KEY(16) ON
1130   ON KEY(17) GOSUB 1520 : KEY(17) ON
1140   '
1150   'Read in password
1160   '
1170   OPEN "password.dat" FOR INPUT AS 1
1180   LINE INPUT#1, PASSWORD$
1190   CLOSE
1200   ON ERROR GOTO 1620
1210   '
1220   'Check user's password entry one char at a time, as entered:
1230   '
1240   CLS
1250   LOCATE ,,1
1260   PRINT "Please enter your password:";
1270   TRY = 0
1280   I = 0
1290   A$ = INKEY$: IF A$ = "" THEN 1290
1300      IF A$ = " ~ " THEN 1420
1310   I = I + 1
1320      IF A$ < > MID$(PASSWORD$,I,1) THEN 1350
1330      IF I = LEN(PASSWORD$) THEN 1420
1340   GOTO 1290
1350      TRY = TRY + 1
1360      IF TRY > = 3 THEN 1480
1370      PRINT "Wrong! Try again from start of password."
1380   GOTO 1280
1390   '
1400   'Access granted
1410   '
1420   PRINT
1430   PRINT TAB(30);"Welcome!"
1440   SYSTEM
1450   '
1460   'Too many attempts, lock system
1470   '
1480   CLS
1490   LOCATE 12,20
```

Fig. 15-4. Continued.

```
1500   PRINT "** System Locked **"
1510   GOTO 1510
1520   '
1530   'Display ignore messages
1540   '
1550   BEEP
1560   READ AH$
1570   PRINT AH$
1580   RETURN
1590   DATA "So there!", "Think you're smart?"
1600   DATA "That won't work either.", "I'm sorry"
1610   DATA "Try harder...", "Okay. Give up now."
1620   RESTORE 1590
1630   RESUME 1560
```

Fig. 15-4. Continued.

Description of PASSWORD.BAS

The following explanation of the PASSWORD program in *Fig. 14-1* is provided for those interested in BASIC programming. It is not required reading, nor necessary to understand if you plan on using PASSWORD in your AUTOEXEC.BAT file. If you're further interested in the BASIC programming language, refer to your library or book store for a complete selection of good, introductory BASIC programming texts.

Lines 1000 through 1060 contain comments about the PASSWORD.BAS program. Line 1070 turns off the function key display on the screen. Lines 1080 through 1130 are responsible for shutting off the functions of Control-C, Control-Break, and Control-Alt-Del. Whenever any of these keys are pressed, BASIC branches to the subroutine at line 1520.

Lines 1170 through 1190 read in the password stored in the PASSWORD.DAT file on disk. This password is assigned to the variable PASSWORD$.

Line 1200 turns on BASIC's error trapping. This is used in conjunction with the subroutine at line 1520, which is called each time Control-C, Control-Break, or Control-Alt-Del is pressed.

Lines 1240 through 1280 prepare the program for entering the password.

Lines 1290 through 1380 do the actual work of comparing characters typed at the keyboard with the characters in the PASSWORD.DAT file. Line 1290 reads one character at a time from the keyboard. Line 1300 is this program's "back door." If at any time the ~ (tilde) character is typed, the program automatically accepts it as the proper password.

Line 1310 increments the character count in variable I. Line 1320 compares the character entered with the character in the same position of the password. If they don't match, program execution branches to line 1350. If they do match, line 1330 checks to see if all the characters are typed. If variable I matches the length of the password on disk, execution branches to line 1420. Line 1340 continues the input loop if all characters in the password have not been entered.

Lines 1350 through 1380 are executed if an incorrect character was entered. Line 1350 keeps track of the attempts at entering the password. Line 1360 tests to see if more than three attempts have been made. If so, execution branches to line 1480. Otherwise, line 1370 displays a warning message and execution continues at line 1280.

Lines 1420 through 1440 are executed after the proper password is entered. Line 1430 displays "Welcome!" and line 1440 exits BASIC and returns the user to DOS.

Lines 1480 through 1510 are executed if the proper password has not been entered after three attempts. Line 1480 clears the screen. Line 1490 positions the cursor in roughly the center of the screen. Line 1500 displays the "** System Locked **" message, and line 1510 contains an endless loop, which locks up the computer.

Lines 1550 through 1610 are executed any time Control-C, Control-Break, or Control-Alt-Del are pressed. Line 1550 beeps. Line 1560 reads one of the six strings held in the DATA statements in lines 1590 through 1610. Line 1570 prints the rude comment, and line 1580 returns from the subroutine.

Lines 1620 and 1630 are the program's error trapping statements. The only error that can occur after the password is read from disk is if the user presses Control-C, Control-Break, or Control-Alt-Del, and all the rude messages have been displayed. Line 1620 restores the DATA statement pointer to line 1590 (so it rereads the same strings again), and line 1630 resumes program execution at line 1560.

To remove the program's back door, replace line 1300 with:

```
1300    REM
```

OTHER WAYS TO PROTECT THE HARD DISK

Besides using a password, there are other ways of keeping unauthorized persons from your computer. In addition to a software password, some computers, such as the 286 and 386 machines, come with a lock and key. After the key is turned, the computer is locked and sits tight until unlocked.

Depending on the make of the computer, the key can do a number of things. With most computers, turning off the key disables the keyboard and prevents the computer from being reset or booted. If you step out of the office for a moment, locking the computer ensures that no one else uses it while you are out. Because the keyboard is turned off, nothing can be tampered with. Your system is secure.

Some systems will boot up and run AUTOEXEC, all with a disabled keyboard. Others will simply sit there until the key is turned on. Still other AT compatibles use the key as a mere "decoration." Internally, the key isn't connected to anything!

In some networked systems, the key might be used to lock your system out of the network, and would prevent other users on the network from accessing your system's hard disk. Again, this depends on the type of computer and networking software available.

One software form of the lock and key is included on the Supplemental Program Diskette. The LOCK.COM program has the effect of putting a giant write-protect tab on the hard disk. After LOCK.COM is run, no file on the hard disk can be changed, renamed, modified, or deleted. It just won't work.

LOCK.COM is a memory resident program. It intercepts all access to the hard disk. When the LOCK is on, LOCK.COM tests to see if the hard disk is being accessed to change information. If so, it immediately tells the operating system, "The hard disk is write-protected." LOCK does allow the hard disk to be accessed for reading information.

The best aspect of LOCK is that it won't allow the hard disk to be reformatted. With the LOCK on, a hard disk FORMAT only verifies information on the hard disk; nothing is erased.

To install LOCK, type LOCK at the DOS prompt:

```
C>LOCK
Your hard disk is not Write- & Format-protected
Run LOCK again to turn it OFF.
```

Any attempt to change anything on the hard disk will produce a write protect error. For example, an attempt to rename the file LETTER to LTTR results in:

```
Write protect error writing drive C
Abort, Retry, Ignore?
```

After LOCK is installed, it can be turned on or off again by typing LOCK at the DOS prompt. For example:

```
C>LOCK
LOCK is now OFF (no hard disk protection).
Run it again to turn it ON.
```

Now the disk is back to normal. Any attempt to change or modify a file on the hard disk will not be stopped. Turn lock on again, and the disk is once again write-protected.

SUMMARY

A password protection scheme is a benefit to any computer system, especially where security is important. Passwords can be implemented via a batch file, BASIC program, or other commercial program. However, DOS offers no direct way to password protect the computer. The methods used are only half best because any DOS computer can be booted from a DOS disk in drive A.

The public domain program LOCK can be used to secure the hard disk against possible change or reformatting, but limits the power of the hard disk by making it a read-only device. In the next chapter, additional security measures are discussed, including making files read-only, hiding, and data encryption.

—————————15—————————
Hidden Files and Data Encryption

IF MORE THAN ONE person uses the computer and a password security system seems limited, or if you're the only one using your computer and you find a password system a bit much, you might look into protecting individual files. This protection can be done with DOS by changing the attributes that DOS describes each file. It also can be done by data encryption.

This chapter discusses disk security measures, some of which are built into DOS. DOS allows certain files to be made invisible; only DOS can see them. DOS also can mark files as read-only, which has the effect of putting a write-protect tab on a single file. As a secondary line of defense, data files can be encrypted or scrambled according to a specific key. Anyone who doesn't know the key would not be able to interpret information in the file.

HOW DOS HIDES FILES

DOS has special ways of describing files on disk. Besides the information displayed by the DIR command, each file has other interesting information associated with it. Part of this information controls whether a file or directory is visible or invisible (hidden from a DIR listing). Anyone who's interested in data security can certainly see how hiding files can be very practical.

Every file in the directory has an attribute byte associated with it. Inside this byte are eight attribute bits that tell DOS a few things about the file. For example, one attribute bit, the modify bit, lets the BACKUP program know if a file has been changed or modified since the last backup. Each time the file is changed or modified, DOS switches this bit's value from 0 to 1. The bits in the attribute byte are shown in *Table 15-1*.

Table 15-1. Bits in the Attribute Byte.

BIT	If on (set to 1) means
7	Nothing
6	Nothing
5	File has been modified since last backup
4	File is a subdirectory
3	File is a volume label entry
2	File is a System file
1	File is invisible
0	File is Read-Only

With regards to bits 4 and 3, every subdirectory and the volume label (name of the disk) take up space in the directory. They are considered files by DOS even though they aren't used as such. Bit 5 is used during BACKUP and XCOPY operations (described in chapter 12). Bit 5 is referred to as the modify, or archive bit.

Bits 2, 1, and 0 are commonly used with system files. Bit 2 informs DOS that the file is a system file, either IBMBIO.COM or IBMDOS.COM. Bit 1 hides a file, making it invisible. And bit 0 puts a protective lock on the file, preventing it from modification or deletion.

Normally, there is no reason to change any of these attribute bytes. DOS assigns them as needed, or to protect its own system files. However, you can manipulate them to add your own level of file security with DOS's ATTRIB command, or the HIDE utility on the Supplemental Program Diskette.

The ATTRIB Command

The ATTRIB, or attribute, command allows you to modify the attributes of any file on disk. ATTRIB will modify subdirectories or other system files. However, all files in a particular subdirectory can be modified with wildcards.

The format of the ATTRIB command is:

ATTRIB [+/−R][+/−A] [d:][path]filename[.ext] [/S]

The R and A switches are used to set or reset the read-only and archive (modify) attributes of the filename listed. The filename can contain wildcards, or be a path to a file in another directory. The optional /S switch is used to change or check the attributes of any files in any subdirectories under the current directory, just as it is with the BACKUP, RESTORE, and XCOPY commands.

If ATTRIB is used without the R or A switches, it displays the attributes of the file (or files) listed:

C>ATTRIB *.*

displays all files in the current directory and their read-only and archive attributes:

A	R	D:\TABHDM\GLOSSARY
A	R	D:\TABHDM\PHOTOS
A		D:\TABHDM\TOC
A		D:\TABHDM\CHAPT11
A		D:\TABHDM\CHAPT08.TXT
A		D:\TABHDM\CHAPT01
A		D:\TABHDM\CHAPT02

An R indicates a read-only status. Any attempt to delete, rename, or modify that file results in an error. An A indicates the file has been modified since the last backup. If there is both an R and A, the file's read-only status was added after the last backup.

To change the attribute of any file, or a group of files, the R or A switch is specified. For example, to protect all files *.WKS with read-only status, use:

C>ATTRIB +R *.WKS

This command adds (+R) the read-only attribute of all files with the extension .WKS in the current directory. Those files can no longer be deleted, renamed, modified, or changed. They can, however, be looked at (read-only).

A good example of making all files in a subdirectory read-only would be DOS. Because you never plan on modifying your DOS files—and there's no reason to delete them (at least not on purpose)—you should make them all read-only. Note: Only IBM-BIO.COM and IBMDOS.COM come as read-only.

To make your DOS files read-only, change to the DOS directory and issue the following ATTRIB command:

C>ATTRIB +R *.*

Or from any directory, specify the files in your DOS subdirectory as follows:

C>ATTRIB +R C:\DOS*.*

If you later discover you need to change or delete a file, switch its read-only status off with:

C > ATTRIB − R NOVEMBER.WKS

This command changes the file NOVEMBER.WKS, removing its read-only protection. To remove the read-only status for all files in the current subdirectory, use:

C > ATTRIB − R *.*

The A switch is a bit more unusual than the R switch. The A attribute is turned on only when a file has been modified. After the file is backed up or XCOPYed, the A status is switched off.

Technically speaking, the bit in the file's attribute byte is set to 1 by BACKUP or XCOPY. When the A attribute is turned on, either by changing the file or by using the ATTRIB command, the bit in the attribute byte is reset to 0.

The only real advantage of changing the A attribute is when backing up or XCOPYing files. When the /M switch is used with BACKUP or XCOPY, those programs only look for files with the A attribute. With ATTRIB, you can selectively turn on or off the A attribute and choose which files will be backed up or XCOPYed.

C > ATTRIB + A *.*

This command sets the A attribute on each file in the current directory. Now every file will appear to DOS as if it were modified since the last backup. To remove the A attribute, and make it seem as though all files have not been modified since the last backup, use:

C > ATTRIB − A *.*

Hiding Files

DOS is capable of hiding files, preventing them from being displayed in a DIR listing. Presently, there is no easy way of hiding files with DOS. The only way to hide a file is to modify its attribute byte directly by using DEBUG or some other disk utility, or by using the file hiding utilities on the supplemental programs diskette.

Three programs on your program diskette, HIDE, UNHIDE, and FINDHIDE, all deal with hiding files and programs on disk. After a file is hidden, it won't be displayed in a DIR listing, nor will it be changed by any command using *.*. You can still, however, use the file or program by typing in its name. The thinking behind hiding files is that others who might be using your system cannot access files and programs they can't see.

To hide a specific program or file, use the HIDE program. The format of HIDE is:

HIDE [d:][path]filename[.ext]

HIDE renders the filename listed invisible. For example:

C > HIDE PASSWORD.DAT

This command hides the file PASSWORD.DAT. The file will no longer be listed in the directory, nor can it be accessed with a *.* wildcard search. It is invisible. Only by naming the file directly can it be used.

Unfortunately, HIDE does not hide subdirectories, nor can it hide a group of files with wildcards. However, you can use the DOS FOR-DO command as follows:

C > FOR %A IN (*.*) DO HIDE %A

This command searches the current directory for the files in the parenthesis (*.* or all files). Each file found is assigned the temporary variable %A. The HIDE command is then used on that file. The above command has the same effect as HIDE *.*. (See chapter 7 for more information on DOS's FOR command.)

After a file is hidden, it can become visible again by using the UNHIDE command. The format of UNHIDE is:

UNHIDE [d:][path]filename[.ext]

Like the HIDE command, this command does not work with wildcards, nor can it UNHIDE any hidden directories. To UNHIDE the file PASSWORD.DAT, use:

C > UNHIDE PASSWORD.DAT

If the file was previously hidden, it will now be visible. If the file was not a hidden file, the UNHIDE utility will inform you, and not change the file in any way.

Because hidden files are invisible to DOS searches, a FOR-DO loop will not work with UNHIDE as it does with HIDE. Hidden files should be individually named after the UNHIDE command, and only one file at a time can be made visible. To help locate hidden files in a specific directory, the FINDHIDE utility is used.

FINDHIDE works like the DIR command, except all files, even hidden files, are listed. This program is included because there is no easy way to locate hidden files with DOS. The format for FINDHIDE is:

FINDHIDE [d:][path]filename[.ext]

Unlike HIDE and UNHIDE, this command accepts wildcards in the filename.

```
C > FINDHIDE *.*
```

This command displays all files in the current directory. Any hidden files are prefixed by an asterisk (*):

```
              .                 ..      *STIME  .ASM   STIME      .COM *ETIME     .ASM
  ETIME   .COM HIDE       .ASM  HIDE    .COM *FINDHIDE .ASM   FINDHIDE .COM
*UNHIDE .ASM  UNHIDE .COM*ASK      .ASM   ASK        .COM *GREET      .ASM
  GREET   .COM
16 Total File(s)
```

In this FINDHIDE listing, all files in the directory that have the ASM extension are hidden. The DIR command will not display them. To change these files back to a visible state, each file needs to be individually unhidden with UNHIDE.

Using DEBUG to Hide Files

As previously mentioned, the HIDE and UNHIDE utilities cannot be used to hide and unhide subdirectories. You need a disk "zapping" utility, or a program like DOS's DEBUG, for subdirectories.

Modifying a directory, especially on a hard disk, is not recommended. Instead, you should format a scratch disk in drive A. Copy a few files from your hard disk to the disk in drive A, then make a subdirectory and copy a few files there as well.

From drive C, use the DEBUG program to load the first track from the disk in drive A into memory. After the files are in memory, the disk's root directory can be located. A file's attribute byte can then be modified in memory, allowing you to make any file in the directory invisible. Finally, with DEBUG, the directory can be written from memory back to disk, making the change permanent. Enter DEBUG by typing:

```
C > DEBUG
```

Debug's L command can be used to load certain sectors from disk into memory. The format is:

```
L memory-address drive-number start-sector length
```

DOS numbers disk drives starting with 0 for drive A. Also, all numbers entered into DEBUG are assumed to be hexadecimal, or base 16. To load in the first 16 (10 hexadecimal) sectors from the disk in drive A to memory, type:

    − L100 0 0 10

This command reads, "Load into memory location 100 from drive 0 (A) starting at sector 0 through the next 10 (16 decimal) sectors." After DEBUG's prompt returns, sectors 0 through 10 (0 through 16 decimal) have been loaded into memory. To examine them, the D (display) command is used. To see the first 256 bytes (100 hexadecimal) on disk now in memory, type:

    − D100 L100

The root directory was loaded into memory with the first 16 sectors of the disk. It is located at memory address B00 hexadecimal. To see the first few entries, type:

    − Db00

Something like *Fig. 15-1* is displayed.

```
0B00   54 45 53 54 31 20 20 20-20 20 20 20 00 00 00 00   TEST1        ....
0B10   00 00 00 00 00 00 1B 72-4B 0E 02 00 54 00 00 00   .......rK...T...
0B20   54 45 53 54 32 20 20 20-20 20 20 20 00 00 00 00   TEST2        ....
0B30   00 00 00 00 00 00 33 73-4B 0E 03 00 55 00 00 00   ......3sK...U...
0B40   54 45 53 54 33 20 20 20-20 20 20 20 00 00 00 00   TEST3        ....
0B50   00 00 00 00 00 00 3A 73-4B 0E 04 00 55 00 00 00   ......:sK...U...
0B60   43 52 59 50 54 20 20 20-20 20 20 10 00 00 00 00   CRYPT        .....
0B70   00 00 00 00 00 00 47 5F-4D 0E 05 00 00 00 00 00   ......G_M.......
```

Fig. 15-1. DEBUG shows the directory of drive A as it is stored in memory.

All files listed in the directory start with the filename and file extension. Other information includes the date the file was last modified, the size of the file, the file's attribute byte, and more. This information is displayed as dots or miscellaneous characters after the file's name.

The attribute byte of each file is at an offset of 11 bytes from the start of the directory entry. For example, the file TEST1 has an attribute of 20 hexadecimal. (Count over 12 bytes from the filename TEST1. The first byte, the letter T, is considered offset 0. So 12 bytes over is actually offset 11.)

The attribute byte for the file CRYPT is 10. (The 11th byte offset from the C in CRYPT is 10 hex.) This identifies the file as a subdirectory instead of a normal file. With DEBUG, you can change the attribute byte to make the entire subdirectory invisible. Refer back to *Table 15-1* for the attribute bytes.

The file CRYPT has bit 4 set to 1 (which is 10 hexadecimal), so it is identified as a subdirectory. To add invisibility to this file, bit 1 of the attribute byte needs to be set. In binary math, this works as follows:

	BIT	7 6 5 4 3 2 1 0	hexadecimal
The file's current attribute:		0 0 0 1 0 0 0 0	10
Bit to change for invisibility:		0 0 0 0 0 0 1 0	+2
File's new attribute should be:		—	
			12 hex

(If you don't understand, just nod your head so as not to confuse those who might be watching you read this.)

To change the attribute byte from 10 to 12, DEBUG's E command is used. The attribute byte for CRYPT is at memory location B6B. (If you're changing the attribute of a file on your scratch disk, enter another appropriate value in place of B6B.)

```
-Eb6b
xxxx:0B6B 10.
```

The xxxx is replaced by a number value which varies from computer to computer. Make sure the number after the colon is 0B6B, or the byte you are modifying (it should end in the letter B). Also, make sure the byte before the period is 10, or the attribute byte of the file you are modifying.

To enter the new value, type 12 and press Enter. This changes the attribute byte of the file CRYPT to invisible. Display the section of memory again to verify the change was made.

```
-Db00
```

Figure 15-2 shows the new attribute byte for CRYPT. Note: The attribute byte is now 12 hexadecimal, which means the file is still a directory entry and is invisible.

```
0B00   54 45 53 54 31 20 20 20-20 20 20 20 00 00 00 00   TEST1        ....
0B10   00 00 00 00 00 00 1B 72-4B 0E 02 00 54 00 00 00   .......rK...T...
0B20   54 45 53 54 32 20 20 20-20 20 20 20 00 00 00 00   TEST2        ....
0B30   00 00 00 00 00 00 33 73-4B 0E 03 00 55 00 00 00   ......3sK...U...
0B40   54 45 53 54 33 20 20 20-20 20 20 20 00 00 00 00   TEST3        ....
0B50   00 00 00 00 00 00 3A 73-4B 0E 04 00 55 00 00 00   ......:sK...U...
0B60   43 52 59 50 54 20 20 20-20 20 20 12 00 00 00 00   CRYPT        .....
0B70   00 00 00 00 00 00 47 5F-4D 0E 05 00 00 00 00 00   ......G_M.......
```

Fig. 15-2. The attribute byte of the CRYPT has been changed to 12 (hex), rendering that subdirectory invisible.

To write this information back to disk and make the change permanent, use DEBUG's Write command. This command has the same options as the Load command, except a W is used:

```
-W100 0 0 10
```

DEBUG writes from memory starting at location 100 to drive A (0), and places that information in sectors 0 through 10 (all numbers are in hexadecimal). To quit DEBUG, type:

```
-Q
```

Now, pull a directory from drive A. The subdirectory CRYPT (or whichever file you changed) is not listed. You can still access the subdirectory with the CD command, or list the visible files in the subdirectory by typing:

```
C>DIR A:\CRYPT\*.*
```

Note: Modifying a disk directly with DEBUG can be hazardous, which is why a scratch disk is used in the example. With a hard disk, or floppy diskette with many sub-directories, locating directory information with DEBUG can be incredibly inefficient. To modify directory information on a hard disk's subdirectory, use a disk zapping utility to locate and modify files. But in all cases, be careful when you do this!

A Very Sneaky Way to Hide Files

DOS allows certain special characters to be used when naming files. Although the DOS manual doesn't specifically state these characters can be used, they are accepted by DOS and serve as an excellent method for file security. You should note that because these characters are not specifically mentioned, this procedure might not work with future releases of DOS.

Normally, a file name may contain any ASCII character (letters, numbers, or punctuation symbols) except the following:

$$. \text{ "} / \setminus [\,] : * \mid < > + = ; , ?$$

Also, a file cannot contain any control character, ^C, ^A, etc., or a space. A wide variety of characters available on the keyboard for naming files. Additionally, certain characters not available on the keyboard can be used for naming files. These are the extended ASCII characters. (See Appendix C.)

The extended ASCII characters can be typed at any time with the Alt key and your keyboard's numeric keypad. (Some utility programs, e.g., Borland's SuperKey, disable this feature.) For example, the Extended ASCII character number 219 is a solid block. To type this character, press and hold the Alt key and type 219 on the numeric keypad. When you release the Alt key, the solid block appears.

Regular ASCII characters can be typed with the Alt key as well. Try typing the following numbers. For each, press and hold the Alt key and type the number. Release the Alt key after the number is entered:

72, 101, 108, 108, 111, 33, 32, 1

The Extended ASCII set contains a variety of characters. However, character 255 is a blank. If a file is renamed with this blank character, it would appear as a mysterious blank in the directory listing. For example, suppose the file TEST1 is on disk. To rename this file as the Extended ASCII character 255, type:

```
C>REN TEST1 [Alt-255]
```

TEST1, now [255], appears as follows in a DIR listing:

```
Volume in drive A has no label
Directory of A: \

                85    2-11-88    2:10p
TEST2           85    2-11-88    2:16p
TEST3           85    2-11-88    2:25p

    3 File(s) 352256 bytes free
```

Unlike hiding a file, [255] is listed; its name is blank, but the size and date show up. The other files in this directory also can be changed to blanks. Remember, no two files can share the same name. So TEST2 could be renamed [255][255], TEST3 could be renamed [255][255][255]. Up to 11 files can be named in a single directory with the [255] (blank) character.

As long as no one else using your computer knows about the Extended ASCII names for files, other bizarre names can be created. Try renaming a file as 224, 225, 226. The new filename appears in the directory as alpha, beta, gamma, the first three letters of the Greek alphabet.

Along the same lines, you should not give certain files obvious names. For example, PAYROLL.WKS is one file any curious office employee might want to take a peek at. Renaming the file SAMPLE.WKS, or even MEMO.DOC, might be enough to keep potentially prying eyes away.

File Transfer with Hidden Files

If hiding files and subdirectories is part of your file security system (along with or in addition to passwords), there needs to be a way of exchanging files between users who aren't aware of other users' hidden directories.

Consider the CompuCard company. Both Jack and Linda have their own subdirectories under \LOTUS. Suppose both directories are invisible, or named using the blank character, each directory contains invisible files. If Linda wants Jack to examine a file, she has to either remove protection on the file or let Jack know what the protection scheme is.

Instead of jeopardizing security measures, a compromise can be reached in the form of a *public* directory. This directory is a common place where all users have access. If Linda wants Jack to look at a file, she simply needs to copy it to the public directory, such as:

```
C > COPY SECRET \ ADMIN \ LOTUS \ PUBLIC \ FORJACK
```

This step copies the file SECRET to the \PUBLIC directory, and names the new file FORJACK. (SECRET might be a secret, or other hidden file.)

Another advantage to a PUBLIC directory is the ability to send messages to other users of the system. Large computers with several users have complete Mailing systems, complete with mailboxes for each individual user. A mail/message system can be set up under DOS with simple batch file commands.

The following batch file can be used to send a message to another user. The file uses EDLIN to type and enter the message. Make sure EDLIN is on the path. Create this batch file using either EDLIN or the COPY command and name it SENDMAIL.BAT:

```
@ECHO OFF
IF N%1==N GOTO CANCEL
EDLIN TEMPMAIL.@
ECHO ====Next Message==== >> \PUBLIC \ %1
TYPE TEMPMAIL.@ >> \PUBLIC \ %1
DEL TEMPMAIL.@
ECHO Message sent
GOTO END
:CANCEL
ECHO No Mail message sent!
:END
```

To use this batch file, type SENDMAIL at the DOS prompt followed by the name of the person you're sending to. For example, to send a message to Sue:

```
C > SENDMAIL SUE
```

The batch file then runs EDLIN, and you can type and enter your message. As with the PASSWORD.BAT program in the last chapter, if nothing is typed after SENDMAIL, the program displays:

No Mail message sent!

After editing is done, the line "= = = =Next Message= = = =" is appended to the person's mail file in the \ PUBLIC directory. Next, the TEMPMAIL.@ file is appended to the person's mail file. Finally, TEMPMAIL.@ is deleted and "Message Sent" is displayed.

SENDMAIL.BAT makes use of the double redirection symbol, > >. If a mail file does not exist, DOS creates it. And if the file does exist, the new message is appended.

The following batch file is used to read mail. It should be part of a password or similar batch file that can identify the user so no one reads anyone else's mail. Again it uses the %1 replaceable parameter as the person's name. Use either EDLIN or the COPY command to create this batch file as READMAIL.BAT:

```
@ECHO OFF
IF N%1 = =N GOTO CANCEL
IF NOT EXIST \ PUBLIC \ %1 GOTO NONE
TYPE \ PUBLIC \ %1 ¦ MORE
DEL \ PUBLIC \ %1
GOTO END
:CANCEL
ECHO Enter a name after the READMAIL command
:NONE
ECHO No mail waiting
:END
```

To use this batch file, type READMAIL followed by your name. For example, if Sue wanted to read her mail, she would type:

C > READMAIL SUE

The batch file first checks to see if any mail is waiting. If so, the mail file is TYPEd to the screen. The MORE filter is used to display the messages one screen at a time. As with SENDMAIL.BAT and PASSWORD.BAT, if nothing is typed after SENDMAIL, the program displays:

Enter a name after the READMAIL command!
No mail waiting

The test is done with the N%1= =N in line 2. After this test, the batch file checks to see if the person has mail waiting. If a file with their name exists, then they have mail. Otherwise, the IF NOT EXIST test passes, the batch file branches to the :NONE label, and "No mail waiting" is displayed.

If mail does exist, it is displayed with the TYPE command. The TYPE command's output is run through the MORE filter to display the messages one page at a time. After the mail file is read, it is deleted.

WHAT IS DATA ENCRYPTION?

Data encryption is the systematic scrambling of information in a file, making that information unreadable. Because the information is scrambled systematically, or according to a specific pattern, it can be unscrambled and returned back to its original form. Scrambling information in this manner is often referred to as *encryption*. Unscrambling is referred to as *decryption*.

Encrypting a file typically involves the use of a key, or password. This key works like the secret decoder rings of old. These decoder rings had two moveable circles on them, one inside the other. On both circles were the alphabet. If the decoding pattern were A-P, the inner circle was turned so that A matched P on the outer circle. The relationship between the characters on both circles looked something like the following:

ABCDEFGHIJKLMNOPQRSTUVWXYZ
PQRSTUVWXYZABCDEFGHIJKLMNO

Kids then used this relationship to translate strings such as:

TPI BPAID BTPA!

Into:

EAT MALTO MEAL!

Encrypting a computer file on disk works surprisingly similar to this. (Who ever would have thought!) Every character of the file is translated using a special key. The key also is used to decrypt the file back to its original state.

Very simple data encryption routines operate like a secret decoder ring. Every character in the file is added or subtracted from a certain key value. However, these schemes usually prove too simple for most practical encryptions. (After all, knowing any kid with a secret decoder ring was capable of reading your encrypted files would prove distressing.) Because of the simplicity, more advanced methods of encrypting computer data are used.

Data Encryption with BASIC

One method for encryption works like the decoder ring, except the decoding key is not a single character but a string of up to 255 characters. This method is used in the file CRYPT.BAS (a BASIC language file) included in the Supplemental Program Diskette. Encrypting files works by adding the key string of characters in sequence to each character in the file. For example, suppose the key string is "TESTING." The file to encrypt contains the following:

now is the time for all good men.

The CRYPT.BAS program works by adding the key string TESTING to each character in the file as follows:

TESTINGTESTINGTESTINGTESTINGTESTI
now is the time for all good men.

The result is a bunch of strange characters that are not easy to read or understand. In fact, unless you know the exact string of characters and their length, decrypting the file would take quite a while. (Keep in mind, this is still an elementary form of data encryption and is not foolproof.)

To decrypt the file, the same key string of characters is subtracted from each character in the file. Only the exact key string of characters can properly decrypt the file. So, by adding the key string to the string of strange characters, the result is:

now is the time for all good men.

This method of encryption works on data and program files, as well as straight text, or ASCII, files. Just don't forget the key string!

The program shown in *Fig. 15-3* demonstrates the encryption routines. It is written in the BASIC programming language. As with the PASSWORD.BAS program in chapter 14, this program is supplied on the supplemental program diskette. However, you can type it in yourself with the BASIC program that came with DOS.

```
100  KEY OFF
110  COLOR 7,0
120  WIDTH 80
130  SCREEN 0,0,0
140  CLS
150  PRINT "A Simple File Encryption Program in BASIC"
```

Fig. 15-3. BASIC program for file encryption.

```
160   PRINT "Written by Dan Gookin, Copyright © TAB Books"
170   PRINT
180   PRINT "Will you be <D>ecrypting or <E>ncrypting? (D or E): ";
190   B$ = INPUT$(1)
200   B$ = CHR$(ASC(B$) AND 95)
210   IF B$><"E" AND B$><"D" GOTO 190
230   PRINT B$
240   PRINT
250   LINE INPUT "Enter the INPUT file: ";FILEIN$
260   LINE INPUT "Enter the OUTPUT file: ";FILEOUT$
270   PRINT
280   LINE INPUT "Enter the keyword pattern: "; KEYWORD$
290   KEY.LEN = LEN(KEYWORD$)
300   IF KEY.LEN = 0 THEN 280
320   REM ****************************
330   REM Encryption/Decryption routines
340   REM ****************************
350   OPEN FILEIN$ FOR INPUT AS 1
360   OPEN FILEOUT$ FOR OUTPUT AS 2
370   FOR X=1 TO KEY.LEN
380      IF EOF(1) THEN 460
390      D$ =MID$(KEYWORD$,X,1)
400      A$=INPUT$(1,1)
410   ON INSTR("DE",B$) GOSUB 480,510
420      PRINT#2,C$;
430      PRINT C$;
440   NEXT X
450   GOTO 370
460   CLOSE
470   END
475   REM ****************************
480   REM Decrypt it:
490   C$ = CHR$((ASC(A$) – ASC(D$)) MOD 255)
500   RETURN
510   REM Encrypt it:
520   C$ = CHR$((ASC(A$) + ASC(D$)) MOD 255)
530   RETURN
```

Fig. 15-3. Continued.

Carefully type in the program, including the line numbers. Double check your work to make certain you don't mistype anything (if you do, use the BACKSPACE key to erase).

Save the Crypt file and exit BASIC by typing SYSTEM. To run the program from DOS, type:

C > GWBASIC CRYPT

The Crypt program displays the following:

A Simple File Encryption Program in BASIC
Written by Dan Gookin, Copyright (c) TAB Books
Will you be < D > ecrypting or < E > ncrypting? (D or E):

Press D or E to decrypt or encrypt a file, respectively. Next the program asks:

Enter the INPUT file:

If you're encrypting, enter the name of the file you'll be encrypting. If decrypting, enter the name of the already encrypted file you'll be decrypting.

Enter the OUTPUT file:

If you're encrypting a file, type the name of a new file on disk, one that will contain the encrypted data. If decrypting, enter the name of the file that will contain the decrypted output. In both cases, the OUTPUT file should be a new file on disk.

Next, you will enter the key string:

Enter the keyword pattern:

Type up to 255 letters, characters, or symbols. Press Enter when you are done. Remember this string! It's the key for encryption.

After you are done typing, the Crypt program reads information from the INPUT file and, depending on whether you selected D or E, it decrypts or encrypts that file's information and saves it to the OUTPUT file.

This simple, yet elegant, method for encrypting files is good as a general purpose security method for protecting your files. It will work on data, text, and program files. Keep in mind that the CRYPT.BAS program and its methods for encrypting your data are not foolproof. Also, remember the key string! The author and publisher take no responsibility for any information lost due to your forgetting your key string.

Description of CRYPT.BAS

The following explanation of the CRYPT.BAS program is provided for those interested in BASIC programming. It is not required reading, nor necessary to understand if you intend on using the Crypt program to protect your files.

Lines 100 through 170 set up the computer screen and display the title of the program. Lines 100 through 140 establish that the screen's function key display is off, the colors used are black and white, the computer is in the 80 column mode, the screen pages are all set to 0, and that the display is clear.

Lines 180 through 240 determine whether the program is decrypting or encrypting. Line 180 displays the prompting message. Line 190 reads one character from the keyboard. Line 200 makes that character uppercase with a logical AND instruction. In line 210, the character entered is compared against E and D. If the input does not match E and D, execution branches back to the input statement in line 190. If the input does match, that letter is displayed.

Lines 250 and 260 get the input and output file names and assign them to variables FILEIN$ and FILEOUT$.

Line 280 gets the encryption keyword pattern and assigns it to the variable KEYWORD$. Line 290 assigns the variable KEY.LEN to the length of the encryption keyword string.

The actual decryption/encryption is done in the FOR-NEXT loop between lines 370 and 450. First, each file is opened in lines 350 and 360. Then, the program incrementally reads a character from the key word (line 390) and from the file (line 400). Line 410 branches to the appropriate encrypting or decrypting routine depending on whether D or E was entered. Line 420 prints the resulting encrypted or decrypted character to the output file, and line 430 prints the character to the screen.

Line 440 completes the loop. Line 450 continues the program until the end of the input file is detected by line 380. After the last character is read from the input file, the IF-THEN test in line 380 branches program execution to line 460 where the files are closed and the program ends.

The actual encrypting routines are in lines 480 through 530. The equation is the same for both, except addition ($+$) is used for description and subtraction ($-$) for encrypting. The MOD 255 function keeps the resulting character within the values of a character to prevent BASIC from producing an error.

Commercially Available Data Encryption Programs

Most commercially available data encryption programs use schemes much more complex than those discussed here. The most popular and foolproof encryption scheme is referred to as the Data Encryption Standard, or DES, which is defined by the National

Bureau of Standards. This encryption scheme is so powerful that the United States Government prohibits the export of programs that use it, even to friendly countries!

Borland's SuperKey memory resident keyboard macro program has two forms of encryption available. Both can use either the DES standard or a special encryption scheme developed by Borland. The two forms of encryption are nontext mode and text mode.

The nontext mode takes the information in a file and scrambles it according to a keyword. The keyword can be any combination of up to 30 characters, upper- and lowercase are considered the same. The resulting scrambled file is the same length and has the same name as the original. As with all encryption, only those knowing the keyword can unscramble the file. Borland makes a special note about attempting to unscramble the file with the improper keyword.

The nice part about the nontext mode is that it won't waste any disk space. Also, because the original file is overwritten by the encrypted file, there's no chance of someone stumbling across it and reading its contents.

When the text mode is used, it places the encrypted information into a second file composed only of uppercase letters of the alphabet. The original file is unchanged. Because the second, encrypted file only contains letters of the alphabet, the program is ideal for use when transmitting files via modem. An encrypted file will be much larger than the original. Text (ASCII), data, and program files can be encrypted in the text mode.

Each file encrypted in the text mode has a special header and footer. Sandwiched between them is the actual encrypted file. For example:

```
***SUPERKEY TEXT-ENCRYPTION START***HFACNAOA
JHLHOEJLGEBHNGGBBCKIKIACPAHPJOFEEFCLNKMNMINKBFKBHKHE
    BFAGNOHMONMD
HNMEENFMMEHKHPLGHLHBKPNLJFIEOPHGAGEEIBKIAGCHHIKOMC
    DHOEGGMFMFODML
KJLGNFDPPHANIMHFJKFALGKCDKPKHPFNIINBPPM
KDPDPDEDAICHJHICJBHJHBOLGLIAMLGGDDKJKBL
***SUPERKEY TEXT-ENCRYPTION END***
```

The drawback to the text mode is that it leaves the original file unprotected on disk. If you're not sending the file to another computer, the nontext mode is the best choice for file security.

SuperKey also can use wildcards, so all the COM and EXE files in your \ DOS subdirectory can be encrypted. This setup could be done in the AUTOEXEC.BAT file before a system password is entered, or by the SHUTDOWN.BAT file at the end of the day. Unless someone knew the proper password, your system would be useless.

SUMMARY

This chapter covered two types of disk security measures. One is provided using the invisible attribute of files and directories on disk, as well as naming files using the special blank character. The second method involved scrambling, or encrypting, information inside files so that only those who know the proper key can unscramble the information. Both measures are reliable and proven methods of adding security to your hard disk.

_____16_____
Tracking Computer Usage

KEEPING TRACK of things is one area computers are very good at. These things can range from the typical recipe file to the national debt. Although most computer users know this, it's amazing how many still rely on pencil and paper when keeping track of simple things. For example, keeping track of your time on the computer.

There are a number of reasons to log computer usage. For example, if you're billing a client by the hour, you need some form of record keeping a bit more convenient than writing the times down (computers are useful for these things after all). Or if a number of people from different departments are using the same machine, having the computer keep track of its usage is reliable and efficient, especially when it can be done automatically.

In this chapter, methods of logging computer usage are covered. Although there really isn't a built-in time manager for IBM computers, it is possible to keep track of computer usage by using batch files and by taking advantage of DOS's redirection commands, > and <.

A BATCH FILE PROGRAM FOR TRACKING USAGE

Because PCs have internal clocks, keeping track of computer time is as easy as looking at the computer's clock, if the clock is set properly every day or the computer has an internal, battery powered clock. To create a usage log, the current time from the computer's clock needs to be written, or redirected to, a disk file.

The best way to keep track of the time you use your computer would be by redirecting the clock's output into a file. For example, a file called LOG could be placed into a special \ USER directory. Recalling from chapter 3, output is redirected from the screen (the standard output device) to a file by using the > symbol. To redirect the time to the \USER\LOG file, the > command is used. This sends all output to the \USER \LOG file instead of the screen.

However, to totally benefit from sending the time to a file, the double redirection symbols, >>, should be used. This way, the time is always appended to the \USER \LOG file. The only problem then is how to get the time out of the computer and into the file. DOS has no built-in "display the time" functions. The time is only seen in a directory listing when a new file is created, or as part of the prompt when the TIME command is issued.

Three utility programs are included on the supplemental program diskette to display the current time. They are STIME.COM, ETIME.COM, and TSTAMP.COM.

These programs were written to assist in creating a usage log. The first two do roughly the same thing: display the current day, date, and time. The only difference is STIME displays "Start Time" and ETIME displays "End Time." TSTAMP.COM displays the time and date without the leading text.

Typing STIME at the command prompt displays something like the following (depending on the date and time):

Start Time = Monday, February 18th, 1991 @ 11:14 am

ETIME displays:

End Time = Monday, February 18th, 1991 @ 11:15 pm

The program TSTAMP.COM is a little more simplistic. Typing TSTAMP at the command prompt displays the current time and date as follows:

23:16:32 02/18/91

All three of these programs read the computer's internal clock and display the current time to the screen. By themselves, these programs are relatively pointless. Yet by redirecting their output to a LOG file, the time you use on your computer system is annotated.

C>TSTAMP >> \USER\LOG

This command redirects the output of the TSTAMP command, the current time and date, to the \USER\LOG file. If \USER\LOG does not exist, DOS creates it. If such a file does exist, the current time and date are appended to the file. Now the current time is stored in \USER\LOG. To view the file, use the TYPE command, and you should get a result like:

12:16:07 02/18/88

If TSTAMP > > \ USER \ LOG is entered at the command prompt again, the current time is appended to the end of the LOG file. Typing the \ USER \ LOG file a second time displays:

```
12:16:07 02/18/88
12:16:44 02/18/88
```

Of course, a file full of dates and times won't mean much unless you know what the times represent. This is why STIME and ETIME were written. Consider this batch file:

```
CD \ ADMIN \ WP \ WS
ECHO Word processing. . . > > \ USER \ LOG
STIME > > \ USER \ LOG
WS
ETIME > > \ USER \ LOG
CD \
```

This batch file first changes to the word processing subdirectory, \ ADMIN \ WP \ WS. The ECHO command is then used to append "Word processing. ." to the \ USER \ LOG file. After that, the current time is appended to \ USER \ LOG by the STIME > > command. Finally, the word processing program WS is run.

After the word processing is done, control returns to the batch file and the current time is appended to the \ USER \ LOG file via > > and the ETIME command. The \ USER \ LOG file now contains something like the following:

```
Word processing. . .
Start Time       = Monday, February 18th, 1991 @ 1:14 pm
End Time         = Monday, February 18th, 1991 @ 2:45 pm
```

If a unique batch file were written for each of your programs, the LOG file might contain something like this at the end of the day:

```
Word processing. . .
Start Time       = Monday, February 18th, 1991 @ 1:14 pm
   End Time      = Monday, February 18th, 1991 @ 2:45 pm
Updating Customer File. . .
Start Time       = Monday, February 18th, 1991 @ 2:51 pm
   End Time      = Monday, February 18th, 1991 @ 3:02 pm
Telecom to Seattle Branch. . .
Start Time       = Monday, February 18th, 1991 @ 3:05 pm
   End Time      = Monday, February 18th, 1991 @ 4:16 pm
```

Backing up files for today:
Start Time   = Monday, February 18th, 1991 @ 4:30 pm
  End Time   = Monday, February 18th, 1991 @ 4:52 pm
System Shutdown:
17:02:26 02/18/91

The TSTAMP program is used at the end of the day to log when the system is shut down. The last program run each day might be a SHUTDOWN batch file (see chapter 12), in which case you should save the shutdown time in the batch file. Also, if a BACKUP is performed, it should be logged to the /USER/LOG file. A couple of the last few lines of the SHUTDOWN.BAT file might be:

```
BACKUP C: \ ADMIN \ WP A: /S/M
ECHO "Backup completed" > >  \ USER \ LOG
ECHO "System Shutdown:" > >  \ USER \ LOG
TSTAMP > >  \ USER \ LOG
```

The only disadvantage to indicating just the start and end time for each job is it still takes a bit of brainwork to figure out how much time was spent on each project. The \ USER \ LOG file helps to show when you started and then stopped work on each project, but does not show totals. This might not be that big of a problem seeing that most time cards show only a start and stop time. However, keep in mind this is a computer and it is capable of next to anything.

COMMERCIALLY AVAILABLE PROGRAMS

One commercially available program capable of keeping track of computer usage is included with the Norton Utilities series of programs. Besides displaying the current time, Norton's TM program also keeps track of elapsed time, just like a stopwatch. By specifying certain parameters, TM can give you the exact number of minutes and seconds elapsed since you've started a particular job. Up to four of these stopwatches can be used to keep track of up to four different elapsed times.

TM is not a memory-resident program. However, it uses a secret portion of low memory at address 4F0 hexadecimal called the *intra-application communications area*, or ICA. In this area, TM stuffs the starting times for each of its four stopwatch functions. When you access TM to display the elapsed time, it looks at memory location 4F0 for the start time, and then displays the elapsed time.

The format of the TM command is:

TM [start¦stop¦comment] [/c*n*][/l][/log][/n]

All parameters are optional with TM. When no parameters are specified, the current time is displayed, right justified on the screen:

11:08 am, Tuesday, February 26, 1991

The optional /L switch is specified to left justify the output:

11:10 am, Tuesday, February 26, 1991

When START is specified, a special stopwatch starts ticking away seconds. The /C switch is used to select one of four stopwatches:

C>TM START /C2

This command starts stopwatch number two. If no /C number is specified, stopwatch number one is used.

To see the elapsed time, type TM STOP. The current date and time are displayed, followed by the elapsed time since TM START was entered:

11:08 am, Tuesday, February 26, 1991
15 seconds

If the TM START command is used again, the stopwatch starts all over. Specifying /C*n* with STOP displays the elapsed time for that particular stopwatch.

The COMMENT option displays a one word comment before the time string. COMMENT can be only one word. Any extra words on the same line after COMMENT are ignored:

C>TM /L STARTING

displays:

STARTING 11:10 am, Friday, February 26, 1988

The /N switch suppresses the listing of the current date and time. TM STOP /N only displays the elapsed time since the last TM START command was issued:

33 minutes, 15 seconds

The /LOG switch is used to add a carriage return/line feed combination to the end of TM's output. As with the utilities STIME, ETIME, and TSTAMP, TM's output can be redirected to a log file. The /LOG switch should be specified to prevent TM's output to the log file from appearing all on one line.

```
TM STOP /L/LOG > \ USER \ LOG
```

This command appends the something similar to the following to the LOG file:

```
11:59 am, Wednesday, February 27, 1991
38 minutes, 9 seconds
```

By using combinations of TM's switches, you can add elapsed time comments to your /USER/LOG file. Because multiple stopwatches can be used, one timer for each user of the computer can be maintained. Consider the following additions to an earlier batch file:

```
CD \ ADMIN \ WP \ WS
ECHO Word processing. . . > > \ USER \ LOG
STIME > > \ USER \ LOG
TM START /C1
WS
ETIME > > \ USER \ LOG
TM STOP /C1/N/L/LOG > > \ USER \ LOG
ECHO "--" > > \ USER \ LOG
CD \
```

TM START /C1 starts stopwatch one. When the job is done, the TM STOP /C1/N/L /LOG produces a left-justified string displaying the elapsed time for stopwatch one. This string is then appended to the \ USER \ LOG file. (ECHO "--" has been added to clean up the \ USER \ LOG file a bit.) At the end of the day, the \ USER \ LOG file will probably look like this:

```
Word processing. . .
Start Time    = Tuesday, September 3rd, 1991 @ 1:14 pm
    End Time  = Tuesday, September 3rd, 1991 @ 2:45 pm
1 hour, 31 minutes, 5 seconds

--

Updating Customer File. . .
Start Time    = Tuesday, September 3rd, 1991 @ 2:51 pm
    End Time  = Tuesday, September 3rd, 1991 @ 3:02 pm
1 hour, 11 minutes, 52 seconds

--

Telecom to Seattle Branch. . .
```

Start Time   = Tuesday, September 3rd, 1991 @ 3:05 pm
   End Time   = Tuesday, September 3rd, 1991 @ 4:16 pm
1 hour, 11 minutes, 6 seconds
--

Backing up files for today:
Start Time   = Tuesday, September 3rd, 1991 @ 4:30 pm
   End Time   = Tuesday, September 3rd, 1991 @ 4:52 pm
22 minutes, 16 seconds
--

System Shutdown:
17:02:26 09/03/91

A special time can be set at the start of each day to keep track of the total time the system was on. For example, suppose stopwatch three were used for this purpose. The elapsed time could then be appended to the \ USER \ LOG file as part of the SHUT-DOWN batch file program:

```
BACKUP C: \ ADMIN \ WP A: /S/M

ECHO "Backup completed" > > \ USER \ LOG
ECHO "System Shutdown:" > > \ USER \ LOG
TSTAMP > > \ USER \ LOG
ECHO "Total up-time today:" > > \ USER \ LOG
TM STOP /C3/N/L/LOG > > \ USER \ LOG
```

This works, assuming the following TM command exists in the AUTOEXEC file:

```
TM START /C3
```

Now the total time the system was on (up-time) can be tracked. This might come in extremely handy for maintenance records or repair work if the average amount of time you use your computer daily is important.

SUMMARY

Keeping track of, or to sound more computerish, *logging* your time is something all PCs are capable of after a fashion. Though DOS doesn't provide any direct means for logging the time, or for even easily retrieving the system time, there are numerous utility programs for that purpose. By combining these programs in a batch file and using redirected output, a simple time tracking system can be developed.

PART THREE
Hard
Disk
Optimization

EVERYTHING COVERED so far in this book, the organizational information provided in Part I and the information on security in Part II, gives you a firm grip on controlling your hard disk. You should be fairly proficient in operating, maintaining, and organizing the hard disk by now. Yet, there are still many interesting things going on behind the scenes that are crucial to hard disk performance. Some of these are governed by DOS, others are controlled at the lowest hardware level of the hard disk. This final part of the book shows you how to take advantage of individual hardware and software controls, allowing you to get the absolute most from your system.

17
Storage Optimization

THERE ARE DOZENS of special tricks for speeding operations on a hard disk, as well as methods for increasing hard disk storage. Surprisingly enough, many of these techniques are deceptively simple. Yet the results are astounding. By using all or a combination of these optimization strategies, you can improve your hard disk's performance by as much as 300 percent!

Storage optimization, or getting the most from your hard disk, is covered in this chapter. There are many techniques for squeezing more performance from a hard disk. Some are software solutions, such as squeezing and sorting a directory or entire disk drive, or storing files in a special, space-saving format. Other solutions are hardware which involve special disk formatting procedures. Not all techniques are things you can do with a screwdriver in your own spare time. In fact, because most of them mess with the actual structure of the hard disk, it's a good idea to have a current backup just in case. However, after the job is done, you'll immediately notice the increased power, speed, and performance of your hard disk.

REVIEW OF DISK FORMATS AND RANDOM STORAGE

When DOS formats a disk, it lays down a series of concentric circles where files and programs are stored. These circles are actually the magnetic tracks and sectors that make up the disk format. (Formatting is discussed in detail in chapter 2.) The number of tracks and sectors are determined by the version of DOS you use, and the size of your disk drives.

Table 17-1. DOS Formats for DOS Versions 1.0 through 4.0.

Formatting command	Size	Comments	DOS
FORMAT /1/8	160K	1 side, 8 sector	1.0
FORMAT /8	320K	2 side, 8 sector	1.0
FORMAT /1/9	180K	1 side, 9 sector	1.1
FORMAT	360K	2 side, 9 sector	1.1
FORMAT /4	360K	1.2M drive	3.0
FORMAT	1200K	2 side, 15 sector	3.0
FORMAT	720K	2 side, 9 sector	3.2
FORMAT /N:9/T:80	720K	1.44M drive	3.3
FORMAT	1440K	2 side, 18 sector	3.3

Each disk contains a root directory and two FAT tables. If the disk is a boot disk, it also contains a boot record with various "wake up" information on it. System disks contain the DOS programs IBMDOS.COM and IBMBIO.COM (or for MS-DOS, MSDOS .SYS and IO.SYS) and the program COMMAND.COM.

Table 17-1 shows the DOS diskette formats that are available from DOS versions 1.0 through 4.0. Hard disks vary, depending on the size of the drive.

The first six formats each use 40 tracks on a diskette. When a diskette is double sided, it really has 80 tracks, 40 to a side. Because the location of the tracks is one above the other, they are often referred to as cylinders. (The tracks occupy a cylinder in space.) A single-sided disk contains 40 tracks and 40 cylinders. A double-sided disk contains 80 tracks and 40 cylinders.

The last four formats are for the IBM PC/AT's high density disk drive and the 3¹/₂-inch drive. These formats have 80 cylinders. (That's 80 tracks on each side of the disk, or 160 total tracks.) The formatting command FORMAT /4 is used to format a 360K disk in the AT's 1200K, or 1.2M disk drive. The /N:9/T:80 switches create a 720K 3¹/₂-inch diskette in a 1.44M drive.

For hard disks, the size varies. There can be any number of physical disks inside a hard disk drive. For example, most 20M hard disk drives contain two physical disks, or platters. Each disk stores 5M on a side, and there is a read/write head on each side. This makes four surfaces for storing information 5M each, or 20M. (With all those surfaces and tracks, you can see why the "cylinder" notation comes in handy.) Each track on each surface holds, on the average, 17 sectors. The number of tracks and surfaces varies depending on the drive. 20M hard disks have about 620 cylinders (2,480 tracks, 42,160 sectors).

After the disk is formatted, programs are placed on the tracks in sequential order, filling the disk from the outside in. As the disk's manager, DOS's job is to fill the disk as efficiently as possible. DOS squeezes as much information as it can on the disk. When it can find no more room for programs, DOS reports the infamous "Disk is full" message.

Clusters

DOS allocates space for programs in chunks called *clusters*. The size of the cluster depends on the size of the disk. For 360K diskettes, the cluster size is two sectors or 1,024 bytes, which means DOS allocates two sectors (for 1K) each time you add a file to disk. Even if the file is less than 1,024 bytes in length, DOS allocates the full 1,024. This number is not reflected by the DIR command; DIR reports the actual, physical size of the program. However, the total bytes free at the end of the DIR command shows the total space left on the disk has decreased by the size of one cluster.

If a program or file's size falls between a cluster size, the larger cluster size is allocated. A 20M hard disk formatted under DOS 3.1 allocated 8,192 bytes for each cluster— 8K! (Which is one reason why DOS 3.1 isn't used today.) That meant even a 27-byte batch file took up 8K on the hard disk. IBM fixed this inefficient use of space by changing the cluster size down to a reasonable 2,048 bytes with DOS 3.2 and later.

File Allocation

When a program is erased, the tracks and sectors it used (its clusters) become available. The clusters don't actually get erased, like rubbing out a pencil mark with a pink eraser. Instead, DOS alters the file's directory entry and marks the tracks and sectors as open in the disk's FAT (File Allocation Table). The tracks still contain the program, only the directory and the FAT show the space as empty. Herein lies the secret behind file recovery programs. Because the physical file is still on disk, these programs can look at the directory entry, examine the tracks and sectors, then repair the FAT and directory to restore the file.

File recovery programs are not foolproof. Because DOS is so efficient with the way it manages space on a disk, it will try to use the available tracks when you save or copy new files. Remember, the tracks are shown as free in the FAT. When a new file actually overwrites the erased file's data on disk, file recovery is impossible. You should be very careful when deleting files, and even more careful (and prompt) when recovering them. (File recovery is discussed in detail later in this chapter.)

To make all this seem a bit clearer, consider a disk as a Disneyland parking lot. A formatted disk is like an empty parking lot. The yellow lines on the pavement marking the stalls are like tracks on a disk. The attendants who direct traffic are like DOS. As cars filter into the parking lot, the attendants direct them to the first available empty space. The cars fill up the parking spaces in sequence. When a caravan of six cars arrives, they all park side by side.

As people leave the parking lot, the space occupied by their cars is made available. New cars arriving fill up the empty spaces starting with the most convenient ones. If a caravan of six cars arrived now, they would fill in the empty spaces as best they could. This might mean that all six cars would not be next to one another.

DOS places programs on disk in the same manner. When a program cannot fit sequentially (all the pieces next to each other on disk, just like the caravan of cars), DOS splits it up according to the available space. DOS further keeps track of all the pieces so the program can be properly accessed or loaded into memory. When a file is split up like this, it is called *fragmented*.

DISK FRAGMENTATION

During the course of using your hard disk, you'll happen across a lot of fragmentation. Because the hard disk can store so many files, and because maintaining, deleting, updating, and creating new files is a big part of using DOS, your hard disk will suffer from fragmentation after a good year of use.

Fragmentation is the official word for what happens when a file does not sit on disk contiguously. For example, suppose that caravan of six cars that arrived late at Disneyland is a file. Three of the cars are parked in sequence close to the front gate. The remaining three had to park elsewhere. One of the cars found a spot a few rows over, and the last two cars found two side-by-side empty spaces further away. If the cars were a single file on disk, DOS would keep track of their locations in the directory and FAT table. When you want to load the file into memory, DOS would pick up the separate pieces and assemble them in sequence in memory.

The CHKDSK will show which files are fragmented in a given directory. CHKDSK displays fragmented files matching the filename specified after CHKDSK. The fragmented filenames are displayed as well as the number of noncontiguous chains (pieces) of the file.

```
C>CHKDSK *.*
```

This command displays all fragmented files in the current directory. If none are found, CHKDSK informs you "All files are contiguous." Otherwise, you might see something like the following:

C:\WP\BOOK\CHAPT12
    Contains 2 noncontiguous blocks.
C:\WP\BOOK\CHAPT2
    Contains 2 noncontiguous blocks.
C:\WP\BOOK\CHAPT8
    Contains 4 noncontiguous blocks.
C:\WP\BOOK\CHAPT10
    Contains 2 noncontiguous blocks.
C:\WP\BOOK\INTRO
    Contains 2 noncontiguous blocks.

All these files are fragmented. Some are split up into two, one (CHAPT8) is split into four separate pieces. Keep in mind, all these pieces are assembled into proper order by DOS as they are loaded into memory. Although CHKDSK does point out which files are noncontiguous, it does nothing to remedy the situation. (The DOS manual recommends you COPY the files to another disk, then copy them back. However, this does not guarantee they will become contiguous, and will generally result in poorer performance from the hard disk.)

Files become fragmented as you use your hard disk. Naturally, as you first put files on the disk they will be in a nice, sequential order. But as you work on your file management, organize the disk, and add and delete files, fragmentation will creep in. After a while, the disk might become seriously fragmented, with pieces of files scattered throughout the disk. Even directories can be fragmented. Have you ever pulled a directory of a large subdirectory and noticed the last few files take forever to appear? Each file appears slowly at the end of the DIR listing, following a lot of disk activity. That's fragmentation in action.

Disks that become severely fragmented lose performance. Obviously, DOS takes longer to pick up and assemble pieces of a fragmented file than an unfragmented file. To repair the disk, each file needs to be unfragmented. All the individual, fragmented pieces need to be picked up and reassembled into a nice, sequential order, like reassembling a jigsaw puzzle. Every file on disk is scanned. If the file is fragmented, its pieces are picked up and put back into sequential order.

Defragmentation

Because hard drives have dropped in price, and several years have passed since folks first started using them, file fragmentation is now a problem most people have to deal with. Coincidentally, the number of file unfragmenting utilities are at an all-time high.

As with most hard disk optimization tricks, unfragmenting files is something DOS doesn't do naturally. Of course, there is a secret way to unfragment your hard disk with DOS: BACKUP, reformat, and RESTORE. Oh? Yeah, I had the same reaction to that one as well. This is why a shareware program, PACKDISK, is included on the supplemental programs disk.

PACKDISK

PACKDISK contains several interesting hard disk utilities. Two of them, LISTFRAG and PACKDISK, deal directly with fragmented files on disk. The other programs, DELDIR, PARK, TRANSDIR, and NAMEDIR are subdirectory manipulating utilities. (Each of these is discussed in detail in chapter 19.)

LISTFRAG displays a list of all fragmented files and subdirectories on a disk drive. To see which files are fragmented, type LISTFRAG followed by an option drive letter (no letter specifies the current drive), and a listing like the following will appear:

The SoftPatch Utility LISTFRAG Version 1.2
(C) Copyright SoftPatch 1985
All Rights Reserved

Fragmented Files in drive C:

\COMMAND.COM
2 noncontiguous chains

\WP\CHAPT1
2 noncontiguous chains

The same information can be obtained with CHKDSK, however, LISTFRAG displays information for the entire drive, or the specified subdirectory and all directories under it. If no fragmented files are found, like CHKDSK, LISTFRAG informs you that all files are contiguous.

The PACKDISK program locates fragmented files and unfragments them. Depending on the severity of your fragmentation, this can take some time. To unfragment files, type PACKDISK followed by the drive letter, or no drive letter if you're unfragmenting the current disk.

The first message PACKDISK gives you is:

WARNING!
Certain copy protection modes may be
incompatible with PACKDISK. If a copy
protected file resides on your disk,
it may be prudent to abort the process
to avoid a loss of information.

If you have a copy protected piece of software on your disk, press Esc. Certain programs rely on tricky copy protection schemes when they are installed on your hard disk. Some of these programs purposely fragment themselves as part of that protection. If you run PACKDISK, it will diligently reassemble the copy protected program into one piece. This might defeat the copy protection and render the program useless. You should use this utility only if you are certain no programs on the disk are copy protected.

If you have no copy protected software, PACKDISK is a safe and reliable program. It unfragments each file on disk, putting them into sequential order. PACKDISK also squeezes any unnecessary space from the disk and from the directories.

After your disk is unfragmented, which could be quite a while depending on the size of the disk, you should immediately reboot. This step is the most important caution regarding any unfragmenting utility. You should always reboot your computer after you've unfragmented the hard disk.

The unfragmenting utility goes about its job by rebuilding the entire diskette. It moves files, then updates the file's location in the directory and in the FAT. DOS uses the FAT to locate files on disk. The FAT is only loaded into memory once when the computer is started. Because the FAT has been updated by the unfragmenting utility, you might see the following message if you do not reset the computer:

Sector Not Found

This is a very bad message to read after messing with your hard disk. However, no real harm has been done. DOS merely needs to load the updated, unfragmented FAT just created. You should reset the computer with Control-Alt-Delete before proceeding.

With your new, unfragmented disk, run the LISTFRAG utility. Don't be surprised when it informs you there are no fragmented files on the disk. You might not notice any improved performance immediately. However, after using the disk a while, and especially if the disk was severely fragmented before, you will notice little things: Directory listings will appear faster, database files will operate quickly, spell checks on word processing documents will proceed faster. And, above all, DOS will load programs into memory much faster than before. The results might not be apparent immediately, but the improvements are there and for the better!

The Mace Utilities

Paul Mace is one of the canonized saints of the Hard Disk Crusades. His Mace Utilities have blossomed into one of the most powerful software packages a hard disk owner needs. As an appetizer, the Mace Utilities claim to fame is that it will actually "unformat" a hard disk drive—the most hazardous thing that can happen to your data can actually be undone by the amazing Mace Utilities.

There are many other saving graces included with the Mace Utilities, most of which are discussed in detail later in this chapter. One of the main features of Mace which pertains to this part of the chapter is file unfragmenting. The F7 option from the main menu in Mace does two things. First, Mace performs a nondestructive read and verify of every sector on your hard disk. If any problems are detected, the program displays a diagnosis and possible treatment. (You can fix the problems by selecting option F5 from the main menu.)

After the diagnosis is complete, the second operation of the F7 option is to unfragment files on your disk. Mace displays a map of your disk (or diskette). You can visibly see the fragmentation and the empty, unused sectors. Each area of the disk is highlighted as Mace works at unfragmenting. Like a child's tile game, you can see the various pieces reassemble into a contiguous structure. Although it's rather fun to watch, the entire process can take up to two hours (depending on how fragmented the disk is). After everything is done, press a key and Mace automatically resets your computer.

One of the advantages of the Mace Utilities unfragment is that it doesn't alter any software copy protection schemes. Mace is aware of almost every copy protected program and scheme out there. The utility carefully skirts around any potential problem areas without risk to your copy protected software.

The entire unfragmenting event is documented by Mace in a file named REPORT.MU (or whichever name you specify). This file must be on a drive other than the one being unfragmented. You can leave the computer unattended and review the proceedings at another time by simply TYPEing the report file. Mace also echoes any bad data to the report or to the printer. If a bad area of the disk is stumbled upon, Mace can correct any problems and restore what it can to the report file.

Power Tools

Power Tools from MLI Microsystems is a complete hard disk utility package. It offers disk utilities, file recovery (unerase), and unfragmenting and disk packing. This program also can be made memory resident. Power Tools can be told to stay in memory so you can access any of its numerous features from any other program you're using.

Power Tools is relatively straightforward and easy to use. DISK OPTIMIZE from the main menu allows you to optimize an entire disk or single files. Then you can pack the files or unfragment them. Packing involves moving all the files toward the start of the disk; in effect, squeezing the empty space, or "air," from between them. Unfragmenting brings the pieces of the files together, just as the Mace and PACKDISK utilities does. Unlike Mace, Power Tools does not check for any copy protection. If you have copy protected files, choose the file-by-file optimizing options and avoid the protected files.

FORMATTING TECHNIQUES FOR INCREASING AND OPTIMIZING STORAGE

Aside from packing and unfragmenting files on disk, there are certain formatting techniques that optimize disk performance on a very low level. As technology races ahead, more and more of these techniques become available. They take standard, middle-of-the-road hard disks and turn them into real storage monsters.

When DOS formats a disk, it lays down a series of tracks and sectors, as discussed earlier in this chapter. Because tracks can be on both sides of a disk, or on the many sides or platters of a hard disk, they are considered cylinders.

Cylinders are numbered starting at the outside of the disk with cylinder 0, and move in sequentially to the highest numbered cylinder. The sectors, however, are not numbered sequentially. Unlike numbers on the face of a clock, sectors are placed around the disk in a specific pattern according to the *interleave factor*.

For example, sectors on a 360K floppy diskette are numbered:

1 2 3 4 5 6 7 8 9

Their physical location on the disk, moving clockwise, is:

1 3 5 7 9 2 4 6 8

This pattern is referred to as a 1-6 interleave. The next sequentially numbered disk sector is actually 6 physical sectors away. The original hard disk in the PC/XT used a 1-6 interleave. The IBM PC/AT's disk drive uses a 1-3 interleave:

1 6 2 7 3 8 4 9 5

Superfast ESDI hard drives on 386 computers use a 1-1 interleave:

1 2 3 4 5 6 7 8 9

Because these computers are so fast, they can keep up with the hard disk controller reading information from the disk.

Disks have an interleave because it spins so fast. After each sector is read from disk, the disk controller performs an error checking calculation on it called a Cyclic Redundancy Check, or CRC. This check assures that the information read from disk is identical to the information on disk. If there is a difference, a CRC error occurs and the controller makes another attempt to read the sector. If after a given number of attempts the sector cannot be read, the disk controller informs DOS and an error message is displayed.

While the disk controller is calculating the CRC, the disk continues to spin. By the time the CRC is calculated on sector 1, sector 2 has already passed and the read/write head is now over sector 3. For the drive controller to read in sector 2, it will have to wait almost one complete disk revolution. To prevent waiting, disk sectors are interleaved. While calculating the CRC on sector 1, the read/write head is over sector 3. When the CRC is done, the read/write head is already in position over sector 2, ready to read in data.

The interleave is invisible to DOS and to your programs. It is maintained by the disk's controller. So when DOS or your program reads information from disk, it is read sequentially, even though the sectors really don't sit that way on disk. As a matter of fact, many technical books leave out the disk interleaving because it is done automatically by the disk's controller.

A potential problem with some hard disk's interleave factor is that they are inefficient. The interleave might be too conservative for the disk controller, or the interleave might be too liberal, causing the controller to skip over sectors and wait a complete revolution for the next sector. Either way, an improper interleave slows the performance of a hard disk.

Several programs are available from Paul Mace Software, the same people who offer the fabled Mace Utilities, for optimizing your hard disk's interleave factor. The Advanced Hard Disk Diagnostics utilities contain two programs for optimum interleave performance: HOPTIMUM and HFORMAT.

HOPTIMUM analyzes hard disk performance. It times the disk drive in a number of situations and determines which interleave factor is the most efficient. This information can be stored and used by a second program, HFORMAT. The HFORMAT program performs a thorough, low-level format of your hard disk based on the optimization scheme provided by HOPTIMUM. Together, both of these programs can result in a more efficient interleave factor for the hard disk, and improve the hard disk's speed.

The only drawback to this brand of optimization is that it performs the dreaded, low-level format of the hard disk, and will definitely erase anything on the disk. Even Mace's UnFormat program cannot recover from a low-level format. You must first BACKUP all files from your hard disk, perform the low-level format, and RESTORE your files. These extra steps are necessary, but the benefits of a higher performing hard disk are worth the time spent backing up and restoring.

CLEANING UP THE DIRECTORY

The order of files in a directory listing can be very important to the speed at which the programs are loaded. Each time you type the name of a program or file, DOS looks three places for it. First, DOS checks to see if it is an internal command. Second, DOS checks the current directory for the file or program. And finally, DOS searches any other directories or drives on the PATH.

When DOS is searching directories, it starts with the first directory entry and reads through the entire directory looking for a match. Files are listed in a directory in the order they were added. Therefore, a simple trick to speed up the time DOS takes to load a program is to put all the COM, EXE, and BAT files at the start of the directory. Even more efficient is to place the most often used programs first in the directory. Unfortunately, this isn't easy to do after the programs are already on your disk. However, it can be done with some interesting utility programs. (Some are discussed at the end of this section.)

Another interesting item about directory searches has to deal with the way files are deleted. When a file is deleted, DOS places a special "available" tag in that file's directory entry. The file isn't actually erased from disk (which is why some special utility programs can undelete deleted files). When DOS searches the directory, it still reads these available directory entries but instead of paying attention to them, it simply skips over them. This adds to the time it takes for DOS to search for and load a program. Not much time is added, but consider if fifty files were deleted from one directory. That's fifty extra stops DOS has to make.

When DOS adds new files to a directory it puts them in one of two places—at the end of the current list of files, or in one of the "holes" left by deleted programs. For example, the following directory has three files:

CFS		4520	1-23-91	5:44p
JOBLOG	88	7516	2-17-92	4:44p
SCHED	WCF	8404	11-11-91	8:08p

If a new file is added, the directory appears as follows:

CFS		4520	1-23-91	5:44p
JOBLOG	88	7516	2-17-92	4:44p
SCHED	WCF	8404	11-11-91	8:08p
LOAN	WKS	3680	11-17-91	11:34p

However, if the file JOBLOG.88 is deleted before the file LOAN.WKS was added, the directory would appear as:

CFS		4520	1-23-91	5:44p
SCHED	WCF	8404	11-11-91	8:08p
LOAN	WKS	3680	11-17-91	11:34p

DOS makes an attempt to fill in the *tombstones* left by deleted files only when new files are added to the directory. By getting rid of the empty directory entries as well as sorting the files in the directory, DOS can search through the entries much faster.

This replacement is not done easily with DOS. You need a special piece of software designed to physically sort a directory on disk. Sorting a directory as it is displayed is quite simple. Recall from chapter 3, the following command is used to sort a directory listing:

```
C > DIR ¦ SORT
```

However, the sort doesn't touch the way the files are physically stored on the disk. It's only for show.

To sort the directory entries on disk, a special utility program is needed. Besides the file's name, each directory entry holds special information about the file used by DOS. This information includes the name of the file, its size, the date and time it was last updated, and other secret, DOS-only stuff. All these details fit in 32 bytes of space in one slot of the directory on disk. The position of the file's slot in the directory is not crucial to the file itself. The actual information telling DOS where on disk the file is located is only referenced by the directory entry. Directory entries can be moved from one slot to another without affecting the content of the files.

The utility programs that sort the directory entries carefully pick up all directory entries and sort them in whichever order you specify. Directory entries can be sorted alphabetically, by extension, size, or date. Additionally, any tombstones left by dead programs are overwritten by the sorting processes. For example, suppose you sort a directory by file extension. The directory contained files with the following extensions:

WKS BAT EXE ASM COM

After the sort, the directory's entries would appear in alphabetical order:

ASM BAT COM EXE WKS

The COM, EXE, and BAT files still won't be put first, so a second technique is required. Before sorting the directory, ensure that the .COM, .EXE, and .BAT files will come first by renaming them. Renaming does not change the contents of the files. However, they will need to be renamed back after the sort. For example, the following commands could be performed before the sort:

```
C>RENAME *.COM *.000
C>RENAME *.EXE *.001
C>RENAME *.BAT *.002
```

In ASCII, numbers take on a lower value than letters. The numbers 0 through 9 have a higher sort priority than the letter A. Make certain there are no other files with the .000 extension in the directory.

After the sort is performed, files in the directory will be listed .000 first, .001 second, and .003 third. Other files will follow based on their extensions. Of course, any tombstones in the directory will be removed. To rename the COM, EXE, and BAT files back to their original names, use:

```
C>RENAME *.000 *.COM
C>RENAME *.001 *.EXE
C>RENAME *.002 *.BAT
```

Note: Files without extensions will appear before any files with extensions. (The character "space" is weighted as the first value by most sorting utilities.) Files without extensions have to be given temporary extensions before the sort to ensure they wouldn't be placed before the COM, EXE, and BAT files. Extensionless files need to be renamed after the sort is completed.

The Mace Utilities

The Mace Utilities comes to the rescue with a directory sorting function. From the main menu, option F6 initiates a directory sort/squeeze. The sorting half deals with placing all the files on your hard disk in any order you specify. Squeezing removes the tombstones left by deleted files.

The sort can take place on four options: filename, filename extension, date and time, or file size. After the options, you are asked if you want the read-only status of the COM, EXE, and SYS files set. Because these files are normally never written to, modified, or deleted, setting the read-only status provides an extra level of protection against accidental erasure. Also, because these files are read-only and are not modified, other operations of the Mace Utilities and hard drive performance in general speeds up.

After this is done, Mace displays each directory on disk as it is sorted. Depending on the size of your hard disk and number of directories and files, the entire operation can take anywhere from ten seconds to about a minute.

The Norton Utilities

Another directory sorting/squeezing program is called DS.EXE or DIRSORT.EXE. This program is part of a group of interesting utilities collectively called the Norton Utilities. The Norton Utilities come from the father of PC disk utilities, Peter Norton.

DS sorts directory entries by filename, filename extension, date, time, or file size. It also can sort with any combination of each. If the optional /S switch is specified, Norton's DS will sort all directories starting with the current directory on down.

To run Norton's DS, type DS on the command line, followed by either N, E, D, T, or S for fileName, filename Extension, Date, Time, or Size, respectively. If the /S slash is included, DS continues to sort all files in any subdirectories under the current directory. DS tells you which directory it is sorting and exactly what it is doing:

DS-Directory Sort, Advanced Edition, (C) Copyright 1987, Peter Norton

C: \ ADMIN \ LOTUS \ SUE . . . reading, sorting, writing, done.

After the entire operation (which happens rather quickly), you are returned to the DOS prompt. You now have a nice, clean, sorted directory.

ARCHIVING PROGRAMS

A hard disk can store a lot of data. But because hard disks hold so much stuff at one time, you might have some seldom used programs that take up a lot of space. If you don't need the programs, you could copy or back them up to floppy disks. But is this really why you have a hard disk? Would organizing the floppy diskettes be more trouble than keeping the programs on hard disk?

The answer comes in shareware programs that archive files, compacting several into one convenient file for storage. These archiving utilities are some of the most popular utility programs for the PC and compatibles. They originated from the electronic Bulletin Board Systems (BBS) that dot the nation. A BBS user saves time by downloading software (copy it from the BBS to their own system) as one file rather than getting 10 or 20 larger files. In the nonelectronic communications use of computers, the archiving utilities allow you to store groups of files in a tight, compact form which saves disk space.

The former champions of the software archiving utility arena were PKARC and PKX-ARC. These utilities had their roots in the ARC program. However, because of legal battles, PKARC was absorbed by the makers of ARC. PKARC went through transitions to PKPAK and PKUNPAK, but was still deemed an unauthorized copy. So PKPAK's author, Phil Katz (the PK part of the filename), came out with a new archiving utility, PKZIP. The other software still exists and, for the most part, both the ARC and ZIP formats are compatible.

The archiving utilities place a number of files into a single file for safekeeping or for transferring over the phone lines to or from a BBS. As the files are stored, they are compressed according to certain computer storage algorithms. Compressed files take up less space than if they were stuck together in one big file.

The flip side of the archiving utilities allows you to unpack, or unARC, the files from their special storage formats. You can get at one or all of the files simply by undoing the archive, like unpacking a box.

For example, suppose you've done your tax returns for the past few years on the computer. You are wise to keep those records around. Rather than store them on floppy, you can put them all into a single, space-saving archive file. You might have files titled 86.ARC, 87.ARC, 88.ARC, and so on.

Because ARC compresses the files, they take up less space on the hard disk. And because files can be added to the ARC file, which means 86.ARC can contain all the tax information for the year 1986, the number of directory slots used is cut down. Now, all your tax information is still stored on hard disk. You can unARC your files and access the data faster and more efficiently than if they had been on floppy.

A version of the PKARC program has been included on the Supplemental Programs Diskette. There are actually two applications, PKARC and PKXARC, that come as a single file named PKXaaAbb.COM. The Xaa refers to the PKXARC version number, and the Abb refers to the PKARC version number. The versions on the diskette are PKXARC 34 and PKARC version 20, which translates into PKX34A20.COM. (By looking at the name of the file you can determine if you have the most recent version.)

To release the files from the PKXaaAbb.COM file, type its name at the DOS prompt. For example:

C > PKX34A20

The PKARC program then proceeds to unfold itself:

PKARC 2.0/PKXARC 3.4   Creation Module   12-15-86
Copyright (c) 1986 PKWARE, Inc. All Rights Reserved.

Performing self-extraction . . .

unCrunching: PKARC.COM
unCrunching: PKARC.DOC
unCrunching: PKXARC.COM
unCrunching: PKXARC.DOC
unCrunching: PKXARCJR.COM
unCrunching: README.DOC

These programs are distributed as shareware. They are not public domain. Shareware refers to software distributed free of charge. Indeed, the distribution scheme expects you to make copies of the programs and give them to your friends. However, if you use the program and find it of value, a donation of $20 is expected.

The files that PKX34A20.COM produces are used for the ARC'ing and unARC'ing of files. The files were originally stored in a crunched format, saving space on disk. They are:

PKARC.COM	Program that creates and maintains .ARC archive files.
PKARC.DOC	The instruction manual for PKARC (a text file).
PKXARC.COM	Program that eXtracts files from .ARC archives.
PKXARC.DOC	The instruction manual for PKXARC (a text file).
PKXARCJR.COM	A special version of PKXARC designed to run on computers without much memory. It is, however, slower than PKXARC .COM.
README.DOC	A text file containing any last minute fixes and changes to the programs.

To archive a single file or a group of files, PKARC is used. The format is:

PKARC [old options] [acdflmuvx] filename[.ARC] [filename. . .]

The numerous options are all described in detail in the PKARC manual, PKARC.DOC. Refer there for details.

The PKARC program is used to create an archive. First, specify the a option for adding files to the archive. Next the ARC file (where the compressed files are stored) is specified, followed by the files you wish to place into the archive. For example, suppose last month's accounting data files all end with the extension ACC. You wish to save them all into an ARC file called JUNE88.ARC.

```
C > PKARC A JUNE88 *.ACC
```

PKARC looks for the file JUNE88.ARC in the current directory. The ARC extension is assumed unless another is specified. If JUNE88.ARC is not found, it is created. Next, it reads all files *.ACC and determines the best way to store them. Depending on what information is in the file, it might be compressed according to one of the following methods: Stored, Packed, Squeezed, crunched, Crunched (with a capital C), or Squashed. PKARC analyzes the file and determines which compacting method works best. As PKARC creates the file and adds the filenames, something similar to the following is displayed:

```
Creating Archive: JUNE88.ARC
Adding:   PAYROLL.ACC  analyzing, (49%) squashing, done.
Adding:   AR.ACC       analyzing, (40%) crunching, done.
Adding:   AP.ACC       analyzing, (41%) crunching, done.
Adding:   OE.ACC       analyzing, (35%) squashing, done.
```

The number in parentheses refers to the size of the file in its compressed form compared to its original size. If the file AR.ACC is 10K long, it will take up only 4K in the ARC file.

After the files are archived, the originals can be deleted, which saves disk space, and is more convenient and handy than backing up.

To retrieve a single file or all files from an archive, PKXARC is used. The format of the PKXARC command is:

```
PKXARC [/c/l/p/r/t/v] filename[.ARC] [d: \ dir. . .] [files. . .]
```

PKXARC's options are all described in detail in the PKARC manual. Refer there for details.

PKXARC's primary function is to extract files from an archive. If no files are specified, all files are extracted. PKXARC can be used to look inside an ARC file. An ARC file might contain hundreds of files, yet appears as only one entry in a directory. To view the files in the archive, the /V switch is used:

C>PKXARC /V JUNE88

This command lists all files in the JUNE88.ARC archive. A single file could be extracted by specifying its name:

C>PKXARC JUNE88 PAYROLL.ACC

This command extracts (and unsquashes) the file PAYROLL.ACC from the JUNE88.ARC archive. The extraction is done quickly and more efficiently than scanning backups on floppy diskettes.

The PKARC utilities are almost a must for your hard disk. By using them alone you can save a lot of space currently taken up by programs "just along for the ride."

CUBIT Optimization software from SoftLogic Solutions does almost the same thing the PKARC programs do—compress data stored on hard disk. The difference is, CUBIT is a memory resident program. This "on the fly" condensing compresses files as they are saved to disk and decompresses files as they are loaded from disk.

Initially, files need to be compressed before the "on the fly" part of CUBIT is used. The CUBIT program itself behaves a lot like PKARC and PKXARC, except there is only one program. CUBIT is smart enough to know when a program or file has been compressed. If the file has not already been compressed, CUBIT compresses it. If the file is compressed, CUBIT decompresses it.

C>CUBIT JUNE.WKS

Suppose JUNE.WKS is a 17K spreadsheet file. CUBIT analyzes the file, first detecting that it is not already compressed. It then proceeds to squeeze JUNE.WKS down by 33 percent to 13K. The squeezing varies from file to file. Text files squeeze down faster than other types of files. For example, a sample 10K word processing file could be crunched by 60 percent to 4K with CUBIT.

The CUBITR program is a memory resident part of CUBIT which intercepts all access to files on disk. The CUBIT manual depicts CUBITR as a traffic cop, directing and intercepting disk activity. CUBITR examines all files you access from disk. If it detects a compressed file, CUBITR decompresses the file as it is loaded. Then, after the file has been updated, CUBITR compresses the file back as it is saved to disk.

Needless to say, this "on the fly" compressing and decompressing takes time. CUBITR ignores files not already compressed on disk. But for compressed files, CUBITR takes about .6 seconds per 1K of file size to compress or decompress the file. Loading a 10K compressed file into a word processor took CUBITR an extra 12 seconds to do the job. (The file was originally 17K.) Another 12 seconds was tacked on by CUBIT when the file was saved back to disk.

CUBIT and CUBITR can cut down on disk space anywhere from 30 to 50 percent, depending on the type of file. The "on the fly" ability means you won't have to PKARC or PKXARC files that are saved in compressed format. On almost full hard disks, CUBIT provides an excellent method of conserving disk space.

HARDWARE SOLUTIONS

The final trick to squeezing performance from a hard disk deals with the actual way information is stored on the disk. The way the bits, the 1's and 0's, sit on disk is important to the amount of information stored on the disk. Although most reference manuals simply state that bytes are placed into sectors one bit at a time, the procedure is much more complex.

There are several popular methods for recording information on disk. Recording 1's and 0's is done by leaving a *magnetic flux reversal* on the surface of the disk. (Don't go running away—this is not going to get overly technical!) The most common method of recording bits on disk is referred to as *modified frequency modulation*. MFM uses a special way of monitoring the flux reversals to mark the positions of the 1's and 0's. MFM can store a lot of 1's and 0's on a disk without too much overhead.

The next best step up from MFM coding is called *run length limited*, or RLL coding. RLL coding allows for an almost 50 percent increase in the amount of information stored on the same disk. The coding scheme squeezes more information onto disk because of the way it looks at the flux reversals. A drive that uses RLL coding can store much more information than an MFM drive.

Maynard Electronics of Casselberry, Florida, has taken RLL coding one step further. With their new Enhanced Run Length Limited (ERLL) coding they are able to improve the storage capabilities of a hard disk by almost 100 percent, and the rate at which the controller accesses the disk by almost 200 percent.

ERLL coding changes the number of sectors on a hard disk from 17 to 33 per track. (This is the same physical disk—the ERLL coding scheme allows more sectors per track.) Because more information is on each track, the controller is able to read in that information twice as fast. Nothing is physically changed on the drive, and it's not spinning twice as fast. Finally, ERLL coding offers unique, foolproof error detection. Maynard's Advanced Error Correcting Code is considered twice as good as the error correcting procedures used on RLL and MFM disk drives.

The ERLL device is a controller card available from Maynard Electronics. Upgrading to an ERLL system does not require that you buy a special disk drive system. Maynard even claims in its literature that you can start using the ERLL controller without reformatting your current hard disk. (With other controllers, you must do a low-level format for the drive to use the new controller.)

The Maynard ERLL controller is totally compatible with the IBM PC/XT and AT hard disk BIOS. It offers a superb way of improving hard disk storage and performance with only one piece of hardware, and is compatible with your existing hardware.

At this writing, the controller is not available on the retail market. Those desiring more information on obtaining a Maynard ERLL controller should contact a local dealer or Maynard Electronics directly. (The address is in Appendix D.)

SUMMARY

This chapter was packed with information about getting the most from your hard disk. A wide variety of topics for hardware and software techniques were covered. These tricks include unfragmenting files; adjusting the hard disk's interleave factor; squeezing, sorting, and cleaning up the directory; archiving files to keep them handy while saving disk space; condensing files "on the fly," and ERLL disk formatting.

These tricks are all more or less physical solutions to optimizing hard disk performance. In the next chapter, you'll see how your computer's memory, or RAM, can be used to maximize disk access and overall computer performance.

18
Disk Access Optimization

COMPUTERS TYPICALLY STORE information in one of two places: internal memory, or on disk. The computer's RAM, or Random Access Memory, is used for the temporary storage of information. Disks are used for permanent storage. In order to hold information in RAM, electrical current must constantly refresh the RAM circuitry. After the power is turned off, any information in RAM is gone, so information needs to be saved to a more permanent site on disk. Disks retain information even when the power is off. (Refer to chapter 1 for an overview of data storage.)

The computer's microprocessor runs programs and stores data in RAM. The microprocessor cannot directly access the information on disk, but it can load that information into RAM, work on it, then save it back to disk. The subject of the book is hard disks and this part of the book deals with optimizing hard disks. Amazingly enough, one interesting way to optimize disk performance is by using RAM.

The previous chapter discussed boosting hard disk performance with various software and hardware tricks. This chapter concentrates on the interaction between the computer's random access memory and disk access. RAM can be used as a fast buffer between your programs and the hard disk. It also can replace some disk operations altogether. Again, the object of all this is to improve disk performance.

OVERLAY FILES

In the old, CP/M days of computing, memory was a scarce commodity. The computer's operating system, programs, and data all had to fit inside a tiny 64K bank of memory. It appears tiny today because PC-DOS computers are now capable of having ten times that much memory for storing the operating system, programs, and data. Even more memory than that, called *expanded memory*, now can be used by the computer in a variety of different ways.

The original IBM PC introduced in 1981 had only 64K of RAM with a potential 640K, which made sense because all other computers at the time also had 64K of RAM. Software houses developing for the PC were used to working in a 64K environment. To make the best use of that space, they divided the 64K RAM up into sections for their own program and for data. For example, the VisiCalc spreadsheet occupied about 30K of RAM and left the rest of memory for spreadsheet data.

If a program required more memory than the computer had, it would swap part of itself in memory with a new part from disk. The new part from disk was referred to as an *overlay file*. For example, suppose one program occupied 32K of RAM. Yet the program was actually 48K in size. The programmers would divide the program code into separate modules. The main part of the program would always be in memory. But the modules, those things in the program that weren't used that often or were only used for special operations, would be kept on disk. The program would then load the modules from disk as they were needed, replacing the modules in memory which weren't used. By juggling data from disk and memory, programs could be quite extensive, yet only use a moderate amount of memory.

As the price of RAM chips dropped, and people were putting more memory into their computers, programs took advantage of it. After a while, the IBM PC was sold off the shelf with 128K of memory standard. When the software houses realized computers were coming with more memory, they started abandoning the overlay file technique. Now, a program could all fit into memory at one time. By removing the overlay files, programs operated faster because they didn't need to access the disk as often.

The IBM PC/XT, which had a 10M hard disk, came with 256K of RAM. For the longest time in PC computing, this was the standard memory size. Amazingly enough, about the same time, most major software manufacturers needed that much memory to run their programs, which led to a belief that programs and programmers were becoming sloppy. After all, the programmers had all that RAM. The belief was further proliferated when the programs requiring 256K had to resort to overlay files to fit into memory.

Currently, the standard memory size in IBM computers is the maximum 640K, a limitation placed on the original PC in 1981. Remember, back then 64K was considered RAM heaven. The designers of the PC figured 10 times that much RAM would be more than enough. They designed the computer and, more importantly, the operating system to use 640K of RAM for running programs. Even at this size, several popular programs have to use overlay files to fit into memory.

Using overlay files is not negative. For example, many programs provide on-line help information with overlay files. The thinking is that later on, after the program is mastered, you won't need the help and can delete those files from your disk to save space. Also, some programs put little-used features on disk as overlay files. This way, if you need the features, they're there. If you don't want them, they won't take up any extra RAM.

EMS MEMORY

As the size of programs increased, the software houses began to see a real limitation with 640K of RAM. Although the PC's microprocessor is capable of talking with up to 1M of RAM, the PC only allotted 640K for storing programs and data. Most standardized programs could get along fine in 640K. But graphics and computer assisted design, or CAD, programs needed more memory. Large spreadsheet users discovered that spreadsheets run out of memory quickly. Software designers were pushing the PC to the limit of its performance. They wanted more RAM.

When the PC AT was introduced, it sported the next generation microprocessor, the 80286. All by itself, this chip is capable of directly addressing 16M of RAM, 16 times greater than the 8088 in the original PC. The 80386 and 80486 extended the amount of memory that could be used by a PC even more. Yet, because computers with those microprocessors are also running DOS, they're subject to the same memory limitations as the 8088; they can only run programs in 640K of their potential megabytes of RAM.

To break beyond the 640K DOS barrier, two software companies sat down and designed an Expanded Memory Specification, or EMS. Lotus, developer of the popular 1-2-3 spreadsheet, and Intel, makers of the PC's microprocessor, teamed up to create the EMS specification to allow IBM PC's to access memory above and beyond the 640K limit. Microsoft, makers of DOS, threw in their approval by announcing support of the EMS standard. (In some circles, the EMS standard also is referred to as the Lotus/Intel/Microsoft, LIM Expanded Memory Specification.)

Note: EMS is not the same as Extended Memory. Extended Memory is memory used in the 80286, 80386, and other processors above the 1M limit. Only non-DOS operating systems, such as OS/2 or Xenix, use Extended memory. However, special software is available that turns that Extended memory into EMS Expanded memory.

With EMS, a PC can access up to 8M of RAM (which includes the basic 640K). No matter how much EMS memory your computer has, it uses only 64K at a time. EMS memory is accessed in four 16K "pages." Each of these pages is a window to 16K of EMS memory. The page system works by swapping a particular 16K chunk of EMS memory with a 16K chunk of memory inside the PC. At any time, up to four pages of EMS memory can be accessed. Although this might seem awkward, especially when dealing with 8M of memory, keep in mind information is read from the hard disk in only .5K (512 byte) chunks. The EMS standard is 128 times more efficient.

The only drawback to all this memory is that you cannot run programs there. Programs must still occupy and run in the first 640K of memory. However, this doesn't necessarily make EMS useless. There are a few programs that take direct advantage of EMS memory for storing their data. Ashton-Tate's Framework, Lotus' Symphony and 1-2-3 spreadsheet, Microsoft's Windows, SideKick Plus, and others all use EMS memory for storing data. Even more programs are on the way. Also, DOS 4 uses expanded memory for storing certain items that cut down on the amount of regular memory available.

If you don't own any programs that take advantage of EMS memory, EMS can be put to use as a Print Spooler, RAM Disk, or as Cache memory. Most of these programs are configured via the CONFIG.SYS file when you start your computer. Each of them helps to speed up operations on the computer, and because they aren't in standard memory, they don't subtract space from running your programs.

PRINT SPOOLERS

Print Spoolers help speed up printer operations. The printer is the slowest part of any computer. When a print spooler is installed, DOS sends characters to the spooler's memory rather than sending them directly to the printer. Now, the computer doesn't have to sit and wait for the printer to finish. The characters stored in the spooler wait until the printer is ready to accept them.

DOS checks the spooler's memory every so often to see if any characters need to be printed. If so, it prints about a handful, then quickly returns to what it was doing before. These quick check-and-prints happen so fast you don't notice them. The printer continues to print and you continue to use the computer.

There are a variety of print spooling programs. DOS's PRINT command isn't a true spooler, though it does act like one. Instead of intercepting characters sent to the printer, PRINT must be directly informed of a document to be printed. Unless you print to disk and then use PRINT to spool, normal printing will continue to slow down your printer.

A RAM disk is a superfast electronic disk drive in memory. DOS offers its own RAM disk driver called VDISK.SYS. A few RAM disk drivers come with EMS hardware. RAM disks are discussed in the next section.

Disk caches are an excellent disk speed-up technique using memory. Not the same as a RAM disk, caches are responsible for quick and efficient disk access. They are discussed later in this chapter.

RAM DISKS AND HOW THEY WORK

RAM Disks go by a number of names: MEMDISK, RAMDISK, VDISK, MEMBRAIN, and so on. Basically, a RAM disk is a superfast disk drive in memory. Because it is in memory, the RAM disk will behave a lot faster than any physical disk drive. Disk access will be quicker and read/write will appear instantaneous. The RAM disk will operate as fast as your computer's memory.

The disk drive is the most mechanical hardware in your computer. Chances are if some piece of hardware is going to fail, it's going to be a disk drive. Floppy drives are the most mechanical and the most susceptible to failure. Hard drives are less so because they're constantly moving. However, nothing moves in a RAM disk. It is all electronic.

Most RAM disks are created with device drivers in the CONFIG.SYS file. CONFIG.SYS is a file read by DOS, even before AUTOEXEC.BAT. CONFIG.SYS's job is to CONFIGure your SYStem. CONFIG.SYS configures and arranges every aspect of your system.

Basically, CONFIG.SYS contains a list of parameters for your system and device drivers. The parameters include information for DOS, such as how many files it can have open at one time, the number of file buffers to be used, even which country and language DOS should operate under.

Device drivers are memory resident controller programs. Some device drivers, like ANSI.SYS, control the way DOS writes to the screen. Others control various devices. For example, the Microsoft Mouse peripheral uses a device driver called MOUSE.SYS. If you want a RAM drive in your computer, include the appropriate RAM disk driver in your CONFIG.SYS file.

To install a device, CONFIG.SYS should contain the word "device" followed by an equals " = " and the name of the driver software and the path if the driver isn't located in the root directory.

DEVICE =

For example, suppose a RAM disk driver named "RAMBO" exists in the \ DOS subdirectory. To install the device driver, and subsequently the RAM disk, the following should be in the CONFIG.SYS file:

DEVICE = C: \ DOS \ RAMBO

When DOS boots, it scans the root directory for the CONFIG.SYS file. If found, DOS reads CONFIG.SYS, sets any parameters, and loads any device drivers. If a device driver is found, DOS loads it into memory and executes the instructions in the driver. In the previous example, DOS would load the RAMBO driver into memory, then execute it. The RAMBO driver would then allocate a certain amount of memory as a RAM disk. DOS then reads the rest of the CONFIG.SYS file, or if done, looks for and executes AUTOEXEC.BAT.

The device driver is the key to running a RAM disk. The driver instructs DOS that it is operating memory as a disk drive. Depending on the driver, DOS assigns the drive a letter and allocates memory to the drive. After space is assigned, the RAM disk allocates space in memory for a directory, FAT, sectors, and clusters. Because DOS knows the RAM device is a disk drive, DOS will treat the RAM disk as if it were another disk. However, the driver also instructs DOS that the RAM disk cannot be formatted. The disk is

Disk Access Optimization **313**

formatted as it is installed. If the FORMAT command is used on the RAM disk, DOS returns the following:

Format not supported on drive D:

Other disk commands, including CHKDSK, XCOPY, SUBST and ASSIGN, all treat the RAM disk just as if it were a real disk drive. The DISKCOPY and DISKCOMP commands might not work with some RAM disks, depending on the size of the RAM disk and the type of device driver used.

Installing a RAM disk in conventional (640K) RAM eats up quite a bit of space. A 360K RAM disk leaves a little over 256K to operate programs and store data. For most cases, this is very efficient. The majority of programs require only 256K of RAM to run. And 360K is exactly the size of one floppy diskette. Backing up the RAM disk is as easy as COPY *.*.

Many RAM disks also can operate in EMS memory, depending on the type of the RAM disk and its device driver. Some RAM disks simply use an extra parameter in the CONFIG.SYS file to install in EMS memory. Other drivers might install only in EMS memory. The advantage is that a RAM disk in EMS memory won't hamper the "tiny" 640K of RAM you have to run your programs. In EMS memory, a RAM disk could conceivably be 8M in size.

The DOS VDISK

A RAM disk driver has been included with DOS, starting with DOS version 3. VDISK.SYS is the name of DOS's Virtual Disk driver. VDISK can create any number of RAM disks in either conventional memory, or in Extended Memory. (EMS memory hardware for PC's and XT's usually comes with its own, customized RAM disk drivers.)

To install a VDISK, the name of the VDISK.SYS device driver must be specified in the CONFIG.SYS file. If VDISK.SYS is not in the root directory, its path also should be specified. VDISK installs itself as the next highest drive letter. If you have drives A through C, VDISK installs itself as drive D. If you're installing more than one VDISK (done by specifying VDISK more than once in the CONFIG.SYS file), each subsequent RAM disk takes on the next highest drive letter.

The format for installing VDISK is:

DEVICE = [path]VDISK.SYS [size] [sector] [dir] [/E:m]

Size is the size of the RAM disk, and can be anywhere from 1 (for a puny 1K RAM disk) to as much memory in your system, minus 64K. VDISK insists at least 64K of RAM be left in the system. If the size parameter is too large, VDISK adjusts itself to allow for that 64K. If a size value is not specified, VDISK installs as a 64K RAM disk.

Sector refers to the size of the sectors used in the RAM disk. DOS usually allocates 512 bytes to a sector, however smaller sizes can be specified to save space in the RAM disk. VDISK allows sizes of 128, 256, or 512 bytes. If none is specified, 128 bytes is the default.

Dir refers to the number of entries, or "slots," allowed in the RAM disk's root directory. This number can be from 2 to 512. VDISK uses 64 if none is specified. Directory slots take space on the RAM disk. Assigning more than you need means less space for program and data storage. If you know exactly what you're using the RAM disk for, liberally estimate the number of files and use that value for the dir option.

Note: VDISK assigns the volume label "VDISK" to each RAM disk it creates. This volume label automatically takes up one directory slot.

The /E switch is used to install the RAM disk into Extended memory (this is not for EMS memory, and will only work with IBM AT's or true compatibles). /E is followed by a value, m, that specifies the number of sectors to be read at a time. The default value of m is 8, although it can be any value from 1 to 8. Lesser values increase the speed of some operations with certain types of *interrupt-driven* software. If your software behaves abnormally with a VDISK installed in Extended memory, decrease the value of the m option.

Each of the options of VDISK, disk size, sector size and directory entries, can be proceeded by an optional comment. For example:

DEVICE=C: \ DOS \ VDISK.SYS DISK SIZE=360 SECTORS ARE=256 62 /E

This statement assigns a 360K RAM disk with 256 byte sectors and 62 directory entries in Extended (/E) memory. The following command in the CONFIG.SYS file does the same thing:

DEVICE= \ DOS \ VDISK.SYS 630 256 62 /E

The following two lines of a CONFIG.SYS file install two RAM disks into conventional memory. The first disk is 64K in size, the second is 128K:

DEVICE=VDISK.SYS
DEVICE=VDISK.SYS SIZE=128

When the computer is booted, and CONFIG.SYS is read, DOS installs the RAM disks into conventional memory. As each disk is installed, information about the disk is displayed:

VDISK Version 3.30 virtual disk D:
    Buffer size adjusted
    Sector size adjusted

Directory entries adjusted
Buffer size: 64 KB
Sector size: 128
Directory entries: 64

VDISK Version 3.30 virtual disk E:
Sector size adjusted
Directory entries adjusted
Buffer size: 128 KB
Sector size: 128
Directory entries: 64

There are now two Virtual Disks in memory. The first is assigned drive D, the second drive E. The first is 64K in size, the second 128K. All other options are at the default settings. Note that having these two RAM disks lower the amount of conventional memory to 330K (on a 640K machine).

MEMBRAIN

MBRAIN12.EXE is a very popular, public domain RAM disk utility. It creates a RAM disk device driver named MEMBRAIN.SYS. With this device driver in your CONFIG.SYS file, you will have a 160K RAM disk installed.

The MEMBRAIN.SYS driver, unlike VDISK, sets its parameters as it's created by MBRAIN12. When creating the MEMBRAIN.SYS driver, the MBRAIN12 options are:

```
MBRAIN12 [size] [sector] [cluster] [dir] [path]
```

Size is the size of the MEMBRAIN RAM disk. It can be a minimum of 64K and a maximum of as much conventional memory that your system has. If a size value is not specified, MEMBRAIN installs a default of 160K. If a value smaller than 64K is specified, MEMBRAIN installs a 64K RAM disk.

Sector refers to the size of the sectors used in the MEMBRAIN RAM disk. MEMBRAIN accepts any sector size as long as it is a multiple of 128. The default value is 512 bytes.

Cluster indicates the number of sectors per cluster. Each file on the RAM disk will be assigned a multiple of this many sectors no matter what its size. The values for cluster can range from 1 to as many sectors that will fit into a 2048 byte cluster. So, for a 512 byte sector size, a maximum of 4 can be used ($4 \times 512 = 2048$). One sector per cluster is used if none are specified.

Dir refers to the number of directory entries allowed in the RAM disk. This can be any number, but the default value is 64.

Path refers to the location of the MEMBRAIN disk drive. For example, to install a RAM disk as drive D, D: \ is used for the path.

To create the MEMBRAIN.SYS file, MBRAIN is typed at the command prompt, followed by any of the above options. MBRAIN alone creates a RAM disk drive with the following parameters:

$<<<<$ M e m   B r a i n $>>>>$
(C) 1984 Dennis Lee
160K MemBrain Created

512 bytes per sector
1 sectors per cluster
64 directory entries
1 reserved sector
1 FAT sector
4 directory sectors
314 data sectors

_____

320 total sectors

This command creates a MEMBRAIN.SYS driver. When included in the CONFIG.SYS file, this driver creates a 160K RAM disk with these characteristics. To activate the driver, as with VDISK.SYS, include MEMBRAIN.SYS in your CONFIG.SYS file:

DEVICE = \ DOS \ MEMBRAIN.SYS

If you wish to change any of MEMBRAIN's options, recreate the MEMBRAIN.SYS file. For example, to create a MEMBRAIN.SYS driver for a 360K RAM disk, the following would be entered:

C > MBRAIN12 360

This command creates a new MEMBRAIN.SYS file, one that will create a 360K RAM disk.

Other RAM Disks

RAM disk drivers are usually available from the same manufacturer that provides your computer's RAM upgrade, or EMS expansion card. For example, when you buy the Intel Aboveboard, you get Intel's own EMS RAM disk driver. When you buy the AST Six Pack, you get AST's RAM disk driver. These RAM disks are tailored specifically to work with their own hardware. They are often easier to use, faster, or offer more power than DOS's VDISK. (Most of them use VDISK as their "benchmark" test, boasting their own software is anywhere from 20 to 80 percent faster.)

RAM Disk Techniques

There are many interesting things that can be done with a RAM disk. Keep in mind the RAM disk's speed, it can do nothing but improve the time disk-intensive operations take. For example, a batch file could be written to copy all your word processing programs and files to the RAM disk for fast operation. As soon as you're done with word processing, the updated files could be copied back to the hard disk.

The following batch file copies all the word processing files from the subdirectory \ WP on the hard disk to the RAM disk, E:. The name of the word processor is WS. All files created with this word processor end in the DOC file extension. After the word processor is finished, any files created are copied to the directory \ WP \ DATA on the hard disk:

```
@ECHO OFF
COPY C: \ WP \ *.* E:
E:
WS
IF NOT EXIST *.DOC GOTO DONE
COPY *.DOC C: \ WP \ DATA
:DONE
C:
ECHO Done!
```

The IF NOT EXIST statement tests to see if any DOC files were created. This statement is executed after the WS program is done. If not, execution branches to the :DONE label. Otherwise, all files with the .DOC extension are copied safely back to the \ WP \ DATA directory.

With the increased size of conventional RAM and the popularity of hard disks, several word processing programs include spell checking and thesaurus software. These utilities are very disk-intensive activities. Copying the dictionaries and using them in RAM improves their performance.

RAM disks really shine when programs lean heavily on disk access. The most marked improvement has happened in the area of software development. Writing, editing, compiling, and linking programs for the PC takes quite a bit of time. It involves a lot of reading and writing to disk. When all these activities are placed into a RAM disk, the time required to create a program can be cut in half.

Data base operations are improved by placing programs and files on the RAM disk (as in the batch file example). Each record on the data base is accessed individually. During a search and sort or an update, there is a lot of disk activity. Placing data base files on a RAM disk speeds up those operations.

Generally, all activities are improved by using a RAM disk. If your computer is equipped with EMS or Extended memory, a RAM disk can come in quite handy.

There's only one drawback for RAM disks. Because the RAM disk is memory, when the power goes off or even if the computer is reset, any information stored on the RAM disk is gone forever. A few RAM disks offer a battery backup option, which saves any data left on the RAM disk while the computer's power is turned off. However, the best rule of thumb when the power goes: The RAM disappears.

Because RAM is so temporary, it should be checked before shutting down your computer. This check could be another function of a possible SHUTDOWN batch file (chapter 12). A good way to test for files in a RAM disk is to include the following statements in a SHUTDOWN.BAT file:

```
REM RAM drive assumed to be drive D:
IF NOT EXIST D: \ *.* GOTO EMPTY
DIR D: /W
ASK Backup the files in the RAM disk (Y/N)?
IF ERRORLEVEL = = 1 GOTO EMPTY
XCOPY D: \ *.* C: \ RAMDISK /S/E
:EMPTY
```

This batch file assumes the RAM disk is drive D. The IF NOT EXIST test determines if the RAM disk is empty. If no files exist (*.*), the batch file execution jumps to the EMPTY label and SHUTDOWN.BAT continues.

If files do exist, a directory is displayed. The ASK statement waits for keyboard input. Either Y or N must be typed before the batch file continues. If Y is typed, an errorlevel of 0 is returned, N sets the errorlevel at 1. (The ASK.COM program is included on the supplemental programs diskette and was discussed in chapter 7.)

If N is pressed, execution branches to the EMPTY label and files in the RAM disk are not saved. If Y is pressed, the XCOPY program is used to copy all files and all subdirectories from the RAM disk to the subdirectory \ RAMDISK on drive C. (This could be replaced with whichever directory you find most appropriate for the files in your own RAM disk.) After the files have been saved, the batch file continues.

DISK CACHING

A *cache* (pronounced "cash") is a secret storage place. Pirates often had a cache of jewels buried on some desert island. Modern day terrorists have caches of weapons hidden somewhere. On a less evil side, squirrels have caches of acorns stowed away for winter. Computers, not necessarily associated with pirates, terrorists, or squirrels, also can use caches. A cache is a secret storage place in memory that speeds up disk operations.

A disk cache is not a RAM disk, although they are similar and easily confused. A disk cache monitors disk activity. It logs all reads and writes from disk, then keeps a copy of what was read or written in its own cache memory. If the computer makes a second request to read information from disk, and that information is already in the cache, the information is read from cache memory instead. In computer jargon, "the read request was satisfied from cache memory." Because the cache is memory, it is much faster than reading from disk.

The disk cache always makes sure whatever it holds in memory is safely saved on disk. When you save a file to disk, a copy is sent to disk and physically stored there. A second copy also is saved in cache memory. Herein lies the difference from a RAM disk where the information is only saved in RAM.

If you want to access the same information again, the cache will intercept the call to disk. Instead of reloading the duplicate information, the cache simply will copy it out of its own RAM. The disk access light will not glow and the information will be loaded much faster.

Disk caches show the best performance with programs using overlay files. Programs using overlays often load their various modules into memory as they are needed. If a disk cache were in operation, it would monitor the overlays loaded and keep a copy of each of them in its cache memory. When the program asks for an overlay from disk and that overlay is already in cache memory, the cache will intercept the disk call and automatically "zap" the overlay into memory. Because overlay files contain program code, they are not modified and there is no need for a second disk access.

Today, programs with overlays aren't that common. The best way to test a disk cache is with a data base or accounting program that uses many modules. Data bases are perhaps the most disk-intensive programs. Each record is read from disk as it is individually called up. In the last section, you read how putting a data base on a RAM disk speeds up certain operations (such as sorting). Using a cache, these operations will still be accelerated. However, unlike the volatile RAM disk, the cache is only a copy of what is already on disk. If a power failure occurs, nothing is lost in the disk cache.

Disk caches are an excellent disk speed-up tool. They function simply on the observation that most disk operations are repetitive. Like unfragmenting your hard disk, you might not notice the full effect of a disk cache until after you've used one a while. The only drawback to a disk cache is that it uses memory. Some can be installed into EMS memory. But if you lack EMS memory and if your standard memory is short on space, a disk cache might eat up too much RAM. However, as long as memory is not a problem, a disk cache is a quick and excellent RAM-based speed-up tool.

One of the most interesting cache programs available comes from Golden Bow Systems of San Diego, California. There are really three versions of Golden Bow's VCACHE program: CACHE is for conventional memory, CACHE-EM is for EMS memory, and CACHE-AT is for Extended memory. Only one program should be used at a time, depending on where you wish to place it in memory.

CACHE can be installed at any time by typing the appropriate program name at the command prompt, or CACHE can be included as part of the AUTOEXEC.BAT file. Unlike many similar programs, CACHE can be removed to free the memory it uses.

The format of the CACHE command varies with version. For most versions, the format is:

CACHE [size] [location] [/drive] [/W][/T][/Q]

CACHE can be either CACHE, CACHE-EM, or CACHE-AT.

Size refers to the amount of RAM used by the cache. The more RAM, the better the improvement. VCACHE keeps as much information in cache memory as it can. The cache keeps track of which items are accessed the most and keeps them in memory with a high priority. Other, less accessed items stay in cache memory on a space available basis.

If size is not specified, CACHE assigns 128K to cache memory, CACHE-EM assigns all available (free) EMS memory to the cache, and CACHE-AT assigns any memory not being used by VDISK to cache memory.

Location is only specified with CACHE-AT. It assigns the starting location above the 1M mark in the AT where the cache is placed. If a location is not specified, the cache uses memory starting at the 1M mark.

The /drive switch is used with special, nonbooting hard disks, for example, a Bernoulli drive. To install CACHE on any of these disks, use a slash followed by the drive's letter. For example, if drive C were a nonbooting Bernoulli drive, the following installs a 128 cache in standard memory:

CACHE /C

The /W switch is used for AT compatibles (and with CACHE-AT) that handle Extended Memory differently than the PC/AT. Refer to the VCACHE manual for information on spotting the noncompatible differences.

/T displays the CACHE timer. A list of cache statistics is displayed on the screen. This list gives a good gauge of how much work the cache is doing, and how much disk access it is saving, as shown in *Fig. 18-1*.

According to the output shown in the figure, 25 percent of the information read from disk was read instead from cache memory. This disk drive did not spin and the information was loaded as fast as the cache memory could go.

The /Q switch turns CACHE off. The memory used by CACHE is released and made available to other programs. If the memory cannot be released (which happens when you

```
Vcache 3.1  serial no. 507877
Copyright (C) Golden Bow Systems 1985-1987

Cache size: 373 kb
Drives cached: C D E
Using options: B=4 T=2
```

```
┌─────────────────────────────┬─────────────────────────────┐
│ Disk Usage Statistics:      │ Error Statistics:           │
├─────────────────────────────┼─────────────────────────────┤
│ Kind  Requested  Actual  %  │  0  Cache Memory Errors     │
│ Reads:      87      22   25 │  0  Disk Transfer Errors    │
│ Writes:      1       1  100 │  0  Errors Ignored by User  │
└─────────────────────────────┴─────────────────────────────┘
```

Fig. 18-1. The output of the CACHE /T command.

have another memory resident program installed after CACHE), a warning message is displayed and CACHE is not disabled.

SUMMARY

Although this is a hard disk book, this chapter dealt with RAM and the various ways RAM can be used to optimize hard disk performance. From the use of overlay files to the new Expanded Memory Specification and its various uses, RAM Disks and RAM disk techniques, VDISK and MEMBRAIN, up to the highly efficient disk caches, RAM can assist in making disk operations smoother, faster, and more efficient.

19

Shareware Programs

MENTIONED throughout this book have been various utilities and hard disk tools. Although most of these are commercial programs available from software dealers, several of them are in the public domain or *shareware* programs. Public domain programs are free to all who use them. The author requests a modest donation if you enjoy and use a shareware program.

PC SIG offers a disk that contains dozens of interesting programs, many of which have been mentioned in this book. Other programs have been included because they are invaluable to a hard disk owner. This chapter tells about the supplemental programs diskette and its contents. It includes a description of each file included on the disk along with instructions on how to use the file and where to find more information.

The programs listed as public domain are free of charge. You may give them to your friends or use them yourself to your heart's content. Shareware programs also are distributed free of charge. However, if you find the program useful, you are encouraged to send in the requested donation. The donation does two things. Primarily, it supports the shareware concept; people writing and distributing helpful programs and asking only moderate charges for them. Secondly, you can use the program free from guilt.

SUPPLEMENTAL PROGRAMS DISKETTE CONTENTS

There are seven files offered by PC SIG on the supplemental programs diskette. Four of the files are held in the special ARC format. These files actually contain dozens of other files, all neatly packed to make the most efficient use of disk space. (See the ARC file program description in chapter 17.) To release these files, you need to unARC them by running the INSTALL batch program.

The directory of the diskette is:

Volume in drive A has no label
Directory of A: \

ABOUT		5475	4-15-87	4:59p
AUTOMENU	ARC	86329	3-16-87	7:13p
DISKTOOL	ARC	62052	3-16-87	7:06p
INSTALL	BAT	450	4-17-87	10:45p
PACKDISK	ARC	25554	3-16-87	7:03p
PKX34A20	COM	58368	3-13-87	1:57p
TOOLS1	ARC	53029	3-30-87	9:19a

      8 File(s) 67584 bytes free

ABOUT is a text file describing the disk. Use the TYPE command to read this file. Press Control-S to pause the display; any other key to resume. Place the supplemental programs diskette into drive A and close the drive door. Log to drive A and type:

    A>TYPE ABOUT

If the MORE filter is on your path, try typing:

    A>TYPE ABOUT ¦ MORE

This command will show the file one screen at a time as you read it.

ABOUT describes the disk and lists all the files on the disk in both ARC and unARCed formats. Also listed are instructions about the INSTALL.BAT program and PKX34A20.COM.

Note: The files will not all fit on a floppy disk in their unARCed format. You must unARC the files to a hard disk.

INSTALLING THE PROGRAMS

The INSTALL.BAT program transfers the files from drive A to drive C and unARCs them. A copy of INSTALL.BAT is listed for your examination. If you think your batch file skills are up to par, try to determine what this one does. (A description follows.)

    ECHO off
    cls

```
ECHO !This program will unpack your Supplemental Programs Diskette
ECHO !and put those programs in the directory \TOOLS on drive C.
ECHO !
ECHO !Make sure this diskette is in drive A.
ECHO !
ECHO !This will take approximately 3 minutes.
ECHO !Press Ctrl C to stop or
PAUSE
c:
cd \
md \tools
cd \tools
copy a:pkx34a20.com
pkx34a20
pkxarc a:automenu.arc
pkxarc a:disktool.arc
pkxarc a:packdisk.arc
pkxarc a:tools1.arc
```

WHAT THE INSTALL.BAT
PROGRAM DOES IN DETAIL

First, INSTALL.BAT creates a directory named \TOOLS on drive C. All the files on drive A will be unARCed and placed in this directory. From there you can further copy the files to any subdirectory you wish. For example, you might want to copy all the Automenu files to their own subdirectory. Do this after the INSTALL.BAT program is run.

After INSTALL creates the \TOOLS subdirectory, it copies the PKX34A20.COM file to drive C. When run, the PKX34A20.COM file "unfolds" itself into the files that do the actual unpacking: PKARC, PKXARC, and their appropriate DOC files along with a few other goodies. After this is done, every other ARC file on drive A is unARCed to the \TOOLS subdirectory by the PKXARC program (the final lines of the batch file).

When the job is finished, you'll be logged to the \TOOLS subdirectory on drive C. You also will have a pretty ungainly subdirectory full of files. Each file on the supplemental programs diskette is listed below in roughly the same order as it will appear in your \TOOLS subdirectory. Following each file name is a description of the name. You can elect to move the file(s) elsewhere or keep them in the \TOOLS subdirectory.

THE MANUAL AND DOC FILES

Several of the programs on the supplemental program disk contain companion DOC files or files titled "MANUAL." These files contain the instructions, or documentation, for the programs that share their name. (MANUAL contains the documentation for the PACKDISK series of programs.) In the public domain/shareware world, instruction manuals are distributed with this kind of documentation.

There are two methods for reading the instructions. One is using the DOS TYPE command. A better way is to print the documentation. A majority of the DOC files (and MANUAL) have been formatted perfectly for a *dump* to your printer. To get a hard copy of them, set your printer so that the print head is at the first line of a sheet of paper. Then, at the DOS prompt, type:

```
C>COPY filename.DOC PRN
```

This command copies the documentation file, filename.DOC, to the printer (DOS's PRN device). Because most of these files are preformatted, they will come out rather nicely on the printer. Some even have headers, footers, and page numbers.

Staple together the various documentation files you produce and put them with the rest of your computer documentation. A hard copy of instructions about a utility is much easier to refer to than trying to memorize commands as DOS TYPEs them.

PKX34A20.COM

The PKX34A20.COM program is one of the latter versions of the PKARC utility. This file unpacks itself into the appropriate PKARC file utilities. PKARC is the version of the ARC program used to compact and store files on the diskette offered by PC SIG. A $20 donation is requested for using this program. For more information on this program, write to:

PKWARE, Inc.
7032 Ardara Avenue
Glendale, WI 53209

PKARC.COM. This program crunches, munches, and scrunches programs, data, and text files. Then it sticks them all into one ARC (archive) file. This compacting makes transmitting a group of files over a modem easy, and a few dozen files are packed into half the space.

PKARC.DOC. This is the documentation file for PKARC.COM.

PKXARC.COM. This program unpacks programs, data and text files from ARC files created by PKARC. Individual files, or groups of files can be extracted. The X in the file title stands for eXtract.

PKXARC.DOC. This file is the documentation file for PKXARC.COM.

PKXARCJR.COM. This file is a special version of the PKARC program for the PCjr. If you don't have a PCjr, this file can be erased.

README.DOC. This file contains a notice to people who distribute the PKX-34A20.COM files and the PKARC files.

AUTOMENU.ARC

The files in the AUTOMENU.ARC file compose the entire Automenu system. They are the same programs you get if you order the Automenu package (version 4.0). The Automenu menu definition system was discussed in length in chapter 11. For more information on Automenu write to:

Magee Enterprises
6577 Peachtree Industrial Blvd.
Norcross, Georgia 30092-3796

AUTO.BAT. A batch file that starts the AUTOMENU program, then runs an AUTO-TEMP batch file.

AUTOCUST.COM. This file is the AUTOMENU customization program.

AUTOEXEC.BAT. A sample batch file included on the Automenu disk. Basically, it contains a few typical AUTOEXEC.BAT statements (PROMPT, VER, etc.), then runs the AUTOMENU program.

AUTOMAKE.EXE. This program builds menus for use by AUTOMENU. It is a combination editor/outliner with an on-line help facility to assist making MDF (Menu Definition) files.

AUTOMENU.COM. This file is the main AUTOMENU program.

AUTOMENU.MDF. A sample menu definition file. It contains some sample menus and can be used as an example for customizing your own MDF files.

AUTOTEMP.BAT. A small batch file that changes to a directory /GAMES and runs a program BACK (for backgammon). It is used in conjunction with the included menu definition file AUTOMENU.MDF.

DOS.MDF. A sample MDF file included with Automenu (and used in AUTO-MENU.MDF) which contains a number of interesting DOS commands and utilities.

ENTER.MDF. A sample MDF file that asks for a password (IBM is the password used). This file can be used for security purposes to limit or prevent access to the Automenu system.

INSTALL.BAT. A batch file that installs the AUTOMENU program. It executes the INSTAL.MDF file which actually does all the installation work.

INSTALL.MDF. A menu definition file that installs Automenu. Install asks you a number of questions, then proceeds to install Automenu on your hard disk.

PRINTER.MDF. A menu definition file that sets printer controls and options such as bold printing, wide printing, and compressed. This sample included with Automenu was tailored to Epson and compatible printers.

READ.ME. A small text file that contains a plug from Automenu's Author, Marshall W. Magee, and an address where to write for additional information.

SW.COM. A "screen swap" program. If you have two monitors installed in your PC, one color and one monochrome, SW switches from the current monitor to the other. Or SW C is used to turn on the color monitor and SW M is used to turn on the monochrome. An interesting extra.

SW.DOC. This file is a text file describing the SW.COM program.

TIME.MDF. A sample menu definition file that shows how a command or program can be executed at a specific time of day.

DISKTOOL.ARC

DISKTOOL is a remarkable collection of disk utilities all in one package. The hacker in you will really admire this program. With DISKTOOL you can change file attributes (make things invisible, etc.), examine the actual bytes on disk, change the bytes, erase files, search for files, rename files—a whole abundance of utilities, all in an easy-to-use package. The author is distributing DISKTOOL as shareware and would like a $20 donation for it. For information, write to:

R.P Gage
1125 6th Street N., #43
Columbus, MS 39701

DISKTOOL.DOC. This file is the documentation for the DISKTOOL program (DT below). If you intend on seriously using DISKTOOL, you should print this out.

DT.COM. This file is the actual DISKTOOL program, which is named DT for some reason. If you like, rename the file to DISKTOOL, or keep it at DT which is easier to type.

DT.PIF. This file is one of those mysterious PIF files which appeared about the same time Microsoft started to sell their Windows environment. PIF stands for Program Information File, and is used by Windows to determine how the program is run. If you don't have Windows, this file should be deleted.

PACKDISK.ARC

PACKDISK contains unfragmenting and directory squeezing programs (PACKDISK and FINDFRAG) as discussed in chapter 17. It also contains several other, interesting directory manipulation programs, as well as a PARK program for certain types of hard disks. The PACKDISK series of public domain programs are shareware and the suggested donation if you use and enjoy the programs is $35.00. For additional information on PACKDISK, write to:

SoftPatch
PO Box 11455
San Francisco, CA 94101

DELDIR.COM. This powerful command deletes a subdirectory, all files in the subdirectory, and all subdirectories and files under those subdirectories. You could say, in the "tree structure" of a disk drive, DELDIR is a chainsaw. Needless to say, DELDIR should be used with extreme caution.

LISTFRAG.COM. This command lists all fragmented files and noncontiguous chains in the specified directory or directories. Unlike CHKDSK, LISTFRAG also displays fragmented directory files and all files in any subdirectories under the one specified.

MANUAL. A text file that contains instructions and documentation for all the PACK-DISK programs. It can be TYPEd at the DOS command prompt, or sent to the printer as described earlier in this chapter.

NAMEDIR.COM. This program renames a subdirectory on disk. (Presently there's no way to do so with DOS.) Be careful of the format of this command; it uses a double backslash, \ \, to denote the new name of the subdirectory.

PACKDISK.COM. This file unfragments files and subdirectories, squeezes the tombstones from directories, and packs files toward the front of the disk.

PARK.COM. This program was included because it is part of the shareware distribution agreement (and as such, cannot be deleted). Because all PARK programs do not work with each hard disk, you might not want to use this program. It will not harm the hard disk, yet it might not work on some hard disks.

TRANSDIR.COM. This utility moves a directory, along with all its files and subdirectories, to another spot on disk. Unlike XCOPY, TRANSDIR also erases the original files and subdirectories. It's more like a move than a copy.

TOOLS1.ARC

These programs are taken from a variety of sources. Where indicated, the author requests money for the program. Otherwise, consider the program public domain and use it freely.

ASK.COM. This program can be used in a batch file to get a yes or no response from the user. It works like ECHO, displaying whatever message is listed after ASK on the command line. Then ASK waits for either the Y or N key to be pressed. Pressing N returns an ERRORLEVEL code of 1, pressing Y returns a code of 0. ASK.COM is discussed in chapter 7.

CRYPT.BAS. This program is a demonstration program written in the BASIC programming language and saved as an ASCII file. CRYPT.BAS takes one file, encrypts its data according to a key string value, and then writes the encrypted data out to a second file. CRYPT.BAS is discussed and demonstrated in chapter 15.

ETIME.COM. This program displays the words "End Time =" followed by the current date and time. It can be used in conjunction with STIME to log the time spent on your computer. ETIME is discussed in chapter 16.

FINDHIDE.COM. This program works like the DIR command, except FINDHIDE displays all files in the current directory. Invisible files are prefixed by an asterisk (*). It is discussed in chapter 15.

GREET.COM. This program is very friendly. It displays Good Morning, Good Evening, or Good Afternoon depending on the time of day. If a message is typed after GREET on the command line, that message is displayed after the time of day greeting.

HIDE.COM. This program hides selected programs on disk. Only single filenames can be listed after HIDE, no wildcards. After a file is hidden, it is excluded from all DOS searches and not listed by the DIR command. HIDE.COM is discussed in chapter 15.

LOCK.COM. This utility program works like a write protect tab on the hard disk. LOCK.COM is a memory resident program that intercepts all writes, changes, and modifications to the hard drive, and returns a Write Protected error to DOS. It can be turned on or off at any time.

LOCK.DOC. This file is the documentation file for LOCK.COM.

PASSWORD.BAS. This program is written in the BASIC programming language and saved as an ASCII file. PASSWORD.BAS is best used in the computer's AUTOEXEC file. It asks for a system password to be entered. If the proper password is not typed correctly after three tries, the system is locked and cannot be reset or rebooted. PASSWORD.BAS is discussed and demonstrated in chapter 14.

PASSWORD.DOC. This file is the documentation file for PASSWORD.BAS.

SDIR5.COM. SDIR5 is Super-Directory version 5. This program contains all kinds of interesting directory and file manipulation utilities. You can sort a directory, change filenames and attributes, rename, TYPE, delete, and copy—a whole variety of options all within this one program. SDIR5 is distributed as shareware and the author requests a donation of $10.00 if you use the program. For more information, contact:

W. Lawrence Hatt
76 Melville Drive
Nepean, Ontario
Canada, K2J 2E1

SDIR5.DOC. This file is the documentation file for SDIR5.COM.

STIME.COM. This program displays "Start Time =" followed by the current date and time. It can be used in conjunction with ETIME to log time on your computer. STIME is discussed in chapter 16.

TREED.COM. This program displays a visual map of the tree structure of your disk. All subdirectories are displayed with links to their parent directories and their own subdirectories.

TREED.DOC. This file is the documentation file for TREED.COM.

TSTAMP.COM. This program displays the current time and date as kept by your computer. It is part of the STIME and ETIME series of programs and is discussed in chapter 16.

UNHIDE.COM. This program unhides hidden programs on disk. Only single filenames can be unhidden, and it does not accept wildcards. If a file is hidden, it can be unhidden with UNHIDE. The FINDHIDE utility is used to display hidden files in the current directory. UNHIDE is discussed in chapter 15.

WHEREIS.COM. This command is a neat utility that locates any file or group of files on disk. Typing WHEREIS *.BAT displays all batch files on disk and the subdirectory where they are located.

WHEREIS.DOC. This file is the documentation file for WHEREIS.COM.

XWORD221.DOC. This file is the documentation file for XWORD223.COM. Although the documentation is for version 2.21, it still applies to the version supplied on disk.

XWORD223.EXE. The XWORD utility (223 is the version number 2.23) transfers text and word processing files between various formats, including: WordStar, MultiMate, XYWrite, WordPerfect, and text formatted files. It also performs a basic data encryption using logical manipulations (NOT, ROL, AND, OR, and XOR) on each character in the file. XWORD is distributed as shareware and the author requests $15.00 if you use the program. For more information, contact:

Ronald Gans
350 West 55th Street
New York, NY 10019

Summary of DOS Commands

BELOW ARE LISTED all major DOS commands through PC-DOS version 4.0. Each command is listed alphabetically by name, whether or not it is internal or external, along with its format and a brief description. Where applicable, there are references to individual chapters in the book where the command is discussed.

Commands particular to DOS 4.0 are noted where they occur. All other commands are for DOS version 3.3.

APPEND   Internal/External

Format: APPEND d:path[;[d:path]] . . .

The APPEND command controls a special search path used to find data files as opposed to PATH, which only locates programs. APPEND works a lot like PATH.

See chapter 5.

ASSIGN   External

Format: ASSIGN [d: =d:]

ASSIGN is used to reassign a drive letter to a certain drive. For example:

ASSIGN A: = B:

This command redirects all attempts to access drive A, sending them off to drive B.

Pretend one drive works like another. By using ASSIGN alone on the command line, all drive assignments will be reset to normal.

ATTRIB   External

Format: ATTRIB [+/−R] [+/−A] [d:] [path] filename[.ext] [/S]

The ATTRIB command changes the read-only and modify attributes of a file or group of files. It can be used to protect files from accidental modification or deletion, or in conjunction with BACKUP or XCOPY to specifically target certain files.
See chapter 15.

BACKUP   External

Format: BACKUP d:path[filename] [.ext] d: [/S] [/M] [/A] [/D:] [/T:] [/F] [L:filespec]

The BACKUP command is used to archive files, typically from a hard disk onto floppies for safekeeping. It is covered in detail in chapter 12.

BREAK   Internal

Format: BREAK [ON ¦ OFF]

The BREAK command is used to turn monitoring of the Control-Break keystroke on or off, as specified by ON or OFF following BREAK on the command line. When used alone, BREAK displays the status of the Control-Break monitoring.

CHCP   Internal

Format: CHCP [nnn]

The CHCP command changes the current code page, which determines formats for the date and time, as well as currency symbol. When specified, the number nnn activates a new code page. CHCP used by itself displays the current code page.

CHDIR   Internal

Format: CHDIR [d:] [path]

The CHDIR command, also abbreviated CD, is used to specify a new subdirectory in which to work. When used by itself, CHDIR simply displays the name of the current subdirectory. See chapter 5.

CHKDSK   External

Format: CHKDSK [d:] [filename] [.ext] [/f] [/v]

The CHKDSK, or check disk, program is used to display statistical information about a disk and memory, as well as examine files on the disk for noncontiguous blocks and bad files. CHKDSK is covered in detail in chapter 4, and also mentioned in chapters 5 and 17.

CLS   Internal

Format: CLS

The CLS command clears the screen.
See chapter 4.

COMMAND   External

Format: COMMAND [/C]

COMMAND is COMMAND.COM, DOS's command processor. It can be run more than once to invoke a new copy of the command shell. This command is primarily used with older versions of DOS to call batch files.
See chapter 7.

COMP   External

Format: COMP [d:] filename[.ext] [d:] [filename] [.ext]

The COMP command is used to compare two files. Any differences in the files are noted and displayed on the screen.
See chapter 4.

COPY   Internal

Format: COPY [d:] filename[.ext] [d:] [filename] [.ext]

COPY is used to copy from one device to another, usually copying one file or a group of files (specified by wildcards) from one disk drive or subdirectory to another.
See chapter 4.

CTTY   Internal

Format: CTTY device

The CTTY command is used to specify another device as the console. For example:

CTTY AUX

This command causes the AUX device (the serial) port, to be used as the console, both keyboard and screen.

DATE   Internal

Format: DATE [mm-dd-yy]

The DATE command is used to enter a new date for DOS. DOS uses that date to time stamp all files created or updated. If the current date isn't specified after the DATE command, DOS will prompt you for it.

See chapter 4.

DEL   Internal

Format: DEL [d:] filename[.ext]

The DEL command is used to delete files from disk.
See chapter 4 and the ERASE command in this Appendix.

DIR   Internal

Format: DIR [d:] [path] filename[.ext] [/P] [/W]

DIR, the most commonly used DOS command, displays a list of files in the current directory. Files can be specified via wildcard, and DIR's two switches can be used to display a directory in wide format (/W) or a page at a time (/P).

See chapter 3.

DISKCOMP   External

Format: DISKCOMP [d:] [d:] [/1] [/8]

The DISKCOMP command compares two diskettes for any differences, similar to the way COMP works to compare files. See chapter 4.

DISKCOPY External

Format: DISKCOPY [d:] [d:]

  DISKCOPY is used to copy (make an exact duplicate of) a floppy diskette. Two floppy drives can be specified for the DISKCOPY, but both must be of the same size.
  See chapter 4.

DOSSHELL External (DOS 4)

  DOSSHELL is a batch file command used to start the DOS 4 shell program.
  See chapter 11.

ERASE Internal

Format: ERASE [d:] filename[.ext]

  The ERASE command removes files from disk. A single file can be specified, or a group of files via wildcards. If you attempt to delete all files in a subdirectory, you are prompted with an "Are you sure" message and must type "Y" or "N" before proceeding.
  See chapter 4.

EXIT Internal

Format: EXIT

  The EXIT command is used to leave a command shell (invoked by COMMAND .COM). It will also return to certain software applications that "shell to DOS."
  See COMMAND.

FASTOPEN External

Format: FASTOPEN d:[=nnn]

  The FASTOPEN command is used to speed access to commonly used files. FAST-OPEN keeps track of recently opened files and their locations. Any additional access to those files will be quicker.

FDISK External

Format: FDISK

The FDISK command is used to initialize and partition a hard drive for use with DOS. FDISK is the step done after a low-level format and before the DOS format. After using FDISK, the computer is reset.
See chapter 2.

FIND   External

Format: FIND [/V] [/C] [/N] "string" [d:] [path] filename[.ext]

FIND is a filter used to search through text files for specific strings of text.
See chapter 3.

FORMAT   External

Format: FORMAT d:[/S] [/1] [/8] [/V] [/B] [/4] [/N:xx] [/T:xx]

The FORMAT command is used to initialize disks, preparing them for use with DOS. Formatting disks is discussed in chapters 1 and 2, a chart of formatting commands appears in chapter 17.

GRAFTABL   External

Format: GRAFTABL [437 ¦ 860 ¦ 863 ¦ 865 ¦ /STATUS]

The GRAFTABL command is used to load a graphics character set into memory, depending on a specific country code specified after the GRAFTABL command.

GRAPHICS   External

Format: GRAPHICS [printer] [/R] [/B] [/LCD]

The GRAPHICS command sets your computer to display graphics on a specific type of monitor, or sets your printer type to work with the IBM graphic character set.

JOIN   External

Format: JOIN [d:] [d: \ path] [/D]

The JOIN command is used to assign a subdirectory name to a disk drive, making DOS think that drive is really a subdirectory. JOIN by itself lists all drives assigned in such a manner. The /D switch is used to disable the joined drives.

KEYB   External

Format: KEYB [xx[,[yyy] [[d:] [path] filename[.ext]]]]

KEYB is used to load a keyboard driver for another country into memory. With KEYB, you can access special characters used in foreign languages or symbols used overseas.

LABEL   External

Format: LABEL [d:] [volume label]

The LABEL command allows you to set, change, or examine a disk's volume label. See chapter 2.

MEM   External (DOS 4)

Format: MEM [/PROGRAM] [/DEBUG]

The MEM command is like the CHKDSK for a disk. MEM displays a list of items in your system's memory, their location, size, and what they are.

MKDIR   Internal

Format: MKDIR [d:] [path] subdirectory

The MKDIR command, also abbreviated MD, is used to create a new subdirectory on disk.
    See chapter 5.

MODE   External

Format: MODE [. . .various. . .]

The MODE command has nine separate uses, most of which are associated with the mode of operation of certain devices in the computer: the display, keyboard, printer, and communications port.

MORE   External

Format: MORE

MORE is a filter used to page the output of files, pausing after each screen of text to display the message "--more--" and wait for a keystroke.

See chapter 3.

NLSFUNC   External

Format: NLSFUNC [filename]

The NLSFUNC command is used in conjunction with CHCP to supply code page information. The filename specified is the COUNTRY.SYS file that comes with DOS.

PATH   Internal

Format: PATH [;] [d:path] [;d:path] . . .

The PATH command is used to specify a series of subdirectories DOS will look through for programs. The PATH command is covered in detail in chapter 5, and various uses of the path command are in chapter 6.

PRINT

Format: PRINT [/d:x] [/b:x] [/u:x] [/m:x] [/s:x] [q:x] [/c] [/t] [/p] [filespec]

The PRINT command activates DOS's printing queue, which is like a print spooler but only for text files specified by the PRINT command. Chapter 19 mentions the PRINT command briefly.

PROMPT   Internal

Format: PROMPT [prompt text]

The PROMPT command changes DOS's system prompt. You can include the date, time, path, directory, or any of a number of text characters in your system prompt, all via the PROMPT command.

See chapter 4.

RECOVER   External

Format: RECOVER [d:] [path] filename[.ext]

RECOVER is used to rescue files, as best DOS can, from damaged diskettes. The files recovered must be renamed and TYPEd at the DOS prompt to determine their former contents.

RENAME   Internal

Format: RENAME filename filename

The RENAME command, which can be abbreviated to REN, is used to change the name of a file on disk.
See chapter 4.

REPLACE   External

Format: REPLACE [d:] [path] filename[.ext] [d:] [path] [/A] [/P] [/R] [/S] [/W]

REPLACE is used to locate files on one disk and replace them with similarly named files on another disk. REPLACE seeks out the older files and replaces them, saving you time when updating software and DOS.
Replace is covered in chapter 12, and REPLACE with an emphasis on replacing DOS is covered in chapter 2.

RESTORE   External

Format: RESTORE d: [d:] [path]filename[.ext] [/P] [/M] [/S] [/B] [/A] [/E] [/L] [/N]

The RESTORE command is used to restore files from a backup diskette back to the original. It is the complement of the BACKUP command, and covered in detail in chapter 12.

RMDIR   Internal

Format: RMDIR [d:] [path]

The RMDIR command, also abbreviated RD, removes a subdirectory from disk. The subdirectory must be empty before it can be removed.
See chapter 5.

SELECT   External

Format: SELECT [A: ¦ B:] [d:] [path] xxx yy

The SELECT command is used to install a new version of DOS, but also adds information regarding the country and keyboard setup.
See chapter 2.

SET   Internal

Format: SET [name[=parameter]]

The SET command is used to place a variable and its associated string into DOS's environment. When used by itself, SET displays the current contents of the environment.

SHARE   External

Format: SHARE [/F:filespec] [/L:locks]

SHARE is a command used in file sharing, primarily to secure access to one file by more than one program or individual.

SORT   External

Format: SORT [/R] [/+ n]

SORT is a filter used to order the lines in a text file alphabetically or reverse alphabetically. SORTing may also be done on a specific column of text using the /+n switch.
See chapter 3.

SUBST   External

Format: SUBST [d:] [d: \ path] [/D]

The SUBST command is used to assign a drive letter to a subdirectory. This makes DOS treat the subdirectory just as if it were its own independent disk drive. (SUBST is the opposite of the JOIN command.) SUBST by itself lists all subdirectories assigned as disk drives. The /D switch disables the substituted drives.

SYS   External

Format: SYS d:

The SYS command is used to transfer the SYStem (the basic DOS files) to another disk which is usually a freshly formatted disk or one with enough space for the system files.
See chapter 2.

TIME   Internal

Format: TIME [hh:mm[:ss[.xx]]]

The TIME command is used to enter a new time for DOS. DOS uses that time to time stamp all files created or updated. If the time isn't specified after the TIME command, DOS will prompt you for it.

See chapter 4.

TREE   External

Format: TREE [d:] [/F]

TREE is a command used to display the tree structure of a disk drive, optionally listing any files found in any subdirectories (with the /F option).

See chapter 5.

TYPE   Internal

Format: TYPE [d:] [path] filename

The TYPE command lists the contents of a file on the screen. It is normally used for viewing text files, although any file can be TYPEd. (Nontext files just don't look pretty, that's all.)

See chapter 4.

VER   Internal

Format: VER

The VER command displays the current version of DOS on the display.
See chapter 4.

VERIFY   Internal

Format: VERIFY [ON ¦ OFF]

The VERIFY command is used to turn automatic verification of disk writes on or off. Used by itself, VERIFY displays the current verify status.

VOL   Internal

Format: VOL [d:]

VOL displays the volume label for the current disk, or a disk drive specified.

XCOPY   External

Format: XCOPY [d:] [path] [filename] [.ext] [d:] [path] [filename] [.ext] [/A] [/D] [/E] [/M] [/P] [/S] [/V] [/W]

XCOPY is a "super COPY" program. Basically it works by quickly copying files by putting them all in memory rather than copying one at a time (as COPY does). XCOPY also contains a number of switches, which makes it far more versatile than the vanilla COPY command.

See chapter 12.

Summary of EDLIN Commands

Insert Line:

I	Inserts a new line at the current line. When creating a new file, I inserts line 1.
nI	Inserts a new line number n.
.I	Inserts a new line at the current line.
#I	Inserts a new line at the bottom of the file.
$+n$I	Inserts a new line n lines down from the current line number.
$-n$I	Inserts a new line n lines up from the current line number.

List:

L	Lists the 11 lines before the current line, the current line, and 11 lines after the current line.
xL	Lists 23 lines starting with line x.
,yL	Lists the 11 lines before line y, line y, and the 11 lines after line y.
x,yL	Lists the lines from x through y.
P	"Page" or print from the current line down 23 lines.
,yP	Print from the current line through line y.
x,yP	Print from line x through line y.

Delete:

D	Deletes the current line.

*x*D	Deletes line *x*.
x,*y*D	Deletes lines *x* through *y*.
,*y*D	Deletes all lines from the current line through line *y*.
x,.D	Deletes all lines from *x* through the current line.

Copy:

x,*y*,*z*C	Copies the block of lines from *x* through *y* and places them at line number *z*.
x,*x*,*z*C	Copies the single line *x* to line number *z*.

Move:

x,*y*,*z*M	Moves the block of lines from *x* through *y* and places them at line number *z*.
x,*x*,*z*M	Moves line *x* to line number *z*.

Search and Replace:

S *string*	Searches for the characters in *string*.
x,*y*S*string*	Searches for the characters in *string* between lines *x* and *y*.
x,*y*?S*string*	Searches for the characters in *string* between lines *x* and *y*, stops and asks "OK?" for each occurrence. Pressing "Y" continues the search, "N" cancels.
R*str1*^Z*str2*	Replaces all occurrences of *str1* with *str2*. ^Z is Control-Z.
x,*y*R*str1*^Z*str2*	Replaces all occurrences of *str1* with *str2* in the range of lines from *x* to *y*.
x,*y*?R*str1*^Z*str2*	Replaces all occurrences of *str1* with *str2* in the range of lines from *x* to *y*. When *str1* is found, replace stops as asks "OK?" Pressing "Y" replaces, pressing "N" cancels.

Edit:

n	Selects line *n* for editing.
−*n*	Selects line *n* lines up for editing.
+*n*	Selects line *n* lines down for editing.
.	Selects current line for editing.

Disk:

*n*A	Appends lines from the disk file into memory. (This command only works if the file being edited is too big to fit into memory.)

*n*T   Transfers text to disk starting with line *n*. If *n* is ommitted, the current line is used

*n*W   Writes a specific number of lines to disk. (Used only for files too large to fit into memory at once.)

End:

E   Ends edit, saves file, renames original file to *.BAK.

Q   Cancels edit, does not save changes.

APPENDIX C

Extended ASCII Chart

ASCII (pronounced ASK-ee) is an acronym for the American Standard Code for Information Interchange. The ASCII codes from 0 to 127 are assigned to letters, numbers, special characters, and other symbols. ASCII codes from 128 to 255 vary from computer to computer. On IBM PC's and compatibles, these characters are referred to as the *Extended ASCII* set. The actual characters displayed on the screen are in the chart at the end of this Appendix.

Char	Dec	Hex	Binary	Code	Char	Dec	Hex	Binary	Code
^@	0	0h	00000000	NUL	^N	14	Eh	00001110	SO
^A	1	1h	00000001	SOH	^O	15	Fh	00001111	SI
^B	2	2h	00000010	STX	^P	16	10h	00010000	DLE
^C	3	3h	00000011	ETX	^Q	17	11h	00010001	DC1
^D	4	4h	00000100	EOT	^R	18	12h	00010010	DC2
^E	5	5h	00000101	ENQ	^S	19	13h	00010011	DC3
^F	6	6h	00000110	ACK	^T	20	14h	00010100	DC4
^G	7	7h	00000111	BEL	^U	21	15h	00010101	NAK
^H	8	8h	00001000	BS	^V	22	16h	00010110	SYN
^I	9	9h	00001001	HT	^W	23	17h	00010111	ETB
^J	10	Ah	00001010	LF	^X	24	18h	00011000	CAN
^K	11	Bh	00001011	VT	^Y	25	19h	00011001	EM
^L	12	Ch	00001100	FF	^Z	26	1Ah	00011010	SUB
^M	13	Dh	00001101	CR	^[	27	1Bh	00011011	ESC

Char	Dec	Hex	Binary	Code	Char	Dec	Hex	Binary	Code
^\	28	1Ch	00011100	FS	C	67	43h	01000011	
^]	29	1Dh	00011101	GS	D	68	44h	01000100	
^^	30	1Eh	00011110	RS	E	69	45h	01000101	
^_	31	1Fh	00011111	US	F	70	46h	01000110	
SPC	32	20h	00100000		G	71	47h	01000111	
!	33	21h	00100001		H	72	48h	01001000	
"	34	22h	00100010		I	73	49h	01001001	
#	35	23h	00100011		J	74	4Ah	01001010	
$	36	24h	00100100		K	75	4Bh	01001011	
%	37	25h	00100101		L	76	4Ch	01001100	
&	38	26h	00100110		M	77	4Dh	01001101	
'	39	27h	00100111		N	78	4Eh	01001110	
(	40	28h	00101000		O	79	4Fh	01001111	
)	41	29h	00101001		P	80	50h	01010000	
*	42	2Ah	00101010		Q	17	51h	01010001	
+	43	2Bh	00101011		R	18	52h	01010010	
,	44	2Ch	00101100		S	19	53h	01010011	
−	45	2Dh	00101101		T	20	54h	01010100	
.	46	2Eh	00101110		U	21	55h	01010101	
/	47	2Fh	00101111		V	22	56h	01010110	
0	48	30h	00110000		W	23	57h	01010111	
1	49	31h	00110001		X	24	58h	01011000	
2	50	32h	00110010		Y	25	59h	01011001	
3	51	33h	00110011		Z	26	5Ah	01011010	
4	52	34h	00110100		[	27	5Bh	01011011	
5	53	35h	00110101		\	28	5Ch	01011100	
6	54	36h	00110110		]	29	5Dh	01011101	
7	55	37h	00110111		^	30	5Eh	01011110	
8	56	38h	00111000		_	31	5Fh	01011111	
9	57	39h	00111001		`	96	60h	01100000	
:	58	3Ah	00111010		a	97	61h	01100001	
;	59	3Bh	00111011		b	98	62h	01100010	
<	60	3Ch	00111100		c	99	63h	01100011	
=	61	3Dh	00111101		d	100	64h	01100100	
>	62	3Eh	00111110		e	101	65h	01100101	
?	63	3Fh	00111111		f	102	66h	01100110	
@	64	40h	01000000		g	103	67h	01100111	
A	65	41h	01000001		h	104	68h	01101000	
B	66	42h	01000010		i	105	69h	01101001	

Char	Dec	Hex	Binary	Code	Char	Dec	Hex	Binary	Code
j	106	6Ah	01101010		u	117	75h	01110101	
k	107	6Bh	01101011		v	118	76h	01110110	
l	108	6Ch	01101100		w	119	77h	01110111	
m	109	6Dh	01101101		x	120	78h	01111000	
n	110	6Eh	01101110		y	121	79h	01111001	
o	111	6Fh	01101111		z	122	7Ah	01111010	
p	112	70h	01110000		{	123	7Bh	01111011	
q	113	71h	01110001		¦	124	7Ch	01111100	
r	114	72h	01110010		}	125	7Dh	01111101	
s	115	73h	01110011		~	126	7Eh	01111110	
t	116	74h	01110100		DEL	127	7Fh	01111111	
	128	80h	10000000			155	9Bh	10011011	
	129	81h	10000001			156	9Ch	10011100	
	130	82h	10000010			157	9Dh	10011101	
	131	83h	10000011			158	9Eh	10011110	
	132	84h	10000100			159	9Fh	10011111	
	133	85h	10000101			160	A0h	10100000	
	134	86h	10000110			161	A1h	10100001	
	135	87h	10000111			162	A2h	10100010	
	136	88h	10001000			163	A3h	10100011	
	137	89h	10001001			164	A4h	10100100	
	138	8Ah	10001010			165	A5h	10100101	
	139	8Bh	10001011			166	A6h	10100110	
	140	8Ch	10001100			167	A7h	10100111	
	141	8Dh	10001101			168	A8h	10101000	
	142	8Eh	10001110			169	A9h	10101001	
	143	8Fh	10001111			170	AAh	10101010	
	144	90h	10010000			171	ABh	10101011	
	145	91h	10010001			172	ACh	10101100	
	146	92h	10010010			173	ADh	10101101	
	147	93h	10010011			174	AEh	10101110	
	148	94h	10010100			175	AFh	10101111	
	149	95h	10010101			176	B0h	10110000	
	150	96h	10010110			177	B1h	10110001	
	151	97h	10010111			178	B2h	10110010	
	152	98h	10011000			179	B3h	10110011	
	153	99h	10011001			180	B4h	10110100	
	154	9Ah	10011010			181	B5h	10110101	

Char	Dec	Hex	Binary	Code	Char	Dec	Hex	Binary	Code
	182	B6h	10110110			219	DBh	11011011	
	183	B7h	10110111			220	DCh	11011100	
	184	B8h	10111000			221	DDh	11011101	
	185	B9h	10111001			222	DEh	11011110	
	186	BAh	10111010			223	DFh	11011111	
	187	BBh	10111011			224	E0h	11100000	
	188	BCh	10111100			225	E1h	11100001	
	189	BDh	10111101			226	E2h	11100010	
	190	BEh	10111110			227	E3h	11100011	
	191	BFh	10111111			228	E4h	11100100	
	192	C0h	11000000			229	E5h	11100101	
	193	C1h	11000001			230	E6h	11100110	
	194	C2h	11000010			231	E7h	11100111	
	195	C3h	11000011			232	E8h	11101000	
	196	C4h	11000100			233	E9h	11101001	
	197	C5h	11000101			234	EAh	11101010	
	198	C6h	11000110			235	EBh	11101011	
	199	C7h	11000111			236	ECh	11101100	
	200	C8h	11001000			237	EDh	11101101	
	201	C9h	11001001			238	EEh	11101110	
	202	CAh	11001010			239	EFh	11101111	
	203	CBh	11001011			240	F0h	11110000	
	204	CCh	11001100			241	F1h	11110001	
	205	CDh	11001101			242	F2h	11110010	
	206	CEh	11001110			243	F3h	11110011	
	207	CFh	11001111			244	F4h	11110100	
	208	D0h	11010000			245	F5h	11110101	
	209	D1h	11010001			246	F6h	11110110	
	210	D2h	11010010			247	F7h	11110111	
	211	D3h	11010011			248	F8h	11111000	
	212	D4h	11010100			249	F9h	11111001	
	213	D5h	11010101			250	FAh	11111010	
	214	D6h	11010110			251	FBh	11111011	
	215	D7h	11010111			252	FCh	11111100	
	216	D8h	11011000			253	FDh	11111101	
	217	D9h	11011001			254	FEh	11111110	
	218	DAh	11011010			255	FFh	11111111	

Control Character Codes:

NUL	-	Null	DC1 -	Device Control 1 (XON)
SOH	-	Start Of Heading	DC2 -	Device Control 2 (AUXON)
STX	-	Start of TeXt	DC3 -	Device Control 3 (XOFF)
ETX	-	End of TeXt	DC4 -	Device Control 4 (AUXOFF)
EOT	-	End Of Transmission	NAK -	Negative AcKnowledgement
ENQ	-	ENQuiry	SYN -	SYNchronous file
ACK	-	ACKnowledge	ETB -	End of Tranmission Block
BEL	-	Bell	CAN -	CANcel
BS	-	Back Space	EM -	End of Medium
HT	-	Horizontal Tab	SUB -	SUBstitute
LF	-	Line Feed	ESC -	ESCape
VT	-	Vertical Tab	FS -	File (or Form) Separator
FF	-	Form Feed	GS -	Group Separator
CR	-	Carriage Return	RS -	Record Separator
SO	-	Shift Out	US -	Unit Separator
SI	-	Shift In	SPC -	SPaCe
DLE	-	Data Link Escape	DEL -	DELete, RUBout

	00	01	02	03	04	05	06	07	08	09	0A	0B	0C	0D	0E	0F
00																
10					(Control		Characters		)							
20		!	''	#	$	%	&	'	(	)	*	+	,	—	.	/
30	0	1	2	3	4	5	6	7	8	9	:	;	<	=	>	?
40	@	A	B	C	D	E	F	G	H	I	J	K	L	M	N	O
50	P	Q	R	S	T	U	V	W	X	Y	Z	[	\	]	^	_
60	`	a	b	c	d	e	f	g	h	i	j	k	l	m	n	o
70	p	q	r	s	t	u	v	w	x	y	z	{	¦	}	~	△
80	Ç	ü	é	â	ä	à	å	ç	ê	ë	è	ï	î	ì	Ä	Å
90	É	æ	Æ	ô	ö	ò	û	ù	ÿ	ö	Ü	¢	£	¥	₧	ƒ

Fig. C-1. Extended ASCII Chart.

A0	á	í	ó	ú	ñ	Ñ	ª	º	¿	⌐	¬	½	¼	¡	«	»
B0	▒	▓	█	│	┤	╡	╢	╖	╕	╣	║	╗	╝	╜	╛	┐
C0	└	┴	┬	├	─	┼	╞	╟	╚	╔	╩	╦	╠	═	╬	╧
D0	╨	╤	╥	╙	╘	╒	╓	╫	╪	┘	┌	█	▄	▌	▐	▀
E0	α	β	Γ	π	Σ	σ	µ	τ	Φ	Θ	Ω	δ	∞	φ	ε	∩
F0	≡	±	≥	≤	⌠	⌡	÷	≈	°	·	·	√	ⁿ	²	■	

Fig. C-1. Continued.

APPENDIX D
Product Names and Addresses

THE FOLLOWING products have been mentioned in this book. The manufacturer or distributor's name has been included for those desiring additional information.

Product	Category	Manufacturer
Ad-PAC 2	Removable Disk	Tandon Corporation 405 Science Drive Moorpark, CA 93021
Bernoulli Box	Removable Disk	IOMEGA 1281 Main Street Holly Pond Plaza Stamford, CT 06902
COREfast	Backup Software	Core International 7171 N. Federal Highway Boca Raton, FL 33431
CUBIT	Disk Optimizer	SoftLogic Solutions 530 Chestnut Street Manchester, NH 03101
ERLL	Disk Controller	Maynard Electronics, Inc. 460 E. Semoran Blvd. Casselberry, FL 32707

Product	Category	Manufacturer
Fastback	Backup Software	Fifth Generation Systems 909 Electric Ave., Suite 308 Seal Beach, CA 90740
400XT Tape Backup System EZTAPE	Tape Backup	Irwin Magnetics 2101 Commonwealth Blvd. Ann Arbor, MI 48105
The Mace Utilities	Disk Utility	Paul Mace Software 123 First Street Ashland, OR 97520
The Norton Utilities	Disk Utility	
The Norton Commander	DOS Shell	Peter Norton Computing 2210 Wilshire Blvd., Suite 186 Santa Monica, CA 90403
POWER TOOLS	Disk Utility	MLI Microsystems PO Box 825 Framingham, MA 01701
Streaming	Book	ARCHIVE Corp. 1650 Sunflower Ave. Costa Mesa, CA 92626
SuperKey	Security Software	Borland International 4113 Scotts Valley Drive Scotts Valley, CA 95066
VCache	Disk Cache	Golden Bow Systems 2870 Fifth Ave., Suite 201 San Diego, CA 92103

APPENDIX E
OS/2 and the Future

THE MAJOR operating system for IBM compatible computers for the bulk of the 1980s has been DOS. Starting with version 1 introduced in 1981 up through version 4, which became widely available in 1989. Although DOS has its problems and drawbacks, it is a functional, useful operating system and it is successful simply given the thousands of software packages available for it.

But DOS isn't forever.

The increasing power of many PC's microprocessors, plus the dwindling prices of RAM and expanding storage capacity of hard disks are all making DOS an old, dying system. Although DOS is bound to be around well into the mid-90's, DOS is really a dead end operating system.

Keep in mind that DOS will still be around and an important piece of software as long as people continue to buy and use DOS computers. But to combat DOS's obsolescence and keep up with the pace of computer technology, a new operating system is available. Endorsed by both IBM and Microsoft, OS/2 will be the operating systems for PCs in the future.

This appendix discusses the implications of the OS/2 operating system. It covers such concerns as what OS/2 does differently than DOS, what efforts are involved to make the upgrade, and what benefits you can expect. More importantly, this appendix briefly covers the subject of whether or not you should upgrade. In any event, as a budding hard disk guru, these are subjects you should think about.

WHAT IS OS/2?

OS/2 came about because of the extended capabilities of the 80286 microprocessor introduced with IBM's PC/AT. This microprocessor has the ability to work with data in

16-bit widths, compared with the older 8088 microprocessor that used a mixture of 16 bits and 8 bits. The 80286 also can access up to 16M of memory, as opposed to 1M on the original PC.

The 80286 comes with a special operating mode, referred to as the *protected mode*. This mode is used to control access to memory, restricting memory for some programs, and granting it to others. The original 8088, as well as DOS, provides minimum memory allocation functions. Any program can (and most do) gobble up all the memory in a PC. In the 80286, programs can be given a specific amount of memory and then be restricted to using that memory by the 80286 itself. Thus, it is known as the protected mode.

When an 80286 computer uses DOS, it is used like an 8088 or 8086. Although the chip still retains its marvelous memory controlling abilities, the 80286 is simply used in a DOS PC like its older brothers. All the power is lost and the end result is just a faster PC. To take advantage of the 80286 and its protected mode, Microsoft and IBM began working on OS/2.

OS/2 was designed from the start as just another DOS upgrade. Originally it was to be DOS 3. Then, when PC-DOS and MS-DOS version 3.0 came out, they decided to call the new operating system DOS 4. But before IBM came out with PC-DOS 4.0, the name OS/2, for Operating System/2, was settled on.

Basically, OS/2 is just an advanced version of DOS. It looks a lot like DOS and uses near identical, but more versatile, commands. Any DOS user will feel at home with OS/2 in a matter of minutes. Yet, OS/2 has many powerful features, all primarily designed to take advantage of the 80286's protected mode.

Because OS/2 was tailored to work with the 80286 (and it will also work with an 80386, 80486, and future microprocessors), it cannot be run on a computer with an 8088 or 8086 microprocessor. Nope, not at all. You must have an 80286 or better to take advantage of OS/2.

BENEFITS OF OS/2

OS/2 solves many problems DOS users have been complaining about for years. Above all, OS/2 gives you megabytes and megabytes of RAM to run your programs. With the present incarnation of OS/2, your PC can have up to 8M of RAM for running programs, which means software can get as big as memory allows (and will probably bloat to that size just because of it). Also, your data files can take advantage of all that memory.

Another advantage of OS/2 allows many programs to work at once. Each program is given its own environment, called a *session*. In one session you could be running the OS/2 command prompt (similar to the DOS command prompt). In a second session, you could be working on your word processor. In a third session, you could be sorting names in a gigantic database. All three activities (or more) can be going on at one time with no noticeable loss in computing speed. Imagine needing an extra formatted diskette and just being able to call up the FORMAT program, format a diskette while you're doing something else, then using that diskette.

Presently, one of the nicest benefits of OS/2 is that it is DOS compatible. You can install OS/2 on a DOS hard disk to coexist with your version of DOS, called the "dual boot option." When your computer starts, you'll be asked to press Enter to run OS/2 or press Esc to run DOS. With the dual boot option, you can have OS/2 on your computer, but use your DOS computer as you did before. Both operating systems coexist on the same disk.

OS/2 also features a DOS "compatibility box." This box is a version of DOS 3.3 that works in an OS/2 session. You can use DOS programs in the compatibility, or 3x box, switching back and forth between OS/2 if you like. The 3x box will eventually fade away as OS/2 gains software and popularity.

Future versions of OS/2 will allow such things as super long (meaning descriptive) filenames, special features for a custom 80386 version of OS/2, and an easy-to-use graphic shell, the Presentation Manager.

SHOULD YOU UPGRADE?

Upgrading to OS/2 requires a few items:

- An 80286 or better microprocessor, without which you cannot run OS/2.
- At least 2M total RAM in your system. That is 1M beyond the 1M used by DOS. (The manual says 1.5M, but the ".5" refers to your computer's first 512K of RAM.) The more memory you have, the better. OS/2 would really like it if your machine sported 4M total RAM.
- A hard disk. You need a hard disk to run OS/2. In fact, OS/2 will eat up 3M of space on that hard disk. And it's sloppy space too: OS/2 puts at least two dozen files into your root directory which must be there. It also requires its own \ OS2 subdirectory. Hard disk management on an OS/2 system will be tougher because of these requirements, but it's still very similar to normal DOS hard disk management.
- Graphics. OS/2 can run on a monochrome monitor. However, to take full advantage of the operating system, you'll need an IBM compatible EGA or VGA display. Especially for the graphical Presentation Manager shell, a VGA monitor is your best bet.
- A mouse. OS/2's graphical interface will make good use of the mouse as an input device. Sure, the mouse is optional and you can run OS/2 without one, but a mouse will be easier to use.
- Money. The average price of DOS has been hovering around the $100 mark ever since it was introduced. OS/2 is $325, or more in the posher parts of town. It's not cheap, and OS/2 software won't be cheap either. Because of everything OS/2 can

do, writing software for it will be expensive for developers. And they will cheerfully pass along the cost to the consumer.

- OS/2 software. Presently there is OS/2 software available. Many utilities, programs, even mainstream applications now can run under OS/2. The problem is, most of these programs are mere copies of what you can get on the DOS side of the PC planet. There will be no compelling reason to move to OS/2 until some of its software becomes desirable, and can only work in the OS/2 environment. When that happens, then you should make the switch.

MAKING THE SWITCH

After you have all the requirements for running OS/2, you can convert your system in one of two ways:

(1) Start over from scratch with an OS/2 system
(2) Run DOS and OS/2 on the same system

Starting over fresh with OS/2 would be a viable option providing you have enough OS/2 software to make the switch. Remember, OS/2 has a DOS compatibility box, allowing DOS software to be run in an OS/2 session. But if you're spending too much time in the compatibility box, you should question your move to OS/2. Otherwise, going with an OS/2 only system would be the most logical choice.

If you're still using DOS applications and need OS/2 only for a few requirements, then the dual boot option of running both DOS and OS/2 on the same system should be your choice. OS/2 will install itself to coexist with DOS. Presently, this type of setup works only with OS/2 versions through 1.1. Version 1.2 employs a new file system, which requires that you reformat your hard drive before moving up to OS/2.

The advantage of a dual boot system is being able to boot DOS when you only need to use DOS. OS/2 remains under wraps while you use DOS. Of course, the OS/2 files will still be there, loud and ugly (and sitting in the root directory!), but DOS will operate as before. When you need to run OS/2, simply press Enter at boot time (or do nothing) and OS/2 will come up.

A third option is simply not to bother with OS/2 until it becomes compelling to do so. Because Microsoft and IBM were so sluggish to bring OS/2 to market, and custom OS/2 software is only now bubbling to the surface, other enterprising developers have come up with alternative methods for solving DOS's problems without forcing you to abandon DOS.

For example, Quarterdeck's DESQview 386 allows 80386 computers to run multiple DOS sessions without having to abandon DOS. It is essentially OS/2 without the price or overhead. Other operating systems are appearing as well, which combined with OS/2's lack of software makes upgrading to OS/2 a difficult choice.

My opinion? Wait. When the right package comes along, then it's time to upgrade to OS/2. Until then, keep your ear to the ground and eyes on popular PC magazines. When the tide turns to OS/2, you'll read about it or hear about it at a user group meeting. Then you'll know it's time to seriously consider the switch.

SUMMARY

OS/2 will be the operating system for PCs through the 1990's. It offers powerful features to take advantage of PC's new microprocessors, and will give users new ways of using their computers. Presently, OS/2 exists as only a sign post of things to come. It's more of a curiosity, a misty haze in a fortune teller's crystal ball. Eventually, when OS/2 specific software arrives, software you can really use, then you should worry about making the switch.

Index

@ subcommand, 127

A

A.BAT, 153
Aboveboard, 316, 319
access arm, 18
access time, 17-19
advanced error correcting code, 306
Advanced Hard Disk Diagnostics utilities, 298
AIX, 27
alphanumeric data, 5-7
ANSI.SYS, 185-192, 312
  calling through DOS escape sequence, 186-187
  CONFIG.SYS file to install, 185-186
  cursor and erase functions, 188
  keyboard reassignment functions, 189
  menu screen displays with, 185-192
  PROMPT to call, 186-188
APPEND, 331
appending files, 68
application programs, batch files to load, 119-121
ARC, 302, 322
archiving, 219, 262, 301-306
ASCII, 6, 195
  data encryption, 274
  EDLIN for, 161

extended character set, 175-177, 346-351
hiding files with, 269
keyboard values, 6
menu screens in WordPerfect, 184
menu screens using, 150
scan codes for, 189-191
ASK utility, 138-139, 141, 142
ASK...IF, 142, 144
ASK.COM, 138, 328
ASSIGN, 313, 331
ATTRIB command, 262-264, 332
attribute bytes, 261, 262, 263
attributes,file, 49
AUTOEXEC.BAT, 39, 41, 75, 123, 124, 127, 144, 145, 151-154, 189, 192, 198, 207, 255, 278, 312
  checking, 124-125
  editing, 125
  printout of, 125
AUTOMAKE, 200-201
AutoMenu, 195-207, 209, 326-327
  automatic blackout feature, 199
  batch files, 200-203
  colors with, 197
  command functions, 202-203
  description entries, 202
  designing menu screens with, AUTOMAKE for, 200-201
  dialog functions, 203-206
  features of, 196
  file encryption with, 206-207

Insert function of, 200
installation of, 198
installing menu systems created with, 207
menu definition files (MDF), 198, 207
menu selections with, 196, 202
menu series vs. submenus, 197, 199
messages and prompts, 199
password security with, 206-207
running, 198-199
screen functions, 202
submenus, 197
titles, 202

B

backing up data, 10, 39, 50, 65, 72, 88, 217-238
  batch files for, 154
  floppy disks, 218
  hard disks, 218
  head crashes and, 218
  Irwin Tape Backup System, 242-244
  streaming tape for, 240, 241
backslash path indicator, 94
BACKUP command, 39, 217-227, 231, 234, 235, 262, 264, 293, 298, 332
backwards loops, 135-136
bad sectors, 85, 87
BASIC, 133, 253, 255
  cassette version, 10

FREE SOFTWARE FOR YOUR HARD DISK

A SPECIAL OFFER TO READERS OF
"Hard Disk Management
with MS-DOS and PC-DOS"

PC-SIG, the world's largest distributor of Shareware and Public Domain software put together a sampler of a few programs from our library to help you get the most from your hard disk. This unique disk contains:

AUTOMENU:
The solution to the problem of learning all DOS commands required to access many different application programs with a single press of a key. It automatically executes commands from an easy to read and understandable menu.

PACKDISK:
A handy tool to eliminate file fragmentation in your hard drive. Packs the root directory and subdirectories and frees subdirectory trailing clusters.

DISK TOOL:
This tool allows you to look at and make changes to what is stored on your DOS disks.

More Hard Disk UTILITIES:
A collection of useful utilities for just about everything. Hide and unhide files; create a RAM disk; map out your many subdirectories on your hard disk for easy access and lock files on your hard disk for protection.

User-supported and public domain software from the PC-SIG Library of over 750 disks and thousands of programs.

User supported software (sometimes called shareware) is an exciting new concept in software distribution. Authors of programs actually encourage the copying of their disks. Satisfied users then send a registration fee directly to the author. Registration, in most cases, entitles you to full documentation and technical support straight from the program author.

Part of the PC-SIG Library is made-up of public domain software from around the country. One of the advantages of public domain software is the ability to get many useful utilities that would otherwise be unavailable on the software market.

As the world's largest distributor of user-supported and public domain software the PC-SIG Library contains thousands of useful and powerful programs. A complete variety of programs are available from word-processing and spreadsheets to communications and games. All programs in the Library are available for only $6 or less per disk.

A partial listing of programs available is included on the next page.